KINtop Studies in Early Cinema – volume 7
series editors: Frank Kessler, Sabine Lenk, Martin Loiperdinger

Pictures of Poverty
The Works of George R. Sims and Their Screen Adaptations

Lydia Jakobs holds a PhD from the University of Trier, Germany, and a Certificate in International Journalism from Hamline University, St. Paul, USA. She was a member of the *Screen1900* research focus at the University of Trier, where she also earned master's degrees in Media Studies, English and Spanish Literature and a Certificate in Gender Studies. She is the editor of the *KINtop* newsletter for early cinema and currently serves as Research Officer for the Magic Lantern Society of the UK.

KINtop Studies in Early Cinema

KINtop Studies in Early Cinema expands the efforts to promote historical research and theoretical reflection on the emergence of moving pictures undertaken by the internationally acclaimed *KINtop* yearbook (published in German from 1992–2006). It brings a collection of anthologies and monographs in English by internationally renowned authors as well as young scholars. The scope of the series ranges from studies on the formative years of the emerging medium of animated photographs to research on the institutionalisation of cinema in the years up to the First World War. Books in this series will also explore the many facets of 19th and early 20th century visual culture as well as initiatives to preserve and present this cinematographic heritage. Early cinema has become one of the most dynamic fields of scholarly research in cinema studies worldwide, and this series aims to provide an international platform for new insights and fresh discoveries in this thriving area.

Series editors: Frank Kessler, Sabine Lenk, Martin Loiperdinger

Pictures of Poverty
The Works of George R. Sims and Their Screen Adaptations

Lydia Jakobs

British Library Cataloguing in Publication Data

Pictures of Poverty:
The Works of George R. Sims and Their Screen Adaptations

Series: KINtop Studies in Early Cinema – volume 7

A catalogue entry for this book is available from the British Library

ISBN: 0 86196 752 0 (Paperback)
ISBN: 0 86196 985 2 (ebook-EPUB)
ISBN: 0 86196 986 9 (ebook-EPDF)

Published by
John Libbey Publishing Ltd, 205 Crescent Road, New Barnet, Herts EN4 8SB,
United Kingdom   e-mail: john.libbey@orange.fr; web site: www.johnlibbey.com

Distributed Worldwide by
Indiana University Press, Herman B Wells Library—350, 1320 E. 10th St.,
Bloomington, IN 47405, USA. www.iupress.indiana.edu

Printed and bound in the UK by Short Run Press Ltd, Exeter.

Contents

List of Figures

Acknowledgements

This book is a slightly revised version of my dissertation *Representations of Poverty in Victorian and Edwardian Popular Media: The Works of George R.Sims and Their Adaptations* completed at the University of Trier (Fachbereich II).

The Konrad Adenauer Foundation provided me both with financial support and the opportunity to discuss my work with brilliant fellow scholars across academic disciplines, which broadened my view and helped me focus it at the same time. I am also grateful to the German Historical Institute, London, which enabled research visits to the British Library and the British Film Institute in London and the Rylands Library in Manchester with a doctoral scholarship.

The scholars of the *Screen1900* research focus at the University of Trier and of the *Early Cinema Colloquium*, a joint initiative of the universities of Trier, Zurich and Utrecht, helped mould my research into the shape it now holds with their well-placed questions and their own considerable expertise. Most especially, I want to acknowledge Martin Loiperdinger, Richard Crangle, Ludwig Vogl-Bienek, Sarah Dellmann, Caroline Braun and Sarah Woike who helped bring this book to print in ways both large and small with their practical assistance, skilled advice and willingness to listen.

I also want to thank the members of The Magic Lantern Society UK, whether they are private collectors, collector-researchers, archivists, artists, performers or scholars. Their generosity in sharing the material in their collections and their immense knowledge with anyone willing to ask nicely never ceases to amaze me.

I want to acknowledge the work of my editors Martin Loiperdinger, Sabine Lenk and Frank Kessler who made this book better with their informed opinions and sensible corrections.

Finally, I want to thank my wife and my family for their encouragement, emotional support and their unending patience throughout the PhD process.

Trier, May 2021

East London lay hidden from view behind a curtain on which were painted terrible pictures: – Starving children, suffering women, overworked men; horrors of drunkenness and vice; monsters and demons of inhumanity; giants of disease and despair. Did these pictures truly represent what lay behind, or did they bear to the facts a relation similar to that which the pictures outside a booth at some country fair bear to the performance or show within?
Charles Booth, *East London* **(1889)**

The poor help the poor. Nowhere are the bonds of human sympathy so strong as down the courts and alleys whose horrors have lately been exhibited in as fierce a light as ever beat upon a throne. We have all painted in strong colours the vices of the people in whom such general interest is now taken – it is only right that their virtues should be brought into equal prominence on the canvas.
George R. Sims, *Horrible London* **(1889)**

Introduction

Mr. BOURKE next asked if the Lecturer was aware that the poem *Christmas day in the Workhouse* was fiction from top to bottom.

The LECTURER referred him to the author.

Mr. BOURKE said it was fiction, and the Lecturer knew that if any man required relief he could get it by going to the relieving officer.

Replying to a question respecting the workhouses, the LECTURER said he believed the Tories built them.

Mr. BOURKE informed him the Liberal party were in power in 1832 when the Poor Law was passed.

The LECTURER, however, thought that was a long way back, and the questioning was rather abruptly terminated by him proposing a vote of thanks to the Rev. J.J. Roumieu (who was present) for the use of the schoolroom.

Mr. PALMER seconded, and the motion was approved, and the meeting terminated in a most amicable manner by Mr. BOURKE proposing a vote of thanks to the lecturer for his lecture, and more especially for the slides exhibiting purely fictitious pictures.[1]

Even apart from Mr Bourke's wonderfully passive-aggressive vote of thanks, this excerpt of a report on a magic lantern performance in the village of Ingham has a lot to offer to the media historian. And it touches on some of the key questions this book aims to discuss and in some cases even answer. When and why are depictions of poverty perceived as realistic? How do we deal with the sheer mass of historical material that has become easily accessible thanks to widespread digitization efforts? Can we reconstruct the audiences and reception contexts of historical media from subjective sources like newspaper reports?

The answer to the last question is a resounding yes – and no. The altercation between our Mr Bourke and the unnamed lecturer during the 1892 General election campaign in Suffolk is a good example for the strengths and weaknesses of newspaper reports as sources. It is rare to see a direct interaction between an audience member and a lecturer documented this extensively. One reason for the length of the report was that the *Bury and Norwich Post* strongly opposed Radical politics and sought to discredit the lecturer by focusing more on the questioning by an audience member associated with the Conservative

---

1   "Radical Speakers Questioned", *Bury and Norwich Post* (12 April 1892): 3.

Party than on the actual content of the lantern lecture. The *Bury Free Press*, a rival Liberal newspaper, also dedicated their political column to the event and painted the actions of Mr Bourke in a slightly different light:

> He and a party of ladies, presumably Primrose dames, swooped down on a Liberal meeting held in the village that evening and he heckled the speakers in a Robin Goodfellow spirit. The intrusion was accepted by the Liberals in perfect good humour, and excellent feeling prevailed on both sides. Indeed, if Mr. Bourke really intends to regularly favour such meetings with his undoubted versatility, and to continue to assist at the close in packing up the obnoxious magic lantern, he ought to be publicly thanked for so markedly contributing to the entertainment and interest of Liberal gatherings.[2]

Did Mr Bourke's relentless questioning expose the lecturer's lack of historical knowledge or were his improper interruptions skilfully deflected by the good-humoured Liberal speakers? We can make educated guesses but we will never know for sure. Still, further research in local newspapers not only reveals additional information about the slide images used to illustrate the lecture, it also sheds light on the use of projected images as tools for political propaganda in Britain more generally.

Leading up to general elections in the summer of 1892, the Liberal party in Suffolk made extensive use of magic lanterns as campaigning devices to illustrate lectures and political events. It is an early example of an electoral campaign that systematically employed projected images, which were only widely used in political campaigns in Britain (and mainly by the Conservative Party) from the mid-1890s.[3] Our as yet unnamed lecturer was a Mr Wade of Stowmarket, one of at least two lecturers associated with the North-West Suffolk Workmen's Liberal Association, who toured the district's schoolrooms to campaign for the Radical candidate and current MP Viscount Sydney Stern. Between February and May of 1892, Mr Wade visited nearly every small town and village across the division to give a lecture on the progress of English liberty over 800 years and on current politics, illustrated with magic lantern slides. On several occasions, this was followed by an illustrated recitation of George R. Sims's famous poem *In the Workhouse. Christmas Day*. The tearful story of an old man who lost his beloved wife because of a merciless workhouse system that denied him out-relief was tied to the lecturer's position on old age pensions:

> Mr. Snell having given the recitation, *Christmas in the Workhouse*, Mr. Wade remarked that for more than six years he had openly expressed his disapproval of

---

2   "Political Quizzing", *Bury Free Press* (16 April 1892): 5. Mr Bourke was secretary of the North-West Suffolk Conservative Association, owned his own magic lantern and gave illustrated lectures for the local Primrose League. See "Ixworth", *Bury and Norwich Post* (23 February 1892): 8, and "North-West Suffolk Conservative Association. The Annual Meeting", *Bury and Norwich Post* (23 February 1892): 5.

3   See Stephen Bottomore, "The Lantern and Cinematograph for Political Persuasion before WWI: Towards an Introduction and Typology", in Richard Crangle and Ludwig Vogl-Bienek (ed.), *Screen Culture and the Social Question 1880–1914* (New Barnet: John Libbey Publishing, 2014), 20–33, here 30.

the way in which parish relief was administered, and strongly advocated that every poor person on reaching the age of 65 should be allowed a sum of 5s. weekly [...].[4]

It is not accidental that George Sims's ballad which had first been published 15 years earlier was met with renewed interest during the Liberal election campaign. The parliamentary franchise had been extended to agricultural labourers only as recently as 1884 (male urban workers had received the franchise with the Reform Act of 1867), which turned them into an electoral force to be reckoned with in Suffolk, where agricultural labour was the main occupation for men according to the 1881 census.[5] The question of outdoor relief and the call for a democratization of poor law elections both became hot-button issues in the 1892 election, following the political radicalization of the Liberal party that had split over the Home Rule question in 1885.[6] Consequently, the second lecturer for the Radical party, a Mr Gathercole, assistant secretary of the Thetford Liberal Association, spoke mainly on the question of Irish independence.[7] For some of his lectures, Mr Gathercole apparently used images from IN THE WORKHOUSE – the lantern adaptation of Sims's popular ballad – as a report in the *Bury Free Press* suggests: "Several capital scenes were depicted upon the canvas showing what life is in the workhouse [...]."[8]

The question of the veracity and truthfulness of the projected images was raised frequently in the popular press and by Conservative politicians in the area. Their joint efforts lead Lord Cadogan, Conservative MP and father of the opposing candidate, to complain about the use of "mendacious cartoons and lying magic-lantern exhibitions" by his political opponents.[9] During a meeting of the Conservative Primrose League at Ampton, he explained jokingly that "their opponents had got a lot of old lanterns which apparently were manufactured, with their slides, between the years 1880 and 1886" (under the Liberal government of William Gladstone), and that these slides "[...] did represent a

---

4 "Hawstead. Liberal Meeting", *Bury and Norwich Post* (29 March 1892): 7.

5 For enfranchisement, see Anthony Brundage, *The English Poor Laws, 1700–1930* (Basingstoke, New York: Palgrave, 2002), 125. For analysis of census data, see A Vision of Britain through Time: "GB Historical GIS / University of Portsmouth, Suffolk RegC through time | Census tables with data for the Poor Law/Registration County" (http://www.visionofbritain.org.uk/unit/10097459).

6 See Brundage, *English Poor Laws,* 126. Up until 1894, boards of guardians, who administered poor law relief and regulated workhouses, were elected by a plural voting system that heavily favoured property owners and well-to do ratepayers, effectively excluding working-class residents of a parish from the management of an institution many of them were dependent on for medical and other forms of relief. Ibid., 125.

7 See "Ampton", *Bury Free Press* (16 April 1892): 6. Judging from the newspaper reports, the slides for his lecture might have been selected from a set of photographic slides produced by Riley Brothers and called IRISH QUESTION (c. 1888, 101 slides) or from another Riley lecture set called IRELAND: ITS BEAUTY AND ITS BLIGHT (c. 1888, 66 slides).

8 "Bardwell", *Bury Free Press* (5 March 1892): 5.

9 "Opening of the Mildenhall Working Men's Club. Speech by Earl Cadogan", *Bury and Norwich Post* (26 April 1892): 8. Interestingly, Gathercole had written to Lord Cadogan in early February to request permission for use of the schoolrooms in several parishes to hold meetings on behalf of MP Stern and to "give an address upon the Irish Question illustrated by magic lantern views", to which Cadogan did not object. See their correspondence, reprinted in *Bury and Norwich Post* (9 February 1892): 5.

state of things really harrowing. He was told that some of those slides had been exhibited at Ingham, and he understood that they were very much blurred, and not very distinct. But of course their age would account for that."[10] However, the Earl did not generally disapprove of the use of projected images for political campaigns, stating that "the magic-lantern system of electioneering might be found to be a very successful one".[11] He recommended that the Conservative Party might "[…] get men to follow these men about with a new lantern, and let them have slides showing the improved condition of Ireland. […] Let them have double slides, one showing boycotting as it took place when Mr. Gladstone was in office and another slide showing that throughout the whole of Ireland there was not a single man boycotted now."[12] The matter was even addressed by Arthur Balfour, formerly Chief Secretary for Ireland, who referred to a magic lantern slide depicting a caricature of himself and a little girl, supposedly imprisoned by him, during a speech in Manchester:

> True it is that, a correspondent informs me, the agricultural labourer, in Suffolk I think it is, is still entertained with magic lantern slides, in which this heroine of 24 years of age, 5ft. 6in., 9st. in weight (laughter), is represented as a little child lying on the prison bed, the Chief Secretary – the late Chief Secretary (laughter) – glaring through the windows and enjoying her sufferings. (Laughter.)

So, while we cannot with any certainty reconstruct the events of one particular meeting from newspaper reports about said meeting, we can with relative certainty assess the wider cultural impact of one particular magic lantern slide mentioned in multiple newspaper reports. It is also a testament to the importance of the local press as a source for media historical practices in specific areas. In recent years, media historians have repeatedly demonstrated the usefulness of different types of periodicals for answering different kinds of research questions. Karen Eifler's analysis of the use of projected images by welfare organizations has foregrounded strategies for attracting and engaging audiences revealed through reports in their own periodicals.[13] Torsten Gärtner has traced itinerant lantern performances of projection vans through reports in the Church Army's publications and sketched the use of projected images in

---

10   "'Seven Hills' Habitation of the Primrose League. Tea and Annual Meeting at Ampton. Speech by Lord Cadogan", *Bury and Norwich Post* (12 April 1892): 8. The Primrose League was a Conservative organization that spearheaded outreach efforts to working-class voters. It made active use of lantern projections and other visual stimuli for local entertainments from the 1880s onwards. The Primrose League campaigned strongly against Irish Home Rule, an issue that had "rocked the country, splitting the great Liberal Party, and revolutionizing political alignments everywhere". Janet Robb, *The Primrose League, 1883–1906* (New York: Columbia University Press, 1942), 189. On magic lantern use, see 88–93.

11   *Bury and Norwich Post* (12 April 1892): 8.

12   Ibid. A few years later, William Palmer of the *Clarion* newspaper utilized precisely these kinds of visual juxtapositions for his socialist campaigning: "In the mid-1890s, Palmer travelled through Britain giving shows in which he projected slides of both luxurious and poverty-stricken communities, alternating the two extremes to create a visual dialectic to counter gross inequality and the status quo […]." Bottomore, "Political Persuasion", 24.

13   See Karen Eifler, *The Great Gun of the Lantern. Lichtbildereinsatz sozialer Organisationen in Großbritannien, 1875–1914* (Marburg: Schüren, 2017), 60–81 for a critical analysis of these publications as media historical sources, and Karen Eifler, "Sensation – Intimacy – Interaction: Lantern Performances in Religious and Socio-Political Education", *Early Popular Visual Culture*, vol. 17, no. 1 (2019): 45–70 for a general overview.

Sunday schools through reports in the *Sunday School Chronicle*.[14] Judith Thissen's work on the changing exhibition practices of nickelodeon theatres in Manhattan's Jewish Lower East Side has repeatedly shown how niche publications can document media practices of minority communities.[15] Richard Abel's recent *Menus for Movieland: Newspapers and the Emergence of American Film Culture, 1913–1916* meticulously documents both the establishment of the American film trade press and the mutually profitable relation that local newspapers and the film industry established in the 1910s.[16] And Paul Moore has proposed a typology of "first notices" about the opening of fixed cinemas based on the different types of reports found in metropolitan, regional and local newspapers in Ontario.[17]

Aside from their function as essential primary sources about the historical media scene, newspapers and magazines were also key agents in discussions of poverty throughout the Victorian period. The popularity and cultural impact of stories and images of ragged children and miserable street urchins can hardly be overstated. This was matched only by the impact of shocking reportages on the living and working conditions of the urban poor and inside the notorious workhouses, which repeatedly stirred up calls for political and social reform. The popularity of these representations of poverty across media and genres is striking. From the 1850s onwards especially, representations of poverty enjoyed a remarkable mobility across different media and genres as evidenced by the large number of novels, newspaper features, poems, pamphlets and works of social investigation dealing with the topic.[18] Visual representations

---

14 See Torsten Gärtner, "The Church on Wheels. Travelling Magic Lantern Mission in Late Victorian England", in Martin Loiperdinger (ed.), *Travelling Cinema in Europe: Sources and Perspectives* (Frankfurt am Main: Stroemfeld, 2008), 128–142, and Torsten Gärtner, "*The Sunday School Chronicle* – eine Quelle zur Nutzung der Laterna Magica in englischen Sonntagsschulen", in Frank Kessler, Sabine Lenk and Martin Loiperdinger (ed.), *KINtop. Jahrbuch zur Erforschung des frühen Films*, 14 / 15: *Quellen und Perspektiven / Sources and Perspectives* (Frankfurt am Main, Basel: Stroemfeld, 2006), 25–35.

15 See, e.g., Judith Thissen, "Jewish Immigrant Audiences in New York City, 1905–14", in Melvyn Stokes and Richard Maltby (ed.), *American Movie Audiences: From the Turn of the Century to the Early Sound Era* (London: BFI Publishing, 1999), 15–28, and Judith Thissen, "Beyond the Nickelodeon: Cinemagoing, Everyday Life and Identity Politics", in Ian Christie (ed.), *Audiences: Defining and Researching Screen Entertainment Reception* (Amsterdam: Amsterdam University Press, 2012), 45–65.

16 See Richard Abel, *Menus for Movieland: Newspapers and the Emergence of American Film Culture, 1913–1916* (Oakland: University of California Press, 2015).

17 Metropolitan dailies only mentioned cinemas if something newsworthy like a fire had occurred there (newsworthy). The dailies of smaller cities would usually publish advertisements before a cinema was going to open (adworthy) and weekly newspapers from towns and villages tended to mention cinemas more or less randomly in their "town topics" or "town gossip" columns. See Paul S. Moore, "The Social Biograph: Newspapers as Archives of the Regional Mass Market for Movies", in Richard Maltby, Daniel Bautereyst and Philippe Meers (ed.), *Explorations in New Cinema History: Approaches and Case Studies* (Malden, Mass., Oxford, Chichester, West Sussex: Wiley-Blackwell, 2011), 263–279, here 268.

18 See, e.g., Ruth Richardson, *Dickens and the Workhouse: Oliver Twist and the London Poor* (Oxford: Oxford University Press, 2012); Peter Keating (ed.), *The Working Classes in Victorian Fiction* (London: Routledge, 1971); Stephen Donovan and Matthew Rubery (ed.), *Secret Commissions: An Anthology of Victorian Investigative Journalism* (Peterborough, Ontario etc.: Broadview Press, 2012); Seth Koven, *Slumming: Sexual and Social Politics in Victorian London* (Princeton: Princeton University Press, 2004); Jacqueline Susan Bratton, *The Victorian Popular Ballad* (Totowa, New Jersey: Rowman and Littlefield, 1975); Geoff Ginn, "Answering the 'Bitter Cry': Urban Description and Social Reform", *The London Journal*, vol. 31, no. 2

abounded in illustrated newspapers and books, paintings, photographs, theatre plays, magic lantern slides and films.[19] Poverty was ubiquitous throughout the Victorian period but the question of why its representations gained such remarkable popularity cannot be answered without reference to George Robert Sims (1847–1922). Sims was one of the most commercially successful playwrights of the late 19th century and possibly the most eccentric. Termed "the quintessential multi-media celebrity of Victorian London" by literary scholar Joss Marsh, the prolific writer Sims published long-running theatre plays, an even longer-running column in a Sunday newspaper, wrote tear-jerking ballads, comic and detective short stories, reflections on his life and times, modelled for one of Madame Tussaud's wax figures and once famously campaigned for a completely ineffective hair restorer.[20]

Sims was neither the most famous Victorian novelist on poverty nor the most widely read poet of the era. He was not even the most notorious journalist, whose exposés most shocked the nation. His theatre plays and ballads tended to follow established formulas and his column was mostly a strange mix of personal anecdotes and political observations with occasional nationalist undertones.[21] Yet, Sims's contemporary notoriety, his extraordinary versatility across genres and his continued popularity for almost four decades make him a worthwhile subject. Sims was also directly involved with the growing efforts in British film production throughout the 1910s: His popular melodramas and literary ballads were preferred subjects for film adaptations, he spoke alongside politicians at cinema trade dinners, discussed trends in film production and cinemagoing in his column for *The Referee*, served as literary advisor to film companies, wrote various original screenplays and personally supervised several adaptations of his works.

Research on poverty and social class in the Victorian period has been too diverse and widespread to exhaustively list here. Statistical, sociological, pictorial, theatrical, photographic, filmic, literary and journalistic representations of

(2006): 179–200; John Marriott and Masaie Matsumura (ed.), *The Metropolitan Poor. Semifactual Accounts, 1795–1910*, 6 volumes (London: Pickering & Chatto, 1999), and Anne Humpherys, *Travels into Poor Man's Country: The Work of Henry Mayhew* (Athens, Georgia: University of Georgia Press, 1977).

19   See, e.g., Peter Schmandt, *Armenhaus und Obdachlosenasyl in der englischen Graphik und Malerei 1830–1880* (Marburg: Jonas Verlag, 1991); Emily Kathryn Morgan, *'True Types of the London Poor': Adolphe Smith and John Thomson's 'Street Life in London'*, PhD diss. (University of Arizona, 2012); Stephanie Spencer, "O.G. Rejlander's Photographs of Street Urchins", *Oxford Art Journal*, vol. 7, no. 2 (1984): 17–24; Michael Booth (ed.), *The Lights o' London and Other Victorian Plays* (Oxford, New York: Oxford University Press, 1995); Kristen Leaver, "Victorian Melodrama and the Performance of Poverty", *Victorian Literature and Culture*, vol. 27, no. 2 (1999): 443–456; Caroline Braun, *Von Bettlern, Waisenkindern und Dienstmädchen: Armutsdarstellungen im frühen Film und ihr Anteil an der Etablierung des Kinos in Deutschland* (Trier: Wissenschaftlicher Verlag Trier, 2018); Crangle and Vogl-Bienek (ed.), *Screen Culture*.

20   Joss Marsh and David Francis, "'The Poetry of Poverty': The Magic Lantern and the Ballads of George R. Sims", in Crangle and Vogl-Bienek (ed.), *Screen Culture*, 64–81, here 65.

21   See Arthur Calder-Marshall, "Introduction. George R. Sims", in Arthur Calder-Marshall (ed.), *Prepare to Shed Them Now: The Ballads of George R. Sims* (London: Hutchinson, 1968), 1–48, here 29, and Philip Waller, "Sims, George Robert", in Henry Colin Gray Matthew and Brian Howard Harrison (ed.), *Oxford Dictionary of National Biography* (Oxford: Oxford University Press, 2004), 721–724, here 722.

poverty have all been studied widely across historical disciplines.[22] Studies on the prolific Mr Sims and editions of his works have often tended to focus on one area of his writing while only touching on others in passing. Brian Crozier, Joachim Frenk, Michael Booth and Richard Higgins discuss various aspects of Sims's theatrical plays.[23] Peter Keating, Geoff Ginn and Anthony Wohl have focused on his journalistic descriptions of London's slums.[24] Keith Wilson covers his editorial work and articles for *Living London*, while Helen Groth and Mark Seltzer mainly discuss specific aspects and themes in his collections of short stories *The Social Kaleidoscope* (1881) and *The Mysteries of Modern London* (1906).[25] Arthur Calder-Marshall and Jacqueline Bratton both provide excellent literary analysis of Sims's ballads and their narrative strategies.[26]

Adaptations of Sims's ballads for the art of projection are discussed at length by Ludwig Vogl-Bienek, who also provides an analysis of *How the Poor Live*, as well as by Joss Marsh and David Francis, who also examine their literary qualities.[27] Somewhat puzzlingly, there have to date been more in-depth analyses of Sims's use of moving image metaphors than of the numerous adaptations of his fiction for the cinema: Helen Groth devotes an entire chapter

---

22   See, e.g., Christian Topalov, "Raconter ou compter? L'enquête de Charles Booth sur l'East End de Londres (1886–1889), *Mil neuf cent*, vol. 22, no. 1 (2004): 107–132; Gareth Stedman Jones, *Outcast London. A Study in the Relationship between Classes in Victorian Society* (Oxford: Clarendon Press, 1971); Linda Nochlin, *Misère: The Visual Representation of Misery in the 19th Century* (London: Thames and Hudson, 2018); Lynda Nead, *Victorian Babylon: People, Streets and Images in Nineteenth-Century London* (New Haven, London: Yale University Press, 2000); Celina Fox, "The Development of Social Reportage in English Periodical Illustration during the 1840s and Early 1850s", *Past and Present*, vol. 74, no. 1 (1977): 90–111; Thomas Prasch, *Fixed Positions: Working-Class Subjects and Photographic Hegemony in Victorian Britain*, PhD diss. (Indiana University, 1994) to name only a few select titles. For a good overview of scholarly literature about representations of the Victorian city, see Anne Humpherys, "Knowing the Victorian City: Writing and Representation", *Victorian Literature and Culture*, vol. 30, no. 2 (2002): 601–612.

23   See Brian Crozier, *Notions of Childhood in London Theatre, 1880–1905*, PhD diss. (University of Cambridge, 1981); Joachim Frenk, "'We have learned the value of poverty': (Re-)Presentations of the Poor in Nineteenth-Century Melodramas", in Barbara Korte and Frédéric Regard (ed.), *Narrating Poverty and Precarity in Britain* (Berlin, Boston: Walter de Gruyter, 2014), 57–74; Booth (ed.), *The Lights o' London*; Richard Higgins, "London on Stage: The Urban Melodrama of George Sims", *Literary London: Interdisciplinary Studies in the Representation of London*, vol. 4, no. 1 (March 2006) , (http://literarylondon.org/the-literary-london-journal/archive-of-the-literary-london-journal/issue-4-1/london-on-stage-the-urban-melodrama-of-george-sims/).

24   See Peter Keating (ed.), *Into Unknown England, 1866–1913: Selections from the Social Explorers* (Manchester: Manchester University Press, 1976); Ginn, "Urban Description and Social Reform"; Anthony Stephen Wohl, *The Eternal Slum: Housing and Social Policy in Victorian London* (London: Edward Arnold, 1977), 202–205.

25   See Keith Wilson, "Surveying Victorian and Edwardian Londoners: George R. Sims' *Living London*", in Lawrence Phillips (ed.), *A Mighty Mass of Brick and Smoke: Victorian and Edwardian Representations of London* (Amsterdam: Rodopi, 2007), 131–149; Mark Seltzer, "The Princess Casamassima: Realism and the Fantasy of Surveillance", *Nineteenth-Century Fiction*, vol. 35, no. 4 (March 1981): 506–534; Helen Groth, "Kaleidoscopic Vision in Late Victorian Bohemia: George Sims's *Social Kaleidoscope*", in Colette Colligan and Margaret Linley (ed.), *Media, Technology, and Literature in the Nineteenth Century: Image, Sound, Touch* (Farnham, Surrey, Burlington, Vermont: Ashgate, 2011), 91–104.

26   See in particular Calder-Marshall, "Introduction", 34–44, and Bratton, *Victorian Popular Ballad*, 122–132.

27   Ludwig Vogl-Bienek, *Lichtspiele im Schatten der Armut. Historische Projektionskunst und Soziale Frage* (Frankfurt am Main, Basel: Stroemfeld, 2016), 272–304 and 205–213; Marsh and Francis, "Poetry of Poverty", 72–78 and 67–71.

to "Flickering Effects: George Robert Sims and the Psychology of the Moving Image", while Stephen Bottomore and Andrew Shail both discuss the role of the cinematograph in short stories by Sims.[28] In contrast, neither the adaptations of his works nor George Sims's personal engagement with British filmmaking have so far been researched systematically. Caroline Braun's analysis of Christmas films in the tradition of the magic lantern, Ian Christie's (supposed) rediscovery of LIVING LONDON (Charles Urban, 1904) and Sally Jackson's article on the film's exhibition in Australia and New Zealand are notable exceptions.[29] This study will attempt a synthesis that connects all of George Sims's fields, highlights their interconnections and covers as yet unchartered territory concerning his engagement with British filmmaking in the 1910s.

The main focus of this book lies on George Sims's popular poverty works and their adaptations for the magic lantern and the cinema. It addresses the question how poverty and poor individuals are depicted in Sims's ballads and his series of articles on the London poor. My approach is interdisciplinary and pledges to take its research objects seriously as elements of Victorian and Edwardian popular culture. Literary analyses of Sims's texts and their adaptations are combined with case studies on historical performance and reception contexts established from contemporary reports in newspapers, trade magazines and periodicals of charity organizations. The focus lies primarily on the period between the first publication of his best-known ballad *In the Workhouse. Christmas Day* in 1877 and the release of the G.B. Samuelson film version of that same ballad in 1914. This time frame coincides roughly with what media historian Richard Crangle terms "the commercial heyday of the magic lantern – the five decades from the 1870s to the 1910s" and the rise of the life model slide genre.[30] The magic lantern was embedded in a highly intermedial context and many of its images were reproductions of classical art, photography, book illustrations, theatre tableaux and so on. The same is true for projected images, which were used on theatre stages and in churches, in music halls and cinemas, on the streets (for example as advertisement) and in classrooms, in contexts of religious and moral instruction, as a children's entertainment, for political campaigning, for ghost raising and, more often than not, to frighten young and impressionable audiences.

---

28 Helen Groth, *Moving Images: Nineteenth-Century Reading and Screen Practices* (Edinburgh: Edinburgh University Press, 2013), 152–176; Stephen Bottomore, "George R. Sims and the Film as Evidence", in Andrew Shail (ed.), *Reading the Cinematograph: The Cinema in British Short Fiction 1896–1912* (Exeter: University of Exeter Press, 2010), 19–36; Andrew Shail, "Reading the Cinematograph: Short Fiction and the Intermedial Spheres of Early Cinema", *Early Popular Visual Culture*, vol. 8, no. 1 (2010): 47–62.

29 Caroline Braun (née Henkes), "Early Christmas Films in the Tradition of the Magic Lantern", in Crangle and Vogl-Bienek (ed.), *Screen Culture*, 96–110; Ian Christie, "The Girl with the Speck of Dust in Her Eye: *Living London* Returns", *Senses of Cinema*, issue 49 (February 2009); Sally Jackson, "The *Living London* Boom", *Senses of Cinema*, issue 49 (March 2009), (http://sensesofcinema.com/issues/issue-49/).

30 Richard Crangle, "The Lucerna Magic Lantern Web Resource", in Crangle and Vogl-Bienek (ed.), *Screen Culture*, 190–202, here 192.

The projected images discussed in this book fall broadly into two categories: magic lantern slides and silent films. The growing availability of high-quality digital editions of primary artefacts and sources has reinvigorated the study of this formerly almost forgotten visual history. In the last decade or so, the study of the historical art of projection has broadened its scope considerably. Lantern slides are relevant to a number of disciplines ranging from archaeology to art history, theatre and media studies, medical and urban history, and the history of learning to name only a few. Whether as documentary sources that captured historical conditions, attitudes and media practices or as material remnants of former teaching practices in university collections.[31] Scholars with varied disciplinary and regional backgrounds have engaged with the surviving historical artefacts using a diverse array of methods and research methodologies from re-enactment to content analysis.[32] Chemical probes have even studied the material qualities of the slides themselves from the provenance of the glass to the pigments of the colours and the different types of resin material used to fix the colours to the glass.[33] The reception contexts of these kinds of projected images have also increasingly come into focus with Ludwig Vogl-Bienek's *Lichtspiele im Schatten der Armut* (2016) and Karen Eifler's *The Great Gun of the Lantern* (2017) as two recent examples for British screen history.[34] This study is narrower in its focus on specific series of lantern slides, how they were produced and who distributed and exhibited them. It aims to provide a

31   See, e.g., Maria Männig, "Bruno Meyer and the Invention of Art Historical Slide Projection", in Julia Bärnighausen et al. (ed.), *Photo-Objects. On the Materiality of Photographs and Photo-Archives in the Humanities and Sciences* (Berlin: Edition Open Access, 2019), 275–291; Deborah Harlan, "The Archaeology of Lantern Slides: The Teaching Slide Collection of the Ashmolean Museum, Oxford", in Richard Crangle, Mervyn Heard and Ine van Dooren (ed.), *Realms of Light: Uses and Perceptions of the Magic Lantern from the 17th to the 21st Century* (Ripon, North Yorkshire: The Magic Lantern Society, 2005), 203–210; Jason Bate, "Projecting Soldiers' Repair: the 'Great War' Lantern and the Royal Society of Medicine", *Science Museum Group Journal* (Spring 2020), (accessed on 29 May 2021, http://dx.doi.org/10.15180/201307). See also the various and varied contributions in the volume *A Million Pictures: Magic Lantern Slides in the History of Learning*, edited by Sarah Dellmann and Frank Kessler (New Barnet: John Libbey Publishing, 2020).

32   See, e.g., Hennig Schmidgen, "1900 – The Spectatorium: on Biology's Audiovisual Archive", *Grey Room*, no. 43 (2011): 42–65; Juliette Wood, "Fairy Tales and the Magic Lantern: Henry Underhill's Lantern Slides in the Folklore Society Collection", *Folklore*, vol. 123, no. 3 (2012): 249–268; John A. Davidson, "How Bright Were Magic Lantern Slides on a Screen? A Photometric Study of Limelight and Notes on Its Use in the Magic Lantern", *The Magic Lantern Gazette*, vol. 22, no. 4 (2010): 3–10; Alejandro Martinez, "Evangelization, Visual Technologies, and Indigenous Responses: the South American Missionary Society in the Paraguayan Chaco", *International Journal of Missionary Research*, vol. 34, no. 2 (2010): 83–86; Peter Heering, "The Enlightened Microscope: Re-enactment and Analysis of Projections with Eighteenth-Century Solar Microscopes", *The British Journal for the History of Science*, vol. 41, no. 3 (2008): 345–367; Mitsue Ikeda, "Reconsideration of *Nishiki Kage-e* (Japanese Magic Lantern) from a Practical Perspective", *The New Magic Lantern Journal*, vol. 11, no. 6 (2013): 4–7; Francisco Javier Frutos Esteban, "El análisis de contenido y la organización de repertorios culturales: El caso de las placas de linterna mágica", *Revista Latina de Comunicación Social*, no. 63 (2008): 265–276.

33   See Rebecca Ploeger, Dominique Scalarone and Oscar Chiantore, "Non-Invasive Characteristics of Binding Media on Painted Glass Lantern Plates Using Mid-Infrared Fibre-Optic Reflectance Spectroscopy", *Journal of Cultural Heritage*, vol. 11, no. 1 (2010): 35–41; Beatriz Rodrigues et al., "Magic Lantern Glass Slides Materials and Techniques: The First Multi-Analytical Study", *Heritage*, vol. 2, no. 3 (2019): 2513–2530.

34   Where Eifler has focused on strategies of audience engagement by welfare organizations, Vogl-Bienek has elaborated on the elements of the dispositif of the historical art of projection.

methodological framework for the analysis of literary adaptations for the art of projection as a multi-medium that combined projected images, spoken words and musical accompaniment.

This book draws from and touches on material studied in several interrelated historical disciplines: social history, art history, media history and literary history. The three introductory chapters approach their subjects from the disciplines' diverse vantage points while also highlighting their intersections. The historical overview in the first chapter sketches those cultural tendencies, media developments and societal discourses of the Victorian era that relate to poverty and resonate in one way or another in George Sims's life and work. The chapter also discusses the New Poor Law of 1834, the single most significant piece of legislation relating to poor relief in the 19th century and the concept of the deterrent workhouse, a cornerstone of the New Poor Law and frequent target for the biting criticism of its detractors.

The second chapter establishes the picturesque and the authentic as two modes of describing and depicting poverty. It posits that both modes are historically contingent and subject to changing interpretations over time. Three short case studies provide examples of the textual and visual strategies that enable them. Henry Mayhew's *London Labour and the London Poor* serves as an example for the use of authenticating strategies that encourage a realistic reading of his descriptions of London street folk. Blanchard Jerrold and Gustave Doré's *London. A Pilgrimage* (1872) introduces the concept of picturesque poverty, while the complicated role photography plays in relation to the authentic is discussed with John Thomson and Adolphe Smith's *Street Life in London* (1877), "the first photographically illustrated study of the urban underclass".[35] The changing perception of what constitutes authentic or picturesque depictions of poverty is explained by contrasting modern scholarly responses to these works with contemporaneous reviews and reactions described in the popular press.

The third chapter introduces George Sims through his media personality presented in ego-documents, newspaper profiles and contemporaneous magazine articles. His melodrama *The Lights o' London* (1881), praised for its *hyper*realism, is discussed as an example of the representation of poverty in Sims's theatrical oeuvre. This chapter also examines the media historical and legal context for adaptations of Sims's popular ballads in the life model slide genre of the historical art of projection. Finally, it sheds light on George Sims's involvement with British film production and provides a timeline for cinematic adaptations of his works.

The fourth chapter establishes the need for a digital source criticism (*Quellenkritik*) that examines the technological principles which govern the selection and presentation of digitized material. Digitized newspapers, magazines and

---

35   Anne Hoy and Katharina Harde-Tinnefeld, *Enzyklopädie der Fotografie* (Hamburg: National Geographic Deutschland, 2006), 159. Translated from the German by the author.

trade journals have become important sources for reconstructing the historical exhibition and reception contexts of popular media. However, a critical examination of the impact of the digitization process on the digitized material and its effect on research is as yet missing.

The case studies of the fifth chapter highlight different aspects of the representation of poverty in three relevant works by George R. Sims and their multiple adaptations. All three address the overarching research questions of how poor characters were represented in lantern images and illustrations, which discourses these images belonged and responded to and which exhibition contexts they were presented in, by whom, to whom and for which purposes. Sims's series of illustrated articles on *How the Poor Live* (1883) is analysed as an example of authenticating strategies that aim to provide readers seemingly unmediated access to the homes of the London poor. The effectiveness of these strategies is established by examining reader responses and reception contexts for lantern lectures based on the series. The ballad *In the Workhouse. Christmas Day* (1877) and its adaptations for the magic lantern (Bamforth, 1890) and the cinema (G.B. Samuelson, 1914) illustrate the changing perception of authenticity and verisimilitude over time. It is also an example of how specific production and distribution processes shaped the form and style of literary adaptations for the magic lantern and early film. The second ballad, *The Road to Heaven* (1882) is an example for the picturesque mode of depicting poverty that references contemporaneous representations of homeless children. A comparative analysis of multiple versions of surviving lantern slides and accompanying readings also addresses fundamental questions about the nature of the slide set.

The conclusion briefly summarizes the research results, reflects on questions of adaptation and stresses the value of critical digital editions of lantern slide series for comparative research into the historical art of projection.

In more general terms, this study posits that popular media commodities like George Sims's ballads – written for recitation – and Bamforth's life model slides – produced for exhibition – can be fruitfully studied with established methods of literary and visual history like close reading and comparative analysis. It also addresses the adaptation of literary sources for the screen, the historical exhibition contexts for projected images accompanied by spoken words and the various intermedial influences on the life model slide genre. With its focus on reports in regional and local newspapers, periodicals of welfare organizations and trade magazines, it highlights the wealth of 'hidden' material that is still waiting to be unearthed by media historians.

1

Historical Perspectives

1.1 George R. Sims – Eminent Victorian?[36]

George Robert Sims was born in London in 1847, ten years after Queen Victoria's accession to the throne of the United Kingdom of Great Britain and Ireland, and he died there in 1922, twelve years after Victoria's grandson had been crowned King George V. Strictly speaking then, George R. Sims lived only two thirds of his life as a Victorian author, although he probably reached the height of his fame in the 1890s and early 1900s following the publication of his Dagonet ballads, pieces of investigative journalism and theatrical successes. Still, adaptations of Sims's ballads and stories – first for the magic lantern and later the cinema screen – made sure that Dagonet remained a household name well into the 1920s.

By 1839 the term "Victorian" was used matter-of-factly to refer to that epoch but, as historians Kelly Boyd and Rohan McWilliam point out, after 1901 its use increased to denote and frequently deride a certain mindset:

> It meant earnestness, prudery, hypocrisy, overly ornate and elaborate design, bold entrepreneurialism, double standards, snobbery, sentimentality, utilitarianism, imperialism, narrow mindedness, cosy but stifling family life, rote-learning, extreme religiosity, racism, respectability, corporal punishment, hard work and drudgery.[37]

The adjective "Victorian", in turn, "came to describe a sepia-tinted age that trumpeted high ideals and Christian virtues but presided over an underworld of poverty and prostitution".[38] For George R. Sims this was not necessarily a contradiction. As a journalist, he wrote extensively about the metropolitan poor (*How the Poor Live*, 1883; *Horrible London*, 1883) and described London's criminal underworld and prostitution schemes in *Watches of the Night* (1907) and *London by Night* (1910). As a dramatist, he put the East End onto the stage

---

36   The second part of the title refers to Lytton Strachey's 1918 book of portraits of the same name, a work that, as Kelly Boyd and Rohan McWilliam state, "really put anti-Victorianism on the map". Kelly Boyd and Rohan McWilliam, "Introduction. Rethinking the Victorians", in Kelly Boyd and Rohan McWilliam (ed.), *The Victorian Studies Reader* (London, New York: Routledge, 2007), 1–47, here 8.

37   Ibid., 1. On usage of the term "Victorian", see also Colin Matthew, "Introduction: The United Kingdom and the Victorian Century, 1815–1901", in Colin Matthew (ed.), *The Nineteenth Century: The British Isles, 1815–1901* (Oxford: Oxford University Press, 2005), 1–38, here 38.

38   Boyd and McWilliam, "Introduction", 1–2.

in his famous, wildly successful play *Lights o' London* (1881). Sims also repeatedly appealed to the Christian charity of his readers and regularly asked them to donate to the *Referee* Children's Dinner Fund and other charitable causes in his weekly column.

The periodization of the Victorian era is approached differently by the two disciplines most relevant to this study. Literary history commonly situates it between the earlier Romantic era and the advent of Modernism around the turn of the 20th century and characterizes it primarily as a period of literary realism and naturalism dominated by the success of the novel form.[39] George Sims's journalistic and theatrical works were certainly influenced by Victorian realism but he also wrote a number of humorous and farcical plays early in his career (*Crutch and Toothpick*, 1879; *Mother-in-Law*, 1881; *The Member for Slocum*, 1881), and ventured into more fantastical and symbolist writing in the 1900s (*Mysteries of Modern London*, 1905; *The Devil in London*, 1908).[40]

Historians disagree on the boundaries of the Victorian period often arguing that it extended beyond the actual dates of Victoria's reign (1837–1901). Many include the earlier reform years of the late 1820s and 1830s, others subsume it within a long 19th century that starts around the time of the French Revolution and ends with the outbreak of the First World War in 1914. While historian Colin Matthew claims that, "nobody then or now would include the 1900s as 'Victorian'", others have argued that the societal changes of the Edwardian Age including women's suffrage and welfare reforms followed developments of the previous century, "making any notion of a decisive break with the past in 1901 questionable".[41] Historians have questioned many of the widely held assumptions about the Victorian age: The notion that an Industrial Revolution fundamentally transformed English society to form a Victorian age characterized by the rise of the middle class and the prevalence of manufacturing, for example.[42] Richard Price has repeatedly argued that instead, a continuity of "basic structures" of society existed from the late 17th to the late 19th century and denied that the notion of Victorian England makes sense.[43] This leads Victorianist Martin Hewitt to conclude that, "the Victorian period has been shaped by a scholarship that has either moulded the terminal dates of Victoria's reign to its own ends, or prefaced studies of the period with the apparently

---

39   See Sean Purchase, *Key Concepts in Victorian Literature* (Basingstoke, New York: Palgrave Macmillan, 2006), 145–146.

40   See Seltzer, "Realism and the Fantasy of Surveillance", 506–513, and Nicholas Freeman, *Conceiving the City: London, Literature, and Art 1870–1914* (Oxford: Oxford University Press, 2007), 152 and 192–193.

41   Matthew, "Introduction", 38, and Boyd and McWilliam, "Introduction", 4.

42   Boyd and McWilliam, "Introduction", 27 and 51.

43   See Richard Price, "Should We Abandon the Idea of the Victorian Period?", in Kelly Boyd and Rohan McWilliam (ed.), *The Victorian Studies Reader* (London, New York: Routledge, 2007), 51–65, and Richard Price, "Does the Notion of Victorian England Make Sense?", in Derek Fraser (ed.), *Cities, Class and Communication: Essays in Honour of Asa Briggs* (Abingdon, Oxon, New York: Harvester Wheatsheaf, 1990), 152–171.

obligatory admission that it doesn't really exist".[44] Another tendency of Victorian Studies pointed out by Boyd and McWilliam is that contemporary influences and issues are reflected in the constantly changing approaches towards the Victorians. Thus, the focal point of influential texts in Victorian Studies has shifted from class-based approaches influenced by Marxist theory in the 1950s and 1960s to studies of gender, race and the nation from the 1980s, often based on concepts developed by Michel Foucault.[45]

1.2 Key Concepts in Victorian Culture

New Media and Poverty

Historian Martin Hewitt has sought to establish a distinct "cultural identity" of the Victorian period by defining five *assemblages*, "compounds of technologies, practices, institutions, knowledges, meanings, values, and ideologies", that allow him to identify "a number of interrelated characteristics of the Victorian as period".[46] Hewitt argues that developments at the start of the Victorian period, most notably the construction of the railways with their high-speed views of landscapes and people in the 1830s and the invention of photographic processes in the late 1830s and early 1840s, "gave the Victorians a fresh visual engagement with the world".[47] Literary historian Renate Brosch states similarly that Victorians witnessed "an explosion of visuality during which new optical devices, new entertainments, new subjects and techniques in representation were accompanied by enormous visual changes in everyday urban life".[48] Legal reforms and new technologies alike enabled this "explosion of visuality", which encompasses the rapid expansion of exhibition cultures (following the Great Exhibition of 1851), performance cultures (the rise of the music hall and melodrama) and an emerging mass market for printed material (illustrated magazines, daily newspapers, multi-volume novels), all of which interacted in various ways.[49]

Representations of the urban poor had been popular since before the Victorian print explosion but from the 1830s in particular, "journalists, painters, illustrators and photographers penetrated urban areas that they found full of

---

44   Martin Hewitt, "Why the Notion of Victorian Britain Does Make Sense", *Victorian Studies*, vol. 48, no. 3 (Spring 2006): 395–438.

45   See Boyd and McWilliam, "Introduction", 18, 24 and 28.

46   Hewitt, "Victorian Britain", 396–397.

47   Ibid., 412.

48   Renate Brosch, "Introduction. Victorian Visual Culture", in Renate Brosch (ed.), *Victorian Visual Culture* (Heidelberg: Universitätsverlag Winter, 2008), 7–20, here 9.

49   On exhibition culture, see Richard Daniel Altick, *The Shows of London: A Panoramic History of Exhibitions* (Cambridge, Mass., London: The Belknap Press of Harvard University Press, 1978). On the proliferation of illustrated printing, see Gerry Beegan, *The Mass Image: A Social History of Photomechanical Reproduction in Victorian London* (London: Palgrave Macmillan, 2008).

unknown phenomena, strong contrasts and shocking experiences".[50] With their first-hand reportages, detailed illustrations, realist paintings and shocking photographs, "[t]hey catered to the public of the new (urban) media".[51] From the 1880s, attempts at systematic classification of poverty and early sociological enquiries were conducted by Charles Booth (*Life and Labour of the People in London*, 17 volumes, 1889–1902) and Seebohm Rowntree (*Poverty: A Study of Town Life*, 1901), who introduced the concept of the poverty line and showed that almost one third of Londoners and 30 per cent of the inhabitants of York lived in poverty.[52] As historian Seth Koven has pointed out the term poor "spanned a considerable spectrum from the homeless to sweated workers [...] to seasonally employed unskilled laborers to regularly employed skilled artisans".[53] And as historians Andreas Gestrich, Steven King and Lutz Raphael state, Victorian attitudes towards poverty, state welfare and charity were likewise situated on a spectrum:

> At one end of this spectrum, the poor might be blamed for their own poverty and left either to sink into abject pauperism or be confined to institutions, sometimes with the full backing of national laws. At the other end of the spectrum, poverty might be associated with the operation of advanced agrarian, urban and industrial systems and the poor might be seen by those who controlled the purse strings as having a legitimate claim on the pockets of those with spare resources.[54]

The depictions of poverty included in this study were similarly located on a spectrum that ranged from authentic, first-hand reports on the living conditions in London's slums to picturesque representations of poor characters as a natural and even entertaining part of urban existence. George Sims collected the material for his stories during slum tours and directly observed the mannerisms, speaking habits and colloquial language he later used to distinguish his fictional characters from polite society. Their authentic expressions and untutored beliefs could be daring, entertaining and colourful in and of themselves.

Sims's fictional texts exhibit a notable downward mobility. The drinking parlours, common lodging houses and casual wards of his ballads and stories are populated by impoverished and fallen women, luckless gamblers and ruined speculators as well as hopeless drunkards of high birth. Whether through no fault of their own or driven by addiction and vice – seemingly anyone could fall into poverty. If you weren't born into it already, that is. Sims's

---

50 Werner Michael Schwarz, Margarethe Szeless and Lisa Wögenstein, "Bilder des Elends in der Großstadt (1830–1930)", in Werner Schwarz, Margarethe Szeless and Lisa Wögenstein (ed.), *Ganz unten. Die Entdeckung des Elends: Wien, Berlin, London, Paris, New York* (Wien: Brandstätter, 2007), 9–17, here 12. Translated from the German by the author.

51 Ibid.

52 See Brundage, *English Poor Laws*, 131.

53 Koven, *Slumming*, 10–11.

54 Andreas Gestrich, Steven King and Lutz Raphael, "The experience of being poor in nineteenth- and early-twentieth-century Europe", in Andreas Gestrich, Steven King and Lutz Raphael (ed.), *Being Poor in Modern Europe: Historical Perspectives 1800–1940* (Oxford etc.: Lang, 2006), 17–40, here 17.

journalistic writings exposed the horrible conditions under which a majority of the honest (i.e. working) poor of London and their children were forced to live:

> The poor – the honest poor – have been driven [...] to come and herd with thieves and wantons, to bring up their children in the last Alsatias, where lawlessness and violence still reign supreme. The constant association of the poor and the criminal class has deadened in the former nearly all sense of right and wrong.[55]

Work and Poverty

The 19th century marks the breakthrough of European capitalism and free trade economics in Britain, epitomized by the repeal of the Corn Laws in 1846 which lifted tariffs on imported grain.[56] Hard work became a core value of Victorian society, historian Colin Matthew even diagnoses a "culture of work" that marked a change from what Victorians considered the "frivolity and corruption" of the 18th century: "Work and the discipline of work, whether in employment, for a charity or a church, for the family and the home, became its own justification: men worked, women worked, children worked, and if they could not work, they went to the workhouse."[57] This "culture of work" was applied to poor-relief as well, differentiating between those unable to work and those unwilling and thus undeserving of aid.

As Gareth Stedman Jones has shown, the twin ideals of work and self-help were advanced even more strictly in the late-Victorian period following economic and social crises in the 1860s and 1880s.[58] Even though in London the problems of seasonal employment, separation of the classes and a growing casual workforce were described by social investigators like Henry Mayhew and Charles Booth, "most unemployment was attributed to the lack of habits of industry and forethought rather than to an excess of supply".[59] Able-bodied men especially were discouraged from seeking either charity or poor relief. The workhouse is symbolic of this application, acting as a deterrent for those unwilling to work and a last resort for those unable to sustain themselves (the aged and infirm, mothers or widows, orphans).[60] Rachel Fuchs locates this shift in Western European attitudes towards poor-relief and the idea of deserving and undeserving poor between 1770 and 1815. She argues that capitalism and the growing industrial sector relied on regulating the workforce: "As a result, poor-relief reformers built the desirability of work into their ideologies."[61] Conversely, conservative historian Gertrude Himmelfarb argues against the widely held notion that a canon of "specifically middle-class values" was

---

55   George Robert Sims, *How the Poor Live and Horrible London* (London: Chatto & Windus, 1889), 11.

56   See Purchase, *Victorian Literature*, xv.

57   Matthew, "Introduction", 4–6.

58   See Stedman Jones, *Outcast London*, 281.

59   Ibid., 277, see also 286.

60   See Rachel Fuchs, *Gender and Poverty in Nineteenth Century Europe* (Cambridge: Cambridge University Press, 2005), 38.

61   Ibid., 38, 40 and 198.

imposed on the British working classes as a means of social control.[62] Himmelfarb claims that there were universal Victorian values held both by the middle classes and "the overwhelming majority of the working classes and even of the very poor".[63] These included "work, thrift, cleanliness, temperance, honesty, self-help" and a set of related virtues that contributed to a Victorian work ethic, namely "promptness, regularity, conformity, rationality".[64]

George R. Sims stressed the *leisurely* aspects of Victorian life in his autobiography, *My Life: Sixty Years' Recollections of Bohemian London*, published in 1917 at a time when many of these Victorian values had become unfashionable. Sims formed important work contacts "during drinking sprees at the Unity Club" and had a penchant for horse races and gambling.[65] His sentimental Dagonet ballads were probably fuelled as much by liquor as they were by Christian concern for the plight of the poor.[66] Even though Sims himself insisted in several interviews in the early 1890s that he only drank weak whiskey and water and smoked his tobacco pipe when working.[67] But Sims was still a prolific and commercially successful writer with an enormous output in prose, poetry and journalism, who for 45 years never once failed to hand in his weekly column for *The Referee*.[68] And when he wrote a short "Autobiography" for *The Theatre* in 1884, his emphasis was less on his Bohemian lifestyle and more on the amount of his writing work:

> At the time *Crutch* [*and Toothpick*] was produced [1879] I was getting through a marvellous amount of work. I was hard at work in the City from ten to five. I wrote for the *Referee* and the *Weekly Dispatch*, and for various periodicals. I edited *One and All*, in which I wrote a novel week by week; and I was filling up my spare time by writing a melodrama, which I hoped one day to induce a manager to look at.[69]

London and Poverty

Increasing urbanization and a rapidly growing population were two key factors that shaped English life throughout the 19th century. While in 1800 London was the only city in England and Wales that had a population of over 100,000, by 1901 "80% of English and Welsh people lived in cities". During that same period the overall population of Great Britain quadrupled.[70] Both trends

---

62 Gertrude Himmelfarb, "In Defence of the Victorians", in Boyd and McWilliam (ed.), *The Victorian Studies Reader*, 209–219, here 214.

63 Ibid.

64 Ibid.

65 Marsh and Francis, "Poetry of Poverty", 65.

66 See George R. Sims, *My Life: Sixty Years' Recollections of Bohemian London* (London: Eveleigh Nash, 1917), 28–29 and 88–89.

67 See, e.g., "Workers and Their Work – No. III. Mr. George R. Sims, Journalist and Playwright", *Pearson's Weekly* (19 September 1891): 135.

68 See "G.R. Sims. Journalist, Dramatist and Bohemian", *The Times* (6 September 1922): 12.

69 George R. Sims, "An Autobiography", *The Theatre* (July 1884): 14–17, here 16.

70 Andrew Saint, "Cities, Architecture, and Art", in Matthew (ed.), *The Nineteenth Century*, 255–291, here 255.

converged in the capital and the population of Greater London increased continually throughout the century from around one million in 1800 to 6.5 million by 1900, which amounted to 20 per cent of the entire population of England and Wales.[71] This growth "resulted from natural increase and immigration, roughly in equal measure", as rural workers and artisans alike sought new employment opportunities in the city.[72] By the early 19th century London had "emerged as a major financial centre" while its docks stored and transferred different goods in a global economy.[73] Unlike the industrial centres of the North (Manchester, Glasgow, Sheffield), London was not characterized by large factories but predominantly "a city of small masters". Its heavy industries actually declined in the latter half of the century while its importance as a banking and insurance centre increased rapidly.[74] This created living and working conditions in London that were in some ways distinct from those in the rest of the country, although it was plagued by the same problems as other growing cities: "Lack of proper housing, overcrowding, inadequate environmental sanitation, polluted water supplies, and malnutrition combined to make the life of the city-dweller, particularly if new, and that of his family, hard, desperate, and hazardous to health and life."[75]

In London the spatial segregation of the rich and poor became especially pronounced throughout the century as the former tended to move to the new suburbs while the latter stayed in or migrated to the overcrowded districts of the centre out of sheer necessity.[76] Insufficient housing was available for the working poor and the growing value of urban land drove up rents which meant that a growing number of people lived in overcrowded areas.[77] As Rachel Fuchs puts it:

> By all standards housing for workers was deplorable and severely overcrowded. Buildings were clustered so close together on narrow streets and alleys that sunlight could not penetrate or air circulate. Green moss and black mold grew within the crevices of the crumbling bricks and plaster inside and out.[78]

---

71   Ibid.

72   Wohl, *Eternal Slum*, 2.

73   Martin Daunton, "Society and Economic Life", in Matthew (ed.), *The Nineteenth Century*, 41–82, here 45.

74   Stedman Jones, *Outcast London*, 29 and 152–153.

75   George Rosen, "Disease, Debility, and Death", in Harold James Dyos and Michael Wolff (ed.), *The Victorian City: Images and Realities*, vol. 2 (London: Routledge, Boston: Kegan Paul, 1973), 625–667, here 625. See also Stedman Jones, *Outcast London*, 32.

76   Harold James Dyos and David Alec Reeder, "Slums and Suburbs", in Harold James Dyos and Michael Wolff (ed.), *The Victorian City: Images and Realities*, vol. 1 (London: Routledge, Boston: Kegan Paul, 1973), 359–386, here 360. Workers, especially those in casual (i.e. unsteady) employment and working women needed to live at walking distance to their (potential) employers as suitable and affordable public transportation only became available in the 1890s. See Stedman Jones, *Outcast London*, 160 and 172. Stedman Jones lists cheaper food and buying on credit as well as elements of working-class culture as other reasons that kept workers in the centre. Ibid., 172–173.

77   See Fuchs, *Gender and Poverty*, 165, and Stedman Jones, *Outcast London*, 20.

78   Fuchs, *Gender and Poverty*, 165.

Fears of contamination and of criminal hotbeds in working-class London were evoked by Edwin Chadwick in his description of *The Sanitary Condition of the Labouring Population* in 1842. But failed legislation (Torrens Act of 1868, Artisans' Dwellings Act of 1875) and repeated slum clearances for railway works and sanitary reasons only made overcrowding in poor districts worse in the following decades.[79] Increasingly, these districts became "an immense terra incognita periodically mapped out by intrepid missionaries and explorers who catered to an insatiable middle-class demand for travellers' tales", as Gareth Stedman Jones puts it.[80] The shocking accounts in George R. Sims's *How the Poor Live* (1883) and Andrew Mearns's penny pamphlet *The Bitter Cry of Outcast London* (1883) brought renewed attention to the living conditions and the supposed moral decay they engendered among the poor. They even brought about a Royal Commission on the Housing of the Working Classes before which Sims appeared as a witness on 22 April 1884.[81] The commission toured the slums of several English cities and its members included the Prince of Wales, who was to be crowned King Edward VII following Queen Victoria's death in 1901, and Radical politician Sir Charles Dilke.

To counterbalance the high level of rents in central London, which was also home to the Parliament, the National and Imperial government and the Court, manufacturers established production in small workshops or sweatshops in an attempt to reduce overhead (the costs of wages, fuel and rent).[82] This meant that workers and working women had to put in long hours in small spaces or work in their own – small and often unsanitary – homes. Sims describes working conditions in London slum houses both in his prose and his journalistic works. In "A Brown Check Suit", a story from his first book *The Social Kaleidoscope* (1881), he gives an account of the sweating system that drastically illustrates its hazards – not only to those whose work it exploited. When a cheap suit is tailored for a large-framed West End customer, its pieces are sewn by various poor workers in their homes to make a profit. One of the sewing-women has a sick child to take care of and when the suit is returned to its owner, he infects a whole village with the scarlet fever when he wears it to his son's birthday.[83] And in *How the Poor Live*, Sims describes rabbit-pulling as one type of work that is hazardous to the health of those who earn a living doing it in their own homes:

> When we open the door we start back half choked. The air is full of floating fluff, and some of it gets into our mouths and half chokes us. When we've coughed and wheezed a little we look about us and gradually take in the situation. [...] They

---

79   See Stedman Jones, *Outcast London*, 163, 188 and 200.

80   Ibid., 14.

81   Sims's testimony appears in the *First Report of Her Majesty's Commissioners for Inquiring into the Housing of the Working Classes* (London: Eyre and Spottiswoode, 1885), 182–189.

82   Stedman Jones, *Outcast London*, 22.

83   George R. Sims, *The Social Kaleidoscope*, First and second series (London: J.P. Fuller, 1881), 46–51. See also Groth, "Kaleidoscopic Vision", 100.

are simply pulling rabbit-skins – that is to say, they are pulling away all the loose fluff and down and preparing the skins for the furriers, who will use them for cheap goods, dye them into imitations of rarer skins, and practise upon them the various tricks of the trade. Floor, walls, ceiling, every inch of the one room these people live and sleep in, is covered with fluff and hair. How they breathe in it is a mystery to me.[84]

George Sims was born, lived and died in London. He was "every inch a cockney" who prided himself on his knowledge of those parts of London inaccessible to many of his fellow citizens.[85] Even theatre critic William Archer, otherwise quite sceptical of the popular Sims, attests that through his work as a businessman, he had acquired an "intimate knowledge of the world – of London – which is peculiar to him, in which no writer, perhaps, has equalled him, since the death of Charles Dickens".[86] Sim's desire to map out the city and understand London in all its facets culminated in his massive editorial work *Living London* (1901–1903), which comprised more than 1,000 pages and 450 illustrations. His first success *The Lights o' London* (1881) was the story of a young couple from the country impoverished and disillusioned by life in the City.

Radical Politics and the Working Class

The late 18th century and the aftermath of the Industrial Revolution in England also marked the introduction of *class* as a concept to describe social differences and power relations. It replaced the older terminology of *ranks* and *orders* as the term *working class* or *working classes* came to describe those "who existed by selling their labour power" instead of deriving income from selling goods they produced.[87] Karl Marx and Frederick Engels posited that this was accompanied by the formation of "class consciousness" and subsequent conflict between those owning the means of production and those dependent on wages.[88] In England this was marked first by the Luddite movement and their "attempts to destroy factories and machinery which competed with workers' labour" and later by "strategies for maintaining and advancing wage levels by means of national trade unions and political campaigns".[89] One of the most notable campaigns was Chartism, a branch of political Radicalism, which historian David Wright characterizes as a "mass working-class movement making a determined bid for political power".[90] Chartists demanded universal male

---

84 Sims, *How the Poor Live* (1889), 14. In his testimony before the Royal Commission, Sims also spoke of women who have to use their own urine to wet the rabbit skins because there is no source of clean water nearby.

85 J.L.O., "Mr. G.R. Sims at Home", *Booksellers' Supplement to the Newsagent & Booksellers' Review* (7 September 1895): 38–40, here 39.

86 William Archer, *English Dramatists of To-day* (London: Sampson Low, Marston, Searle, & Rivington, 1882), 297–298.

87 David Graham Wright, *Popular Radicalism: The Working Class Experience, 1780–1880* (London, New York: Longman, 1988), 3.

88 See ibid., 7–8.

89 Ibid., 8.

90 Ibid., 112.

suffrage (among other things).[91] The movement arose from a working-class frustration with the Reform Acts of 1832, "which enfranchised property while abolishing old franchises which had previously allowed some working-class representation".[92] Small bursts of violence and public disorder in the late 1830s and the early 1840s somewhat discredited the movement and fuelled Conservative fears of "mob rule" but political Radicalism remained influential throughout the century.[93]

The Chartists formulated a Charter of six demands, which George R. Sims quotes fully in his memoir. Sims reminisces about his grandfather John Dinmore Stevenson, whom he describes somewhat hyperbolically as "one of the leaders of the Chartist movement".[94] The influence of George R. Sims's Chartist grandfather and his Suffragette mother on his writing is noted by most modern commentators[95] and Sims repeatedly mentioned his mother's activism in magazine articles.[96] It is not a coincidence that his first effort at public speaking was a lecture at a Radical Club in Tower Hamlets, one of London's poorest boroughs in 1880. This lecture was also the starting point for his social investigation into the living conditions of the urban poor in Southwark which his *How the Poor Live* articles were based on. Poverty was not the only social issue that Sims raised in newspaper articles. He focused on the "white slave traffic" in *London by Night* and *Watches of the Night* and campaigned to ban children from public houses in *The Cry of the Children* and *The Black Stain* which eventually became law. In *The Tribune* he focused public attention on *The Bitter Cry of the Middle Class* (1906) and argued against state "pampering" of the poor. A state of affairs that – as one reader reminded him – he himself had helped to bring about with his dramatic tales of working class suffering.[97] This may have proven an unfortunate choice since, as historian Phillip Waller argues, it "forfeited him the goodwill of progressives" and Sims's obituary in *The Times*

---

91   In 1831 only five per cent of the adult male population were enfranchised and even after electoral reforms, political representation was only achieved through property (male householders), education (seats for universities) or businesses and anyone who received aid through the Poor Law (paupers) subsequently lost their vote for at least one year. See Purchase, *Victorian Literature*, 116, and Colin Matthew, "Public Life and Politics", in Matthew (ed.), *The Nineteenth Century*, 84–133, here 94–95.

92   Matthew, "Public Life", 100. Further electoral reform acts in 1867, 1884 and 1918 extended the franchise to eventually include most men and a limited number of women. Ibid., 93.

93   Purchase, *Victorian Literature*, 117–118 and 138.

94   Sims, *My Life*, 9. An article in the *Worcester Journal* (28 September 1843): 3 calls Stevenson "the leader of the Chartists of Worcester", and another states that he will be sent to the National Convention as representative of the Worcester Chartists; see *Worcester Journal*: (26 April 1848): 4. Another article from the Conservative paper refers to him as "a personage", who worked as a fishmonger in November 1842, when he ran for Town Councillor and polled one vote – his own. *Worcester Journal* (3 November 1842): 3.

95   Keating, *Into Unknown England*, 65; Marsh and Francis, "Poetry of Poverty", 66; Higgins, "London on Stage"; Philip Waller, "Altercation Over Civil Society: The Bitter Cry of the Edwardian Middle Classes", in Jose Harris (ed.), *Civil Society in British History: Ideas, Identities, Institutions* (Oxford, New York: Oxford University Press, 2003), 115–134, here 118.

96   See for example John Pearce, "Mr. George R. Sims", *'House and Home' Popular Biographies*, no. 1 (1882): 3–12, and *The Gentlewoman* (11 July 1891): 42.

97   See Waller, "Civil Society", 123.

neglected to mention any of his various social causes except that "he would champion the cause of the unfortunate middle classes, who, he maintained, were being steadily taxed out of existence by vote-catching politicians".[98]

The main political issues of the 19th century were the so-called "Condition of England" question raised by politicians (Benjamin Disraeli) and novelists (Elizabeth Gaskell, Charles Dickens) from the 1830s to the 1850s in response to "the miseries and deprivations suffered by the British working classes" and the Irish Famine of the mid-1840s.[99] Later, many of the same issues resurfaced during discussions of the "Social Question" following further revelations about the living and working conditions of the urban poor in Britain's larger cities. Colonial uprisings in India (Sepoy Mutiny, 1857) and Africa (Boer Wars, 1899–1902) and the question of Irish Home Rule (1880s, 1890s) likewise threatened the stability of the British Empire. Lastly, the changing role of women in society was marked by the Suffragette movement which began in the late 1860s.[100] The involvement of George R. Sims's mother Louisa in the Suffragette movement has already been noted and may have provided some inspiration for the heroine of his play *The Member for Slocum* (1881), "a lady of pronounced views on the equality of the sexes".[101] Sims also wrote a series of pseudo-memoirs from various female perspectives including that of a young housemaid (*Mary Jane's Memoirs*, 1887; *Memoirs of a Mother-in-Law*, 1892; *Memoirs of a Landlady*, 1894) and he invented a "pioneering woman detective" named Dorcas Dene (first series 1897, second series 1898).[102] Sims's revolutionary detective eventually made it onto the film screen in a miniseries of four two-reel episodes, produced under his personal supervision, that was set for international distribution in Spain and South America.[103]

Death and Poverty

Death and mourning were ubiquitous in Victorian society, "woven into the very fabric of Victorian daily existence" according to art historian Terri Sabatos.[104] Queen Victoria's very public life-long mourning for Prince Albert was only the most obvious example of the Victorian preoccupation with mourning rituals.[105] Receiving a proper burial was considered so important that many poor persons joined so-called "funeral clubs" during their lifetime to be able

---

98   Waller, "Sims", 722, and *The Times* (6 September 1922): 12.

99   Purchase, *Victorian Literature*, xiv.

100 Janet Howarth, "Gender, Domesticity, and Sexual Politics", in Matthew (ed.), *The Nineteenth Century*, 63–193, here 187.

101 Sims, *My Life*, 114. On Mrs. George Sims (Louisa), see also Elizabeth Crawford, *The Women's Suffrage Movement in Britain and Ireland: A Regional Survey* (London, New York: Routledge, 2006), 174 and 178.

102 Waller, "Sims", 723.

103 See "George R. Sims' Stories to Be Screened", *Kinematograph Weekly* (1 May 1919): 91; see also the advertisement for "Aventuras de Dorcas Dene, Investigadora de Crímenes" in *Kinematograph Weekly* (6 November 1919): 166.

104 Terri Sabatos, *Images of Death and Domesticity in Victorian Britain*, PhD diss. (Indiana University, 2001), 3.

105 Ibid. For a description of Victorian mourning rituals, see 13–23.

to afford it. The contempt poor Victorians felt for the workhouse was exacerbated after the passing of the Anatomy Act of 1832 which "legalized the use of dead bodies from workhouses, hospitals and gallows, for use in medicinal science".[106] Effectively this equated workhouse inmates who died in "the house" with murders and other criminals executed for their deeds.[107]

Average life expectancy rose steadily throughout the 19th century, however, it remained as low as the early 50s for the poor well into the 20th century.[108] The combination of close quarters, unsanitary sewerage systems and unclean water supply made for a deadly combination in larger cities (Glasgow, Manchester, London, Liverpool). Poverty and its resultant effects of malnutrition, overcrowding and lack of heating was seen as the main cause for the high mortality rates (especially of poor infants) by Victorian medical professionals.[109] But contagious diseases like cholera, typhoid, tuberculosis and venereal diseases affected all strata of society (if not at the same rate) and caused a number of epidemics throughout the century. Albert, the Prince Consort, died of typhoid in 1861.

Concerns for those living under unsanitary conditions in overcrowded houses and working as sweated workers were often mixed with fears of contamination of well-to-do neighbourhoods from the unhygienic and unsanitary slums.[110] This led to the appointment of medical officers who, by mid-century, reported regularly on the sanitary conditions in London's parishes and districts following Edwin Chadwick's influential report on the "sanitary condition" of England in 1842.[111] The physical presence of dead bodies became especially problematic in this context since the "sheer numbers and visibility of the dead throughout the country forced the authorities to construct more and more cemeteries, with eight new graveyards being built in London alone".[112] In 1843 Edwin Chadwick published his *Report on the Practice of Internment in Towns* and described the common practice among the poor of keeping the bodies of dead family members at home until they could afford a proper funeral.[113] Forty years later George R. Sims still reported on similar cases in *How the Poor Live*: "It often happens there is no money to pay for the funeral, and so, with that inertness and helplessness bred of long years of neglect, nothing at all is done,

---

106   Purchase, *Victorian Literature*, 35.

107   See Richardson, *Dickens*, 228.

108   Purchase, *Victorian Literature*, 34. For statistics on death rates, see Eric Edwin Lampard, "The Urbanizing World", in Dyos and Wolff (ed.), *The Victorian City*, vol. 1, 3–57, here 10 and 19–20.

109   George Rosen names William Farr and John Simon as examples. See Rosen, "Disease", 628 and 651.

110   For a short overview of factory regulation legislation, see ibid., 646.

111   See Anthony Wohl, "Unfit for Human Habitation", in Dyos and Wolff (ed.), *The Victorian City*, vol. 2, 603–624, here 604.

112   Purchase, *Victorian Literature*, 35.

113   Sabatos, *Images of Death*, 15.

no steps are taken, and the body stops exactly where it was when the breath left it."[114]

Children were especially at risk of dying in the Victorian period and the mortality rates of infants remained alarmingly high (fluctuating around 150 per 1,000 births) in England and Wales.[115] While infant deaths "occurred in all social classes", according to historian George Rosen, "the greatest number occurred among workers and the poor".[116] In his ballad *The Street Tumblers* George Sims tells the story of the poor wife of a street artist who learns to be thankful for her station in life when she observes the sudden death of the baby of a countess during the boy's christening.[117] Death frequently functions as a narrative resolution in Sims's ballads (e.g. *The Road to Heaven, Billy's Rose*). Jacqueline Bratton describes it as Sims's "[…] chief narrative device for neutralizing the pain and injustice he describes […]: justice and happiness in Heaven are overtly offered as a redress for suffering on earth, both in order to calm the conscience, and as a reason the sufferers might be expected to accept for not rising up in their own defence."[118]

Death also directly affected Sims's personal life as the author was widowed twice. The death of his first wife was announced in a short note in *The Referee* on 26 December 1886: "Our dear friend DAGONET has this week suffered one of the calamities to which we are all in turn subject. Very early in the week his dearly beloved wife, Sarah Elizabeth (Bessie), died, after a lingering illness, which made death a happy release to her."[119] In March of 1888 Sims married Annie Maria Harriss and in August 1901, widowed again, Sims married Elizabeth Florence Wykes, who outlived him.[120]

1.3 The New Poor Law, Poor Relief and Private Charity

The so-called New Poor Law (Poor Law Amendment Act of 1834) was the most important piece of legislation relating to poverty and poor relief in the 19th century. It was an attempt to curb rising poor rates, minimize outdoor relief to able-bodied paupers and centralize poor law administration. As such it replaced the more than two centuries old Elizabethan Poor Law (1601), which had "set up a mandatory system of publicly financed poor relief through-

---

114 Sims, *How the Poor Live* (1889), 60. As a remedy, Chadwick had proposed that dead bodies should be brought to mortuary houses to examine them and prepare them for burial. However, when George Sims wrote his articles in 1883, he complained that some districts were still without a mortuary.

115 See Rosen, "Disease", 649. According to contemporary medical statistics by William Farr, infant deaths even increased in the late 19th century. In total, they accounted for around one quarter of all deaths while infants under the age of one accounted for one fifth. See Purchase, *Victorian Literature*, 35.

116 Rosen, "Disease", 649. Rosen cites the immediate employment of new mothers after birth, the use of drugs and strong alcohol to pacify children and "improper feeding of infants" as the main causes. Ibid., 650.

117 See George R. Sims, *The Lifeboat and Other Poems* (London: J.P. Fuller, 1883), 49–58.

118 Bratton, *Victorian Popular Ballad*, 125–126.

119 *The Referee* (26 December 1886): 5.

120 See Waller, "Sims", 723.

out England and Wales".[121] Poor relief was administered and poor rates were raised on a local level at the parish unit. Each parish (more than 15,000 in total) was responsible for its own poor, whose settlements were defined (and re-defined) in settlement legislation throughout the 17th century.[122] Any poor person could only apply for relief in their place of settlement and even those merely in danger of becoming impoverished could be removed to their original settlement. This caused both considerable hardships for poor families and especially unwed mothers threatened by removal as well as increasing litigation between parishes attempting to reduce the burden on their ratepayers.

The first workhouses (or poorhouses) were institutions that housed the aged and infirm paupers of a parish and towards the end of the 18th century the wages of rural workers were occasionally subsidized to help them maintain their families.[123] The annual cost of poor relief rose steadily throughout the century and following the war against Napoleon and a combination of cyclical depression and bad harvests in the first quarter of the 19th century, attempts were made to reform the Old Poor Law. Both the findings of a Royal Commission (1832–1834) and influential writings by economic theorists (Malthus, Bentham, Ricardo) informed the New Poor Law.[124] Its key features were the creation of poor law unions as administrative units, a severe restriction of outdoor relief to the able-bodied and the principles of less-eligibility and the deterrent workhouse.[125]

The principle of less-eligibility presumed that if living conditions inside workhouses were made worse than the standard of living for poor labourers, able-bodied paupers would choose not to seek relief from the parish and seek work instead. However, as historian Derek Fraser notes, living standards especially in times of rural depression or cyclical unemployment were "[…] so low that it was quite impossible for less-eligibility to operate. […] Critics of poor relief were reminded time and time again that the food, income and accommodation of paupers was often superior to that of their poorest independent neighbours."[126] The so-called workhouse test operated under a similar assumption to determine whether or not an applicant for relief was actually in need of it by offering them only *the house*. It followed that only those willing to submit to the strict rules inside the workhouse were truly in need of relief and thus truly poor. But in effect, as the Liberal politician William Rathbone

---

121 Brundage, *English Poor Laws*, 9.

122 On settlement, see also Michael Rose, "Settlement, Removal and the New Poor Law", in Derek Fraser (ed.), *The New Poor Law in the Nineteenth Century* (London, Basingstoke: Macmillan, 1976), 25–44.

123 See Brundage, *English Poor Laws*, 28–29.

124 See Michael Rose, "The Disappearing Pauper: Victorian Attitudes to the Relief of the Poor", in Eric Sigworth (ed.), *In Search of Victorian Values: Aspects of Nineteenth-Century Thought and Society* (Manchester: Manchester University Press, 1988), 56–72, here 58–59.

125 Unions were formed of 20 to 30 parishes and managed by boards of guardians. See Peter Higginbotham, *The Workhouse Cookbook* (Stroud: The History Press, 2008), 8.

126 Derek Fraser, "Introduction", in Fraser (ed.), *The New Poor Law*, 1–24, here 18–19.

put it, the workhouse test "was felt so deeply to degrade the pauper that the best of the working class will rather starve – often do rather starve – than apply for it".[127] George Sims similarly criticized the workhouse test in his most famous ballad *In the Workhouse. Christmas Day* in which a starving elderly woman refuses to enter the workhouse for fear of being separated from her husband and dies when he is refused out-relief. And in a short poem titled *The Workhouse Test* Sims sarcastically lauded the effectiveness of the principle:

> It is better they die in their pauper pride,
> Inch by inch, for the lack of bread,
> Than the workhouse test be left untried,
> And the ratepayers saved so much per head.
>
> Hurrah! hurrah! For the workhouse test;
> Of all the schemes by our Bumble planned,
> The quickest and harshest, and so the best,
> Of pauper vermin to rid the land.[128]

With the New Poor Law, poor law reformers also strove to draw a clearer distinction between poverty, "the lot of most of the manual labouring classes" and pauperism, "a degenerate state in which the will to work was lost, the urge to self help was broken, and dependency and degeneration were the results".[129] Paupers were those dependent on relief by the parish and able-bodied pauperism in particular "was seen as the result of the irregular administration of relief, combined with individual indolence and improvidence", according to David Ashforth.[130] In theory, while those considered deserving poor (the old, sick or orphaned) were to be cared for in special institutions (workhouses and poorhouses, asylums, hospitals), those considered undeserving (the able-bodied, idle, vagrants) were to be deterred from seeking institutional relief and 'encouraged' to seek employment instead and migrate to areas where workers were needed. If only statistics are taken into account, the New Poor Law was successful in this respect since the number of paupers (those in receipt of poor relief) in relation to the total population declined constantly throughout the century.[131]

It should be noted that alongside public institutions, private charity – reserved mainly for those considered deserving poor – played a significant role in poor relief as Victorian society "made charity something of a social imperative for the new urban elite".[132] Indeed, according to Norman McCord, the amount

---

127 Quoted in ibid., 21.

128 George R. Sims, *The Land of Gold and Other Poems* (London: J.P. Fuller, 1888), 107–109. First published in *The Referee* (25 March 1883): 7.

129 Rose, "Disappearing Pauper", 57.

130 David Ashforth, "The Urban Poor Law", in Fraser (ed.), *The New Poor Law*, 128–148, here 129.

131 Historian Michael Rose cites the following numbers of paupers in England and Wales: "In 1841–42, they were between eight and nine per cent, falling to four or five per cent in mid-century, to two and a half per cent by 1900 and two per cent on the outbreak of the First World War. Within these overall totals, the old, the sick and the orphaned were always dominant." Rose, "Disappearing Pauper", 63.

132 Fraser, "Introduction", 9.

of annual "voluntary philanthropic activity" in London alone surpassed Poor Law expenditure for the entirety of England and Wales in the 1860s and generally, "unofficial far outweighed official exertion".[133] The foundation of the Charity Organization Society (C.O.S.) in 1868 marked an attempt to centralize and re-organize private charity by channelling all applications for relief through one organization that determined which specific charity an applicant would be referred to. Another aim was to separate charity more clearly from public poor relief: "The C.O.S. finally provided a rigorous discipline for what had previously been informally acknowledged; the deserving should be aided by charities, the undeserving by the Poor Law."[134] George Sims was often critical of the organization in his column for *The Referee* and noted in 1883:

> It seems to me that the whole question of charity requires overhauling, and the middlemen who absorb 60 per cent of the money ought to be abolished. I give credit for all the honesty and all the sincerity of purpose, but I say that as long as it costs £80 to distribute £20 it is the middle classes who are benefiting by charity, and not the poor.[135]

After a surprisingly smooth passage in parliament, the New Poor Law was met with strong opposition from several directions. While political opposition in parliament was unable to stop the law, critics used their newspapers to agitate against it.[136] As Chartism gained momentum towards the end of the 1830s, calls for workers' suffrage and political reform were combined with resistance to the New Poor Law and its treatment of the poor.[137] Moreover, local officials were often hesitant to implement the new policies and unwilling to cede power to a central body.[138] And, as David Green has pointed out, the poor as subjects of the New Poor Law were not without agency. Even if they did enter the workhouse, inmates used a diverse array of protest forms:

> They fought, stole, broke property, threatened officials, wrote letters, organized petitions and took out summonses against arbitrary authority. They flitted between the workhouse and gaol, and when given temporary leave of absence they not infrequently returned late or drunk.[139]

---

133 Norman McCord, "The Poor Law and Philanthropy", in Fraser (ed.), *The New Poor Law*, 87–110, here 96–97.

134 Fraser, "Introduction", 10–11.

135 Dagonet [George R. Sims], "Mustard and Cress", *The Referee* (9 December 1883): 7.

136 See Norman Longmate, *The Workhouse* (London: Temple Smith, 1974), 58–59 and 109.

137 See Nicholas Edsall, *The Anti-Poor Law Movement* (Manchester: Manchester University Press, 1971), 171.

138 Historian David Ashforth even goes so far as to state: "This was the great common denominator amongst opponents of the New Poor Law, and many who were otherwise prepared to accept the new system could not stomach the thought of being ruled by 'three Big Wigs in London'." Ashforth, "Urban Poor Law", 130.

139 See David Green, "Pauper Protests: Power and Resistance in Early Nineteenth-Century London Workhouses", *Social History*, vol. 31, no. 2 (May 2006): 137–159, here 159.

Journalists and writers like Charles Dickens, James Greenwood and George Sims also repeatedly criticized the treatment of paupers in parish institutions, which contributed to a general hatred for the workhouse.

The Deterrent Workhouse

The New Poor Law of 1834 did not create the institution of the workhouse but according to historian Norman Longmate, workhouses only became a noticeable presence, especially in rural Southern England, following the Poor Law reform: "In market towns they dwarfed the surrounding shops and cottages; in the depths of the countryside, they stood gauntly in hitherto untilled fields or on desolate stretches of waste land."[140] These newly constructed workhouses were almost exclusively built in a similar prison-like style:

> Usually they consisted of a bleak, two-storey block, built round a courtyard with vegetable gardens lying behind it. At the front there was a narrow gate, guarded by a porter's lodge, with a large bell hanging above it, and the premises were invariably surrounded by a high wall.[141]

These new workhouses were to be governed and poor relief was to be administered by boards of guardians in each union or parish. Any form of relief was to be channelled only through the workhouse except in "Cases of sudden and urgent Necessity".[142] Although the deterrent function of the workhouse was not a new feature, the first workhouses built in the late 17th century had simply provided food and sometimes shelter and education to the old, young and impotent poor of a parish.[143] By the early 18th century some lawmakers and local administrators proposed that workhouses could save ratepayers money since the impotent poor would be cared for in the house and the able-bodied discouraged from applying for relief. More than 150 new workhouses were built following the passage of the Knatchbull Act in 1723, "which authorised any parish to set up its own workhouse".[144] The assumption turned out to be false since paying paupers a small weekly allowance was often cheaper than maintaining them inside a workhouse and poor rates rose steadily throughout the century.[145] By the early 19th century, however, the Rev. Robert Lowe of Bingham had figured out how to reduce poor-rates and discipline the able-bodied and idle poor of his parish by "virtually abolishing out-relief and offering instead food and shelter in the workhouse, where conditions were made so strict that soon all its former occupants [...] had voluntarily moved

---

140   Longmate, *The Workhouse*, 13.

141   Ibid.

142   *An Act for the Amendment and Better Administration of the Laws Relating to the Poor of England and Wales: With Explanatory Notes and a Copious Index*, 2nd edition (London: B. Fellowes, 1834), 58, Article 54.

143   See Longmate, *The Workhouse*, 23–24.

144   Ibid., 24.

145   As Norman Longmate puts it: "In mid century the universal claim had been that the poor rates were halved by building a workhouse. Now it was clear they had, instead, doubled, trebled or increased tenfold." Ibid., 33.

out".[146] This type of deterrent workhouse became a cornerstone of the New Poor Law of 1834 and the able-bodied poor its main focus. Since living conditions outside the workhouses were frequently worse than inside, Poor Law Commissioners proposed specific measures to discourage applicants: "The pauper would be forced to undergo such indignities as wearing a prison-style uniform, he would be subjected to the hardest and most tedious labour human ingenuity could devise, and, above all, he would be separated from his wife and children."[147] Other means of making inmates' lives miserable inside the workhouse were the bland and repetitive food as well as close and uncomfortable sleeping quarters.[148]

Not all unions implemented the regulations of the New Poor Law with equal fervour and out-relief remained a common practice for several decades, but a stream of workhouse scandals that were published in the popular press and in medical reports quickly turned public opinion against the institution. The most notable one was the Andover workhouse scandal of 1845.[149] Andover, Hampshire, was considered a "model union" for its strict adherence to the Poor Law Commissioners' recommendations and had stopped all out-relief to the able-bodied.[150] Politicians and the public were shocked when reports in *The Times* revealed that starving workhouse inmates at Andover were habitually eating the marrow and any scraps of meat they found on the bones they were crushing to make fertilizer.[151] A Select Committee of the House of Commons later found that the paupers at Andover were routinely undernourished while the workhouse master had ordered good food and liquor for himself at the expense of the inmates' rations. His other misdeeds included the sexual abuse of female inmates. The practice of bone crushing was subsequently banned in all workhouses, but food rations were later reduced again at Andover and the meagre workhouse diet remained a recurring topic in popular portrayals of the workhouse – especially in times of economic depression. In April of 1881 the Radical newspaper *The Referee* printed its own revelations about a workhouse in London's East End. They published the full dietary table of the Whitechapel Union Infirmary and testimony by a visiting gentleman who alleged that patients were not allowed visitors on Sundays and that "the meat is occasionally uneatable, that the other articles are of commensurate quality, and that such comforts for the dying as lemonade and barley water are unknown in the

---

146 Ibid., 45.

147 Ibid., 55–56. For the type of work carried out, see ibid., 251–256. The tasks included bone-crushing and oakum picking.

148 Ibid., 94.

149 See Ian Anstruther, *The Scandal of the Andover Workhouse* (London: Bles, 1973), and Longmate, *The Workhouse*, 122–135. Literary historian Ruth Richardson also lists the reports on malnutrition and starvation of parish children at a pauper farm by surgeon Dr Thomas Pettigrew in 1836 and those by Dr Joseph Rogers, a Poor Law Medical Officer at Cleveland Street Workhouse, in the 1850s and 1860s as examples. See Richardson, *Dickens*, 281–283 and 291–296.

150 See Longmate, *The Workhouse*, 122.

151 Ibid., 124–125, and Anstruther, *Andover Workhouse*, 139–141.

Whitechapel Infirmary".[152] In the following year several cases of deaths from starvation in the Whitechapel infirmary were reported in other newspapers, however, they were all attributed to the already poor health of the patients. Still, these cases illustrate the aversion that even those completely without the means of subsistence felt towards the deterrent workhouses. In the following issue of *The Referee*, George Sims published the substantially larger rations given to prisoners and sarcastically recommended the superior quality of food and life in prison. And in his popular melodrama *The Lights o' London*, which premiered later that same year, Sims had a poor character quip: "Fools goes to the workhouse, rogues goes to prison. Why, cause every man a goes to the workhouse is a fool for not being a rogue."[153] In Sims's ballads, the workhouse appears frequently as a backdrop when the protagonist is or reluctantly becomes a workhouse inmate (*One Winter Night*, *The Street Tumblers*, *The Land of Gold*) or as a place that is to be avoided at all costs – even death (*In the Workhouse*, *The Old Actor's Story*).

Historian Derek Fraser concedes that "workhouses were depressing and life inside them was monotonous" but remains doubtful "if they ever really became the harsh prisons of popular myth".[154] And David Green points out that contrary to popular belief, paupers could not be held in the workhouse against their will:

> Paupers could discharge themselves at any time from the workhouse, and many regularly came and went, secure in the knowledge that officials had an obligation to readmit them and that failure to do so, particularly for those who were obviously in need, was always liable to invite scrutiny by local magistrates, the press and not infrequently the Poor Law Commissioners themselves.[155]

Still, as this chapter has shown, the principle of less-eligibility fostered an attitude towards the workhouse that George Sims sums up succinctly:

> Over and over again society professes to be astonished that men and women commit suicide rather than go into the house. There are some things which to men with a scrap of self-respect are more horrible than death. The workhouse 'as arranged for endurance' is one of them.[156]

152　"Christian Charity", *The Referee* (17 April 1881): 5.

153　Act 3.1, lines 25–27, see Booth, *The Lights o' London,* 129.

154　Fraser, "Introduction", 20.

155　Green, "Pauper Protests", 139.

156　Dagonet, "Mustard and Cress", *The Referee* (24 April 1881): 7.

2

Modes of Depicting Poverty

2.1 From the Picturesque to the Authentic

Shortly after the publication of *How the Poor Live* (1883), which had caused quite a stir in London, George Sims commented on the public's new-found interest in the lives of the poor:

> The question of the housing of the poor still continues to excite general interest all over the country. All the great centres of industry have felt the wave, and we have in Liverpool, Birmingham, Manchester, and Leeds special commissioners making revelations to the local journals which vie with those which the London Press are daily publishing.[157]

Sims also put himself in an imagined lineage of authors and artists who had previously examined the living conditions of the poor in London:

> To this very question which now engages every hand that can wield a pen, dozens of good men and true have for years devoted their untiring energies. Charles Dickens and Henry Mayhew worked at it; Mr. Sala and Mr. James Greenwood have worked at it for years; ever since I had a public journal to write in I, too, in my humble way, have worked at it.[158]

Sims's descriptions of the homes of the poor and Frederick Barnard's sketches were influenced by those who came before them and relied on the familiarity of their readers both with illustrated reports and social investigative journalism. After pointing out general tendencies in the depiction of poverty in 19th century Britain, this chapter will discuss in more detail three examples of illustrated descriptions of the London poor. These will serve as examples for two categories central to the understanding of Victorian depictions of poverty: the picturesque and the authentic.

John Ruskin, one of the leading proponents of Victorian aesthetic theory wrote about the picturesque in 1849: "Probably no word in the language, (exclusive of theological expressions,) has been the subject of so frequent or so prolonged dispute; yet none remain more vague in their acceptance [...]."[159] The term

---

157 Dagonet, "Mustard and Cress", *The Referee* (18 November 1883): 7.

158 Ibid.

159 John Ruskin, *The Seven Lamps of Architecture*, 6th edition (Orpington, Kent: George Allen, 1889), 188. Reprinted from Ruskin's Venetian notebooks of 1840–1850.

picturesque was adapted into English from the French *pittoresque* and the Italian *pittoresco* in the early 18th century and simply designated an object, a person or a landscape as either "suitable for a picture" or "having the elements or qualities of a picture" according to the *Oxford English Dictionary*.[160] The concept gained popularity through the travel books of the Reverend William Gilpin published from the 1780s. Gilpin was also a painter and introduced "the Picturesque" as a particular way of designing gardens and viewing landscapes that would evoke pleasure in the viewer. He also suggested precise spots and scenes in the English and Scottish countryside that would provide readers with agreeable pictures for both viewing and painting which led to a "vogue for Picturesque tourism in Britain".[161] The objective of picturesque travel as proposed by Gilpin in his *Observations on the River Wye* (1770) was of

> [...] not barely examining the fact of a country; but of examining it by the rules of picturesque beauty: that of not merely describing; but of adapting the description of natural scenery to the principles of artificial landscape; and of opening the sources of those pleasures, which are derived from the comparison.[162]

There are several key characteristics of Gilpin's conception of the picturesque that I will adopt for my use of the term and that, I would argue, remain accurate even when the term is redefined, modified and criticized throughout the 19th century. First and foremost, the picturesque is an aesthetic operation initiated by the viewer that provides a pleasurable experience. The picturesque allows the viewer to gain pleasure even from observing objects (and people) not ordinarily considered beautiful or pleasant. According to Malcolm Andrews,

> [...] as Picturesque tastes develop, the visual delight in scenes of decay and dereliction is fully indulged as feelings of moral repugnance are subordinated. The Picturesque licenses a new appreciation of what the moral sense would deem as ugly, deformed.[163]

From the outset, scenes of rural poverty were a staple of the picturesque aesthetic and thus a possible source of pleasure. Thomas Gray, a pioneer of picturesque travel, offered the following description of "one of the sweetest landscapes, that art ever attempted to imitate" in his *Journal of a Visit to the Lake District* (1769) in North West England. Of a village situated on Grasmere lake, he paints the following picture:

> Just opposite to you is a large farm-house at the bottom of a steep smooth lawn embosomed in old woods, which climb half way up the mountain's side, and discover above them a broken line of crags, that crown the scene. Not a single red tile, no flaming [sic] Gentleman's house, or garden-walls, break in upon the prose

---

160   Lemma "picturesque, adj. and n.", Oxford English Dictionary Online (Oxford: Oxford University Press, January 2018), (http://www.oed.com/view/Entry/143510).

161   Malcolm Andrews, "Introduction", in Malcolm Andrews (ed.), *The Picturesque: Literary Sources & Documents*, vol. 1: *The Idea of the Picturesque and the Vogue for Scenic Tourism* (Mountfield: Helm Information, 1994), 3–37, here 7.

162   William Gilpin, "Observations on the River Wye in the Summer of 1770", reprinted in Andrews (ed.), *The Picturesque*, vol. 1, 241–278, here 243.

163   Andrews, "Introduction", 7.

of this little unsuspected paradise, but all is peace, rusticity, and happy poverty in its neatest, most becoming attire.[164]

In his highly influential *Essays on the Picturesque*, published in dialogue form around the turn of the 19th century, Uvedale Price defined as picturesque a class of "numberless objects which give delight to the eye, and yet differ as widely from the beautiful, as from the sublime".[165] Here again "giving delight" is cited as the main effect a picturesque aesthetic has on the viewer. Later, Price states that both sublime and beautiful "visible objects" have always "excited the emotions of astonishment, and of pleasure" and that their pictorial representation would evoke similar but less powerful emotions.[166] As Carrie Tirado Bramen notes, the picturesque was defined by its proponents as an alternative to the two Burkean modes of aesthetic reception: "Not requiring the classically trained eye necessary to detect beauty, and not possessing the infinite awe of the sublime, the picturesque is somewhere in the middle, a domesticated sublime that transforms shock into mild surprise."[167]

Price provided a list of objects he considered picturesque which included abandoned buildings that were signs of rural dilapidation like ruins, old mills and barns. But the picturesque could also be found in people, namely "among the wandering tribes of gypsies and beggars" who, he claimed, "bear a close analogy to the wild forester and the worn out cart-horse, and again to old mills, hovels, and other inanimate objects of the same kind".[168] Price admired the paintings of Thomas Gainsborough like *Landscape with Gipsies* (1753–1754) and while in actuality such scenes of rural poverty were not considered beautiful or morally acceptable, some could appreciate them for their aesthetic potential.[169] In Price's conception, the picturesque thus becomes "a symptom of special cultivation: it distinguishes the man of refined taste from the general observer", according to Malcolm Andrews.[170] It could also serve to repress feelings of sympathy for the rural poor: "This connoisseur elitism of the Picturesque goes hand in hand with the view that the Picturesque aesthetic was an elaborate kind of moral *an*aesthetic, a means of numbing the human sympathies when confronted with a scene of rural poverty and decay."[171] As literary historian Nancy Armstrong points out: "From its inception the pictur-

---

164 Thomas Gray, "Journal in the Lakes", in Edmund Gosse (ed.), *The Works of Thomas Gray in Prose and Verse*, vol. 1, reprint of 1884 edition (New York: AMS Press, 1986), 249–281, here 266. See also Andrews, "Introduction", 13.

165 Uvedale Price, *Essays on the Picturesque, As Compared with the Sublime and the Beautiful; And, on the Use of Studying Pictures, For the Purpose of Improving Real Landscape*, vol. 1 (London: J. Mawman, 1810), 43.

166 Ibid., 211.

167 Carrie Tirado Bramen, "The Urban Picturesque and the Spectacle of Americanization", *American Quarterly*, vol. 52, no. 3 (2000): 444–477, here 451.

168 Price, *Essays*, vol. 1, 63.

169 See **Uvedale** Price, *Essays on the Picturesque, As Compared with the Sublime and the Beautiful; And, on the Use of Studying Pictures, For the Purpose of Improving Real Landscape*, vol. 3 (London: J. Mawman, 1810), 272–275.

170 Andrews, "Introduction", 25.

171 Ibid., 26.

esque aesthetic had been uniquely geared to the task of turning poverty into art."[172]

This detached attitude towards scenes of poverty was criticized in the first half of the 19th century as apolitical by Charles Dickens and George Eliot and as nonsensical by Jane Austen.[173] Dickens was shocked by the scenes of urban misery he witnessed in Naples, a destination favoured by British tourists. Many claimed that its slums contributed to the picturesqueness of the South Italian city. Dickens summarily rejected the notion of a picturesque appreciation of such poverty: "The condition of the common people here is abject and shocking. I am afraid the conventional idea of the picturesque is associated with such misery and degradation that a new picturesque will have to be established as the world goes onward."[174] Victorian art critic John Ruskin obliged and presented a new theory of the picturesque in the mid-19th century more adapted to the changing realities of Victorian cities, where the poor were no longer "loitering at the boundary of one's country estate, or visible only on one's summer tour to the Highlands or North Wales".[175] Rather, all classes were living in close proximity and repeated outbreaks of the cholera in London spurred fears of contamination as sanitary reports shed light on the miserable living conditions of the poor. Ruskin criticized those who regarded scenes of poverty and decay merely as pleasurable sights as lovers of a low or "surface picturesque": "All other men feel some regret at the sight of disorder and ruin. He alone delights in both; it matters not of what. [...] Poverty, and darkness, and guilt, bring in their several contributions to his treasury of pleasant thoughts."[176] From this he distinguishes the "true, or noble picturesque", which does not necessarily exclude poverty as a subject for pictorial repre-sentation but "the dignity of the picturesque increases from lower to higher, in exact proportion to the sympathy of the artist with his subject".[177] Both artists and viewers are thus differentiated by their reaction to picturesque poor subjects – depending on whether they merely take delight in them or whether they sympathize with their fate. Such fine distinctions were not necessarily felt by most Victorian readers as popular depictions of poverty proliferated throughout the century. In his series of articles on *How the Poor Live* George Sims lamented "the difficulty of getting that element of picturesqueness into these Chapters which is so essential to success with a large class of English

---

172 Nancy Armstrong, *Fiction in the Age of Photography: The Legacy of British Realism* (Cambridge, Mass.: Harvard University Press, 1999), 95.

173 See Andrews, "Introduction", 26–29.

174 Quoted in Malcolm Andrews, "The Metropolitan Picturesque", in Stephen Copley and Peter Garside (ed.), *The Politics of the Picturesque: Literature, Landscape and Aesthetics since 1770* (Cambridge: Cambridge University Press, 1994), 282–298, here 286. On Dickens and his opposition to the picturesque mode, see Nancy Klenk Hill, *A Reformer's Art. Dickens' Picturesque and Grotesque Imagery* (London, Athens: Ohio University Press, 1981), 9–43.

175 Andrews, "Metropolitan Picturesque", 288.

176 John Ruskin, *Modern Painters*, vol. 5: *Of Mountain Beauty* (London: George Allen, 1906), 10.

177 Ibid., 13.

readers".[178] For him any "truthful account of 'How the Poor Live'" offered "little to attract those who read for pleasure only".[179]

A second characteristic of William Gilpin's picturesque that I consider relevant to my topic is its close connection to tourism and the visiting of picturesque sights. As film scholar and visual historian Giorgio Bertellini points out, the picturesque style of the 18th century and its emphasis on "painterly effects of irregularity, variety, and roughness of design" was inextricably linked with the travels of the Grand Tour and became "the pictorial style that Northern European élites most often adopted to render their cultural experience of Mediterranean Europe".[180] This included depictions of both the wild Italian landscapes and the human element of "notoriously vicious bandits, or banditti, [who] came into view as romantic and colorful outlaws".[181] These Italian bandits are mirrored in Uvedale Price's appreciation of "gypsies and beggars" as picturesque objects; and like the landscapes of Southern Italy, English "gipsy encampments became objects of tourist curiosity" and sites for excursions by holiday parties around the turn of the 19th century.[182] Around the same time, numerous Northern European intellectuals like Johann Wolfgang von Goethe and Madame de Staël published influential accounts of their visits to the Italian South as part of the Grand Tour in a style that combined "learned references from highbrow literature with the iconic vocabulary of picturesque representations".[183] Goethe reminisced about looking down from the summit of Mount Etna: "I no longer saw Nature, but pictures; it was as if some very skilful painter had applied glaze to secure a proper gradation of tone."[184] More than a half-century earlier, William Gilpin had published his first description of what he considered an exemplary picturesque landscape; the gardens of a Lord Cobham at Stow [sic], Buckinghamshire. Gilpin reimagined the visit in the form of a dialogue between two visitors to the gardens, who commented at length on the "beautiful Objects, and all so happily disposed, [which] make a most delightful Picture".[185] In various volumes of his *Observations, relative chiefly*

---

178 Sims, *How the Poor Live* (1889), 45.

179 Ibid., 44.

180 Giorgio Bertellini, *Italy in Early American Cinema: Race, Landscape, and the Picturesque* (Bloomington: Indiana University Press, 2010), 4.

181 Ibid.

182 See Andrews, "Introduction", 26.

183 Bertellini, *Italy in Early American Cinema*, 33. Notably, American photographer Alfred Stieglitz as late as 1896 reminisced about photographs taken in the streets of Venice: "Nothing charms me so much as walking among the lower classes, studying them carefully and making mental notes. They are interesting from every point of view. I dislike the superficial and artificial, and I find less of it among the lower classes." Quoted in "Alfred Stieglitz and his Latest Work", *Photographic Times*, vol. 28, no. 4 (1896): 161–169, here 161. In 1897 Stieglitz published his *Picturesque Bits of New York and Other Studies*, which, according to Giorgio Bertellini, "captured the movement of the picturesque from its traditional urban European settings to urban America." Bertellini, *Italy in Early American Cinema*, 52.

184 Quoted in Bertellini, *Italy in Early American Cinema*, 34.

185 William Gilpin, *A Dialogue upon the Gardens of the Right Honourable the Lord Viscount Cobham at Stow in Buckinghamshire* (London: Printed for B. Seeley, Sold by J. and J. Rivington, 1748), 14.

to Picturesque Beauty, Gilpin recommended specific natural scenes and locations that tourists in search of the picturesque might visit in Britain. As Malcolm Andrews points out, "most popular Picturesque tours of the later eighteenth century were to the non-arable regions of Britain: north Wales, the Scottish Highlands and the Lake District".[186] This appreciation of rugged scenery and wild nature was also a response to the radical alteration of the English countryside by systematic agricultural cultivation and those people left behind could be appreciated as part of the picturesque aesthetic.

Picturesque sights could also be found in Victorian cities: throughout the 19th century, London inspired a number of guide books with titles like *Picturesque Sketches of London* or *Pictorial Half-Hours of London Topography*.[187] And for some affluent West-End denizens the poor areas of the East End became sites of thrilling amorality and picturesque human variety.[188] Pierce Egan's *Life in London* published from 1821 and illustrated by George and Richard Cruikshank is representative of this "social Picturesque", its comic representations provided "the compensatory, voyeuristic attractions of eccentricity, spontaneity and angularity for an austerely self-disciplined, middle-class readership".[189] Egan metaphorically positioned his readers as viewers of a camera obscura showing a series of East London pictures "as a trope to emphasise the detachment between the reader and the scene".[190] And in 1872, journalist Blanchard Jerrold promised readers of his *London. A Pilgrimage*, illustrated by Gustave Doré, that they would see "the most picturesque features of the greatest city on the face of the globe".[191] Seen through the eyes of the artist, Jerrold exclaimed, London was far from ugly – contrary to popular opinion: "We soon discovered that it abounded in delightful nooks and corners, in picturesque scenes and groups, in light and shade of the most attractive character."[192] Urban poverty formed part of the visual spectacle of the Victorian city and Jerrold even recommended a tour guide of sorts should readers wish to revisit some of the slums visited by him and Doré:

> You put yourself in communication with Scotland Yard to begin with. You adopt rough clothes. You select two or three companions who will not flinch even before

---

186 Andrews, "Introduction", 19.

187 See Andrews, "Metropolitan Picturesque", 290.

188 In his autobiography George Sims reminisced about his forays into London's notorious criminal areas in the 1860s: "The rowdy night life of London in the 'sixties was not confined to the West End. It was quite the thing for the 'Corinthians' of the 'sixties to make excursions to the East, and when I first became a student of 'life as she is lived' my studies occasionally took me after nightfall in the direction of Ratcliffe Highway, and I have a vivid remembrance of weird and wonderful scenes in the dancing saloons attached to Paddy's Goose, which was in the notorious Highway, the Mahogany Bar, which was close by, and in the disreputable dens for they were dens and they were disreputable of Tiger Bay." Sims, *My Life*, 100–101.

189 Andrews, "Introduction", 32. The French edition of 1822 was titled *The English Diorama, or, Picturesque Rambles in London*.

190 John Plunkett, "Moving Books / Moving Images: Optical Recreations and Children's Publishing 1800–1900", *19: Interdisciplinary Studies in the Long Nineteenth Century*, issue 5 (2007): 1–27, here 9.

191 Gustave Doré and Blanchard Jerrold, *London. A Pilgrimage* (London: Grant & Co., 1872), x.

192 Ibid., ix.

the humours and horrors of Tiger Bay: and you commit yourself to the guidance of one of the intelligent and fearless heads of the detective force.[193]

Similarly, in the penultimate chapter of *How the Poor Live* (1883), George Sims urged his readers to visit the London Docks themselves early in the morning when work is allotted among the day labourers. With his usual mixture of hyperbole and a grain of truth, Sims later claimed that his articles caused a slumming craze in the 1880s.[194] Slumming was situated at the intersection of the authentic and the picturesque: it provided the opportunity to see poverty and squalor first hand but slummers were frequently accompanied by police-men or guided along established routes that favoured certain picturesque spots.[195] By the 1900s slumming was so well established in London that George Sims promised readers to find new pathways and take them "Off the Track in London" (1905) in a series of illustrated articles for *Strand Magazine* that inevitably highlighted the picturesque qualities of certain areas. Sims particu-larly recommended a visit to Little Italy, so that readers might themselves appreciate the "picturesque colony of Italian peasants in the heart of London". He even provided his readers with a travel itinerary: "Sunday morning is the best time to make the Little Italian trip, because not only are most of the inhabitants at home, but the poor Italians scattered about in other parts of London make the main street of the colony their rendezvous."[196] Later in the chapter Sims's description of the impression made by dimly lit houses in the neighbourhood completed the picturesque tour:

> On a dark winter's night there is a weirdness in the streets of Little Italy that would have appealed to Doré. Here and there you see an open way through the narrow passage of a house, and the dull yellow light of a lamp in a street perched high up at the back and approached by a flight of stone steps.[197]

---

193 Ibid., 141–142.

194 See Sims, *My Life*, 136. This referred of course only to those who went into the slums seeking thrills and entertainment. At the same time, as historian Seth Koven notes, "there were hundreds of private charitable institutions and agencies in the metropolitan slums, each visited regularly by scores of donors, trustees, and volunteer and paid workers. No doubt slumming was merely an evening's entertainment for many well-to-do Londoners, but for many others, the slums of London exercised powerful and tenacious claims over their minds and hearts, drastically altering the course of their lives." Koven, *Slumming*, 1.

195 Giorgio Bertellini notes about slum tourism in New York: "[G]uided tours took tourists safely to Chinatown and 'the Ghetto.' Through postcards, stereographic views, and photographic albums, American tourism patterned a respectable sightseeing experience of the Lower East Side that would anticipate, inform, and later parallel film spectators' voyeuristic access to immigrants' miserable quarters and lives. This process was defined by the familiar and transnational aesthetic of the picturesque, which in New York acquired conspicuously American features." Bertellini, *Italy in Early American Cinema*, 140.

196 George R. Sims, "Trips About Town. III. Round Little Italy", *Strand Magazine*, vol. 29, no. 173 (May 1905): 510–516, here 510, and George R. Sims, *Off the Track in London* (London: Jarrold & Sons, 1911), 154–155. The book combined two series of articles originally published in *Strand Magazine* called "Off the Track in London" (vol. 27 and vol. 28, both 1904) and "Trips About Town" (vol. 29 and vol. 30, both 1905), which contained a number of additional illustrations by Thomas Heath Robinson.

197 Sims, *Off the Track*, 160. Doré's interplay of light and shadow, captured in the *chiaroscuro* technique popular for picturesque illustrations, is most apparent in his rendition of the Bull's Eye lantern that casts both a literal and metaphorical light on those usually hidden from view. On the symbolism of the Bull's Eye lantern, see **Vogl-Bienek**, *Lichtspiele*, 214–222.

Destinations for picturesque tourism could thus not only include beautiful landscapes and forgotten architecture but also the slums of Naples, the gypsy camps of Northern England and the Italian quarters of London and New York.

The third characteristic of the picturesque that makes it relevant to the analysis of depictions of poverty is that from its initial conception its subject is always already mediated. The proponents of the picturesque did not advocate a direct appreciation of the countryside (or the people living and working in it) – but required a knowledge of certain pictorial representations which could be compared to those scenes found in nature. Initially, those were the Dutch and Italian landscape paintings of the 17th century by artists like Claude Lorrain and Salvator Rosa. In the 18th century, picturesque tourists often used a so-called Claude-glass, a small convex mirror to convert the landscape in front of them (or, more accurately, behind them) into an image that resembled Lorrain's landscape paintings:

> It offered an instant pictorialising of the landscape, reducing a sprawling view to a compact composition and also giving to the composition a consistent tonality. [...] Like its descendant, the modern camera, the glass gave the tourist a means quickly of translating nature into art: the tourist's drawing or painting would be based on the image in the mirror as much as on the view immediately in front of him.[198]

Similarly, George Sims's description of a pair of Italian lovers (a staple of the picturesque aesthetic) in "Trips About Town" views the pair entirely in terms of other artistic representations of the familiar subject:

> They walk with clasped hands, looking into each other's eyes and heedless of all the world. The look that is in their faces is the look that an artist puts in his pictures of 'Love's Young Dream,' with a southern sky above and a blue sea in the background. [...] But they make a living picture of 'Italian Lovers' framed in the mirk of a London night.[199]

One way to achieve a picturesque aesthetic of poverty is by referring to previous pictorial representations of the subject and repeating visual patterns either in paintings and prints or increasingly in photographs. One obvious example would be the representation of poor barefooted children dressed in rags which can be traced from the genre paintings of Bartolomé Esteban Murillo to the pictorial photographs of Oscar Rejlander and the adaptations of George Sims's ballad *The Road to Heaven* as life model slides.[200]

The use of models to represent picturesque poverty was not limited to studio photographs. Henry Peach Robinson advised amateur photographers on the proper use of models to represent peasant girls in his treatise on *The Elements of a Pictorial Photograph* (1896) – ideally unbeknownst to the casual observer:

198 Andrews, "Introduction", 14.

199 Sims, "Trips About Town", 516.

200 Such representations relied on the familiarity of viewers with a motif while the plain backgrounds amounted to a reduction of complexity often associated with the stereotype.

Fig. 1: Bartolomé Esteban Murillo - *The Young Beggar* (c. 1645), Public domain, Wikimedia Commons.

Fig. 2: Oscar Gustave Rejlander - *Poor Joe* (c. 1860), Mirrored reproduction, Public domain, J. Paul Getty Museum open content program.

> With a well-trained model, always supposing you do your work properly, you can get nearer to nature than nature itself. This seems a bold saying, but is quite true. Besides being extremely difficult to manage, very awkward and self-conscious, it is not easy to explain what you want to a fresh caught peasant. Sometimes she is superstitiously afraid of being photographed, at other times she remembers having been told to 'keep quite still' – words that have spoilt many a photograph – and becomes another being, rigidity taking possession of her [...].[201]

Peter Henry Emerson whose impressionistic photographs of rural south-East England evoke traditional picturesque landscapes similarly advised students: "[...] you must choose your models most carefully, and they must without fail be picturesque and typical. The student should feel that there never was such a fisherman, or such a ploughman, or such a poacher, or such an old man, or such a beautiful girl, as he is picturing."[202] Robinson's claim that his pictures could get "nearer to nature than nature itself" leads me to the second mode of depicting poverty – the authentic.

In literary studies, 'authenticity' can be defined as an intrinsic quality of texts. Authentic can be understood both in a legal or theological sense as verified or original as opposed to copied, but also more broadly as "having the quality of verisimilitude" according to the *Oxford English Dictionary* definition of the

---

201 Henry Peach Robinson, *The Elements of a Pictorial Photograph* (Bradford: Percy Lund, 1896), 98.

202 Quoted in Jennifer Marion Green, "The Right Thing in the Right Place: P.H. Emerson and the Picturesque Photograph", in Carol Christ and John Jordan (ed.), *Victorian Literature and the Victorian Visual Imagination* (Berkeley, Los Angeles, London: University of California Press, 1995), 88–110, here 94.

term.[203] It can also refer to the legal / historical provenance of documents and the psychological truthfulness of a person to their inner self. Rather than assuming a truthful representation of an objective reality, most modern uses of the term "authenticity" reject the notion of an unmediated access to the real and stress its subjective qualities instead. As media scholar Thomas Schierl points out:

> Authenticity can refer solely to a possible congruity between an individual's experience of reality and the referencing of that reality in a specific reproduction. The possible point of reference for authenticity is not reality as such but merely the subjective apprehension of reality shaped by an individual's interpretation, selection and perspective.[204]

"Authenticity" is thus always situational and can be defined as "the result of authenticating techniques of representation", according to media historian Jan Berg.[205] Film scholar Guido Kirsten has introduced the concept of "realistic ostentation" to describe the deliberate *presentation* of certain (historically contingent) aesthetic markers that signal filmic realism.[206] Similarly, Manfred Hattendorf analyses "authenticating strategies" of documentary films and states that "[…] the plausibility of an event that is being depicted is thus dependent on the effectiveness of filmic strategies of authentication at the moment of reception. Authenticity is based as much on the formal composition as it is on the reception."[207] The intrinsic authentic potential of texts (and of photographs and films) can thus be realized or nullified (or at the very least influenced) at the moment of reception – depending on the reception or exhibition context. Or, as literary scholars Wolfgang Funk, Florian Groß, and Irmtraud Huber put it: "the authentic is realized as a performative effect", the result of a communicative process and the "interplay between production, aesthetic object, context, and reception".[208]

203 Lemma "authentic, adj. and n." *Oxford English Dictionary Online* (Oxford: Oxford University Press, January 2018), (www.oed.com/view/Entry/13314). For an exploration of the multiple meanings and etymology of the term, see Susanne Knaller, *Ein Wort aus der Fremde. Geschichte und Theorie des Begriffs Authentizität* (Heidelberg: Universitätsverlag Winter, 2007), 7–35.

204 Thomas Schierl, "Der Schein der Authentizität: Journalistische Bildproduktion als nachfrageorientierte Produktion scheinbarer Authentizität", in Thomas Knieper and Marion Müller (ed.), *Authentizität und Inszenierung von Bilderwelten* (Köln: Herbert von Halem Verlag, 2003), 150–167, here 159. Translated from the German by the author.

205 Jan Berg, "Techniken der medialen Authentifizierung Jahrhunderte vor Erfindung des 'Dokumentarischen'", in Ursula von Keitz and Kay Hoffmann (ed.), *Die Einübung des dokumentarischen Blicks. 'Fiction Film' und 'Non Fiction Film' zwischen Wahrheitsanspruch und expressiver Sachlichkeit 1895–1945* (Marburg: Schüren, 2001), 51–70, here 56. Translated from the German by the author.

206 See Guido Kirsten, *Filmischer Realismus* (Marburg: Schüren, 2013), 28–29.

207 Manfred Hattendorf, *Dokumentarfilm und Authentizität. Ästhetik und Pragmatik einer Gattung* (Konstanz: Ölschläger, 1994), 67. Translated from the German by the author. Jan Berg on the other hand stresses the universality of certain authenticating strategies and applies his definition of authenticity equally to the present time, pre-enlightenment times and classical antiquity.

208 Wolfgang Funk, Florian Groß and Irmtraud Huber, "Exploring the Empty Plinth", in Wolfgang Funk, Florian Groß and Irmtraud Huber (ed.), *The Aesthetics of Authenticity: Medial Constructions of the Real* (Bielefeld: transcript Verlag, 2012), 9–21, here 13.

In literary history, the authentic that is the notion of a text being "true to life", is closely linked to the rise of narrative realism in the 19th century. In his introduction to the second series of *The Social Kaleidoscope* (1881), a collection of short stories on London life, George Sims declared the picturesque incompatible with realism:

> 'Realism' is the only quality which it is necessary these sketches should possess. They do not belong to the golden realms of fiction; the scenes are laid in the not always too picturesque land of fact. […] There shall be no picture found in the gallery which is not painted from life, – in which the figures are not drawn from living, breathing models.[209]

For Sims, modelling his narration on the ever-changing forms and shapes of the kaleidoscope and likening it to a stroll through a picture gallery was not incompatible with still labelling it as realistic and "painted from life". Literary historian Nancy Armstrong has argued that the visual descriptions of Victorian Realism did not refer to any immediate reality but rather to "visual representations" of that reality.[210] She continues: "Moreover, whenever Victorian fiction presumed to enlighten the reader by stripping away some euphemizing image so as to reveal the social reality beneath, that fiction was referring not to some object behind the image, but to another, somehow more adequate image."[211] Still, the authentic mode held the promise of unmediated access to a perceived social reality (e.g. the living conditions in London's slums). Accordingly, I understand the authentic not necessarily as a representation of any unmediated reality but as the result of authenticating strategies. These could be textual references to the circumstances of production like the repeated assurances throughout *How the Poor Live* by George Sims that his companion Frederick Barnard had taken his sketches "on the spot" and that "what I have written about I have in every case seen with my own eyes, and in no case have I exaggerated".[212] It also meant that the pictures and scenes from the homes of the poor did not make for pleasant viewing and were often shocking to better-off readers many of whom sent relief money to the newspaper which had published Sims's articles. Such authenticating strategies could also purposely exaggerate and even augment the realism of their depiction as in the case of Jacob Riis's *How the Other Half Lives*: "Despite his claims of realism, Riis knowingly manipulated his photographic images by exaggerating the effects of the flash, arranging the dirt and chaos of the domestic interiors, and using 'jagged-edge' framing to convey a sense of instantaneous reporting."[213]

That the reception context of a text or an image can help to determine whether or not it is considered authentic follows Roman Jakobson's remarks on literary realism. Jakobson, a linguist and member of the Russian formalists, had

---

209 George R. Sims, "Introduction", *The Social Kaleidoscope*, 2nd series (London: J.P. Fuller, 1881), iii–iv.

210 Armstrong, *British Realism*, 3.

211 Ibid., 26.

212 George R. Sims, *How the Poor Live* (London: Chatto & Windus, 1883), 37.

213 Bertellini, *Italy in Early American Cinema*, 156.

outlined his views still under the impression of Victorian realism but also considered modernism and futurism in his essay titled *On Realism in Art* (1921). Jakobson differentiates between various meanings of the term realism variously referring to "the aspiration and intent of the author" or the judgement of a reader: "A work may be called realistic if I, the person judging it, perceive it as true to life."[214] Jakobson bemoans that the conflation of both meanings has led to an overemphasis of personal and subjective readings: "The question as to whether a given work is realistic or not is covertly reduced to the question of what attitude I take toward it."[215] In extension, as Jennifer Green-Lewis points out, since "readership is historically contingent, what best represents the real, according to this view, will be largely a matter of time and place".[216]

Another authenticating strategy was the use of actual poor people as models for representations of poverty that are generally considered proto-documentary. This includes Richard Beard's daguerreotypes for Henry Mayhew's *London Labour and the London Poor* (from 1850), John Thomson's photographs for *Street Life in London* (1877) and lantern slide series like SLUM LIFE OF OUR GREAT CITIES (Archer & Sons, 1892) and STREET-LIFE: OR THE PEOPLE WE MEET (Riley Brothers, in or after 1887). Photography, "The Pencil of Nature" as Fox Talbot had termed it, seemed predestined for authentic representations of poverty because it claimed to eliminate the human influence of the artist.[217] John Thomson argued that the "unquestionable accuracy" of photography would allow him "to present true types of the London Poor" and Richard Beard posed and photographed actual street-sellers in his studio; the daguerreotypes were then copied and printed from woodcuts.[218] Advertisements for SLUM LIFE OF OUR GREAT CITIES promised buyers "direct photographs from Life in the Slums" which according to the accompanying lantern reading were taken with a hand camera, sometimes before the subjects themselves noticed the apparatus.[219] The lecture was frequently used to promote temperance as the dire situation particularly of the children that were depicted was attributed to the evil of alcoholism. But despite its accusatory tone and unhappy subject, some of the photographs could still hold a picturesque appeal. This is also evident from the similar lantern slide series STREET-LIFE: OR THE PEOPLE WE MEET. It was advertised as "photographed from life" and the accompanying lecture

---

214 Roman Jakobson, *Language in Literature* (Cambridge, Mass., London: The Belknap Press of Harvard University Press, 1987), 20.

215 Ibid.

216 Jennifer Green-Lewis, *Framing the Victorians: Photography and the Culture of Realism* (Ithaca, London: Cornell University Press, 1996), 27. See also Jakobson, *Language in Literature*, 22–24.

217 Other photographers like Henry Peach Robinson attempted to elevate photography to the rank of the traditional arts and created elaborately constructed composite photographs that emphasized the role of the photographer in the creation of an artistic photograph.

218 John Thomson and Adolphe Smith, "Preface", *Street Life in London* (London: Sampson Low, Marston, Searle & Rivington, 1877, Reprint New York, London: Benjamin Blom, 1969).

219 See Ludwig Vogl-Bienek, "A Lantern Lecture: Slum Life and Living Conditions of the Poor in Fictional and Documentary Lantern Slide Sets", in Crangle and Vogl-Bienek (ed.), *Screen Culture*, 34–63, here 54.

promised viewers they would be brought "face to face with a number of people […] who, collectively, give life and animation and colour to the gloomy streets of our great cities and towns".[220] The catalogue of lantern slide distributor Riley Brothers emphasized that many of the "various characters met with in everyday life" would be "most amusing, and all are exceedingly realistic".[221] Images like "The Italian and Monkey" move the series towards what literary historian Carrie Tirado Bramen has termed the "urban picturesque":

> At its most fundamental level, the urban picturesque afforded a new way of apprehending urban space by making inequality and immigrant diversity expected elements of modernity. It signaled a constellation of aesthetic practices and meanings that rendered the heterogeneity of the city as 'charming' and 'quaint' rather than exclusively deleterious.[222]

George Sims's monumental editorial work *Living London*, that began just after Queen Victoria's death in 1901, is perhaps the most notable example of this picturesque representation of poverty as part of modern city life in his works. D. L. Woolmer's introductory remarks in an article titled "Scenes from London Slum-Land" serve as a good example of this: "Slums may be contemptible in themselves as the backyards of a noble city and the ruins of castles in the air, but they are the scenery of life's quaintest comedies and darkest tragedies."[223] At twelve (cloth) and sixteen shillings (half-leather) the lavishly illustrated volumes were clearly aimed at a middle and upper-class readership.[224] Reviews commended the "fine descriptions of the lower parts of the City with their dens and eating houses", and praised the "interesting and picturesque work".[225] Compared with Frederick Barnard's black-and-white sketches for Sims's *How the Poor Live* (1883), the coloured illustrations (often from paintings) did not present individual characters but rather strove to represent the typical and

---

220 Quoted in ibid., 40.

221 *Catalogue of Photographic Lantern Transparencies and Apparatus* (Bradford: Riley Brothers, 1891), 32.

222 Bramen, "Urban Picturesque", 445–446. Both Bramen and Giorgio Bertellini note that late 19th century representations of New York's racial variety in a picturesque aesthetic usually did not include either Chinese immigrants or African Americans. See Bertellini, *Italy in Early American Cinema*, 10, and Bramen, "Urban Picturesque", 452 and 464. Rather, as Bertellini points out: "Southern Italian immigrants often found themselves at the center of this newly articulated urban picturesque". Bertellini, *Italy in Early American Cinema*, 137.

223 D.L. Woolmer, "Scenes from London Slum-Land", in George R. Sims (ed.), *Living London: Its Work and Its Play, Its Humour and Its Pathos, Its Sights and Its Scenes*, vol. 3 (London etc.: Cassell & Co., 1903), 109–114, here 109.

224 For prices, see ad for first volume by publisher Cassell & Co. in the *Pall Mall Gazette* (17 April 1902): 9. Even a respectable workman with a good weekly income would have had to spare more than half of his 30 shillings to purchase the leather-bound volume. See Arthur Morrison, "Family Budgets: I. A Workman's Budget", *Cornhill Magazine*, vol. 10, no. 58 (April 1901): 446–456, here 446. For reference, twelve shillings roughly equalled one week's rent for a poor family of six in London's West End as cited in the third edition of Arthur Sherwell's *Life in West London: A Study and a Contrast* (London: Methuen, 1901), 112. The fortnightly instalments of *Living London*, which usually contained five articles with illustrations, were sold for sevenpence – or seven times the price of the popular weeklies *Penny Illustrated Paper* and *Reynolds's Newspaper*.

225 "Book Reviews", *Lichfield Mercury* (6 December 1901): 6, and "Living London", *The Globe* (25 March 1903): 5.

Fig. 3: "The Italian and Monkey", Slide 18 of STREET-LIFE: OR THE PEOPLE WE MEET
(Riley Brothers, in or after 1887, 50 slides), illuminago Collection / Karin Bienek and Ludwig
Vogl-Bienek Frankfurt am Main, reproduced with permission.

familiar London types like the flower girl, the organ grinder, the policeman or the dosser.[226]

There was also a strong association of (immigrant) poverty with dirt and squalor, which some identified as the source of its picturesque appeal, as American poet Carl Sadakichi Hartmann remarked in his *Plea for the Picturesqueness of New York* (1900): "For filth – as disagreeable as it is in actual contact – is the great harmonizer in the pictorial arts, the wizard who can render every scene and object – even the humblest one – picturesque."[227] The association of Italian immigrants with poverty and dirt was well established by the early

226 The flower seller as a London type was also included in a later book of colour photochromes of London (mainly its buildings and sights) with a foreword by George Sims. *Fifty Colour Photographs of London. Reproduced by an Exclusive Process with Short Descriptions* (London: The Photochrome Company, 1913).

227 Quoted in Bertellini, *Italy in Early American Cinema*, 149.

1900s, so much so that George Sims was clearly surprised by the tidiness of London's Little Italy upon his visit for "Trips About Town" (1905): "With thirty years' experience of the slums and poverty areas of London, the cleanliness and good sanitary order of the houses in Little Italy were, when I first made a thorough inspection of the district, startling revelations to me."[228] However, in the same chapter, Sims praises the aesthetic (i.e. picturesque) value of their italianized poverty:

> In the streets that lie off the main thoroughfare there are houses painted in bright colours in the Italian style, and when the window of one of these opens and an Italian woman in her native head-dress looks out the eye of the artist is charmed. London has vanished. It is a spring morning in some southern Italian town. The people may be poor, but the note of squalor which makes our English poverty so terrible is not to be found here.[229]

I would argue that few depictions of poverty in the 19th and early 20th century were strictly picturesque or strictly authentic but rather located on a spectrum between the two extremes. Most combined elements of both modes to appeal to the desire for entertainment of Victorian readers *and* to their moral sensibilities and desire for societal change. As commodities to be bought and sold these popular depictions of poverty oscillated between the requirements of an authentic depiction of poor people and a picturesque desire for visual pleasure and aesthetic appreciation of difference.[230]

2.2 Henry Mayhew – *London Labour and the London Poor* and Authenticity

Among the most influential pieces of journalism on London poverty were the contributions by Henry Mayhew on "Labour and the Poor" published in the *Morning Chronicle* in 1849 and 1850. They formed the basis and established the basic format and method for his later series *London Labour and the London Poor* (1851–1852 and 1861–1862). After the initial letters in the *Morning Chronicle* (1840–1850), Mayhew continued the series as weekly pamphlets (1850–1852).[231] These pamphlets comprised eighteen pages and included a woodcut illustration and a section with "Answers to Correspondents" on the wrappers.[232] Two bound volumes produced from the pamphlets in 1851 and 1852 also included the illustrations but not the "Answers to Correspondents" where Mayhew had mainly reflected on his theories and methods. For the first

228   Sims, "Trips About Town", 513.

229   Ibid., 511.

230   On the link between the picturesque aesthetic and commodity culture, Nanna Verhoeff states: "The [picturesque] aesthetic promotes a colonizing mode of looking that is a form of appropriation. In contrast to the sublime, [...] the picturesque produces a viewer who hardly risks anything but whose thrill comes from the sense of visual ownership." Nanna Verhoeff, *The West in Early Cinema: After the Beginning* (Amsterdam: Amsterdam University Press, 2006), 252.

231   The last issue of the pamphlet series appeared on 21 February 1852, when a court case was brought against Mayhew by his printer. See Humpherys, *Henry Mayhew*, 24.

232   See Rolf Lindner, *Walks on the Wild Side. Eine Geschichte der Stadtforschung* (Frankfurt, New York: Campus Verlag, 2004), 52.

book versions, Mayhew "added an index, a list of errata (typographical errors in figures), a dedication to his father-in-law Douglas Jerrold, and, most important, a preface".[233] These two bound volumes later formed the first two volumes of the better known 1861 edition of *London Labour and the London Poor*, to which was added a third volume, "more rambling and disorganized", and a fourth one in 1862, which mostly comprised texts written by Mayhew's contributors about prostitutes, beggars and thieves.[234] A major issue in scholarly discussions of Mayhew's work on the poor is this complicated publication history. Although well documented, it has given rise to widely differing interpretations of his work as the different approaches of each editor are reflected in their selection: While Edward Palmer Thompson and Eileen Yeo focus on Mayhew's articles in the *Morning Chronicle*, Peter Quennell uses only material from the first three volumes of the 1861 edition.

On 18 October 1849 the editors of the *Morning Chronicle* announced a new "series of communications", which would present a "detailed description of the moral, intellectual, material, and physical condition of the industrial poor throughout England" and claimed that it would "equal, perhaps surpass, official or Parliamentary reports in impartiality, authenticity, and comprehensiveness".[235] Henry Mayhew reported as special correspondent from London for the Metropolitan Districts and in his first contribution on the following day, laid out his definition of the poor as "all those persons whose incomings are insufficient for the satisfaction of their wants".[236] His aim, according to historian Eileen Yeo, was "to establish conditions of employment, especially wage levels, in the metropolitan trades, relate these to the life style of the poor and, at the same time, explore the industrial causes of low wages and poverty".[237] His method was to correlate official statistics about wages, unemployment, crime, prices etc. with the lived experiences of individual workers gathered in interviews – often in their own homes. After a while, instead of conducting individual interviews with workers, Mayhew "arranged large and apparently well-publicized meetings", where "members of a particular trade or group were invited to give information about their work and wages".[238] In the 82 letters that appeared between October 1849 and December 1850, Mayhew covered a wide variety of London trades and industries:

---

233 Humpherys, *Henry Mayhew*, 76–77.

234 Gertrude Himmelfarb, "The Culture of Poverty", in Dyos and Wolff (ed.), *The Victorian City*, vol. 2, 707–736, here 710. See also Edward Palmer Thompson, "Mayhew and the *Morning Chronicle*", in Edward Palmer Thompson and Eileen Yeo (ed.), *The Unknown Mayhew: Selections from the Morning Chronicle 1849–1850* (London: Merlin Press, 1971), 11–50, here 41–42.

235 *Morning Chronicle* (18 October 1849): 4. The articles followed in the wake of a cholera epidemic in London and an investigation by Mayhew into one of the areas hit worst by the disease published in the *Morning Chronicle* (24 September 1849). See Humpherys, *Henry Mayhew*, 16.

236 *Morning Chronicle* (19 October 1849): 5.

237 Eileen Yeo, "Mayhew as a Social Investigator", in Thompson and Yeo (ed.), *The Unknown Mayhew*, 51–95, here 55.

238 Humpherys, *Henry Mayhew*, 46. For a contemporaneous description of such a meeting, see *Reynolds's Newspaper* (16 June 1850): 3.

He wrote about seamstresses and tailors, dock workers and seamen, joiners and cabinet makers, hat- and dressmakers, sawyers and carpenters, coopers and tanners, hawkers and street musicians, costermongers and street vendors, a true panorama, an encyclopedia of working London with a special emphasis on the traditional London industries.[239]

Mayhew's project was cut short when he left the *Morning Chronicle* in October 1850 over repeated disputes with the editors about alterations to his articles.[240] On 14 December of the same year, Henry Mayhew started the publication of twopenny weekly pamphlets under the familiar heading *London Labour and the London Poor* from his newly established London office.[241] Unlike the title suggests, they focused almost exclusively on those making their living on the London streets, as historian Gertrude Himmelfarb has pointed out:

> From the beginning of the pamphlet series, Mayhew took as his explicit theme the street-folk, reprinting from the *Chronicle* (in revised form) only those articles on the street-traders and laborers, and omitting, except for passing references, those on the more conventional occupations.[242]

His emphasis had shifted from the systematic analysis of the correlation between low wages and poverty to a taxonomy of London street folk, who, as he himself stated, made up only "about a fortieth-part of the entire population of the metropolis".[243] This typological method is evident in the – newly added – preface to the first bound volume of *London Labour and the London Poor* published in July of 1851:

> The subject of the Street-Folk will still require another volume, in order to complete it in that comprehensive manner in which I am desirous of executing the modern history of this and every other portion of the people. There still remain – the *Street-Buyers*, the *Street-Finders*, the *Street-Performers*, the *Street-Artizans*, and the *Street-Laborers*, to be done, among the several classes of street-people; and the *Street Jews*, the *Street Italians and Foreigners*, and the *Street Mechanics*, to be treated of as varieties of the order.[244]

Mayhew also dabbled in contemporary racial theories and phrenology in his introduction, classifying his subjects (e.g., vagrants, beggars, street-sellers, prostitutes) as belonging to the "wandering tribes" and "nomadic races of England" characterized by a variance in physiognomy and morality:

> Whether it be that in the mere act of wandering, there is a greater determination of blood to the surface of the body, and consequently a less quantity sent to the

---

239 Lindner, *Walks on the Wild Side*, 49–50. This and all subsequent quotes from Lindner's book were translated from the German by the author. See also Humpherys, *Henry Mayhew*, 49 for a general overview of the contents of Mayhew's letters for the *Morning Chronicle*.

240 For a detailed account, see Humpherys, *Henry Mayhew*, 20–21.

241 See Thompson, "Mayhew and the *Morning Chronicle*", 41–42. Such an undertaking required little capital since unsold parts were simply stitched together and sold in monthly parts or bound up as regular volumes. See Humpherys, *Henry Mayhew*, 24. The last one appeared in March of 1852.

242 Gertrude Himmelfarb, "Mayhew's Poor: A Problem of Identity", *Victorian Studies*, vol. 14, no. 3 (March 1971): 307–320, here 310.

243 Henry Mayhew, *London Labour and the London Poor*, vol. 1, *The London Street-Folk* (London: George Woodfall and Son, 1851), 6.

244 Mayhew, *London Labour*, iv.

brain, the muscles being thus nourished at the expense of the mind, I leave physiologists to say. But certainly be the physical cause what it may, we must all allow that in each of the classes above-mentioned, there is a greater development of the animal than of the intellectual or moral nature of man, and that they are all more or less distinguished for their high cheek-bones and protruding jaws – for the use of a slang language – for their lax ideas of property – for their general improvidence – their repugnance to continuous labour – their disregard of female honour – their love of cruelty – their pugnacity – and their utter want of religion.[245]

Most modern editors have excused or outright ignored these tendencies but as historian Thomas Prasch remarks:

> Mayhew never abandoned his beliefs in the racial basis for differences in station. Had he abjured racial notions, he would not have reiterated them in 1862, when, discussing criminality, he explicitly rejected explanations that ascribed crime to the environment, population density, or poverty, instead reasserting a two-race theory.[246]

Mayhew's work was almost unanimously praised by contemporary commentators and continues to be cited as a prime example of early sociological and ethnographic work on the city. Peter Quennell calls Mayhew "a pioneer in this particular type of sociological record", Rolf Lindner a "pioneer of urban ethnography", and Edward Palmer Thompson a "systematic empirical sociologist".[247] Even critical scholars like Thomas Prasch who bemoans "his biological determinism, his conflation of labor and poverty, his failure to propose concrete reforms (and his distrust of many existing reform efforts, especially ragged-school education), the dubiousness of his statistics, and his frequent rhetorical excesses" still acknowledge his influence.[248]

Mayhew's direct observation and the fact that he (partially) let the poor speak for themselves distinguish his work from countless other enquiries (medical or otherwise) published before his "Labour and the Poor" letters.[249] The articles are interspersed with direct and indirect quotes by those he interviewed for each piece, a method that he continued to use for his *London Labour and the London Poor*. His second letter on "Labour and the Poor" in the *Morning Chronicle* began with the assertion that "hardly a line will be written but what a note of the matter recorded has been taken upon the spot".[250] He also included a detailed account of the circumstances of his investigation of the Spitalfields weavers:

---

245 Ibid., 2–3.

246 Prasch, *Photographic Hegemony*, 214.

247 Peter Quennell, "Introduction", in Peter Quennell (ed.), *Mayhew's London* (London: Bracken Books, 1984, Reprint 1987), 17–28, here 20; Lindner, *Walks on the Wild Side*, 43; Thompson, "Mayhew and the *Morning Chronicle*", 45. Quennell refers to the three-volume edition of *London Labour* of 1861, while Thompson refers to Mayhew's *Labour and the Poor* series for the *Morning Chronicle*.

248 See Prasch, *Photographic Hegemony*, 214–215 and 213 respectively.

249 See Lindner, *Walks on the Wild Side*, 48.

250 *Morning Chronicle* (23 October 1849): 5. The article was not included in *London Labour and the London Poor*. On the evolution of Mayhew's interview method, see Humpherys, *Henry Mayhew*, 40–45.

> In the first place, having put myself in communication with the surgeon of the district, and one of the principal and most intelligent of the operatives, it was agreed among us that we should go into a particular street, and visit the first six weavers' houses that we came to.[251]

In his initial contributions, Mayhew included such detailed accounts of his research methods and the interviews he conducted as a way to authenticate his claims and build up the trust of his readers.[252] That trust was shaken in April of 1850 when in a letter to the *Morning Chronicle*, Alexander Anderson, secretary of the Ragged School Union, claimed that he had questioned some of those interviewed by Mayhew for his letters on the London Ragged Schools and "charged Mayhew with leading his witnesses and with omitting information which contradicted his own point of view".[253] Similar charges were brought against him by a George Martin, Secretary to the Street Traders' Protection Association, a newly founded body of the London street folk.[254] In a series of letters to the editor published in *Reynolds's Newspaper* from June through September 1851, Martin attempted "to draw public attention to the gross misrepresentations and ridiculous inaccuracies" in Mayhew's work.[255] He also made strong allegations concerning the veracity of Mayhew's interviews:

> The 'unvarnished language' to which he alludes, is neither ours, nor of those belonging to us. But that Mr. Mayhew has charged us with vices he cannot prove – that he has misrepresented our labour and our earnings – that he or his agents have used petty and disgraceful tricks to elicit statements from poor men addicted to intoxication – that he has exaggerated the information received, and that he has caricatured, and sneered, and vilified, and exposed the worst and hidden the best of our nature […].[256]

However, neither his attack nor that of the Ragged School Union had any lasting impact and according to Anne Humpherys, Mayhew's articles "were not only lauded by the most established journals, clergymen, and philanthropists; but they were also praised by those members of the working classes who read them, including some of the most radical".[257]

---

251 *Morning Chronicle* (23 October 1849): 5.

252 Mayhew's short-lived pamphlet series also included a section titled "Answers to Correspondents", where he reflected on his theories and methods. See Humpherys, *Henry Mayhew*, 76–77.

253 Ibid., 58.

254 The London street-sellers also held two meetings in London in May and June of 1851 both reported on in *Reynolds's Newspaper* to refute "the statements put forth by Mr. Mayhew in his work". *Reynolds's Newspaper* (18 May 1851): 14. The chairman of the meeting left little doubt as far as his opinion on Mayhew's work was concerned, stating that he "had got up his book to suit the tastes and views of the upper and middle classes, and he had selected a helpless class to be the victim of his slanders – the butt and target to be fired at by public scorn and ridicule." Ibid.

255 *Reynolds's Newspaper* (15 June 1851): 14. See also (20 July 1851): 3, (17 August 1851): 3, and (7 September 1851): 7. The fact that his critique was not picked up by any other major newspaper suggests that he did not succeed. Possibly, the paper attempted to cater to its radical working-class readership with the publication of his letters, and they freely admitted that they could not prove themselves that Mayhew had "deliberately outstepped the bounds of truth". *Reynolds's Newspaper* (25 June 1851): 14. However, the initial reviews of *London Labour and the London Poor* had expressly praised his "plain and truthful style", so a deliberate campaign against him seems unlikely. *Reynolds's Newspaper* (30 March 1851): 2.

256 *Reynolds's Newspaper* (15 June 1851): 14.

In addition to the direct quotes, Henry Mayhew also repeatedly posited himself as an authoritative eyewitness and used descriptions of his own actions and surroundings to authenticate his work: "We knocked at the door of the first house, and, requesting permission to speak with the workman on the subject of his trade, were all three ushered up a steep staircase, and through a trap in the floor into the 'shop'."[258] In his articles for the *Morning Chronicle*, Mayhew occasionally evoked the dangers and surprises that he encountered on what he later termed his travels "in the undiscovered country of the poor".[259] In this he followed the established patterns of travel accounts and urban exploration.[260] And in the preface to *London Labour and the London Poor* (1851), he eventually combined his claims of personal observation and accurate documentation to ascertain the authenticity of what was to follow:

> It surely may be considered curious as being the first attempt to publish the history of a people, from the lips of the people themselves – giving a literal description of their labour, their earnings, their trials, and their sufferings, in their own 'unvarnished' language; and to portray the condition of their homes and their families by personal observation of the places, and direct communion with the individuals.[261]

Unlike Mayhew's texts, the illustrations for *London Labour and the London Poor* have seldom been of concern to historians: "Whatever disagreements historians have had over Mayhew's text, there is nearly unanimous silence on the employment of sketches based on photographic images to illustrate that text in both the pamphlet and book editions."[262] These "Engravings of the scenes and the people described, copied from Daguerreotypes", as they were advertised in the *London Evening Standard*, were a novel feature of the weekly twopenny pamphlets that Mayhew published from December 1850.[263] That the woodcuts were based on photographs was supposed to add authenticity to the depictions and as one review in the *Leeds Times* illustrates, Mayhew's contemporaries were inclined to trust in the realism of photography:

> We must not omit to say that the part before us contains several engravings on wood, admirably executed, and of whose accuracy, as pictures of the persons and objects represented, it is sufficient to say that they have been engraved from daguerreotypes taken expressly for this work.[264]

257 Humpherys, *Henry Mayhew*, 19.

258 *Morning Chronicle* (23 October 1849): 5.

259 Mayhew, *London Labour*, iii.

260 See John Marriott, *The Other Empire: Metropolis, India and Progress in the Colonial Imagination* (Manchester: Manchester University Press, 2003), 114, and Prasch, *Photographic Hegemony*, 220–221.

261 Mayhew, *London Labour*, iii.

262 Prasch, *Photographic Hegemony*, 219.

263 *London Evening Standard* (3 December 1850): 1. The short-lived *Penny Illustrated News* had previously published illustrated excerpts from Mayhew's *Labour and the Poor* series with their own black and white sketches. See Humpherys, *Henry Mayhew*, 32 and 159.

264 *Leeds Times* (25 January 1851): 6.

Indeed, the daguerreotypes were of actual costermongers and others from the London streets, who were taken to Richard Beard's photographic studio and asked to pose for them.[265] After that, woodcuts of the photographs were drawn by Henry George Hine and Henry Anelay, who erased "all traces of the studio" and in some cases added "hints of street background", and then engraved by Edward Whimper (birth name Elijah Whymper) and Walter George Mason.[266] As Thomas Prasch notes, the published illustrations were thus "several procedural (and interpretive) steps removed from the photographic process".[267] Indeed, one contemporaneous reviewer noted that the engravings were not lifelike (i.e. true to life) anymore:

> The engravings from Daguerrotypes, by Beard, are wonderfully minute, and yet forcible; though whether it is owing to the sun by whom the portraits are painted in the first instance, or to some other cause, we know not, but the costermongers depicted to us have rather a holiday look about them, which does not exactly agree with our recollections of the class as a whole.[268]

The three volumes of *London Labour and the London Poor* reprinted in 1861 together numbered roughly 1,500 pages and included a total of 70 illustrations most of them either sketches or sketches based on photographs.[269] The respective captions "From a Daguerreotype by Beard", "From a Sketch taken on the Spot", "From a Photograph" and in one case "Partly from a Photograph, and partly from a Sketch" clearly identify and authenticate the various types of depictions for the reader. According to Thomas Prasch, different techniques were used for different purposes:

> Crowd scenes and night views are represented through sketches, which embody and continue a caricature tradition of representing poverty; individual figures are favored by the photographer's eye, with studio, darkroom, and sketch-production work operating to disguise the studio as the site of photography.[270]

The illustrations in the first volume are almost exclusively from Beard's daguerreotypes taken in the studio. The subjects are posed frontally or turned slightly to one side, some looking directly into the camera and shown with the tools or wares of their trade.

The final sketches thus followed the iconographic tradition of the *Cries of London*: "These prints depicted street merchants and other characters shouting out their presence and advertising their goods or services for sale. Their cries

---

265 Beard was Daguerre's London licensee and in 1841 had opened Europe's first studio for photographic portraits. See Humpherys, *Henry Mayhew*, 70.

266 See Prasch, *Photographic Hegemony*, 220, and Fox, "Social Reportage in English Periodical Illustration", 110.

267 Prasch, *Photographic Hegemony*, 220.

268 *Northern Star and Leeds General Advertiser* (4 January 1851): 4.

269 The following refers to the illustrations in the three volumes of *London Labour and the London Poor* published in 1861 by Griffin and Bohn, London. In the first volume, they are identical to those of the 1851 edition. The original plates of Beard's daguerreotypes have been lost. See Prasch, *Photographic Hegemony*, 220.

270 Ibid., 192.

Fig. 4: *The London Costermonger*, engraving by Edward Whimper after drawing by Henry George Hine, based on a daguerreotype by Richard Beard, from Henry Mayhew, *London Labour and the London Poor*, vol. 1 (1851), Public domain, Digital Collections and Archives, Tufts University.

appear as captions within or below the images, often transcribed phonetically to reproduce the seller's accent or street patois."[271] A few are individualized in Mayhew's textual description, which otherwise seldom references the pictures. One example is "The Hindoo Tract Seller" who remains silent in the text: "The man whose portrait supplies the daguerreotyped illustration of this number is unable to speak a word of English, and the absence of an interpreter, through some accident, prevented his statement being taken at the time appointed."[272] But overall, the subjects are not depicted as individuals but as types assumed to represent a class ascribed to them in the caption (e.g. "The Irish Street-Seller", "The Blind Boot-Lace Seller"). In the second volume, Mayhew sorts his subjects into ever finer categories, for example he differentiates both textually and visually between several different kinds of street sweepers ("The Able-Bodied Pauper Street-Sweeper", "The Boy Crossing-Sweepers"). As Thomas Prasch notes, "[o]ne of the most frequent strategies for constructing 'the real' was the typological claim". This notion of true types in turn "constructs a highly problematic notion of 'the real' poor" repeated in depictions of poverty throughout the 19th century.[273] This idea of the real is reinforced in *London Labour and the London Poor* by the recurrence on the seemingly objective medium of photography, even if the original photographs could not be printed yet. The limits of mid-century photography also become evident in the second volume where illustrations from sketches were used to represent workers in places with little or no natural

---

271 Morgan, *True Types*, 160. See also Sean Shesgreen, *Images of the Outcast* (Manchester: Manchester University Press, 2002), 2–3 and 167–170.

272 Mayhew, *London Labour*, 242. He is also one of the few non-white persons depicted in the volumes.

273 Prasch, *Photographic Hegemony*, 31–32.

Fig. 5: *The "Kitchen", Fox Court, Gray's-Inn-Lane*, engraving by Walter George Mason after drawing by Henry Anelay, from Henry Mayhew, *London Labour and the London Poor*, vol. 1 (1851), Public domain, Wellcome Collection, Attribution 4.0 International (CC BY 4.0).

light sources (e.g., the sewers, below-deck on a ship, the coal-wharf), or individuals whose occupation was based on movement that the camera could not capture (e.g., street acrobats, street artists on stilts). Sketches also were not based on photographs when larger groups were shown indoors such as "A Dinner in a Cheap Lodging-House" or "Fox Court".

Here, the poor appear as a menacing group with evil faces and are associated with crime, drunkenness and vulgarity in the accompanying text:

> The illustration presented this week is of a place in Fox-court, Gray's-inn-lane, long notorious as a 'thieves' house, but now far less frequented. On the visit, a few months back, of an informant (who declined staying there), a number of boys were lying on the floor gambling with marbles and halfpennies, and indulging in savage or unmeaning blasphemy. One of the lads jumped up, and murmuring something that it wouldn't do to be idle any longer, induced a woman to let him have a halfpenny for 'a stall;' that is, as a pretext with which to enter a shop for the purpose of stealing, the display of the coin forming an excuse for his entrance.[274]

These disorderly crowds of poor people were juxtaposed with the orderly classified individual types of the studio daguerreotypes.

2.3 Gustave Doré and Blanchard Jerrold – *London. A Pilgrimage* and the Picturesque

Unlike Henry Mayhew's cheap pamphlet series, which was widely read across Victorian society, Gustave Doré's and Blanchard Jerrold's *London. A Pilgrimage*

---

274 Mayhew, *London Labour*, 254.

was marketed mainly as an artistic work to be owned and displayed in affluent households. At five shillings a piece the twelve monthly instalments published by Grant & Co. from 1 January 1872 cost thirty times as much as Mayhew's twopenny pamphlets.[275] The bound edition issued just in time for Christmas sale in 1872 was a luxury item sold at £3 10s: "The text, framed in double red lines, was perfectly printed on thick creamy paper, and each illustration was lovingly protected by a tissue."[276] Accordingly, it was advertised as the "gift book of the season", and "the handsomest Christmas present".[277] Note that the pleasure derived from the book came not from reading it or looking at the images but from giving it away, owning it and presenting it in the drawing-room. One review explicitly recommended the book as "an elegant addition to the drawing-room table".[278]

The collaboration between renowned French illustrator Gustave Doré and English journalist Blanchard Jerrold was announced as early as August of 1869 when several London newspapers reported that the pair was undertaking "a systematic exploration of London from Wapping to Kensington, among high and low, with the view to a great work on the great capital".[279] They were accompanied by Doré's friend and collaborator Émile Bourdelin:

> For our trips round and about London in search of material for our sketches and studies of character from the life, two private detectives had been placed at our disposal; and every night we spent hours in populous London districts such as Lambeth, Clerkenwell, Bayswater, and the Docks. It was a real pleasure to watch Doré, dressed in some ragamuffin style or other, hurrying in and out of the streets and alleys, and rapidly taking notes with the rarest precision – notes which served him for the composition of his blocks.[280]

Apart from Bourdelin, who added the detailed backgrounds, houses and monuments, Doré also relied on his own workshop of trusted engravers to complete the engravings.[281] Stylistically, as Alexander Roob has shown, his depictions of the London poor followed the pictorial traditions of illustrated newspapers and in particular the work of Henri Durand-Brager for *Une excursion dans les quartiers pauvres de Londres* (1865) published in the illustrated travel magazine *Le Tour du Monde* by French journalist Louis Laurent

---

275   An early sample of the first chapter was published and sent to London newspaper offices around Christmas of 1871 and advertised as "The Handsomest Christmas Present" in the *Pall Mall Gazette* (20 December 1871): 14.

276   Eric de Maré, *The London Doré Saw: A Victorian Evocation* (London: Allen Lane, 1973), 9.

277   *Sheffield Daily Telegraph* (4 November 1872): 3; *Western Times* (12 November 1872): 3.

278   *Western Times* (12 November 1872): 3. On the representative function of the drawing-room in Victorian households, see Judith Flanders, *Inside the Victorian Home: A Portrait of Domestic Life in Victorian England* (New York, London: W.W. Norton, 2003), 168–213.

279   *Morning Post* (13 August 1869): 5; see also *London Daily News* (13 August 1869): 4.

280   Quoted in Blanche Roosevelt, *Life and Reminiscences of Gustave Doré* (London: Cassell, 1885), 368–369.

281   See Melton Prior Institute for reportage drawing & printing culture: Alexander Roob, "Gustave Doré in der Tradition der London – Reportage III: Dritte Männer", *Feature*, October 2016 (http://www.meltonpriorinstitut.org/ pages/textarchive.php5?view=text&ID=122).

Simonin.[282] Durand-Brager's drawings prefigured several of Doré's emblematic motifs from *A Pilgrimage* including a bull's eye lantern shedding light on poor people and a group of homeless sleeping in one of the stone recesses of London Bridge.[283]

Henry Mayhew had promised his readers a "cyclopedia of the condition and earnings of those that will work, those that cannot work, and those that will not work" in the subtitle of his work. Blanchard Jerrold repeatedly cautioned his readers that Doré the artist and he himself were mainly looking to present them with "the most striking types, the most completely representative scenes, and the most picturesque features of the greatest city on the face of the globe".[284] The picturesque – like the typical – is a central concept in Jerrold's text and the adjective is used multiple times in his introduction: "And, in starting on our pilgrimage, let me warn the reader once again that we are but wanderers in search of the picturesque, the typical."[285] As art historian Peter Schmandt points out the term picturesque was used from the late 18th century to designate the visual appeal a place held for tourists, and as I have shown in the previous chapter it was also applied to the artistic rendition of scenes of human misery.[286] Jerrold's enumeration of the sights of London thus includes images of urban poverty like homeless children, "a pawnbroker's shop on Saturday" and the workhouse ("outside the casual ward; the stone yard in the morning").[287]

According to art historian Alan Woods, the picturesque functioned as "a Victorian escape route" that "enabled the artist or writer to avoid the issues raised by any presentation of the poor by a kind of aesthetic indifference to the characters described, which left him free to concentrate on the attractive nature of rags in sunlight, or the delights of accidental arrangements of figures".[288] The appeal of picturesque poverty is evident in Jerrold's description of Doré's reaction to the homeless on London Bridge:

> He had been deeply impressed with the groups of poor women and children we had seen upon the stone seats of the bridge one bright morning on our way to Shadwell. By night, it appeared to his imagination, the scene would have a wonderful grandeur. We went. The wayfarers grouped and massed under the moon's light, with the ebon dome of St. Paul's topping the outline of the pictures,

---

282 Ibid.

283 Ibid.

284 Doré and Jerrold, *London*, x.

285 Ibid., 15.

286 Schmandt, *Armenhaus und Obdachlosenasyl*, 50.

287 Doré and Jerrold, *London*, viii.

288 Alan Woods, "Doré's London: Art and Evidence", *Art History*, vol. 1, no. 3 (1978): 341–359, here 354. Unlike Jerrold, Gustave Doré is not guilty of this according to Woods because he leaves the poor in groups and in their surroundings instead of presenting them as isolated individuals and thus as a general problem of society, which individual acts of charity cannot solve. Peter Schmandt provides a different reading and argues convincingly that Doré's adaptation of Christian iconography in images like "Scripture Reader in a Night Refuge" makes his illustrations pointed visual propaganda for Christian welfare organizations. Schmandt, *Armenhaus und Obdachlosenasyl*, 80.

Fig. 6: Gustave Doré - *Asleep Under the Stars*, from Gustave Doré and Blanchard Jerrold, *London. A Pilgrimage* (1872), Public domain, British Library.

engrossed him. In the midnight stillness, there was a most impressive solemnity upon the whole, which penetrated the nature of the artist. 'And they say London is an ugly place!' was the exclamation.[289]

The production process thus becomes part of the narrative through the descriptive force of the text. In *The Life of Gustave Doré*, Blanchard Jerrold later described Doré's working methods and stated that the Frenchman relied on his excellent memory to reconstruct what he saw: "I could seldom prevail upon him to make a sketch on the spot [...] notes or scenes [...] were the utmost he would take on the scene. He made his old answer: J'ai beaucoup de collodion dans la tête."[290] Doré likening his artistic process to the workings of the photographic apparatus was by then a common metaphor and highlights the importance Victorian artists and critics placed on detail:

> Painters of contemporary life like Frith relied on photographs to build up their minutely accurate canvasses, and even classicists such as Alma-Tadema and Lord Leighton were slaves to the demand for historically accurate settings and accessories. Some critics seemed to feel that to spot an error of detail was to reveal the work as bad art.[291]

Despite his photographic memory, there were notable and numerous factual inaccuracies in Doré's illustrations, as architectural historian Eric de Maré points out:

> [H]e wilfully placed French baskets on the arms of London flower girls, allowed at least fifty horses to run in the Derby, and designed slum chimneystacks, in that

289 Doré and Jerrold, *London*, 6.

290 Quoted in Woods, "Art and Evidence", 344.

291 Idem.., 342.

scene of railway arches so beloved by social historians, with a waste of brickwork that would scandalise any speculative builder.[292]

Similarly, contemporaneous reviews of the first number of *London. A Pilgrimage* focused on the lack of verisimilitude in Doré's illustrations with the often-repeated reprimand that his subjects looked "too French". A reviewer for the *Morning Post* remarked:

> It would be tedious to mention in detail each sketch which lacks local resemblance; suffice it to say that the general impression left on the mind is that M. Doré never actually drew from life on the spot, but contented himself with carrying away his recollections merely, which in many cases must have been filled up with figures after he got back to France.[293]

The same commentator praised the artistic composition of Doré's images and complimented his use of light and shadow: "Those figures applying for admittance at the night refuge are striking, and the grouping and arrangement of light are admirable; but the scene might be anywhere, and the men are evident Frenchmen of the lowest class."[294] The skilful interplay of foreground and background and of light and shadow in Doré's illustrations was central to their picturesque appeal which foregrounds execution over subject matter as in the following review for the *Morning Advertiser:*

> *Hayboats on the Thames*, a full-page engraving, presents us with a picturesque moonlight scene with which all Cockneydom must be familiar – the hayboats lying close up under the shore, whilst a forest of masts and rigging is dimly seen on the opposite side of the river. A night scene at the docks has some good bits of chiaroscuro, but is slightly overdone as regards the general that is going on amongst the dock labourers.[295]

This sentiment is echoed in a review for the *Illustrated London News* whose author also points towards Doré's shortcomings as a realist:

> Then, no such rigging was ever seen of a barge as in the hay-boats on the Thames. Again, the figures in the night scene at the docks and the night refuge exist only in the artist's imagination. [...] The 'get-up' of the part is perfect; there are some beautiful examples of the wood-engraver's art, and, setting aside the falsity of the representation, some very artistic effects of light and shade.[296]

Conversely, Doré's illustrations – especially those of East End scenes – were frequently taken at face value by modern scholars, as art historian Alan Woods has pointed out: "The London illustrations are increasingly regarded not as works of art but as evidence; and their 'realism' has been taken for granted. They are accepted as accurate and objective records of the age."[297] A tendency that has already been observed for Beard's daguerreotypes for *London Labour*

---

292   De Maré, *The London Doré Saw*, 9. According to Roob, the railway arches were probably based on a design by Bourdelin and bear his stylistic signature.

293   *Morning Post* (30 November 1872): 6

294   Ibid.

295   "Gustave Doré's 'London'", *Morning Advertiser* (1 January 1872): 3.

296   "Fine Arts", *Illustrated London News* (6 January 1872): 18.

297   Woods, "Art and Evidence", 341.

and the London Poor, which Anne Humpherys calls "some of the most accurate pictures that we have of the actual facial features and dress of the people making their living in the streets of London at midcentury".[298] The impact of structuralist and constructivist theories has led to critical reevaluations of the interplay between seeing and social control in Doré's London illustrations and Thomson's *Street Life in London*. Modern critics like Griselda Pollock, Alan Woods and Tanushree Ghosh who stress the merit of Doré's illustrations often do so on account of images of the poor 'looking back' at the reader.[299] The stare becomes an act of resistance that renders the safe viewing position precarious as in Wood's interpretation of an East End mother depicted in *Houndsditch*:

> She is staring straight at us. She obviously has no hope. She is not asking for sympathy; she is not asking for charity. She is questioning our right to be there, looking at her family. She accuses us and our society which enables the conditions in which she and her family and her neighbours live to continue.[300]

In contrast, a reviewer for the *Sheffield Daily Telegraph* of June 1872 seemed entirely unfazed by the intense stare of the poor woman and complimented Doré's artistic ability and "his unrivalled power of delineating abject human nature".[301]

The illustration is found in chapter XVII "Whitechapel and Thereabouts", where Doré and Jerrold (seemingly) embark on a separate travel within their pilgrimage.[302] Literary historian Tanushree Ghosh states that Jerrold's and Doré's "choice of sites and situations when portraying the East End" aims to "provide the upper-class reader with access to the kinds of scenes that they would not encounter in everyday life".[303] Throughout the chapter Jerrold reverts to the familiar tropes of social exploration like the representation of the poor as an alien race: "We dismiss our cab: it would be useless in the strange, dark byeways, to which we are bound: byeways, the natives of which will look upon us as the Japanese looked upon the first European travellers in the streets

---

298 Humpherys, *Henry Mayhew*, 70.

299 Griselda Pollock, "Vicarious Excitements: *London. A Pilgrimage* by Gustave Doré and Blanchard Jerrold, 1872", *New Formations*, no. 4 (Spring 1988): 25–50; Tanushree Ghosh, "Gifting Pain: The Pleasures of Liberal Guilt in *London. A Pilgrimage* and *Street Life in London*", *Victorian Literature and Culture*, vol. 41, no. 1 (2013): 91–123. See also Alan Wood's reading of the Newgate prison scenes and the Bull's-Eye lantern, "Art and Evidence", 351–353.

300 Woods, "Art and Evidence", 355. Woods argues that Doré's depictions of the poor "are radically different from those of mainstream Victorian culture" (350), a reading based mainly on his Newgate and Bull's-Eye illustrations as they show authority figures as being outnumbered by prisoners and East End denizens. Conversely, Peter Schmandt situates Doré firmly within a Conservative mindset that favoured the traditional model of Christian benevolence and charitable engagement towards the poor. See Schmandt, *Armenhaus und Obdachlosenasyl*, 66.

301 *Sheffield Daily Telegraph* (8 June 1872): 6.

302 Jerrold was accompanied by a police officer and a number of other slummers: "Prince Charles Bonaparte, who, as a thoughtful and serious observer, made the tour of the East End one night (February 5, 1872) with me; accompanied by the Marquis of Bassano, and Monsieur Filon, tutor to the Prince Imperial." Doré and Jerrold, *London*, 148.

303 Ghosh, "Liberal Guilt", 99.

Fig. 7: Gustave Doré - *Houndsditch*, from Gustave Doré and Blanchard Jerrold, *London. A Pilgrimage* (1872), Public domain, British Library.

of Jeddo."[304] He also highlights the dangers and thrills of his exploration to provide an experience of armchair-travel: "At dark corners, lurking men keep close to the wall; and the police smile when we wonder what would become of a lonely wanderer who should find himself in these regions unprotected."[305] Since the slumming party is accompanied by Sergeant Meiklejohn "an intelligent, a reflective, and courageous professional student of the criminal classes", Jerrold focuses on the correlation of poverty, crime and drugs on their patrol through common lodging-houses and dark streets: "In his company they will see the policeman's bull's-eye turned on extraordinary faces and figures such as we marked in a card-playing scene; while they will listen to very instructive stories of the devious ways in which men and women reach Newgate."[306]

The London represented in Doré's 180 illustrations and Jerrold's 21 chapters is a city dominated by work and divided into "three major components", according to art historian Griselda Pollock:

> [A] working centre focused geographically in the City and the port of London, a vagrant and criminal East where the multifarious activities by which the population attempts to survive (the street trades of Mayhew) are barely credited as labour or work, and finally a leisured West End.[307]

304 Doré and Jerrold, *London*, 144.

305 Ibid., 146.

306 Ibid., 138.

307 Pollock, "Vicarious Excitements", 39. See also 32. Woods provides a helpful classification of Doré's illustrations in five categories: 1. "Work-a-day London" (c. 40 illustrations: docks, markets, warehouses); 2. "The poor and their environment" (c. 35 illustrations: working and non-working poor, homeless, criminals); 3. "Character studies" (c. 25 small illustrations of "those engaged in some of the stranger and more colourful trades"); 4. "High society life and leisure" (c. 30 illustrations: parks, zoos, Boat Race and Derby); 5. "London and its landmarks" (c. 25 illustrations). Woods, "Art and Evidence", 357.

Fig. 8: Gustave Doré - *Orange Woman*, from Gustave Doré and Blanchard Jerrold, *London. A Pilgrimage* (1872), Public domain, Digital Collections and Archives, Tufts University.

Doré's small sketches of street vendors with their wares are reminiscent of the *Cries of London* tradition and Beard's daguerreotypes for Mayhew. The street sellers are included in the volume on account of their picturesqueness which, in Jerrold's logic, separates them from the badly dressed ordinary poor: "An English crowd is almost the ugliest in the world: because the poorer classes are but copyists in costume, of the rich. The exceptions are the followers of street trades – the costermongers, the orange-women, and the tramps."[308]

The picturesque is thus established throughout *London. A Pilgrimage* as a descriptive category that poor subjects and depictions of poverty can be judged by: "Indeed, poverty itself in *London. A Pilgrimage*, is categorized into picturesque and unpicturesque – a division that speaks to how the text catered to scopophilic desires of the upper classes."[309]

2.4 John Thomson and Adolphe Smith – *Street Life in London* and Photography

Literary historian Tanushree Ghosh defines scopophilia as "the pleasure that arises from looking at another as an object".[310] When the term is applied to the production and consumption of images of the poor, it "foregrounds the inequality inherent in the field of vision by indicating who can look and who is looked at".[311] Thus, the notion is closely linked to works that offer a categorization and representation of "true types" of the poor, who are selected, photographically captured and reproduced for a paying middle- and upper-

---

308   Doré and Jerrold, *London*, 35.

309   Ghosh, "Liberal Guilt", 104.

310   Ibid., 94. In psychoanalysis, the term also refers to the interplay between voyeurism and sexual desire.

311   Ibid., 95. Tanushree Ghosh discusses *London. A Pilgrimage* and *Street Life in London* as two examples of "reformist material" that was also "being sold and consumed as luxury items". Ibid., 92.

class readership. Another important example of this genre is *Street Life in London* by photographer John Thomson and journalist Adolphe Smith.[312]

The series was published in monthly parts by Sampson Low, Marston, Seale & Rivington from 1 February 1877, each issue containing "three permanent photographs" by Thomson and accompanying texts by either Smith or Thomson. What distinguished the work from its predecessors was not only the use of photography to document poverty but that of a new printing process for photographs, the Woodburytype. Patented by Walter Woodbury in 1864, the ink-based process produced high quality photomechanical prints barely distinguishable from an original photograph and guaranteed long durability – unlike earlier prints on coated paper (hence the description as permanent photographs).[313] However, since Woodburytypes had to be cut and glued individually for published works it "resulted in a more expensive product because of the hand labor involved in assembling the work".[314] Individual parts of *Street Life in London* were sold at 1s. 6d. (eighteenpence), which equalled a day's labour for the London Boardman depicted in one of Thomson's photographs.[315] As art historian Emily Morgan points out, the price "[…] put the serial well beyond the means of any of the people depicted inside the book, but it does not represent a deliberately exclusionary measure by the authors. Rather, 1s. 6d. was simply the publisher's standard price for its photographically-illustrated serials […]."[316] Additionally, a single bound volume of *Street Life in London* was issued in November 1877 for the Christmas trade and reviewed in the Gift and Christmas books sections of London newspapers.[317] It sold at 25 shillings but apparently, the book did not sell and the publisher Low & Co. cancelled the monthly serial in January of 1878. Emily Morgan points out that the single volume might have been an effort to counter poor sales with a Christmas Book, but "when reviewers panned the book and the public appeared indifferent to it, the publisher decided instead to cancel the series".[318] In 1881, an abbreviated version of the work was published as *Street*

---

312 For biographical information on Thomson, see Stephen White, *John Thomson: A Window to the Orient* (New York: Thames & Hudson, 1985). Biographical details and writings of Thomson and Smith relevant to *Street Life in London* are provided by Morgan, *True Types*, 48–81 and 82–127 respectively.

313 For details of the Woodburytype process, see Morgan, *True Types*, 179–181, and Luis Nadeau, "Woodburytype", in *Encyclopedia of Printing, Photographic, and Photomechanical Processes*, vol. 2 (Fredericton, New Brunswick: Atelier Luis Nadeau, 1990), 469. Nadeau notes that "Woodburytypes are permanent in the sense that they are light-fast […]." Ibid.

314 Jeff Rosen, "Posed as Rogues: The Crisis of Photographic Realism in John Thomson's *Street Life in London*", *Image*, vol. 36, nos. 3–4 (Fall / Winter 1993): 8–39, here 38.

315 Thomson and Smith, *Street Life*, 99.

316 Morgan, *True Types*, 184. The claim in the Publisher's Note to the 1969 edition that Street Life was "priced low enough for the very worker whose plight it depicted to afford" is thus easily disproven.

317 "Gift-Books", *Athenaeum*, no. 2616 (15 December 1877): 778; *Morning Post* (6 December 1877): 2, and *London Evening Standard* (13 December 1877): 2.

318 Morgan, *True Types*, 188. In 1881, an abbreviated version of the work was published as *Street Incidents*. The 21 entries were selected exclusively from parts published in the ultimate seven months of the serial. Thus, Morgan's claim that this was "solely the publisher's endeavour to recoup expenditures on this unsold material" (189) seems very likely.

Incidents. The 21 entries were selected exclusively from parts published in the ultimate seven months of the serial. Thus Emily Morgan's claim that this was "solely the publisher's endeavour to recoup expenditures on this unsold material" seems very likely.[319]

The first issue established *Street Life in London* in the visual tradition of the London street cries and directly referenced Henry Mayhew's observations on *London Labour and the London Poor*. Thomson began his description of London street life with a reference to Mayhew's classification of the poor in his introductory essay "London Nomades": "Hence it is that in London there are a number of what may be termed, owing to their wandering, unsettled habits, nomadic tribes."[320] But while Mayhew promised his readers a taxonomy of London street-folk, the nomadic tribes of Thomson's *Street Life* "render abortive any attempt at systematic classification".[321] As a result, individual biographies ("'Caney' the Clown", "Cast-Iron Billy", "'Hookey Alf' of Whitechapel") and less familiar occupations ("The 'Wall Worker'", "Public Disinfectors", "The London Boardmen") appear much more prominent throughout the work.[322] But descriptions of familiar London types ("Covent Garden Flower Women", "Street Doctors", "The Street Fruit Trade") and what are considered typical representatives of certain trades and their wares are also included: "The horse is typical of the class of animal used for the work – large and powerful, so as to stand the strain of incessant journeyings to and fro, and of the weight of water in the tank. The man is a fair type of his class, being attired in a manner peculiar to watering-men."[323]

In the preface Smith and Thomson explicitly acknowledge their debt to Mayhew, whose work "is still remembered by all who are interested in the condition of the humbler classes" but promise to actualize it through "the precision of photography".[324] The medium's "unquestionable accuracy", they suggest, will finally make good on the often-repeated promise to "present true types of the London Poor and shield us from the accusation of either underrating or exaggerating individual peculiarities of appearance". The printed photographs are thus presented as authentic visual depictions of poverty, but they mainly serve "in illustration of our subject".[325] It is worth noting that photographs as such were not a novelty for readers in the 1870s, indeed following the *carte-de-visite* craze of the 1860s many (if not most) Londoners had had their own portrait taken before (as the lower middle-class clientele of

---

319   Ibid., 189.

320   Thomson and Smith, *Street Life*, 9. Mayhew's first chapter in *London Labour and the London Poor* was titled "The Street-Folk. Of Wandering Tribes in General".

321   Ibid.

322   Many of these occupations were related to changes in media usage and advertising like the itinerant photographer of Clapham Common or the "walking advertisements" of the London Boardmen.

323   Thomson and Smith, *Street Life*, 103.

324   Ibid., Preface.

325   Ibid.

the Clapham Common photographer also indicates) or had at least seen one. Engravings made "from a photograph" or "from a daguerreotype" had also been used for several decades. Henry Fox Talbot's *The Pencil of Nature*, the first book of photographic prints in England (using the calotype process), was published as early as 1844. But photographic prints of superior quality and size were still a rarity when *Street Life in London* was published, and it wasn't until the invention of half-tone printing in the 1890s that combinations of texts and photographs in print reached mass distribution. Indeed, by the early 1880s it might be more likely that an average Victorian media user would have seen a projected photograph than a printed one.[326]

Newspaper ads for the single volume publication of *Street Life in London* praise the 37 photographs as "taken from life" – not from a photograph and not in a studio – which enhances their claim to authenticity.[327] Smith and Thomson also employed various textual strategies to authenticate their work like referencing personal familiarity with the subject and direct quotes in working-class vernacular. In the preface they promised their readers "careful observations among the poor of London", and in a later chapter Adolphe Smith explicitly advised his readers to seek out the poor for themselves to discover such characters as were described in the book. Fittingly, it was Smith who mainly established the initial connections with those depicted in *Street Life in London* and collected facts and figures about each street occupation from various informants (who were sometimes mentioned in the texts).[328]

Like Mayhew, Smith and Thomson frequently used verbatim quotes of their poor subjects transcribed in their dialect. Thomson also directly referenced his own note-taking in the text and vouched for the truthfulness of his jottings. He concludes his initial chapter on "London Nomades" with the following assurance: "I hastened to note down as fast as possible the information received word for word in the original language in which it was delivered, believing that this unvarnished story would at least be more characteristic and true to life."[329] And in a footnote to the unsigned chapter "The Dramatic Shoe-Black" the author (probably Thomson as well) insists that the quotations by Jacobus Parker "were jotted down as they were uttered".[330]

326　Jacob Riis used his photographs of working-class tenements in New York mostly for projection during his lantern shows while many of the pictures in his books were merely illustrations based on photographs. See Beate Althammer, "Die Faszination des Elends. Sozialreportagen um 1900", in Herbert Uerlings (ed.), *Armut – Perspektiven in Kunst und Gesellschaft* (Darmstadt: Primus, 2011), 215–223, here 220.

327　See, e.g, *The Examiner* (20 October 1877): 1344.

328　See Morgan, *True Types*, 97. Of the 36 chapters, 24 were written and signed by Adolphe Smith, two by John Thomson and ten remained unsigned but were probably either written by Thomson or collaborations between the two. See ibid., 279. Thomas Prasch notes that Thomson's writing style clearly differed from Smith's in three key aspects: "[A] greater inclination to discuss the circumstances that produced the photograph itself [...]; a strong commitment to direct quotation of street people's own words, usually with deliberate stilting of language to reflect the speaker's accent and style [...]; and a habit of comparing London to China, reflecting Thomson's own previous photographic experience [...]." Prasch, *Photographic Hegemony*, 193, note 5.

329　Thomson and Smith, *Street Life*, 3.

The interplay of images and text distinguished *Street Life in London* from the two previously discussed works. The life stories of the individuals depicted in the photographs were portrayed in the accompanying essays which sometimes also provided additional information on the production of the picture and the various street occupations. Art historian Angela Vanhaelen argues that ideological frictions between text and image permeate the entire work and that in an effort to resolve them, "the text of the book prompts specific readings of the photographs, often working against the images in order to convey an ideological point".[331] Sometimes, the text indeed dramatically altered the meaning of the photographs as in the case of Mary Pradd, depicted in the first chapter, who, Thomson is shocked to learn during a return visited, has been murdered since the photograph was taken.[332] In another case the change is less dramatic but equally notable. The boy pictured in the photograph *Cheap Fish of St. Giles's* is dressed like a stereotypical homeless boy with his bare feet and ill-fitting clothes. The accompanying essay clarified that he is actually seventeen years old but "only reaches the height of three feet ten inches" and that his attire is by choice: "His bare feet, I should add, are not necessarily symptoms of poverty; for, as a sailor, and during a long voyage to South Africa, he learnt to dispense with boots and shoes while on deck."[333]

While the texts were collaborations between Adolphe Smith and John Thomson, the latter was solely responsible for the 37 photographs collected in *Street Life in London*.[334] And contrary to the reception of Mayhew's *London Labour and the London Poor*, in the case of *Street Life in London*, modern scholars have focused almost exclusively on the photographs and their documentary qualities.[335] Literary scholar Richard Stein calls it "one of the most important examples of early urban photography" and art historian Angela Vanhaelen states that Thomson is considered "one of the pioneers of documentary street photography".[336] Thomson's use of the wet-plate technique required sufficient light and exposure time which meant that by necessity all of his subjects were

330 Ibid., 55.

331 Angela Vanhaelen, "Street Life in London and the Organization of Labour", *History of Photography*, vol. 26, no. 3 (Autumn 2002): 191–204, here 198.

332 Thomson and Smith, *Street Life*, 2. In a later chapter, Thomson relates this anecdote about a would-be photographic subject not pictured in the book: "Another well-known crawler had consented to have her portrait taken in company with that of the woman whose circumstances I have already described, but on the previous evening a gentleman gave her sixpence while she was strolling down Albemarle Street. This enabled her to indulge in a night's lodging, and she was so unaccustomed to the luxury of a bed, that she overslept herself and thus missed the appointment!" Ibid., 83.

333 Thomson and Smith, *Street Life*, 59–60.

334 See Morgan, *True Types*, 97. For a possible timeline of Thomson's photographs, see 189–194.

335 For an extensive discussion of scholarly works about Thomson and *Street Life*, see Morgan, *True Types*, 25–44. On Thomson's reception in different historical disciplines, Thomas Prasch notes: "Historians have neglected Thomson's continuation of Mayhew's exploration. Social historians have ignored him altogether. [...] Historians of photography, on the other hand, have hailed him as a founder of the documentary photography tradition." Prasch, *Photographic Hegemony*, 230.

336 Richard Stein, "Street Figures: Victorian Urban Iconography", in Christ and Jordan (ed.), *Victorian Visual Imagination*, 233–263, here 247, and Vanhaelen, "Street Life", 196.

Fig. 9: John Thomson - *Cheap Fish of St. Giles's*, Woodburytype, Plate 6 in *Street Incidents* (1881), Public domain, The Art Institute of Chicago.

posed for the camera or at least required to stand still for some time.[337] Apart from the individual poses, the selection of subjects, arrangement of groups and especially the lighting were the results of Thomson's careful artistic composition. As art historian Sylvia Sukop points out the aesthetic of Thomson's photographs was clearly influenced by the compositional conventions of painted portraits.[338] While Thomas Prasch sees Thomson's photographs unequivocally in the visual tradition of the *Cries of London*, Morgan argues that contemporary criticism and requests by the publishers made Thomson choose a "more traditionally typological imagery" throughout the course of the serial. She consequently offers a more nuanced consideration of the photographs: "Conventional or familiar street figures get conventional treatment; unconventional or unusual street figures may be – but are not always – depicted in less stylistically-conventional ways."[339]

---

337 See Vanhaelen, "Street Life", 196. The blurred face of a young boy in the photograph for the chapter "The Old Clothes of St. Giles" illustrates the results if those being photographed did not stand still long enough. Ghosh details the various steps required to produce a photograph with the wet-plate process (posing the subjects, focusing the lens, coating, bathing and loading the plate) and concludes that subjects would have had to hold their pose for at least ten minutes to produce satisfactory results. Ghosh, "Liberal Guilt", 119. The fact that a dog standing in the foreground of the photograph "A Convict's Home" is (relatively) clearly visible would seem to contradict such a long exposure time.

338 See Sylvia Sukop, "Die soziale Wirklichkeit als Bild. John Thomsons *Street Life in London*", in Bodo von Dewitz and Roland Scotti (ed.), *Alles Wahrheit! Alles Lüge! Photographie und Wirklichkeit im 19. Jahrhundert. Die Sammlung Robert Lebeck* (Dresden: Verlag der Kunst, 1996), 201–209, here 206. On Thomson's compositional technique, see also Prasch, *Photographic Hegemony*, 235–236.

339 Morgan, *True Types*, 245.

Fig. 10: John Thomson - *Black Jack*, Woodburytype, from *Street Life in London* (1877),
Public domain, The Art Institute of Chicago.

In several cases, the negatives were cropped or altered to produce the printed photographs. Art historian Jeff Rosen cites "two images that bear evidence of either close cropping, obvious enlargement, and excessive manipulative highlighting around the figures" and others which "appear to have had the entire background of the image removed".[340] The latter is clearly visible in the depiction of a hawker on his cart that is reminiscent of Beard's studio daguerreotypes. These alterations to the photograph apparently bothered contemporaneous reviewers less than their staged nature. One critic complained: "[T]here is little of the magic we call 'spontaneity' in them; even the donkey owned by *Black Jack*, […] stands here, as it were to be 'taken'."[341]

340   Rosen, "Posed as Rogues", 34.

341   "Gift-Books", *Athenaeum*, no. 2616 (15 December 1877): 778. The reviewer also lamented that photographs by their very nature as neutral records lacked the touch of the artist: "Such pictures as those before us, not being produced by an able artist, but by an intelligent 'operator,' have that 'dead and alive' look which is always present in works of this class." Ibid. The *London Daily News* also bemoaned the lack of "artistic spirit" in the photographs but still admitted that, "as records of the life of the poor in our days, these groups are not without interest". *London Daily News* (26 November 1877): 2.

A similar complaint was made against the picture *Cheap Fish of St. Giles's* in the *British Journal of Photography*, where the critic regretted that "it is somewhat apparent that some of the group were far from unconscious of the fact that they were standing for their portraits".[342] As a critic for a photographic journal the reviewer would have been aware both of contemporary photographic practice and the fact that all of Thomson's subjects were conscious of being photographed. Especially since the accompanying texts by Thomson explicitly mention that many of his subjects previously consented to having their picture taken. Indeed, some of the people in the background gathered behind the fish stall and two posed customers in the foreground are looking directly at the camera, something that Thomson's individual models generally avoided. That the different social status of the readers (and reviewers) and the subjects of *Street Life in London* also played a significant role in its reception becomes apparent from a review in the *London Evening Standard*:

> This book contains photographic portraits true enough no doubt as photographs, alas! must be, but for the most part very unlovely. *The Convict's Home*, *Black Jack*, *The Temperance Sweep*, and the *London Cabmen*, are no doubt very like the persons and things they represent; but those persons and things do not make pretty pictures. The photograph of a tramp or a cadger is generally as uninteresting as the tramp or cadger himself. We should promptly show 'Cast Iron Billy' the door if he came to visit us. Why should we cherish that tipsy old bus driver's portrait painted with all its imperfections by the sun?[343]

Tanushree Ghosh rightly points out that the question of who is photographing and who is being photographed was closely linked to questions of class: "Class and social status, in fact, were encoded within photographic practice itself: while upper-class photographers felt free to roam into lower-class neighbourhoods to photograph people and places, the presence of photographers in upper-class areas was declared to be a public nuisance."[344]

---

342   *British Journal of Photography* (10 August 1877): 382, cited in Rosen, "Posed as Rogues", 34. On contemporary reactions to Thomson's photographs, see also Vanhaelen, "Street Life", 196. For reviews in papers and trade press, see Morgan, *True Types*, 185–188.

343   *London Evening Standard* (13 December 1877): 2.

344   Ghosh, "Liberal Guilt", 104.

3

The Popular Poverty Works of George R. Sims and Their Adaptations

This chapter approaches the question of George R. Sims's popularity and the adaptations of his works from various angles. First, Sims is introduced as a popular media personality whose authority as an eyewitness was established through a personal narrative repeated in interviews with newspapers and magazines. The second section examines Sims's *The Lights o' London* (1881), his most popular melodrama and an example for the use of authenticating strategies on the theatre stage. The following sections provide an overview of the various adaptations of Sims's popular works for the historical art of projection and the cinema made between the early 1880s and the 1920s. Both explore the question of what kind of material was chosen for adaptation and why and provide an analysis of the artistic, legal and economic factors that shaped these adaptations.

3.1 George R. Sims – Creating a Media Personality

In an article titled "An Autobiography" for the monthly magazine *The Theatre* in July 1884, George R. Sims reviewed his journalistic and dramatic career. He was born on 2nd September 1847 in London and sent to preparatory school in Eastbourne at 8 years old.[345] He made his first "essay at journalism" at Hanwell College where he also published his first article, "a flippant comment upon certain details of the school management" in the *Hanwell College Gazette*.[346] Interestingly, in a later portrait for the "Weekly Gallery of Celebrities" this innocent article had already become "a bold and trenchant comment on certain details of the school management to which he objected, and, as such, an interesting earnest of his future unsparing castigations of abuses in the larger world outside school".[347] After studying in Paris and Bonn, Germany, where

---

345   See Sims, "An Autobiography", 14. In his actual autobiography, published in 1917, Sims states that he was 9 years old when he was sent to boarding school in The Grove, Eastbourne. See Sims, *My Life*, 20.

346   Sims, "An Autobiography", 14. The George R. Sims Collection at Rylands Library holds several issues of the *Hanwell College Gazette*, articles by Sims are signed "G.R.S.".

347   GB 133 GRS/10/3 (probably 1888): 84–85. This and all other items from the George R. Sims Collection at Rylands Library, Manchester, will be cited with their archive reference and – if available – page number and date given on the object. Another portrait of Sims called the essay "a sweeping denunciation [...] of the scheme of the school management". Helen C. Black, "Half-Hours with Celebrities. Mr. George R. Sims", *Lloyd's Weekly* (30 June 1885): 8.

Sims developed "a taste for roulette", he entered his father's office to work as a mercantile clerk at 19 years old.[348] In his later autobiography Sims elaborated on their trade: "My father was at that time a wholesale and export cabinet-manufacturer and plate-glass factor, and he carried on his business on historical premises which were his freehold property."[349] He stressed how the personal interactions of his office work served as inspiration for him as an author: "Quaint characters came to the office and to the warehouse from all parts of the kingdom, and I remembered them with great advantage when I began to write stories professionally."[350] During the ten years that Sims worked on his father's premises at Aldersgate Street, he "'scribbled' a great deal" and "sent poems and short stories right and left" but never saw them published.[351] More importantly, however, Sims "took to studying character", as he put it.[352] In order to "see life as it is among the masses" he used to "go into back streets, bar parlours, penny gaffs, to stand outside workhouse doors, to hang about the early markets and the dock-gates".[353] All in an effort to "get at the plain, unvarnished truth", as a profile points out, while Sims himself stated that "the material I then acquired for the novel that was never written has been exceedingly useful to me in many ways".[354]

His "Autobiography" appears to be one of the first instances that Sims posits himself as an eyewitness who relates his own first-hand experiences. This assertion reappears frequently both in his journalistic works and in later interviews and serves to establish him as a trustworthy expert on London's byways – even if that effort wasn't always successful. In 1889, literary journalist Charles Whibley sarcastically remarked:

> There is not one of his ballads of misery and virtue in the slums which a school-girl might not have written, though she had never seen an alley in her life. His books are one and all compacted of battered and threadbare conventionalities. It is difficult to believe that he has ever studied life outside the Britannia […].[355]

But more frequently, Sims was defended from contemporaneous critics and praised for his powers of observation like in this excerpt from a portrait in *Pearson's Weekly*:

> The critic sneers and says, that his so-called ballads are only sentimental drivel, but said critic has never faced an audience when a reciter has given *Billy's Rose*, or *The Lifeboat*, and he knows nothing of that subtle power underlying Mr. Sims'

---

348 Sims, "An Autobiography", 14.

349 Sims, *My Life*, 31–32.

350 Ibid., 35.

351 Sims, "An Autobiography", 15.

352 Ibid.

353 Ibid. The term "studying character" does not only refer to class differences but also carries racial and physiognomic undertones, according to Kate Flint: "The idea was widespread, in the mid-century, that different social types, and different types of character, were physiognomically distinguishable." Kate Flint, *The Victorians and the Visual Imagination* (Cambridge etc.: Cambridge University Press, 2010), 14.

354 GB 133 GRS/10/3 (probably 1888): 84–85, and Sims, "An Autobiography", 15.

355 Charles Whibley, "Modern Men. George R. Sims", *Scots Observer* (23 November 1889): 11–12, here 11.

work which comes to him from perfect knowledge of the life and struggles of the poor. He is their poet and he talks to them in their language putting their own words into telling periods or simple and effective rhyme.[356]

Similarly, literary critic William Archer opined in *English Dramatists of Today* (1882): "The minutiae of middle and lower class life in London – its heroism, its pathos, its humour, its rascality, its barbarism – are known to Mr. Sims from personal observation [….]."[357] It should be noted that in these instances the authenticity ascribed to Sims explicitly refers to his fictional (i.e. dramatic and poetic) works; not his journalistic reports. I would argue that this stems in part from the narrative George Sims constructed about himself and his literary career in countless interviews, newspaper portraits and, perhaps most importantly, his autobiography *My Life: Sixty Years' Recollections of Bohemian London* (1917), which is frequently cited and referenced by modern scholars. Instead of providing a factual overview of his life and works, this chapter will reconstruct the media personality that George Sims successfully created.

The more than 30 newspaper portraits, news cuttings, interviews and caricatures analysed for this chapter – a selection made from Sims's personal papers now kept at the Rylands Library in Manchester – are filled with recurring quotes and anecdotes. The four remaining scrapbooks in the archive are only a fraction of Sims's larger original collection. A reporter for *The Princess*, who was invited into Sims's London home in 1895, wrote that he had already amassed 64 volumes "containing Press notices" by then.[358] The fact that Sims was interviewed quite frequently is repeatedly mentioned in the articles and one interviewer jokes that he is unsure, "if a public portrait of George R. Sims has appeared since he altered the trim of his beard".[359] Sims's popular appeal is ridiculed in *Judy, or the London Serio-Comic Journal* in 1890:

> 'You've caught on rather,' I say to G.R.S. 'It's not so very surprising, after all. The public like their plots to be familiar, their comedy not too high, and their sentiment hot and strong – in fact, pathos tells all the better when spelt with a *b*. You have taught future generations of aspiring authors that the secret of success is to talk about your own – and that if a man desires others to write about him, he should industriously write about himself.'[360]

Not surprisingly, most articles praise Sims and even those critical of his works usually admit that he is enormously popular. The aforementioned Charles Whibley bemoans that Sims's success with working class readers "proves more

---

356 "Workers and Their Work – No. III. Mr. George R. Sims, Journalist and Playwright", *Pearson's Weekly* (19 September 1891): 135.

357 Archer, *English Dramatists*, 297–298.

358 Anne Morton Lane, "'Dagonet' at Home", *The Princess* (9 November 1895): 2–5, here 4.

359 Joseph Keating, "George R. Sims", *The Idler* (September 1904): 284–288, here 284.

360 Paul Pry, "Lions of the Day in Their Dens. No. 14–Mr. Geo. R. Sims in Regent's Park", *Judy, or the London Serio-Comic Journal* (17 September 1890): 137. Just how many others wrote about "George R. Sims" (or, indeed, Sims wrote about himself) can be guessed at from a full-text search of that term in the British Newspaper Archive, which yields nearly 16,000 results between 1880 and 1900 as of December 2020.

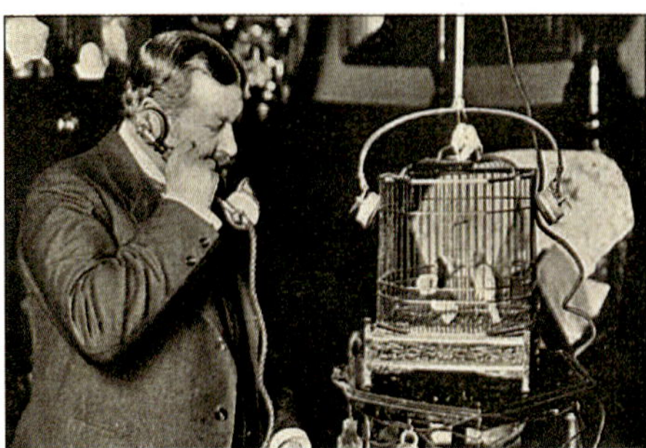

Fig. 11: George Robert Sims and his canary Richard Yea and Nay, Photograph, *The Illustrated Sporting and Dramatic News* (21 June 1902): 646, Public domain.

conclusively than any research could do that the bulk of the British public neither recognises nature nor appreciates art", but he cannot deny it: "He has crammed a hungry public with 'works' by the hundred thousand. Is there a single cottage home in England where the blameless and persuasive Dagonet is not?"[361] Accordingly, many articles stress Sims's popularity among lower-class readers, praising him as "the poet of the people" and mention his intimate knowledge of the "highways and byways of life".[362] The appreciation of those classes he writes about lends additional credit to his depictions of poverty both as a journalist and a writer:

> He is perhaps the only writer of the present day who really reaches the hearts of the humblest reader; and even in the midst of the scenes he writes of his works are known and read with avidity. On Saturday night in Whitechapel Road, the street hawker will do a roaring trade in any work by 'Jarge Har Sims,' while at the street corner one will see a sympathetic crowd listening, with eager interest, and often with tearful eyes, to some peripatetic reciter giving them *Billy's Rose*.[363]

George Sims also seems to have been popular among fellow journalists as evidenced by the Jubilee Dinner for his 50th birthday, which was attended by "a large number of his personal friends – including most of the best-known journalists in and around Fleet-street".[364] In several cases these personal friends wrote flattering newspaper profiles about him: The George R. Sims Collection holds several personal letters to Sims from John Latey then of the *Penny Illustrated Paper* who later interviewed Sims for *The Sketch* in 1902.[365] In the same year, a profile on Sims appeared in the *Illustrated Sporting and Dramatic News* written by Spencer Edwards who had worked with Sims at *The Referee* under the pen-name Carados. Both portraits included numerous photographs of Sims in his writing rooms, with his family, his personal typewriter (the person, not the machine) and of course his various pet animals like horse "Faust-up-to-date", named after one of his plays, or the canary "Richard Yea and Nay".[366] In 1901 and 1902, Sims was happy to invite journalists into the

---

361 Whibley, "Modern Men", 11.

362 J.L.O., "Mr. G.R. Sims at Home", 38.

363 GB 133 GRS/10/3 (probably before 1883): 54.

364 *Illustrated Police News* (11 September 1897): 8.

365 John Latey, "G.R. Sims at Home to *The Sketch*", *The Sketch* (12 February 1902): 140–141.

366 Even Sims's pets, which he often mentioned in his "Mustard and Cress" column, gained some notoriety. In 1895, Sims printed invitations for the christening of his bulldog Barney Barnato.

"Living-London-room" of his Regent's Park home to promote his current editing project in interviews and photographs.

Most articles on George Sims resemble one another and use similar quotes even down to the same curious details. One example is a recurring anecdote which underlines his ability to work well under pressure. Sims told the magazine *Pearson's Weekly* in September of 1891 that when *The Referee* ran a column short one time, he asked the printer boy to wait while he wrote down some verses and "that was about the best thing he ever wrote in his life".[367] The anecdote is repeated almost verbatim in a portrait of Sims from *The Search Light* in 1892.[368] Another article from January 1892 tells a very similar story. This time about a theatre manager anxiously waiting for the "final act of his play" from Sims who proceeded to write his Dagonet column and the play alternately for a few hours and of course, "the act written under these disadvantageous circumstances contained some of the smartest dialogue of the play".[369] It is not possible to determine if the authors and interviewers simply copied from one another (a common practice in contemporaneous journalism) or if Sims successfully sold his narrative. Another aspect of this narrative is his perseverance in the face of constant rejection. In *The Theatre*, Sims remembered his initial frustration with London's publishers:

> I sent poems and short stories right and left, but I never had one accepted. I turned out of an old box the other day a book in which I had entered the address of every magazine and periodical published in London and I sent some of my stories to each one in turn, until I got to the end of the list.[370]

Sims had been writing both in his free time and during work hours after he was employed by his father in 1866, but it wasn't until 1874 that Sims started contributing regularly to *Fun* magazine, edited by Henry Sampson, and only in the early 1880s that he finally quit his day job to focus solely on his writing career: "I could not possibly put in eight hours a day in the City, write a play a month, and contribute regularly to three weekly papers."[371] One of those papers was *The Referee* a weekly newspaper that focused on sports and dramatic criticism and from the first issue of 19 August 1877 until his death in 1922 featured Sims's column "Mustard and Cress" as well as the occasional Dagonet ballad. The fact that *The Referee* appeared on Sundays, its affordable price of

---

367 "Workers and Their Work – No. III. Mr. George R. Sims, Journalist and Playwright", *Pearson's Weekly* (19 September 1891): 135.

368 GB 133 GRS/10/3: 117, "Mr. George Robert Sims, of the *Referee*", *The Search Light* (1892): 74.

369 GB 133 GRS/10/3: 123, "About Well-Known People, Mr. George R. Sims", *Unknown Magazine*, vol. 7, no. 161 (16 January 1892).

370 Sims, "An Autobiography", 15. The assertion was later repeated in a portrait of Sims for *Lloyd's Weekly Newspaper*.

371 Sims, *My Life*, 126. The fact that he had apparently indebted himself quite heavily to a loan-shark might have had something to do with his initial hesitance to quit his work in the City: "The fees I had so far received had not been sufficient to clear off the trifling sum of a thousand pounds for which I had in some way managed to become indebted to certain gentlemen who only charged sixty per cent interest for the accommodation." Ibid. On Sims's financial situation, see John Russell Stephens, *The Profession of the Playwright: British Theatre, 1800–1900* (Cambridge etc.: Cambridge University Press, 2006), 65–66.

one penny and its political Radicalism all suggest that the paper was aimed at a broad readership that included the working class. Under the pen-name Dagonet, the jester to editor Henry Sampson's Pendragon (King Arthur), Sims wrote wittily about a broad range of topics from current affairs, London life and society to his frequent travels and health issues as well as his family life.[372] On the latter, one interviewer jokingly remarked:

> The story of George R. Sims everybody knows: his life of tragic endeavour against the tyranny of a despotic liver and a digestive apparatus that won't work. But in spite of the combined efforts of these miscreants, the poet, playwright, novelist, and journalist goes on his vigorous way.[373]

Sims's popularity as a journalist was surpassed only by his success as a dramatist. Arthur Calder-Marshall calls him the "most successful English playwright of his age" and according to Philip Waller, Sims was the first dramatist to have "four plays running concurrently in West End theatres [...] with, additionally, a dozen touring companies performing his work".[374] Many of his plays enjoyed extraordinarily long runs, which secured substantial revenue for the author. His best known melodrama, *The Lights o' London* (1881), was played "somewhere in the world non-stop for thirty-five years".[375] The play made George Sims "indubitably, liberatingly rich" and his villa in Regent's Park, where many journalists visited him, soon became the symbol of his success as an author.[376] One newspaper reported that he made over £25,000 from that play alone but Sims himself was at times hesitant to speak about his wealth – probably because he lost a considerable amount of the money he made through his gambling. His statements in *The Theatre* about his first successful play *Crutch and Toothpick* (1879) are typical in this respect: "It has brought me up to date £150. I state this solely for the benefit of the Commissioners of Income-Tax and others, who have been greatly deceived by paragraphs concerning my income from play-writing."[377] Sims often worked in collaboration with other authors (e.g., Henry Pettitt, Arthur Shirley, Clement Scott) for his plays and many of them were adapted as feature films in the 1910s and 1920s.

Sims's "Mustard and Cress" was "a pioneer gossip column" that "acknowledged and created Sims as a personality", according to James Marsh and David Francis: "'Dagonet' became the late-Victorian epitome of the 'familiar stranger' of modern celebrity studies, famous for being the famous George R. Sims."[378] Many of Sims's ballads were first published in *The Referee* and when his *Dagonet*

---

372 Many portraits refer both earnestly and jokingly to Sims's liver problems, and funny quips of his niece Florence Wykes (known as child performer Minty Lamb) appeared frequently in his column in the late 1900s.

373 Keating, "George R. Sims", 284.

374 Calder-Marshall, "Introduction", 16, and Waller, "Sims", 722–723.

375 Waller, "Sims", 722.

376 Marsh and Francis, "Poetry of Poverty", 65.

377 Sims, "An Autobiography", 16. Conversely, Sims also speaks about "Arrangements with American managers which have made my pieces excellent properties in the States". Ibid., 17.

378 Marsh and Francis, "Poetry of Poverty", 66.

Ballads were released in book form in 1879, they were an enormous success according to Sims himself: "[…] already considerably over 100,000 copies of my 'poems' have been sold […]. For poetry to pay is so rare an occurrence that I cannot refrain from mentioning the large and still daily increasing sale of the 'Dagonet' Ballads."[379] The number of 100,000 sold copies seems to have originated with Sims's article in *The Theatre* and is repeated by most scholars including Philip Waller, Norman Longmate as well as Joss Marsh and David Francis.[380] As Dagonet, Sims did not hesitate to promote his other publications and activities in the *Referee* column. On 11 November 1883 he wrote:

> I have received from Messrs. Chatto and Windus an announcement that they will publish early in the week a shilling volume, entitled *How the Poor Live*, written by George R. Sims, and illustrated by Mr. Frederick Barnard, the artist who accompanied the author on his journey through outcast London in the spring of the present year.[381]

And on 21 December 1884 'Dagonet' announced a new series of short stories that he preemptively defended from critics:

> The series of stories which the author of *How the Poor Live* commences in the *Weekly Dispatch* of January 4 are, I am told, founded upon actual facts. I have not the slightest doubt that his sketches *In Black and White* will be described as exaggerations or improbabilities by those who never believe anything possible that does not happen within the narrow circle of their own acquaintances.[382]

By likening his factual reports to his fictional stories, which, as he assured his readers, were nevertheless "founded on actual facts", Sims reiterated his claim to authentic story-telling. The fact that he appeared as a witness before the Royal Commission on the Housing of the Working Classes in April of 1884 to answer questions about the living conditions in Southwark only cemented his authority as an expert on London's poverty. Sims himself only mentioned his testimony in passing in *The Referee* and in his autobiography, whereas multiple articles claimed that his revelations in *How the Poor Live* and *Horrible London* "helped to focus public opinion on the housing of the working classes, and brought about a Royal Commission".[383]

Another facet of Sims's public persona was that he used his popularity and newspaper column to support various charitable purposes. Together with a Mrs Burgwin Sims founded The *Referee* Children's Dinner Fund in the early 1880s and asked his readers to donate money or food, usually around Christmas. By 1900 it was the largest charity of that kind in London and "was generating £4000 a year".[384] The donations bought meals for thousands of

---

379   Sims, "An Autobiography", 17.

380   Longmate, *The Workhouse*, 223; Marsh and Francis, "Poetry of Poverty", 67; Waller, "Sims", 722.

381   Dagonet, "Mustard and Cress", *The Referee* (11 November 1883): 7.

382   Dagonet, "Mustard and Cress", *The Referee* (21 December 1884): 7.

383   *The Search Light* (1892): 74, and Black, "Half-Hours with Celebrities", 8. See also Mrs. George Augustus Sala, "Famous People I Have Met", *The Gentlewoman* (11 July 1891): 42.

384   Waller, "Sims", 722.

schoolchildren in Southwark whose families could not afford to feed them properly during the winter. On 20 December 1885 Sims appealed directly to his readers: "This year the distress is greater than ever; only one-half of the children attending the four Southwark Board schools can pay the one penny a week school fee. We select for our dinners only the absolutely destitute cases."[385] Donors in turn received a mention by name in the next column and Sims was praised as a philanthropist in portraits: "The man who writes his epitaph, when he requires one, may write that by the power of his pen he threw a flood of sympathetic light on 'How the Poor Live', and collected thousands of pounds to feed the starving little ones of London."[386] Sims also frequently engaged directly in charitable activities like in July of 1883, when he "provided for six hundred little children, from one of the poorest districts in London, a pleasant day in the country at Ashtead".[387]

Despite the recognition and praise of his contemporaries, the longevity of his "Mustard and Cress" column and the success of his ballads, Dagonet ceased to be a household name soon after Sims died on 4 September 1922. As already mentioned, his obituary in *The Times* focused mainly on his theatrical work and neglected to mention any of his various social causes except that "he would champion the cause of the unfortunate middle classes, who, he maintained, were being steadily taxed out of existence by vote-catching politicians".[388] Historian Philip Waller, who wrote Sims's entry in the *Oxford Dictionary of National Biography* when Sims finally re-entered the national canon, sums up his reception:

> Sims never received a native honour. His literary output was too prolific and ephemeral, and his social crusading, while spirited and arresting, was spread across too many causes. Yet he possessed uncommon flair and imagination, together with curiosity and concern about people.[389]

Literary historian Richard Higgins similarly struggles to explain why Sims lacked critical acclaim: "A symptom, perhaps, of the opportunistic and derivative nature of this very prolific man's writing, the lack of interest in Sims is belied by his contemporary popularity. Sims was interested in giving his audience what they wanted."[390] The incongruence between his popularity with contemporaneous audiences and his literary afterlife might be attributed to the type of audience Sims mainly appealed to, which theatre historian Brian Crozier describes as follows:

---

385 Dagonet, "Mustard and Cress", *The Referee* (20 December 1885): 7.

386 "Mr. G.R. Sims Interviewed by G.S. Edwards", *Illustrated Sporting and Dramatic News*, vol. 46, no. 1221 (6 February 1897): 896–898, here 898. On the outings and activities of the Children's Dinner Fund, see also *Penny Illustrated Paper* (2 February 1895): 72.

387 *Peterhead Sentinel and General Advertiser for Buchan District* (1 August 1883): 8.

388 *The Times* (6 September 1922): 12.

389 Waller, "Sims", 723.

390 Higgins, "London on Stage".

Essentially, these were the readers of the penny papers, the habitués of the pit and gallery, for whose custom the music halls and theatres competed, and whose patronage sustained the institutions of entertainment which Gareth Stedman Jones cites as the pillars of late Victorian popular culture. With this audience, Sims's success was probably unrivalled.[391]

3.2 "The last word on realism" – *The Lights o' London* (1881)

The Lights o' London, the first of many melodramas George R. Sims wrote for the theatre stage, premiered at the Princess's Theatre, "the headquarters of West End melodrama in the 1880s and 1890s", on 10 September 1881.[392] The title was taken from a short Dagonet ballad, *The Lights of London Town*, first published in the collection *Ballads of Babylon* (1880) and instantly popularized through a song version composed by Louis Diehl. The title of the ballad was in turn inspired by a real-life incident, according to Sims. In his autobiography he remembered meeting a young couple who were tramping to London: "The darkness fell as we tramped along, and as we came to Highgate the lights of the City were just visible in the rather misty darkness. 'Look, Liz', exclaimed the man eagerly to his wife as he stretched out his hand towards the City 'paved with gold'. 'Yonder are the lights o' London'." [393]

Newspaper advertisements for the play appeared in most London papers and some included several stanzas of the ballad, which told the story of a young couple who come to London filled with hope and ambition ("O gleaming lamps of London that gem the City's crown / What fortunes lie within you, O Lights of London Town.") only to be bitterly disappointed and return to their village after years of sorrow ("O cruel lamps of London, if tears your light could drown / Your victims' eyes would weep them, O Lights of London Town").[394] In the play George Sims elaborated on this opposition between London's promises and the reality of life in the city for most migrants and added typical elements of sensational melodrama.[395] As most contemporaneous reviewers noted, there was little originality in the plot and the characters were the familiar types of Victorian melodrama. The hero wrongly accused of a crime (Harold Armytage), the suffering, passive woman (Bess), the comic man and woman (the Jarvises). As Brian Crozier points out, melodrama remained popular with Victorian audiences precisely because of its predictability, not in spite of it: "Audiences knew to a considerable extent what sort of entertainment awaited them before they entered the theatre. The product's consistency was the price paid for its enormous and sustained success as a popular form of entertain-

---

391 Crozier, *Notions of Childhood*, 82–83.

392 Michael Booth, "Introduction", in Booth (ed.), *The Lights o' London*, ix–xxvi, here xxi–xxii.

393 Sims, *My Life*, 83.

394 George R. Sims, "The Lights of London Town", *Ballads of Babylon* (London: J.P. Fuller, 1880), 101–102.

395 For a detailed summary of individual scenes including audience reactions during the first run, see "The London Theatres", *The Era* (17 September 1881): 5.

ment."[396] The *London Daily News* summed up the conventions for heroes and villains presented in *The Lights o' London* as follows:

> The elements of its story present, it is true, little that is new; they even savour strongly of an exploded class of pieces in which virtue and vice are painted in the strongest colours with little artistic relief of any kind, the wicked personages, compassing the ruin of the innocent with incredibly fiendish cold-bloodedness and perseverance, while the innocent suffer endless trials with an heroic fortitude and a noble resignation hardly within the conceivable capabilities of our weak nature.[397]

Similarly, Brian Crozier states that characters were rarely developed in melodramas: "Individuals are rare in melodrama. By and large the process of characterization was one of modifying already existing stereotypes to fit given situations."[398] Despite this conventional treatment, audiences were enthusiastic about *The Lights o' London* and initial reviews rightly predicted a long and successful run. By way of explanation, *The Morning Post* declared that "experience proves that nothing in the way of theatrical entertainment is more attractive to Londoners than a drama truthfully descriptive of life and manners in their own city".[399] Crozier describes Sims's subtle modifications to the melodramatic genre in similar terms: "Sims takes the customary sentimental or comic interlude whose traditional role was merely to provide an emotional change of pace, and turns it into a panoramic view of London life which brought the play instant acclaim."[400] A review in the *Pall Mall Gazette* confirms that audiences reacted especially to Sims's depictions of poverty and misery in London: "Again and again a loud burst of applause attested how keenly the public appreciated the exactitude of the reproduction of scenes with which it is most familiar."[401] Even famous dramatic critic William Archer stressed the play's verisimilitude: "*The Lights o' London* is a picture of low-class life painted with a fidelity which is almost without precedent on our stage."[402]

Indeed, as Archer's choice of words indicates, the various representations of poverty in *The Lights o' London* combined characteristics of the authentic ("fidelity") and the picturesque ("picture of low-life"), as established in the second chapter. As the reviewer for the *Morning Post* noted, with its rapidly changing stage scenery and fast-paced action, the play quite literally presented

---

396 Crozier, *Notions of Childhood*, 59.

397 "Princess's Theatre", *London Daily News* (12 September 1881): 2.

398 Crozier, *Notions of Childhood*, 55.

399 "Princess's Theatre", *Morning Post* (12 September 1881): 6.

400 Crozier, *Notions of Childhood*, 84. By contrast, literary historian Richard Higgins calls into question the verisimilitude of Sims's representations of London life on the stage and reads *The Lights o' London* as an attempt to render the city legible and palatable to a middle-class audience. See Higgins, "London on Stage". His underlying assumption that "*Lights o' London* was played primarily for middle class audiences" will be challenged below. Brian Crozier on the other hand claims that melodrama functioned as "a form of journalism" for Sims and discusses his plays variously as "dramatised journalism" and "dramatised documentary". Crozier, *Notions of Childhood*, 84, 103 and 86, respectively.

401 "A Drama of the Streets", *Pall Mall Gazette* (16 September 1881): 11.

402 Archer, *English Dramatists*, 310.

Fig. 12: Sir Luke Fildes - *Applicants for Admission to a Casual Ward* (1874),
Black-and-white reproduction, Wellcome Collection, Public Domain Mark.

viewers with a "picturesque diversity of 'spectacle'": "The scene-shifters are kept continually on alert, exhibiting to the audience a series of finely-painted views, rural, urban, and architectural, which pass before their eyes with panoramic splendour, and as much rapidity as the lucid action of the plot will permit."[403] Following the pictorial traditions of Victorian melodrama, two well-known paintings were recreated on the stage. The second scene of the fourth act showed paupers at the casual ward of a workhouse and recalled Luke Fildes's *Applicants for Admission to a Casual Ward* first exhibited at the Royal Academy in 1874.[404] The painting was lauded for its authenticity and showed a variety of poor men, women and children waiting to receive permits that would secure them admission to the casual ward for the night.

Fildes claimed that he was walking by a similar scene outside a police station after a dinner one night and modelled his painting on studies he made of the "poor wretches".[405] Fildes's son remembers how his father had actual poor people pose in his studio for the painting: "None of these twenty-one figures was a professional model [...] and he had difficulty in getting them to his studio."[406] The use of actual poor people as models has already been discussed as an authenticating strategy and George Sims and Wilson Barrett successfully employed it for *The Lights o' London*. The opening scene of the fifth act became an instant sensation with audiences at the Princess's, while a reviewer for the

---

403 *Morning Post* (12 September 1881): 6.

404 The painting itself was a reworking of a woodcut from *The Graphic*. For the changes made by Barnard, see Schmandt, *Armenhaus und Obdachlosenasyl*, 90–93.

405 Quoted in ibid., 107.

406 Quoted in ibid., 108.

Nottingham Evening Post called it a "repulsively realistic representation of 'The Borough, Saturday night'".[407] *The Era*, the main theatrical paper of the capital, was decidedly more impressed if no less overwhelmed by the scene: "How can we describe it? We give up the task. Mr Barrett and Mr Sims have imported the Borough wholesale, and costermongers and organ-grinders and street cadgers are all here to the life."[408] Sims and Barrett recruited actual street-sellers to represent a busy market scene and a large, well-managed crowd to frame the climatic fight between the main hero and the villain. To present the coster-mongers in their proper surroundings, "[...] great care was taken to ensure the duplication on stage of a street market and the shops behind. Eight coster-mongers' barrows were set out and stocked with goods such as vegetables, fruit, haddock, bloaters, whelks, and oysters."[409]

Actor-manager Wilson Barrett assumed the leading part of Harold Armytage while a Mr Harry Jackson acted as stage-manager and received considerable praise for his management of the crowds. The sheer scale of the market scene, the mass of people and amount of detail must have been almost overwhelming for theatre audiences as Clement Scott's often-quoted description indicates:

> This scene of the Saturday night marketing in the Borough, with its hundreds of varied supernumeraries, men, women, and children; its grim squalor and hideous depravity, its drunkenness and its dirt, its fierce unbridled animal passion and wild-beast fighting, its street row and police-court mêlée is realism out-realised. I am not saying that such scenes are pleasant; they are horrible enough in actual life, and they don't delight me personally. But if public taste pronounces them legitimate, I do not see how they can possibly be better done.[410]

Critic William Archer similarly struggled to explain how such an unmediated (i.e. authentic) representation of poverty on the stage could produce the pleasure and excitement noted in all first-night reviews:

> It even seems ludicrous and degrading that such should be the case; but a very little analysis is sufficient to show that the pleasure excited is neither quite irrational nor altogether contemptible. [...] I neither entirely defend nor entirely condemn the scene from the point of view of art, but content myself with 'constating,' as the French would say, its merits from the point of view of stage-technique, together with the vivid effect it produced upon the audience.

Indeed, the seeming chaos of the market and the public houses was safely contained within a pictorial framework. It evoked Frederick Barnard's painting *Saturday Night in the East End*, which was presented at the Royal Academy exhibition in 1876 and was lauded for its realism.[411] The following description from the *Illustrated London News* struggles to impose coherence on the

---

407   "Literary and Art Notes", *Nottingham Evening Post* (14 September 1881): 4.

408   "The London Theatres", *The Era* (17 September 1881): 5.

409   Booth, "Introduction", xxiii. The New Cut Market was also described by Henry Mayhew both in his *Morning Chronicle* series and in *London Labour and the London Poor*. See Humpherys, *Henry Mayhew*, 67.

410   C.S., "The Playhouses", *Illustrated London News* (17 September 1881): 275.

411   See Martin Meisel, *Realizations: Narrative, Pictorial, and Theatrical Arts in Nineteenth-Century England* (Princeton: Princeton University Press, 1983), 398–400.

"crowded composition" and human variety of Barnard's painting (and, one imagines, could easily be referring to Sims's play):

> To describe the crowd of seedy, dirty, and dissipated men, women, and children which jostles and squeezes, barters and bawls; here making room for a sorry cab laden inside and out with drunken sailors, there giving way to a virago fighting at the gin-shop door, is next to impossible.[412]

However, while the painting was aimed squarely at a (paying) West End audience, melodrama patrons were drawn from a more diverse background. Richard Higgins has argued that *"Lights o' London* was played primarily for middle class audiences" and that it functioned as a comfortable form of slumming:

> By creating the illusion that audiences were transported into the midst of urban destitution, melodrama collapses the distance between [the] audience and the city's spectacle while simultaneously ensuring that spectators could travel back to the refuge of their West End and suburban homes.[413]

This follows a common criticism of Sims's work as aimed at middle-class sentimentality, yet it is somewhat at odds with contemporaneous reviews of the play. Most London newspapers published long reviews of the first night of the play and correspondents for smaller provincial papers included shorter reviews in their weekly columns from the city. Almost all noted the enthusiastic reaction of the first night audience, one stating that the final 'situation' (the hero and heroine in front of a police station) was met with a "roar of acclamation that seems to make the walls of the Theatre vibrate. On Saturday night it was nearly deafening".[414] As far as the make-up of the Princess's audience was concerned, the London correspondent for the *Sheffield Daily Telegraph* was quite clear as to what sort of people George Sims's reputation brought to the theatre: "If Mr. Wilson Barrett likes to fill his pit and gallery with the social cream of Seven Dials he must of course please himself, but to call such a composition as *The Lights o' London* a play is an outrage even on the lowest form of the drama."[415] The pit and gallery were the cheapest category of seats and, as Brian Crozier points out, were "within reach for most of the seventy per cent of the population who were not in actual want, and for these people circumstances at least up to the late 1890s were fairly favourable for theatre-going".[416] Urban melodrama in particular was the "distinctive form of the upper working and lower middle classes", and while the number of seats

---

412 "Royal Academy Exhibition. Third Notice", *Illustrated London News* (12 May 1876): 475.

413 Higgins, "London on Stage".

414 "The London Theatres", *The Era* (17 September 1881): 5. Multiple reviews also state that the audience demanded to see the author after the third act. Sims declined to appear because he wanted to wait for their final verdict. See, e.g., *Reynolds's Newspaper* (11 September 1881): 8.

415 "Our Private London Correspondence", *Sheffield Daily Telegraph* (12 September 1881): 2. Unlike most reviewers for the London papers, the correspondent was particularly displeased with Sims's ample use of colloquial language and cockney dialect: "Most of the characters talk a slang which is quite unintelligible to educated people, but is immensely relished by Mr. Sims' admirers. There is not a single stroke of real humour or sentiment in all the five acts of this dull exhibition."

416 Crozier, *Notions of Childhood*, 35.

in pits and galleries of West End theatres was reduced towards the end of the century in favour of the more expensive stalls, together they still made up almost half of the available seating in 1880.[417] All this points to an economically diverse audience drawn from almost all classes of London society as does this first-hand observation given by Clement Scott in the *Illustrated London News*. Walking by the Princess's Theatre in the first week, he finds it almost completely sold out:

> 'Stalls full! Dress-circle full! Boxes full! Standing room only in the Pit!' A success has been made that has been communicated to all classes of society. Every single individual up to that time who had seen *Lights o' London* had no doubt been pleased with it, and had gone home spreading the news in hundreds of directions. This is how successful plays are advertised.[418]

The play was undoubtedly a success. In his autobiography published in 1917, George Sims claimed that it had been played "somewhere on the face of the earth ever since that September evening in 1881".[419] It was reprised with some minor alterations at Aldwych Theatre in London in 1914 to favourable reviews that stressed the good acting and strong emotions it still elicited but made no mention of the Borough market scene. The play was also adapted for the movie screen at least twice by The Magnet Film Company (Barker Motion Photography) in 1914 and by British Gaumont in 1923 while the eponymous ballad "The Lights of London Town" was adapted for the magic lantern as THE LIGHTS OF LONDON by York & Son in 1892.

The Lights o' London serves as an example of the spectrum described in the previous chapter. Its depictions of poverty oscillate between comic relief and sympathetic portrayals of individual poor characters while the staging combined "realism out-realised" with the pictorial traditions of Victorian melodrama.[420] John Ruskin had identified "the sympathy of the artist with the subject" as an essential criterion for the noble picturesque.[421] It is perhaps not accidental that William Archer praised Sims for his treatment of the subject:

> [W]e feel that this writer is not a mere manufacturer of scenes, treating the life of the 'lower orders' as so much useful and paying material, but a man whose eye leads straight to his heart and brain, whose intimate knowledge of the people has produced that tolerance, pity, and admiration which are summed up in the word sympathy.[422]

The various images of London life in Sims's play present a panorama of poverty reminiscent of Blanchard Jerrold's introduction to *London. A Pilgrimage* (1872):

> The casual ward when the claimants for shelter crowd around its doors; the bleak refuge offered by the less exposed portions of the parks; the steps upon which the

---

417   Ibid., 245; see also 43 for seat ratios.

418   C.S., "The Playhouses", 275.

419   Sims, *My Life*, 129.

420   C.S., "The Playhouses", 275. On pictorial traditions of melodrama, see Booth, "Introduction", xiv.

421   Ruskin, *Modern Painters*, 13.

422   Archer, *English Dramatists*, 311.

tramp sinks in exhaustion, to be driven on by the voice of authority; the street market with the loud-voiced costermongers shouting themselves hoarse in the attempt to sell their wares; the tavern-door through which the penniless and fuddled artisan is ignominiously thrust, the lobby of the police-station with the unkempt and wild-eyed vagabonds pressing for admission [...].[423]

The streets and public houses of the Borough and the East End were depicted as bustling, vibrant locales of working-class culture and sites of debauchery by both Frederick Barnard and George Sims in works lauded for their realism. The homes of the poor offered no such pleasures but were places of quiet suffering and deprivation in Barnard's illustrations and Sims's descriptions of *How the Poor Live* (1883), which will be discussed in the following chapter. Sims himself was well aware of the fact that truly authentic depictions of poverty were unsuitable for a theatre audience:

> My dear sir, you can have too vivid a realism upon the stage. [...] Besides, no English audience would tolerate for a moment a faithful reproduction of an East-end garret in all its filth and squalor. [...] I should like to know who would stand five acts of 'slum'. No, you must have the comedy as well as the pathos, the beauty as well as the squalor [...].[424]

3.3 The Bigger Picture – The Historical Art of Projection and the Magic Lantern

George Sims's popularity was at a peak in the 1880s and 1890s. His ballads were enormously popular in print and as recitation pieces performed in exhibition contexts that ranged from charity concerts, elocutionary competitions and temperance entertainments to political events and street recitations.[425] Producers of magic lantern slides seized the opportunity and adapted a significant number of his poems and stories for the historical art of projection. The function of the slide images was illustrative, they could hardly be understood without the spoken words of the recitation or reading that accompanied them. Sims's poetry was not modified for the adaptations, on the contrary manufacturers' catalogues often included instructions on where to find and purchase the collections that held the original text. Quite a few were collected in a selection of popular pieces chosen specifically for public recitation by George Sims himself and published as *The Dagonet Reciter and Reader* in 1888.[426]

---

423   "A Drama of the Streets", *Pall Mall Gazette* (16 September 1881): 11.

424   George Sims interviewed for "Mr. George R. Sims's New Melodrama, 'The Last Chance'", *Pall Mall Gazette*, vol. 41, no. 6260, supplement no. 41 (7 April 1885): 19.

425   They were also translated into a number of other languages, as George Sims related in *The Referee*: "Since I printed the Danish version of a 'Dagonet Ballad', I have received copies of others in almost every language under the sun. 'The Lifeboat' in Chinese I was going to print as a curiosity but the resources of Wine Office-court are not equal to this occasion. The following, however, is a verse of a remarkably able translation of 'The Lights o' London' by Herr Wilhelm Brand, a well-known German journalist." Dagonet, "Mustard and Cress", *The Referee* (21 September 1884): 7.

426   George R. Sims, *The Dagonet Reciter and Reader; Being Readings and Recitations in Prose and Verse, Selected from His Own Works by G.R. Sims* (London: Chatto & Windus, 1888).

The first adaptation of one of George Sims's texts for the magic lantern dates from 1884 although the majority was first produced and performed in the 1890s.[427] Of the 32 different Sims texts adapted for the magic lantern, 24 came from the Dagonet ballads published in *The Referee* and various collections of poems. A portrait of Sims published in a book trade magazine in 1895 describes their popularity as follows:

> As to the *Ballads* themselves, who does not know them? who has not heard *Christmas Day in the Workhouse*? or, to turn to the *Ballads of Babylon*, what open-air reciter has not tried his dramatic power, in terrible earnest, with a rendering of *Ostler Joe*, or to reap a harvest of coppers with *Little Jim*? In drawing-room and on deck in mid-ocean, *The Lifeboat* has been given with every variety of delivery or elocutionary effect, and *The Land of Gold* has run the round of penny readings and private recitals.[428]

By that time all of the cited ballads (safe the very short *Little Jim*) had also been issued as lantern slide series.[429] Several ballads were adapted by more than one slide manufacturer (e.g., *Ostler Joe*, *The Magic Wand*, *A Bunch of Primroses*) or produced in multiple versions (e.g., *The Road to Heaven*, *Nellie's Prayer*, *In the Signal Box*), which adds up to a total of 47 known adaptations. According to Joss Marsh and David Francis, Sims was the most popular living writer for lantern adaptations: "Sims was virtually the only living writer in Britain whose name sold slides. Only Dickens rivalled him for lantern slide popularity – and emphasis on the 'Social Question'."[430]

Many of Sims's ballads selected for adaptation were explicitly set in London (*Told to the Missionary*, *The Land of Gold*, *The Road to Heaven*, *A Bunch of Primroses*, *Billy's Rose*, *The Magic Wand*), others played out in nondescript villages or small sea towns (*The Level Crossing*, *In the Signal Box*, *Ticket o' Leave*, *The Lifeboat*, *In the Harbour*, *Ostler Joe*), and at least one in Ireland (*Kate Maloney*). Others tell of characters tramping (*One Winter Night*) or travelling showpeople on the road (*Fallen by the Way*, *The Street Tumblers*). For characters in the country, London is often a faraway place of sin, where their women and sons are lost to vice (*Ostler Joe*, *The Lifeboat*), and of disappointed hopes, where honest workers are reduced to poverty (*The Lights of London Town*, *In the Workhouse*). The ballads often depicted social ills like child poverty or adult drunkenness or dramatic and heroic episodes on the bounds of respectable society told by sailors and fishermen, street artists and itinerant puppeteers. The majority of the protagonists in Sims's ballads chosen for adaptation fit somewhere on the spectrum of poverty described in the introduction. Most are characterized as deserving poor, whose poverty is the result of adverse circumstances – whether they are hard-working, honest adults, innocent children or aged poor. Even those who

---

427   The first adaptation, a set of photographic slides titled Outcast London: or, How the Poor Live (York & Son, c. 1884, 40 slides) based on George Sims and Frederick Barnard's articles of the same name has been tentatively dated based on newspaper reports.

428   J.L.O., "Mr. G.R. Sims at Home", 40.

429   For a timeline and list of adaptations for the magic lantern, see Appendix B.

430   Marsh and Francis, "Poetry of Poverty", 73.

commit crimes are described in sympathetic terms if they do so out of hunger or desperation (*A Man Hunt, One Winter Night*) or were reformed through the events described in the ballad (*Told to the Missionary, The Matron's Story*).

Most ballads followed a simple formula that literary historian Jacqueline Bratton describes as follows: "Each character tells or has told about him, a story of a characteristic or climatic moment in his life, often in language which is a skilful modulation of colloquial speech, so that the ballad seems to be an artless tale told in the hero's own words."[431] Quite a few featured female protagonists, who either told their own stories (*The Street Tumblers*) or, more often, had them told by another character or an omniscient narrator (*The Matron's Story, In the Harbour, Kate Maloney, One Winter Night, A Bunch of Primroses, Nellie's Prayer, The Magic Wand*). Recurring motifs included death (*Fallen by the Way, A Man Hunt, In the Workhouse*) followed by translation to heaven in the case of children (*Billy's Rose, A Bunch of Primroses, The Road to Heaven, One Winter Night*), loving relationships between siblings, spouses and parents and their children (*Billy's Rose, A Bunch of Primroses, In the Harbour, The Magic Wand, Nellie's Prayer*) and the simple, untutored faith of the poor (*Billy's Rose, The Road to Heaven, Told to the Missionary, The Magic Wand*). In the tradition of melodrama, families and lovers are often reunited through chance after long suffering (*The Land of Gold, The Lifeboat*) or being believed dead (*Nellie's Prayer, The Old Actor's Story*). Many tales also featured dreams, visions or flashbacks that were illustrated with projection effects or effect slides (*Nellie's Prayer, The Magic Wand, The Land of Gold*).

Most lantern adaptations were made in the photographic life model slide genre while drawn or painted slides were chosen for some of Sims's short stories (*The Fatal Sneeze, Mrs Three-Doors-up*). In the remainder of this chapter, I will outline the technical developments that led to a significant growth of lantern related activities in Britain in the 1890s. I will also work out intermedial influences on the life model slide genre.[432] The 19th century marked an important turning point in the history of the art of projection shaped by the impact of technical innovations and a growing standardization of production processes and modes of presentation.[433] By the last decades of the century, images and apparatuses for projection were produced and distributed by a growing number of firms and magic lantern performances took place in varying exhibition contexts and reached large audiences across Great Britain.

---

431 Bratton, *Victorian Popular Ballad*, 123.

432 The following paragraphs look especially at the developments of the art of projection in England with London as a focal point, although similar tendencies of professionalization and standardization can be observed in other European countries and North America.

433 On standardization of image format, see Richard Crangle, *Hybrid Texts: Modes of Representation in the Early Moving Picture and Some Related Media in Britain*, PhD diss. (University of Exeter, 1996), 116. The 3 ¼ by 3 ¼ inches format (the size of a stereo card broken in two) was used mainly in Great Britain. According to Ine van Dooren, the standard format was 4 ¼ by 3 ¼ inches in America and 10 by 8.5 centimetres in continental Europe. Ine van Dooren, *Devices and Desires: The Magic Lantern and the Life Model Drama Presentations in a History of Screen Practices*, MA diss. (University of East Anglia, 1989/1990), 12.

And in a separate sphere, smaller toy lanterns and slides were a common feature in many middle-class households.[434]

The invention of limelight, used for lantern projections from 1837, significantly improved the quality of the projected image and allowed for larger crowds that were not necessarily confined to the small darkened rooms of the phantasmagoria shows, the private salons of learned ladies or gentlemen and the living rooms of those entertained by the itinerant *galantee* showmen.[435] However, the transport and handling of easily inflammable and highly explosive gases required highly skilled operators and there were frequent reports about fatal explosions.[436] The introduction of acetylene burners and electric lamps in the 1880s and 1890s eventually "offered a safer alternative to the dubious practices of transporting and burning pressurised flammable gases in public places", as Richard Crangle has put it.[437] Brighter light sources meant that the apparatus could now be placed further away from the screen while the audience was often placed in-between the two: "Limelight, and the front projection it made possible, turned the lanternists who embraced the dissolving view into showmen-educators, expounding their marvels in full view of their much-enlarged audiences [...]."[438] Apparatus, interface (screen) and the operator who handled the projection device were usually visible for the audience while a lecturer recited texts, narrated the images or gave connective readings.[439]

As far as the manufacturing of lantern slides was concerned, the 19th century saw the introduction of new processes for transferring images to glass slides (printing and photography).[440] In 1823, optician and lantern maker Philip Carpenter from Birmingham patented the so-called copper-plate sliders, which allowed serial production of the same image: "These were manufactured

---

434   On toy lanterns, see, e.g., Meredith A. Bak, "'Ten Dollars' Worth of Fun': The Obscured History of the Toy Magic Lantern and Early Children's Media Spectatorship", *Film History*, vol. 27, no. 1 (2015): 111–134.

435   On the history of itinerant projection in the 17th and 18th century, see Deac Rossell, *Laterna magica / Magic Lantern*, vol. 1 (Stuttgart: Füsslin, 2008), 102–140; see also Rossell's articles in the *eLaterna Companion* "Apparatus" section at https://elaterna.uni-trier.de. On the phantasmagoria, see Mervyn Heard, *Phantasmagoria: The Secret Life of the Magic Lantern* (Hastings, East Sussex: Projection Box, 2006).

436   See John Barnes, "The History of the Magic Lantern", in Dennis Crompton, Richard Franklin and Stephen Herbert (ed.), *Servants of Light: The Book of the Lantern* (Ripon, North Yorkshire: The Magic Lantern Society, 1997), 8–33, here 25.

437   Crangle, *Hybrid Texts*, 118.

438   Joss Marsh, "Dickensian 'Dissolving Views': The Magic Lantern, Visual Story-Telling and the Victorian Technological Imagination", in Jeffrey Geiger and Karin Littau (ed.), *Cinematicity in Media History* (Edinburgh: Edinburgh University Press, 2013), 21–34, here 23.

439   On the different roles of lecturers, see Crangle, "The Lantern Lecture in Britain", 39–47. For a comparison of the role of lecturers in early cinema and lantern cultures, see Joe Kember, *Marketing Modernity* (Exeter: University of Exeter Press, 2009), 60–83.

440   For a detailed description of the three main techniques to put images on glass lantern slides (painting, printing and photography), see Francisco Javier Frutos, "From Luminous Pictures to Transparent Photographs: The Evolution of Techniques for Making Magic Lantern Slides", *The Magic Lantern Gazette*, vol. 25, no. 3 (2013): 3–11.

using engraved copper plates to print outlines on glass discs, which were fired, coloured by artists and set in mahogany frames."[441] The wet collodion process, introduced in the early 1850s, allowed the fixing of a photographic negative on a collodion-coated glass slide, which could then be developed into any number of positive copies. This was faster and cheaper than painting slides by hand even if the black-and-white photographic slides were often hand-coloured during post-production.[442] Consequently, in the last decades of the 19th century, the production of magic lantern slides shifted from manufactured, hand-painted slides to mass production of mostly photographic slides.[443] This also meant that a range of new subjects and genres were introduced into lantern culture. Photographic and lithographic reproductions of works of art and photographic representations of foreign lands and people were used in educative contexts.[444] Photography also gave rise to a particular genre of fictional photographs for projection introduced in the late 1870s, the life model slides. They were produced to illustrate the events of an existing narrative or song by posing models (mostly inside a studio, sometimes in natural surroundings) in settings that usually featured painted backdrops and props. Their heyday roughly coincided with what Joss Marsh terms "the palmy years of the magic lantern, in England, from the 1860s to the 1890s, when perhaps twelve hundred lantern lecturers criss-crossed the country by railway and lantern companies splurged on studios, supplies and slide catalogues that were the size of bricks".[445]

Most empirical research about the scope of production of magic lanterns and lantern slides in Britain is based on a small but continually growing number of sources, chief among them catalogues of slide and lantern producers and dealers.[446] Richard Crangle sums up the scope of British slide production in the 1890s as follows:

---

441 Phillip Roberts, "Building Media History from Fragments: A Material History of Philip Carpenter's Manufacturing Practice", *Early Popular Visual Culture*, vol. 14, no. 4 (2016): 319–339, here 322. The labour-intensive process leads Roberts to discard the often-repeated claim that Carpenter's copper-plates revolutionized slide production. See ibid., 324.

442 See Olive Cook, *Movement in Two Dimensions* (London, 1963), reprinted in Stephen Herbert (ed.), *A History of Pre-Cinema*, vol. 3 (London, New York: Routledge, 2000), 115. On the colouring of slides, see Stephen Herbert, "An Indescribable 'Something'...: The Magic Lantern and Colour", *Living Pictures*, vol. 2, no. 2 (2003): 14–25.

443 The use of gelatine dry plates from the 1880s further simplified the process although wet collodion negatives remained in use for some time. See Jens Ruchatz, "The Magic Lantern in Connection with Photography: Rationalisation and Technology", in Simon Popple and Vanessa Toulmin (ed.), *Visual Delights: Essays on the Popular and Projected Image in the 19th Century* (Trowbridge: Flicks Books, 2000), 38–49, here 48, note 17.

444 For a good overview of the different subjects of photographic slides, see van Dooren, *Devices and Desires*, 13–16.

445 Marsh, "Dickensian Dissolving Views", 21.

446 More than 50 catalogues from various European and American firms are available through the "Magic Lantern and Lantern Slide Catalog Collection (1840s–1920s)" at the Media History Digital Library. As of December 2020, data from more than 200 catalogues of English, Scottish, American, German, Austrian, French, Belgian and Dutch slide producers and dealers is available through Lucerna – The Magic Lantern Web Resource.

> A very simplified sketch of the 1890s slide trade in Britain could picture about ten companies, all family-based concerns, covering almost the entire volume of commercial slide production; a slightly larger number of major wholesale or clearing-house businesses [...] and a more widespread network of local dealers and hirers, many of which were sidelines of related businesses such as chemists or opticians.[447]

Still, the scope of lantern slide production could not be compared to that of cinematograph films on equal terms, as Crangle concedes:

> The lantern never had access to venture capital in the way that the Cinematograph did as soon as it became perceived as a way of making quick money [...]; it never really had the same industrialised supply and distribution of products for consumption; and it never had national chains of venues like those which the cinema began to develop from the late 1900s onwards [...].[448]

Geographically speaking, London was the centre of both production and trade with smaller regional centres around the industrial towns of Liverpool and Birmingham and several firms based in the larger Scottish cities of Glasgow and Aberdeen. The trade followed a lantern season that by the 1890s "was almost formally established, and clearly demarcated in the trade press, as the period between about October and about April", according to Richard Crangle.[449] There was a marked increase of business and lantern shows around Christmas while manufacturers used the summer months for the preparation and production of new slide sets. The two firms with the largest stock for sale or hire, producer Bamforth & Co. and slide dealer Riley Brothers, were based in small towns in West Yorkshire.[450] In the case of Bamforth, many inhabitants of Holmfirth posed as models for their life model slide images and the railway company even permitted photographer James Bamforth the use of their tracks and platform for stories photographed on location like the Sims adaptation IN THE SIGNAL BOX (1889, 9 slides).

Research on lantern performances points to an extensive use of projected images in non-commercial, welfare and religious contexts.[451] Temperance organizations like the UK Band of Hope Union or the Church of England Temperance Society relied heavily on lantern projections and later cinematographic projections and had their own lantern departments and stocks of

---

447 Richard Crangle, "What Do Those Old Slides Mean? or Why the Magic Lantern is Not an Important Part of Cinema History", in Popple and Toulmin (ed.), *Visual Delights*, 16–24, here 18.

448 Ibid.

449 Crangle, *Hybrid Texts*, 120.

450 Lucerna – The Magic Lantern Web Resource currently lists over 20,000 individual slides in 1,419 sets produced by Bamforth & Co. and over 40,000 slides in 1,849 sets that were in the stock of Riley Brothers (searched on 7 December 2020). This number of course does not account for multiple copies of slide sets and reproductions of existing slides produced on demand. James Bamforth himself claimed in interviews with the trade press in 1900 that his company had over two million slides and produced 600 new subjects a year. See Philip Reynolds, "Sentiment to Order", *Harmsworth Magazine*, vol. 5, no. 28 (October 1900): 337–343, here 343.

451 One reason for that is that publications of organizations active in these fields like the *Church Army Gazette* or the *Sunday School Chronicle* meticulously documented the use of lanterns and lantern performances for their work and have consequently been one of the main sources for research in this area.

Fig. 13: Slide 1 of In the Signal Box (Bamforth, 1889, 9 slides),
Nicholas Hiley Collection, reproduced with permission.

slides that were hired out to local branches.[452] During their temperance
entertainments, biblical stories and 'scientific' representations of the evils of
drink were combined with dramatic depictions of social decline caused by
alcoholism and tragic-heroic children whose escape from drunk and often
violent parents practically inevitably ended with their death and ascension to
heaven. The headquarters of religious organizations like the Church Army, the
Sunday School Union or the Salvation Army were based in London, where
their missionary efforts aided by projections were focused as well.[453] Anti-
capitalist and labour organizations like the Co-operative Movement focused

---

452 See Eifler, *The Great Gun of the Lantern*, 128–157 for a comprehensive overview of the various lantern,
     lecture and slide departments and projection activities of religious, welfare and socialist organizations.

453 See Karen Eifler, "Between Attraction and Instruction: Lantern Shows in British Poor Relief", *Early
     Popular Visual Culture*, vol. 8, no. 4 (2010): 363–384, here 366.

their efforts more on the Manchester region.[454] Mobile projection units, so-called "lantern vans" or "mission vans" and touring lecturers reached audiences in rural areas all over the country.[455]

Life Model Slides, Photography and Melodrama

The precise origin of the life model slide genre is unclear. One of the earliest examples, a comic set titled DIOGENES AND THE BOYS OF CORINTH based on book illustrations by Wilhelm Busch, was sold by Pumphrey Brothers of Birmingham by 1872 and the term was used by the London-based lantern and slide dealer W. C. Hughes in their 1878 catalogue.[456] The first life model sets by York & Son appeared in the early 1880s and James Bamforth started producing them as an offshoot of his photographic studio in Holmfirth around 1887. Richard Crangle has shown that the concept of *bricolage* is helpful in understanding how the practice of posing live models for fictional photographs was established: "[A] new textual practice borrowed features of a pre-existing practice and used them alongside features borrowed from a range of other practices."[457] This section will trace some possible influences and similar practices in the performing and fine arts.

In terms of production processes and techniques, life model slides share a number of similarities with studio photography. This includes the use of props, costumes and painted backdrops which serve to establish characters and settings. Unlike portrait photographs that documented the models' status and looks, life model slides illustrated fictional stories. However, according to Richard Crangle, *carte-de-visite* photographs, which became popular across Europe from the 1860s, sometimes included fictional representations and stereo cards used life models to illustrate fictional narratives and topics.[458] For their combination photographs that emulated classical paintings, Oscar Rejlander and Henry Peach Robinson combined parts of various negatives to produce fictional scenes like *Two Ways of Life* (1857) and *Fading Away* (1858). Unlike these combination prints and portrait photographs, life model slides were usually available in colour if customers were willing to pay for it. The tinting was done manually by female workers who used a range of translucent colours. In a sense, these coloured photographic slides were more lifelike than

---

454   Ibid.

455   For projection vans, see Torsten Gärtner, "The Church on Wheels".

456   See Crangle, "What Do Those Old Slides Mean", 17 and the record for DIOGENES AND THE BOYS OF CORINTH (Pumphrey Brothers, 7 slides) in the Lucerna database (http://lucerna.exeter.ac.uk/set/index.php? id=3005272). In catalogues of French slide dealers, life model slides were described as *d'après nature* (in contrast to *d'après gravures* or *d'après dessins*).

457   Richard Crangle, "'Next Slide Please': The Lantern Lecture in Britain, 1890–1910", in Richard Abel and Rick Altman (ed.), *The Sounds of Early Cinema* (Bloomington: Indiana University Press, 2001), 39–47, here 46.

458   See Richard Crangle, "Zweidimensionales Leben. Die britischen Life model-Dias", translated by Jens Ruchatz, *Fotogeschichte*, vol. 19, no. 74 (1999): 25–34, here 25. Crangle cites Julia Margaret Cameron's photographic illustration of Tennyson's *Idylls of the King* as one example.

contemporaneous black-and-white photographs or news illustrations and Richard Crangle argues that

> [a]lthough the colouring of these slides could appear crude in the hands of amateurs or the smaller commercial manufacturers, the workforces of the larger producers were capable of highly-skilled delicate tinting which at its best could give a very convincing impression – even by modern photographic standards – of realistic colouring.[459]

Realistic images of everyday life combined with explanatory texts were also found in genre paintings and in the 1850s and 1860s, some photographers staged real models in tableaux based on famous paintings. These widely circulated stereo cards also showed restagings of illustrations and caricatures and sometimes quotes or poems to explain the narrative image.[460] Finally, series of plates like William Hogarth's *Harlot's Progress* and George Cruikshank's *The Bottle* or William Powell Frith's *Road to Ruin* also employed visual storytelling to show narrative progress through images.

From a performance standpoint, recitations illustrated with life model slides shared similarities with contemporary theatre practice and certain visual fairground attractions in their use of images to illustrate spoken words or narrative. Art historian Wojciech Sztaba likens the presentation of images on fairgrounds to multimedia shows with images, music and spoken commentary.[461] The so-called *Moritatensänger* (literally: murder ballad singers) accompanied the presentation of their picture boards, sheets or painted canvases with songs that told a fictional narrative. However, unlike life model slides, the images showed almost exclusively scenes of murder, theft, arson and other violent crimes.[462] Peepshows offered their paying customers a glimpse into a wooden box that showed them three-dimensional scenes (often using a combination of lenses and mirrors).[463] The peepshow men changed the images inside the box by hand or by turning a handle and also accompanied their images with exciting stories and spoken commentary. The coloured images were of particular interest to rural audiences and showed them "the sights and adventures of the age", according to Richard Balzer: "What wondrous sights there were to visit: distant lands, never before seen and perhaps never before even heard of, ferocious battles and stately monuments, images to startle and delight."[464] For centuries, projections of hand-painted magic lantern slides had occasionally presented narrative sequences and media historian Sarah Dellmann found that around

---

459 Crangle, *Hybrid Texts*, 140.

460 See Denis Pellerin and Brian May, *The Poor Man's Picture Gallery: Stereoscopy versus Paintings in the Victorian Era* (London: The London Stereoscopic Company, 2014), 9–12.

461 Wojciech Sztaba, "Die Welt im Guckkasten. Fernsehen im achtzehnten Jahrhundert", in Harro Segeberg (ed.), *Die Mobilisierung des Sehens. Zur Vor- und Frühgeschichte des Films in Literatur und Kunst* (Munich: Fink, 1996), 97–112, here 103.

462 Ibid.

463 See Richard Balzer, *Peepshows: A Visual History* (New York: Abrams, 1998), 17–21 on the origins of the peepshow.

464 Ibid., 12.

1870 magic lantern slides were beginning to be offered in sets, usually with accompanying readings.[465]

The style of the painted backdrops used for life model slides photographed in the studio was similar to the painted stage backgrounds of contemporary theatrical practice as was the use of theatrical gestures and poses by the models.[466] These visual codes were particularly meaningful in melodrama, the most popular genre of Victorian theatre. Melodrama's popularity resulted partly from legal interference with common theatre practice as the Licensing Act of 1737 expressly forbade the staging of dramatic productions outside the city of Westminster.[467] Other theatres took to staging "illegitimate dramas" (burlesques or melodramas) that circumvented the ban by combining music, songs and movement.[468] The spoken word was necessarily of secondary importance in the interactions between performers and the auditorium. Literary historian Juliet John describes melodrama audiences as

> [s]ocially mixed and often, in illegitimate theatres, predominantly drawn from the traditional working classes and the constituency Ledger calls the 'literate nonelite'. Melodrama evolved with an uneducated audience in mind, thus offering an ideal aesthetic template through which to reach those often excluded from serious literature.[469]

This "uneducated audience" was addressed with simplified visual codes combined with exaggerated theatrical gestures to provide easily legible narratives. This became a simple necessity in larger theatres with their often bad acoustics.[470] Magic lantern performances also entertained large (and often less educated) audiences and depended on a similarly simplified visual display. The use of life models contributed to the easy legibility and emotional impact of the aptly named slides. As Olive Cook has stated, "the introduction of living models endowed the projected image with a more vivid human interest, a form of realism more readily intelligible to the unsophisticated, and a wider emotional range than it had so far been able to command".[471] Producers of life model slides also adopted certain representational conventions that contemporaneous audiences were familiar with. This included the outward appearance and poses of the models as well as the settings and props: "Facial

---

465 Sarah Dellmann, *Images of Dutchness: Popular Visual Culture, Early Cinema and the Emergence of a National Cliché* (Amsterdam: Amsterdam University Press, 2018), 82.

466 Crangle, "Zweidimensionales Leben", 27–28.

467 The "patent theatres" of Drury Lane and Covent Garden had held a monopoly on dramatic productions in London from 1662. This was only lifted through the Theatre Regulation Act of 1843 at a time when both theatres had already adapted the successful formula of smaller theatres and presented similar visual spectacles. See Johann Schmidt, *Ästhetik des Melodramas. Studien zu einem Genre des populären Theaters im England des 19. Jahrhunderts* (Heidelberg: Universitätsverlag Winter, 1986), 36–37, and Juliet John, "Melodrama and its Criticism: An Essay in Memory of Sally Ledger", *19: Interdisciplinary Studies in the Long Nineteenth Century*, no. 8 (2009): 1–20, here 2–3.

468 See Schmidt, *Ästhetik des Melodramas*, 37.

469 John, "Melodrama", 1–2.

470 See Schmidt, *Ästhetik des Melodramas*, 316–317.

471 Cook, *Movement in Two Dimensions*, 103.

expressions, postures and gestures of the life models changed during the specific scenes into 'pictures', which followed an iconographic pattern that could be understood by the spectators."[472]

Aside from the adoption of melodramatic aesthetics by their models, the theatrical practice of posing actors in so-called *tableaux* (or pictures) can be considered structurally similar to life model slides.[473] Literary historian Johann Schmidt describes *tableaux* as carefully orchestrated arrangements of characters in 'dramatic groupings' that often followed very dynamic scenes. They were part of the standard repertoire of any melodrama ensemble, according to Schmidt, and used frequently at the close of a play and occasionally as climatic effects of individual scenes or acts.[474] Theatre *tableaux* sought to present memorable scenes that were often based on well-known paintings or illustrations and sometimes printed on the playbills to aid recognition by the audience.[475] Similarly, producers of life model slides often adapted previous illustrations of their material:

> Composition of the images in Life Model sets often depended to some extent on emulation of existing sources of illustration, especially for sets relating to previously-published narrative prose, and manufacturers appear to have had few scruples about reusing or blatantly copying each others'[sic] images and conceptions of a scene.[476]

Theatre historian Martin Meisel has argued that the pictorialism of 19th century theatre was not merely part of a general drive towards visual spectacle on the theatre stage but an essential element of dramaturgy, which he expressly compares to a magic lantern performance:

> The play creates a series of such pictures some of them offering a culminating symbolic summary of represented events, while others substitute an arrested situation for action and reaction. Each picture, dissolving, leads into consequent activity, but to a new infusion and distribution of elements from which a new picture will be assembled or resolved. The form is serial discontinuity, like that of the magic lantern, or the so-called 'Dissolving Views'.[477]

What Meisel describes as a serial presentation of dramatic groupings linked through a fictional narrative in some ways prefigures the life model slide genre. In 1880, the entire stage of a London theatre was fitted with a golden frame

---

472   Ludwig Vogl-Bienek, "'From Life': The Use of the Magic Lantern in Nineteenth-Century Social Work", in Gestrich, King and Raphael (ed.), *Being Poor in Modern Europe*, 467–484, here 467. On the pictorial conventions of life model slides, see also Crangle, *Hybrid Texts*, 139–149.

473   Schmidt uses the terms *tableaux* and pictures synonymously. The term *tableau* is however not to be confused with the similar practice of the popular *tableaux vivants*, which recreated paintings with life actors: "Both present a readable, picturesque, frozen arrangement of living figures; but the dramatic tableau arrested motion, while the tableau vivant brought stillness to life." Meisel, *Realizations*, 47.

474   Schmidt, *Ästhetik des Melodramas*, 303 and 307.

475   See ibid., 306. Representations of theatrical scenes photographed in studio settings with actors or models were also produced and distributed as series of stereoscopic images in England and France in the 1850s and 1860s. See May and Pellerin, *Stereoscopy versus Paintings*, 12.

476   Crangle, *Hybrid Texts*, 139.

477   Meisel, *Realizations*, 38.

and the critic Percy Fitzgerald described the effect as follows: "[…] the whole has the air of a picture projected on a surface."[478] By October of 1883, Captain Evatt Acklom, a popular reciter and elocutionist, had added "illustrated dramatic recitals" to his repertoire. For this novel entertainment, Acklom combined recitations of well-known favourites like Dickens's *Gabriel Grub* and Sims's *The Lifeboat* with dissolving views and music.[479] Acklom gave three concerts with varied programmes in October and November 1883 at London's Steinway Hall with seat prices ranging from 1s. to 5s. Acklom's other recitations – presumably also accompanied by lantern slides – were *A Christmas Carol*, *Jane Conquest*, *Gray's Elegy* and *The Vagabonds* by John Trowbridge. Lantern slide series (some painted, some with life models) based on these texts were produced in the 1880s by two London-based slide producers, York & Son and Newton & Co., it thus seems likely that Acklom used their slides for his recitals. The *London Daily News* gives an elaborate description of the arrangement on the stage, which suggests that it was not an established practice yet:

> A novel feature of the entertainment was the way in which it was illustrated by means of dissolving views. One half of the stage was arranged as a platform with a reading desk for the reciter, and on the other half was a blind upon which, as he progressed with the story, the various incidents were graphically illustrated.[480]

From reports in other London newspapers and the trade press it seems that Acklom was one of the first public reciters who used projected images (and life model slides) to accompany his recitations.[481] While his recitations included several popular pieces, the reviews suggest that his performances were aimed mainly at an educated audience: *The Era* noted that Acklom "deserved the greatest praise" for his elocution and that "the entire entertainment is of a refined and intellectual character", and the *Musical World* assured readers that even the "most strictly puritanical section of the public could not possibly object" to this type of entertainment.[482]

Copyright Legislation and Life Model Slides

Arthur Calder-Marshall has claimed that Sims did not receive any royalties for lantern slide adaptations of his poems.[483] However, at least one slide manufacturer did apparently secure permission from Sims for the use of his ballad *The Magic Wand* adapted as THE FAIRY WAND (J.H. Steward, in or before 1888) and described explicitly as "By special permission of G.R. Sims, Esq. (Dagonet)".[484]

---

478 Quoted in ibid., 44.

479 See "Captain Evatt Acklom's Recitals", *The Era* (3 November 1883): 6.

480 "Captain Acklom's Recitals", *London Daily News* (30 October 1883): 5.

481 See for example *London Magnet* (5 November 1883): 2, *Morning Post* (3 December 1883): 2, and *Musical World* (10 November 1883): 710.

482 *The Era* (27 October 1883): 12; *Musical World* (10 November 1883): 710.

483 Calder-Marshall, "Introduction", 45.

484 *J. Theobald and Company's Extra Special Illustrated Catalogue of Magic Lanterns, Slides and Apparatus* (London: Theobald & Co., c. 1893), 76.

A similar claim, "by permission of G.R. Sims", appears on paper slips attached to several surviving slides of the set THE LIFEBOAT by York & Son (registered for copyright in 1886, 7 slides). It is notably absent from later sets by that manufacturer, which do however still use the addendum "By G.R. Sims" after the set title.[485]

It could be argued that the epithet "from life", which appeared on paper slips in Bamforth slides together with the word *copyright*, is meant to indicate a realistic depiction of life and thus a promise of authenticity. While that might have been one component, I would argue that both the name and the practice of life model slides were also related to considerations of copyright legislation at the time. The inscription "from life" appears frequently in newspapers to denote that an illustration of a person or scene was taken directly and not reproduced "from a photograph" or "from a painting". The phrase "life models" also referred to people posing for other forms of reproduction of life namely painting or sculpture. Photographs taken directly from life did not infringe on existing copyrights or require money to buy the copyrights as would have been necessary for a direct reproduction. Original photographs were however protected under the 1862 Fine Arts Copyrights Act and both York & Son as well as Bamforth usually registered some of the photographs for each new life model slide series at the Stationers' Hall to secure their own copyright. Bamforth brought at least two cases of copyright infringement to court. One against a Professor Hermann (Edmund Wright) of Liverpool, who had sold pirated copies of lantern slides.[486] The other involved "sending one of his principal female models, Hannah Hinchcliffe to New York to appear as a witness", according to Robert McMillan, who also notes that James Bamforth "was rigorous in suppressing any infringement of his copyright by competitors".[487]

Buying copyrights for reproduction of an original painting, drawing or photograph could be quite expensive as documented by a letter addressed to George R. Sims in his private papers at Rylands Library, Manchester.[488] In the letter his collaborator Frederick Barnard writes that he was approached by "our magic lantern friend" who apparently intended to reproduce Barnard's sketches for *How the Poor Live* first published in the *Pictorial World*. Barnard states that he was offered 50 pounds "for his share in the thing" and asks Sims

---

485   See slide from the Nicholas Hiley collection reproduced in Lucerna – The Magic Lantern Web Resource (http://lucerna.exeter.ac.uk/slide/index.php?id=5015501).

486   See "Piracy of Copyright Lantern Slides", *The Optical Magic Lantern Journal*, vol. 12, no. 144 (May 1901): 56.

487   Robert McMillan, "James Bamforth. A Talk Given by Robert McMillan to the Magic Lantern Society of Great Britain on 29th April, 1978", *The New Magic Lantern Journal*, vol. 1, no. 2 (February 1979): 12–15, here 14.

488   The letter is not dated but Barnard sent other letters from the same address between January 1882 and July 1884. Richard Crangle notes that the crossing out of the address and a handwritten "out" could suggest that the letter was posted soon after Barnard moved – sometime in or before 1888, after which date he was no longer listed under that address in the London electoral roll (Private e-mail correspondence, 3 July 2014). For a full transcript of the letter, see Appendix D.

if he knows the new proprietors of the *Pictorial World*.[489] If this is taken as a representative amount, it would not have been feasible for producers of lantern slides to directly copy existing illustrations by photographing them. Life model representations presented a cheaper alternative. Taking into account that dressing and staging models and painting sets requires a substantial amount of time and resources in comparison with simply photographing or transfer printing from an existing image, lower production costs were certainly not the main reason for the use of life model slides to represent existing images.[490] In December of 1883, George Sims gave permission to Captain Evatt Acklom to base an illustrated lecture on his articles about *How the Poor Live*. Acklom presented the lecture in various cities across England. In January of 1884, the *Liverpool Mercury* announced: "Enlarged copies of the powerful drawings which Mr. F. Barnard provided for Mr. Sims' book will be shown in the course of the lecture [...]".[491] This could have referred to photographic reproductions of Barnard's illustrations that formed a set of 40 lantern slides called OUTCAST LONDON: OR, HOW THE POOR LIVE and produced by York & Son. Whatever else it may reveal about copyright negotiations between artists and producers of magic lantern slides, the letter clearly shows that George Sims was aware that adaptations of his work were made for the historical art of projection even if details on the business arrangements remain sketchy.

The question of copying versus representation was raised again in the so-called "Living Pictures" court case of 1894 that very probably got the attention of life model slide producers in England. The German publishing company Franz Hanfstaengl sued the Empire Palace for an interlocutory injunction to stop their "living pictures" which represented several of Hanfstaengl's copyrighted paintings.[492] They consisted of *tableaux vivants* exhibitions on a stage with painted backgrounds that were taken from photographs of those paintings and enclosed in a gilt frame. Hanfstaengl cited the 1862 Fine Arts Copyright Act which (for the first time) awarded the author of an original painting, drawing or photograph "the sole and exclusive right of copying, engraving, reproducing, and multiplying such painting or drawing and the design thereof, or such photograph and the negative thereof, by any means and of any size, for the term

---

489   The paper had changed hands right after the final instalment of *How the Poor Live* was published. By January 1886, the *Pictorial World* was looking for capital again and sold to the newly formed 'Pictorial World' Company. Richard Clay remained on the board of directors and Fred Barnard was listed as a member of the Consulting Art Committee. See announcement in *St James's Gazette* (5 January 1886): 16. It remains unclear to me if the new proprietors offered Barnard 50 pounds for his share to sell the pictures to a magic lantern slide maker or if the maker negotiated directly with Barnard.

490   I am thankful to Richard Crangle for this thought.

491   *Liverpool Mercury* (2 January 1884): 6.

492   He also sued two illustrated newspapers, the *Daily Graphic* and *Westminster Budget* for reproducing sketches from the events at the Empire. Both cases were eventually decided against Hanfstaengl. See Walter Arthur Copinger, *The Law of Copyright, in Works of Literature, Art, Architecture, Photography, Music and the Drama: Including Chapters on Mechanical Contrivances and Cinematographs*, 5th edition (London: Stevens and Haynes, 1915), 182–183.

of the natural life of such author, and seven years after his death […]".[493] If accepted by the court, this would have redefined what constituted a reproduction of an original. This might have included life model slides that copied existing book illustrations, as they so often did, considering that the practice of posing characters in front of painted backdrops was also their basic production technique. Hanfstaengl lost and an appeal to the Court of Appeals was also dismissed.[494] The Lord Justice Lindley distinguished in his decision between copying and representing of pictures: "It does not say that the author of a picture shall be entitled to prevent anybody from representing his picture. It is intended to protect the author of the picture from anybody's producing a painting, drawing, or photograph of his pictures so as to compete with him in the market."[495] One year later, however, Hanfstaengl was awarded 65 pounds in damages against London-based magic lantern and slide dealer Walter Tyler, who had produced several magic lantern slides from Hanfstaengl's reproductions of paintings in his copyright.[496] Still it meant for producers of life model slides that seeking 'inspiration' from one another or previous illustrations of a subject remained lawful.

3.4 To the Silver Screen – Film Adaptations

If scholars have written little about George R. Sims's literary works, even less has been written about their filmic adaptations and Sims's involvement in them.[497] This is somewhat surprising since George Sims himself was very interested in the new medium.[498] As early as January of 1897, in a short sketch from *The Referee* titled *Our Detective Story*, Sims imagined a cinematograph as the key witness in a court case of marital infidelity: First it records the wife's illicit affair in Madrid, then later displays it to the husband as part of a variety theatre programme at the Alhambra.[499] In the 1910s, Sims wrote repeatedly of his experiences with cinema-going for his column in *The Referee* and in the foreword to his 1902 collection of short stories titled *Biographs of Babylon: Life-Pictures of London's Moving Scenes*, he described his manner of storytelling akin to a film act during a music-hall programme:

---

493 Walter Arthur Copinger, *The Law of Copyright, in Works of Literature and Art: Including that of the Drama, Music, Engraving, Sculpture, Painting, Photography, and Ornamental and Useful Designs*, 2nd edition (London: Stevens and Haynes, 1881), 389.

494 Copinger (1915), 183. However, the court held that the painted backgrounds were an infringement of the copyright.

495 Quoted in Copinger (1915), 181.

496 *Manchester Courier and Lancashire General Advertiser* (17 January 1895): 6. See also Walter Tyler, "Hanfstaengel [sic] v. Tyler", *Optical Magic Lantern Journal*, vol. 6, no. 70 (March 1895): 52–53.

497 This may have something to do with the fact that in his autobiography, Sims wrote only very little about "moving images" and nothing about his involvement with them.

498 Judging from the photographs of his home published in the 1900s, Sims was generally interested in new technologies, proudly displaying his canary listening to opera via the electrophone for the *Illustrated Sporting and Dramatic News* and posing on the telephone for *The Sketch*.

499 See Andrew Shail, "Reading the Cinematograph", 47 and 49. Shail also discusses a second short story by Sims published in 1902 about a side-show pianist. Ibid., 57–58.

> Because in the biograph we watch human figures pass and repass and their lips are dumb, because in the 'scenes' which they work together to make they are often ignorant of another's presence, I have called these pictures of Babylon 'Biographs' also. They are all taken from life. As they happened so you will see them reproduce themselves. So much by way of note upon the programme, that you may read it when the lights go down, and in the darkened house the first of the series of *Biographs of Babylon* is shown on your sheet.[500]

Sims's media metaphor combined a claim to realism ("taken from life") and the promise of providing an authentic, unmediated access – at least by human interference – to London life stories ("as they happened so you will see them reproduce themselves"). This echoed his introduction to *The Social Kaleidoscope*, published twenty years earlier, in which Sims had promised readers pictures "painted from life" and asked them to "look into the kaleidoscope and see the first picture".[501] As Joss Marsh and David Francis have noted, Sims had a preference for visual metaphors: "His preferred master-metaphors were strikingly visual: the 'social kaleidoscope' (1881); the 'cinematograph' of urban existence (from the 'Prologue' to *Living London*, 1901–1903); the cosmopolitan 'moving scene' and 'life-Picture' (from the 1902 volume *Biographs of Babylon*)."[502] In 1901 Sims prefaced the first issue of his monumental editorial work *Living London* with another elaborate visual metaphor staking his claim to authenticity and verisimilitude; this time via the cinematograph:

> I step modestly forward to speak the Prologue. If I have chosen the metaphor of the theatre, it is because in these pages there is to be enacted for us a great human drama. In them we are to find a breathing, pulsing panorama of Living London. Panorama is hardly the word – cinematograph would be a better one, for it is not a London of bricks and mortar that will pass before our eyes, but a London of flesh and blood.[503]

Living London was in every sense the culmination of Sims's decades-long efforts to penetrate, record and represent his native London. In three bound volumes (or 37 issues published fortnightly), Sims and his august contributors aimed to describe all aspects of current life in the Edwardian metropolis in chapters ranging from "Cycling London", "Wig and Gown in London", "Cat and Dog London" to "London's Toilet".[504] The 175 articles, of which Sims contributed 28 himself, amount to more than 1,100 pages with 450 illustrations, many of them photographs taken expressly for the project:

500 Quoted in Groth, *Moving Images*, 164. See also 165–166.

501 Sims, *Social Kaleidoscope*, iv. On the media imagery of *The Social Kaleidoscope*, see Groth, "Kaleidoscopic Vision", 91–104.

502 Marsh and Francis, "Poetry of Poverty", 74.

503 George R. Sims, "Prologue", in George R. Sims (ed.), *Living London: Its work and Its Play, Its Humour and Its Pathos, Its Sights and Its Scenes*, vol. 1 (London etc.: Cassell & Co, 1902), 3–6, here 3.

504 *Living London* was published by Cassell & Co. in 36 fortnightly instalments at sevenpence between October 1901 and March 1903 and in three bound volumes issued in 1902 and 1903 at twelve shillings (cloth) or sixteen shillings (half-leather) each. A new, updated edition in 37 fortnightly instalments with coloured plates of London types was then issued between October 1904 and February 1906.

Wherever photography has been practicable it has been relied upon, because no other process of reproduction is at once so actual and so convincing. Nearly all the photographs have been specially taken by the Publishers; but in many phases of London life this method of illustration has been impossible, and the artist has been called in. Drawings and sketches have been made where the fixing of a camera was out of the question, and the subject was too big and animated for the snapshot.[505]

The second edition featured specially advertised Rembrandt photogravures. The photogravure process was invented by Karl Klic in 1879 and considered "the ultimate facsimile process for the reproduction of etchings because the lines it reproduces are indeed etched in the printing plate".[506] The Lancaster-based Rembrandt Intaglio Printing Company, "the first modern gravure plant in the world", used a mechanical adaptation of the process that was also available in colour.[507]

The coloured photographic reproductions of artists' drawings included in *Living London* showed the traditional "London types" that followed the pictorial traditions of the *Cries of London* and the urban picturesque: "Londoners, rich and poor, at work and play, by night and day, are all depicted here. King and coster, duke and dock labourer, are all shown at their different occupations."[508] Poverty in *Living London* forms an integral part of London's human panorama. As literary historian Keith Wilson notes, "at least half of *Living London* concerns itself with the lives of the underprivileged".[509] The working poor, the home-less, Jewish, Asian and Italian immigrants are discussed in chapters such as "London Street Characters", "Sweated London", "In a London Workhouse" or "Scenes from London Slum-Land" that, according to Wilson, "can often seem to generate a journalistic equivalent to the classed voyeurism of slum tour-ism".[510] Abject poverty and "alien" customs alike held a picturesque appeal that was promoted by the publisher and lauded by reviewers: "The name of Mr. George R. Sims as Editor is a guarantee that the subject will be ably and picturesquely treated, for no one knows his London better than Mr. Sims, and no one can furnish us with more vivid pen-pictures of the varied lives within its bounds."[511]

By the beginnings of the Edwardian period, George Sims had established and continued to promote himself as an expert at describing and depicting London and its inhabitants – particularly those living under less fortunate

---

505 Sims, "Prologue", 6.

506 Luis Nadeau, "Photogravure", in *Encyclopedia of Printing*, vol. 2, 372–374, here 372.

507 Luis Nadeau, "Rembrandt Photogravure", in *Encyclopedia of Printing*, vol. 2, 414–415, here 414.

508 Interview with George Sims for "How London Lives", *Illustrated Mail* (26 October 1901): 6.

509 Wilson, "George R. Sims' *Living London*", 140.

510 Ibid., 141. On the treatment of race and class in *Living London*, see 142–145. On Jewish immigrants in *Living London* as part of the urban picturesque, see Judith Walkowitz, "The Indian Woman, the Flower Girl, and the Jew: Photojournalism in Edwardian London", *Victorian Studies*, vol. 42, no. 1 (Autumn 1998 / 1999): 3–46, 31 and 39.

511 Review from the *Daily Mail*, quoted in advertisement in *Pall Mall Gazette* (21 October 1901): 4.

circumstances than he himself and the majority of his readers. In the first chapter of his series of illustrated newspaper articles "Off the Track in London", illustrated by Thomas Heath Robinson and first published in April 1904 in *Strand Magazine*, Sims practically bragged:

> It is many a long year since I first began to find delight in wandering through the least-known districts of the capital, in visiting strange quarters inhabited by strange people, in penetrating dim, mysterious regions where thousands of our fellow-citizens live, cut off from the rest of the populace by a network of streets and slums into which it is nobody's business but the inhabitants' to enter, and where a visitor from beyond is rarely seen. [...] So it has come about that to-day I can not only survey the streets of the strange lands in the capital of King Edward, but I can enter the houses and take my notes from the cellar to the roof. I am privileged to sit around the coke fire in lodging-houses where an ordinary stranger would meet with scant courtesy; and the mysteries of 'How the Poor Live' are freely unveiled to me.[512]

Sims was thus a logical choice for German-American film pioneer Charles Urban of the newly founded Charles Urban Trading Company to collaborate on a film version of *Living London*.[513] Throughout the summer of 1904, four Urban camera operators recorded material all across London, presumably attempting to capture people unaware in the tradition of snapshot photography:

> Mr. Urban's junior Bioscope proved particularly suitable for this task. It is no bigger than a hand camera, taking a hundred feet of films, can be re-charged in daylight, and does not require a tripod. In order to still further conceal their fell intent, the Bioscope operators disguised their machines as cigar boxes. In this way they were able to obtain some wonderfully 'natural' studies.[514]

The extent of Sims's actual involvement in the production is unclear, it was, however, expressly advertised as "LIVING LONDON, with Co-operation of Mr. Geo. R. Sims".[515] It seems plausible that beyond his name and the publicity it entailed, Sims also lent his expert knowledge to the project – possibly for the selection of suitable filming locations, like he did as editor of the *Living London* serial: "East and West I have been seeing the aristocrats at play as well as the poor at work, and after I had been all over the Metropolis it was mapped out into different sections, and a staff of specialists set to work with pen and camera

---

512 George R. Sims, "Off the Track in London. I. In Alien Land", *Strand Magazine*, vol. 27, no. 160 (1904): 416–423, here 423. The "Off the Track in London" series was followed by another titled "Trips About Town" also published in *Strand Magazine* in 1905, both were republished together as *Off the Track in London* by Jarrold & Sons in 1911, the above passage now amended to read "in the capital of King George".

513 Urban had made a name for himself as managing director of the London-based Warwick Trading Company, a producer and distributor of high quality non-fictional and proto-documentary films. See Luke McKernan, *Charles Urban: Pioneering the Non-Fiction Film in Britain and America, 1897–1925* (Exeter: University of Exeter Press, 2013), 17–22.

514 "A Development in the History of Animated Photography", *The Entr'acte* (21 January 1905): 6.

515 Charles Urban was an ingenious promoter of his films and the Urbanora brand in advertisements and interviews with the trade press. In 1905, the London theatrical paper *The Entr'acte* even featured a regular column titled "Urban Notes" (later Urbanora) that reported weekly (or even several times a week) on current and upcoming company projects in what essentially amounted to press releases.

to depict every phase of the life I had seen."[516] The final LIVING LONDON film was composed of 280 "views", and at 2,500 feet it ran a whooping 45 minutes making it "literally the longest film of its kind at that time".[517] According to film historian Tom Gunning, the so-called "views" (or actualities) followed a specific aesthetic in presenting their subjects:

> To my mind the most characteristic quality of a 'view' lies in the way it mimes the act of looking and observing. In other words, we don't just experience a 'view' film as a presentation of a place, an event or a process, but also as the mimesis of the act of observing. The camera literally acts as a tourist, spectator, or investigator, and the pleasure in the film lies in this surrogate of looking.[518]

In this vein LIVING LONDON appears as an early example of a genre that Gunning terms "place films": "Unlike the single shot films typical of the turn of the century, the 'place films' from at least 1906 on edit together a series of shots in order to provide a rich and varied sense of locale."[519] From late January 1905, it was one of the first films shown at the Urbanora matinées at London's Alhambra music hall where Frank Stevens, a well-known lecturer on natural history, provided a live commentary.[520] Sims himself was full of praise for the "wonderful series" of pictures in his Dagonet column claiming with his usual hyperbole: "The fireworks at the Crystal Palace are so realistic that the people in the stalls sit back to avoid the rocket sticks."[521] From March of 1905, seven companies successfully toured England's opera houses, town halls and music halls exhibiting LIVING LONDON under the Urbanora brand and by 1906 it caused a veritable sensation in Australia.[522] No complete copy of the film survives but contemporaneous newspaper notices described it as "a panoramic view of the busy life in the principle thoroughfares in London, from the fashionable West to the populous East" and "a journey of observation across London from Hyde Park to the Ghetto".[523] The scenes recorded in the streets

---

516 Interview with George Sims for "How London Lives", *Illustrated Mail* (26 October 1901): 6.

517 Jackson, "The *Living London* Boom". In 1903, the average film length was only around 300 ft. with single shot films of non-fictional subjects being the dominant genre around the turn of the century. See McKernan, *Charles Urban*, 35.

518 Tom Gunning, "Before Documentary: Early Nonfiction Films and the 'View' Aesthetic", in Daan Hertogs and Nico de Klerk (ed.), *Uncharted Territory: Essays on Early Nonfiction Film* (Amsterdam: Stichting Nederlands Filmmuseum, 1997), 9–24, here 15.

519 Ibid.

520 The two-hour matinées were given from 9 January 1905 in addition to the regular twenty-five-minutes of Urban bioscopes shown as part of the Alhambra's varied evening programme from August of 1903.

521 Dagonet, "Mustard and Cress", *The Referee* (5 February 1905): 15.

522 Local newspapers ran advertisements for performances in Bath, Bournemouth, Oxford, St. Helens and Jersey in March and April alone.

523 "Gossip", *The Stage* (2 February 1905): 18, and *London Daily News* (26 January 1905): 4. An eleven minute fragment discovered in the National Film and Sound Archive Australia by Ian Christie and screened at the Giornate del Cinema Muto in Pordenone in 2008 has since been identified as Urban's slightly later production of the same bent THE STREETS OF LONDON (1906). See Luke McKernan's comments on his article in The Bioscope: Luke McKernan, "London loves…" (accessed on 7 December 2020, https://thebioscope.net/2008/10/24/london-loves/). According to McKernan the surviving footage matches the description of THE STREETS OF LONDON in Urban's 1906 catalogue shot by shot, although he notes that "it may have re-used film from the earlier series". Indeed, the "pictures" listed for the first

of the East End were of particular interest. *The Entr'acte* stating, "[n]ever has life in the East End been brought more vividly before the public gaze". While a review in the *Jersey Weekly Press* noted: "Much amusement was created by the views in the Ghetto, including 'Petticoat Lane' at the height of business on Sunday morning and East End life generally."[524] LIVING LONDON transposed to the movie screen both the picturesque mode of displaying poverty in the London street cries and the early documentary tradition of snapshot photography.

In the late 1900s, George Sims's involvement with film production began in earnest. In 1908, he was commissioned by British Gaumont to write the filmic adaptation of one of his short stories titled *Lady Letmere's Jewellery*.[525] *The Era*, London's leading theatrical paper at the time, noted the novelty of such an agreement – in particular concerning the common practices of film adaptations:

> Many farseeing business men in the cinematograph trade have said that the time must come when the authors and owners of copyrights, which have been so frequently plundered for the cinematograph stories, would find out for themselves that there was a fruitful source of profit in this industry. The Gaumont Company with their characteristic enterprise have been the first to carry this idea to fruit by co-operating with Mr. Geo. R. Sims in the production of a high-class series of authorised cinematograph films.[526]

The release of the 20 minute (1,105 ft.) film in November of 1908 coincided with the arrival of the first French *films d'art* (art films) in the United Kingdom, making it one of the earliest examples of a film "exploiting performers borrowed from the legitimate stage as production value".[527] Like LIVING LONDON four years earlier, LADY LETMERE'S JEWELLERY was an early example of a coming trend in cinematic storytelling, described by film historian Tom Gunning: "The period from 1907 to about 1913 represents the true narrativization of the cinema, culminating in the appearance of feature films which radically revised the variety format. Film clearly took the legitimate theatre as its model,

part of THE STREETS OF LONDON in the 1906 Urban Catalogue match most of those given for the first section of LIVING LONDON in the company's 1905 catalogue. See catalogue cutting in Bottomore, "Film as Evidence", 36.

524 "Urban Novelties. Important New Films at the Alhambra", *The Entr'acte* (4 February 1905): 7, and "'Urbanora' At the Opera House", *Jersey Independent and Daily Telegraph* (25 March 1905): 3. Interestingly, a short notice about a performance of the film given at the Alhambra for 250 children from the Foundling Hospital likewise notes how the "series of pictures proved vastly amusing and instructive to the little visitors". *London Daily News* (9 February 1905): 4.

525 It was part of a round of stories titled *The Life We Live* published as a book by Chatto & Windus and in weekly instalments in *Lloyd's Weekly Newspaper* (10 January 1904): 16.

526 "'Lady Letmere's Jewellery'. A Remarkable Gaumont Film", *The Era* (21 November 1908): 28.

527 Andrew Shail, "The Invention of Cinematic Celebrity in the United Kingdom", in André Gaudreault, Nicolas Dulac and Santiago Hidalgo (ed.), *A Companion to Early Cinema* (Chichester: Wiley-Blackwell, 2012), 460–486, here 471.

producing famous players in famous plays."[528] André Gaudreault similarly notes the "profound changes" occurring in the industry around 1908 as cinemas "began to attract bourgeois and petty-bourgeois audiences", noting how "[…] such attempts to 'upgrade' audiences must have involved a parallel 'upgrading' of subjects. This explains why the cinema at this time began systematically turning towards established literary and theatrical values, of which the *film d'art* was an early manifestation in France."[529] Before the start of the film, the theatre actresses and actors starring in LADY LETMERE'S JEWELLERY were presented in portrait shots with their names and their roles on cards, which was a distinct novelty at a time when the importance of film stars had yet to be established.[530] Sims as the author of the piece was also presented, bowing to the audience in a credit shot supplied after the ending. In Australia, most advertisements for the film utilized his name, several stating that it was "founded on a story written especially for the Biograph by G.R. Sims".[531] In the following year, George Sims also collaborated with Gaumont on a drama based on the trials of Adolf Beck titled THE MARTYRDOM OF ADOLF BECK. Beck appeared as himself in the film (released shortly before his death in December of 1909), while George Sims was credited as script writer. The film was probably based on a book Sims had released under the same title in August of 1904, which was advertised as "containing the official session reports taken at the Beck trial at the Old Bailey" as well as Sims's articles published on behalf of Beck in the *Daily Mail*.[532]

As Leslie Wood notes in *The Miracle of the Movies*, copyright provisions at the time did not yet extend authors' copyrights to cinematic adaptations of their works, "so that film producers found themselves at liberty to adapt any well-known stories by popular authors which took their fancy".[533] Familiar stories also had the distinct advantage of making it easier for audiences to follow the filmic narrative – especially when such films were screened without recitations or other spoken commentary. In the case of George Sims, this included no less than four American adaptations of his notorious ballad *Ostler*

---

528   Tom Gunning, "The Cinema of Attractions: Early Film, Its Spectator and the Avant-Garde", in Thomas Elsaesser and Adam Barker (ed.), *Early Cinema: Space, Frame, Narrative* (London: British Film Institute, 1990), 56–62, here 60. Or in this case, mildly famous players but a wildly famous author. But in any case, as Andrew Shail notes, "the modest fame of the performers was less important than the idea that Gaumont's films warranted the employment of stage professionals". Shail, "Cinematic Celebrity", 471.

529   André Gaudreault, "Showing and Telling: Image and Word in Early Cinema", in Elsaesser and Barker (ed.), *Early Cinema*, 274–281, here 278.

530   Andrew Shail even calls the absence of stars "one of early cinema's clearest distinguishing features". Shail, "Cinematic Celebrity", 460.

531   See for example "Queen's Hall", *Daily News*, Perth (27 February 1909): 1 and 5.

532   See advertisements in *Leeds Mercury* (27 August 1904): 9, and *Leeds Mercury* (2 September 1904): 3. Sims had campaigned vigorously for Beck's release, who was wrongfully imprisoned twice in a spectacular case of mistaken identity that secured him (and Sims) a lasting place in Britain's legal history. See Waller, "Sims", 723.

533   Leslie Wood, *The Miracle of the Movies* (London: Burke Publishing, 1947), 149.

Joe.[534] The first was made in 1908 by David Wark Griffith for the American Mutoscope and Biograph Co., the second directed by Edwin Stanton Porter for his Rex Motion Picture Company under the title THE PRICE in 1911, while two others by Edison and Comet were released within two weeks of one another in 1912.[535] Also in 1912, a film version of Sims's ballad *The Magic Wand* starring Harriet "Baby" Parsons was produced by Essanay Chicago after a scenario written by Louella O. Parsons.[536] The Imperial Copyright Act of 1911 finally stipulated that the copyrights of "literary, dramatic or musical works" extended to "any record, perforated roll, cinematograph film, or other contrivance by means of which the work may be mechanically performed or delivered".[537] Consequently, the producers of several adaptations of Sims's ballads accompanied by various spoken word schemes were careful to announce that they had acquired the rights to produce his poems. In 1913, the American Novelty Poem-o-graph Company of Cleveland, Ohio, announced to *The Billboard* that it had purchased "the world's rights" to three poems, among them Sims's *In the Workhouse. Christmas Day,* "to be produced in moving pictures, and a first-class dramatic man is engaged reciting these poems to fit every action on the screen, making it a human voice talking picture".[538] In the following year, the British elocutionist Eric Williams announced to *The Bioscope* that he had "in active preparation the famous story of 'The Lifebelt,' [Lifeboat] by Geo. R. Sims, from whom he has bought all the film rights".[539] Williams appeared as the protagonist in film adaptations of famous poems and stories that he recited synchronously as the films were shown. In contrast, a series of twelve one-reel adaptations of Sims's ballads (including *The Road to Heaven*) produced by the Master Film Company in 1922 appears to have been entirely silent.[540] As an unenthusiastic reviewer noted for *Variety:* "The sub-titles are taken from the verse, but in some cases this has been beyond the scenarist, and prose has been invented to meet the case. The production work is considerably better than the material."[541]

---

534   The poem about the elopement and misfortunes of an ostler's wife had "scandalised America" after it was publicly recited in Washington in early 1886. Marsh and Francis, "Poetry of Poverty", 75. It was subsequently reprinted in over 1,200 newspapers and recited in 290 theatres, according to Sims, who never received any royalties from the poem. See Sims, *My Life,* 187–189.

535   See David Mayer, "The Victorian Stage on Film", *Nineteenth Century Theatre*, vol. 16, no. 2 (Winter 1988): 111–122, here 116 **and Appendix C.**

536   A review in the *Moving Picture World*, vol. 13, no. 7 (17 August 1912): 663 makes no mention of Sims.

537   *Copyright Act*, 1911. Part I. Section 1.2 (d).

538   "Purchase Poem Rights", *The Billboard* (23 August 1913): 15.

539   "A Remarkable Record. Mr. Eric Williams", *The Bioscope* (9 April 1914): 217.

540   The British Film Institute holds three copies of one of the films, SIR RUPERT'S WIFE. The story of the poem is explained in intertitles while the actors and their characters are first introduced with lines from the poem. The film about an unfaithful stage actress features a car chase and a dramatic climax at a cliff.

541   Gore, "Famous Poems", *Variety*, vol. 68, no. 10 (27 October 1922): 42. In the same review, *The Road to Heaven* is derided as follows: "He is an expert in laying on treacle with a trowel and to him every little beggar boy is a saint who wants to go to heaven, wakes up in the hospital ward and thinks it heaven, with the house surgeon impersonating God." Ibid. For other reviews, see also "Poems by Geo. R. Sims", *The Bioscope* (14 September 1922): 59.

As film producers were increasingly looking for longer narratives to fill the theatre circuits and cinema chains with new material, they again turned to the stage. In the early 1910s, with further development of filmic narrative and the growing establishment of feature films (upwards of three reels), popular theatrical plays were frequently selected for adaptation to the cinema screen.[542] As Ben Brewster and Lea Jacobs note:

> With the rise of the feature film in the 1910s, films became much more like plays in the kind of narratives they related – indeed, many, perhaps most of them were adaptations of stage plays, ancient and modern. In this new, longer form, the pictorial theatre again became a model, but the established practices of filmmaking were not simply abandoned for a photographic record of stage performances.[543]

Melodramas in particular with their emphasis on action over dialogue and as "the form of theatre enjoyed by the class which patronized the picture palaces" were a preferred material, both written works and entire theatre productions readily available for filming.[544] George Sims was one of the most popular and prolific melodrama writers of his age. He produced 70 plays over four decades, many of them enjoying extraordinarily long runs.[545] Consequently, between 1914 and 1923, fifteen adaptations of plays by Sims and contributors Henry Pettitt and Robert Buchanan were produced by eleven different production companies in England and the United States with film lengths between three (THE ROMANY RYE, Neptune, GB 1915) and seven reels (THE LIGHTS OF LONDON, Gaumont, GB 1923). In 1914, an adaptation of Sims's most famous play *The Lights o' London* (1881) by Barker Motion Photography was released just as the play itself was reprised at London's Aldwych Theatre to favourable reviews.[546] The film's distributor, the Magnet Film Company even prominently referenced the concurrent theatre production in its advertisements.[547] A review in *The Globe* stressed that the film had been "produced under the personal supervision of Mr. Sims" and lauded the "vivid sensationalism" of this "model cinema-drama", that would "make a strong appeal to all habitués of the picture theatre".[548] And between September 1914 and May 1915, the

---

542 See Ben Brewster and Lea Jacobs, *Theatre to Cinema: Stage Pictorialism and the Early Feature Film* (Oxford: Oxford University Press, 1997), vi.

543 Ibid., 213.

544 Rachael Low, *The History of British Film 1906–1914* (London: George Allen & Unwin, 1949), 192.

545 See Booth, "Introduction", xxii.

546 The *Sheffield Evening Telegraph* noted: "Mr. G.R. Sims, the author, has altered the piece very little. His funny people drag in references to the kinema, theatres, supper clubs, and the half-penny press, but in essentials the play remains the same as it was a generation ago." "Town Talk", *Sheffield Evening Telegraph* (13 April 1914): 4. Other alterations are listed in "The Lights o' London", *Dundee Evening Telegraph* (17 April 1914): 2.

547 See Jon Burrows, *Legitimate Cinema: Theatre Stars in Silent British Films 1908–1918* (Exeter: University of Exeter Press, 2003), 108.

548 Leonard Donaldson, "A Guide to the Cinemas", *The Globe* (22 April 1914): 4. Another report claimed that *The Lights o' London* had "been written as a filmplay by George R. Sims" but that could not be confirmed. Charles F. Ingram, "Film Gossip", *Illustrated Films Monthly*, vol. 2 (March–August 1914): 172. The film was acquired by the World Film Corporation for American distribution which presumably has led Dennis Gifford to include it as a separate Sims adaptation in his list of *Books and Plays in Films,*

newly-founded British Neptune Film Company under the management of Percy Nash released adaptations of no less than five popular military and nautical dramas co-written by Sims to promote the new venture.[549] HARBOUR LIGHTS (3,000 ft.), the adaptation of a play Sims had written with Henry Pettitt, was apparently the first big production of the new company and advertised widely in the trade press.[550]

The works by George R. Sims selected for filmic adaptation in the first two decades of the new medium in some ways mirror the changing character and reception contexts of moving pictures in Britain: First came actualities and short fictional films in the tradition of the illustrated lecture and magic lantern mode of recitation with various schemes that combined spoken words and moving images. This was followed by a phase of intense competition between film producers who, seeking to distinguish their brands and establish familiarity with audiences, recruited theatre personalities to film adaptations of the works of popular authors from around 1908. As longer feature films increasingly dominated film production from the 1910s, several of Sims's popular theatre plays were made into long films and advertised furiously. This was followed by a burst of short adaptations of Sims's Dagonet ballads released shortly after his death in 1922. They formed part of several series of adaptations produced that year by the Masters Film Company and based on famous plays, operas and "tense moments from great authors", all condensed into one-reel films.[551] The brevity of the features was a conscious decision by producer H. B. Parkinson to counter the trend for ever longer films. Parkinson thought that the cinema public would prefer shorter pictures with a narrative condensed into few, well-produced scenes instead of being "obliged to watch scene after scene, played by dashing heroes and dainty heroines, which are of little or no consequence to the story".[552] A trade show review of the "Famous Poems" series similarly stressed the "ever-increasing demand for variety" of cinema audiences in recommending the twelve featurettes to exhibitors.[553] Banking on Sims's popularity, the familiarity of audiences with his ballads and the appeal of better-known British actors filmed on location in exciting scenes, the films were distributed widely across England and Scotland.[554]

1896–1915: Literary, Theatrical and Artistic Sources of the First Twenty Years of Motion Pictures (London etc.: Mansell, 1991), 139. See also the list of releases by the World Film Corporation provided by Kevin Lewis, "A World across from Broadway II: Filmography of the World Film Corporation, 1913–1922", *Film History*, vol. 1, no. 2 (1987): 163–186, here 164.

549   See "The Neptune Film Company. A New All-British Producing House", *The Bioscope* (1 October 1914): 17, and "Neptune Co.'s 'In the Ranks'. Popular Sims Drama Filmed", *The Cinema* (17 December 1914): 53.

550   See, e.g., "The Neptune Film Company's First Trade Show. 'Harbour Lights,' by G.R. Sims and Henry Pettitt", *The Bioscope* (8 October 1914): 150–151, "Harbour Lights", *Pictures and the Picturegoer*, vol. 7, no. 39 (14 November 1914): 212–214, and "Interview with Mr. Douglas Payne. Mark Helstone in Neptune Film Company's Production 'Harbour Lights'.", *The Bioscope* (29 October 1914): 427.

551   "Potting the Classics", *The Picturegoer* (August 1922): 34.

552   Ibid.

553   See "Attractive Additions to the Programme", *The Bioscope* (31 August 1922): 36.

4

Newspapers as Sources – Towards a Digital Source Criticism

4.1 The Historical Art of Projection and Digitized Sources

The authentic and the picturesque have been identified as two relevant modes of depicting poverty in various 19th and early 20th-century popular media. The designation "popular culture" refers both to well-selling media commodities and their wide appeal, following literary historian Denis Denisoff's broad definition:

> The term 'popular culture' is widely understood today to refer to those beliefs, practices and forms of entertainment and leisure activity that are common to the general population, and not specific to any single class field. Within the Victorian context, scholars see these as including mainstream, everyday activities and objects of pleasure and leisure such as street ballads, broadsides, melodrama and music halls.[555]

It has also been established that the authentic or picturesque potential of media representations is tied inextricably to their specific reception contexts. Reconstructing the reception contexts of George Sims's popular depictions of poverty and their adaptations thus becomes an essential part of their analysis. By elaborating on the various performance contexts for specific lantern slide series, this approach responds to the call for further micro-historical studies of magic lantern practices made by media historian Martin Loiperdinger:

> Until more exhaustive micro-studies are conducted on the media history of lantern shows on the local level, not much more can be said than, all in all, there were a great number of lantern lectures and entertainments (whatever lecture and entertainment might have meant in the local context and time).[556]

Its focus on the reception contexts of visual (and textual) media puts this book thematically within the broad field of exhibition and reception history. The study of the historical art of projection has tended both towards a performance or reception-oriented historiography that puts the physical artefacts in a wider

---

554 See "'Dagonet' for the Screen", *The Bioscope* (27 July 1922): 46, and "Four Northern Counties", *The Bioscope* (26 October 1922): 62.

555 Dennis Denisoff, "Popular Culture", in Francis O'Gorman (ed.), *The Cambridge Companion to Victorian Culture* (Cambridge: Cambridge University Press, 2010), 135–155, here 136.

556 Martin Loiperdinger, "The Social Impact of Screen Culture 1880–1914", in Crangle and Vogl-Bienek (ed.), *Screen Culture*, 8–19, here 12.

historical context and towards national or regional studies of lantern practice. Over the last decades, a number of articles and monographs have traced the spread of the art of projection in various countries while micro-historical studies have elaborated on magic lantern practices in rural areas and individual cities.[557] The phrase "art of projection" (*Projektionskunst, Art de la projection*) describes the technical and creative potential of projections. According to media historian Ludwig Vogl-Bienek, "It included all aspects of design and projection techniques related to the use of classic hand-painted lantern slides, photographic lantern slides, all kinds of projection effects and early film projection."[558] The study of the historical art of projection has profited immensely from the adoption of digital methods in media historical research. Most recently, Mary Borgo Ton has applied topic modelling and mapping to magazine reports about magic lantern performances and the associated metadata collected in the Lucerna database.[559]

The study of the historical art of projection is embedded within the study of screen history as a larger media historical research agenda, which examines the concept of the screen as the place of an ephemeral performance:

> Screen Studies and the practice of writing screen history is therefore not about privileging particular media, practices and practitioners and not about conceiving this history as a set of phases or stages that are linear and successive (one practice / medium following another). It is about engaging with a plurality of histories, discourses and meanings within each medium and between the media.[560]

As a historical subdiscipline, the study of screen history relies heavily on textual secondary sources where primary artefacts (films, slides) or practices (film

---

557 See, e.g., Francisco Javier Frutos and Carmen López San Segundo, "Media Archeology in Spain: The Audiovisual Projections with Magic Lantern (1692–1899)", *Media History*, vol. 22, no. 1 (2016): 1–12; Laurent Mannoni, *Le grand art de la lumière et de l'ombre. archéologie du cinéma* (Paris: Nathan, 1995); Charles Musser, *The Emergence of Cinema: The American Screen to 1907* (New York: Scribner, 1990), 20–48; Kevin Rockett and Emer Rockett, *Magic Lantern, Panorama and Moving Pictures Shows in Ireland, 1786–1909* (Dublin: Four Courts Press, 2011). For local studies, see, e.g., Niamh McCole, "The Magic Lantern in Provincial Ireland, 1896–1906", *Early Popular Visual Culture*, vol. 5, no. 3 (November 2007): 247–262; Damer Waddington, *Panoramas, Magic Lanterns, Cinemas: A Century of 'Light' Entertainment in Jersey 1814–1914* (Jersey: Tocan Books, 2003). For non-European traditions, see, e.g., Elizabeth Hartrick, *Consuming Illusions: The Magic Lantern in Australia and Aotearoa / New Zealand 1850–1910*, PhD diss. (University of Melbourne, 2003); Alina Novik, "'The awakening of our taste for natural science': The Magic Lantern and Popular Education in Imperial Russia (1721–1871)", *Early Popular Visual Culture*, vol. 17, no. 1 (2019): 34–44, and Kenji Iwamoto, *Gentō no seiki: eiga zenya no shikaku bunkashi* [= Centuries of Magic Lanterns in Japan] (Tokyo: Shinwasha, 2002).

558 Ludwig Vogl-Bienek, "Turning the Social Problem into Performance: Slumming and Screen Culture in Victorian Lantern Shows", in Marta Braun et al. (ed.), *Beyond the Screen: Institutions, Networks and Publics of Early Cinema* (New Barnet: John Libbey Publishing, 2012), 315–324, here 315.

559 Mary Borgo Ton, "Magic Lantern Shows through a Macroscopic Lens: Topic Modelling and Mapping as Methods for Media Archaeology", *Early Popular Visual Culture*, vol. 17, nos. 3–4 (2019): 341–360.

560 Frank Gray, "Engaging with the Magic Lantern's History", in Crangle and Vogl-Bienek (ed.), *Screen Culture*, 172–180, here 179. Although one has to be careful not to neglect the importance of oral and even corporeal aspects of the cinema and lantern tradition represented by the *Filmerklärer* or lantern lecturer. See Martin Loiperdinger, "Missing Believed Lost: The Film Narrator, Then and Now", in Kaveh Askari et al. (ed.), *Performing New Media, 1890–1915* (New Barnet: John Libbey Publishing, 2014), 87–94, and Joe Kember, *Marketing Modernity*.

narrators, lecturers) have been lost or were not recorded. Historical periodicals are thus frequently consulted by screen historians and students of the history of projection to provide information on the content and context of screen performances. Aside from personal accounts, the periodical and trade press are perhaps the essential resource for film and screen historiographies that focus on the reception of projected images.[561]

In recent decades, digital reproductions of newspapers, journals and the trade press have been made available to an unprecedented extent both in commercial and non-commercial databases and collections.[562] Massive efforts in digitization have allowed scholars to search unprecedented amounts of press articles and receive almost instantaneous results. The search tools utilized in these collections are so ubiquitous that most researchers now take them for granted:

> They allow researchers to simultaneously search the full text of multiple periodicals, filter these searches by date, genre, title and relevancy, and then display the results as a list of images. Most allow users to construct more complex searches using 'logical' and 'proximity operators', 'wildcards' and 'fuzzy searches', and also make it possible to browse through individual issues.[563]

With the help of these analytical search tools and OCR software that permits full-text searches of databases, researchers are able to engage with enormous volumes of digitized texts in radically new ways. These vast amounts of digitized historical sources call for a new kind of historical critical consideration (*Quellenkritik*). Based on the traditional source criticism practiced by historians, digital source criticism widens the scope to include the impact of the digitization process on historical material and research. Many scholars have argued that digitization does not only change the quantity but also the quality and even the very nature of the sources being digitized:

> There is a danger in this process of forgetting that newspapers were material objects that were bought, read and passed around, and that the location and presentation of individual articles is of central importance in understanding how

---

561 For examples of the use of personal accounts of magic lantern performances in memoirs, see Ludwig Vogl-Bienek, "Lichtspiele", 49–52, and Richard Crangle, "Next Slide Please", 44.

562 See the various collections in Gale Cengage's commercial historical newspaper archives, which also include two collections of 19th century British periodicals, or the "Early Cinema Collection (1855–1930)" at the non-commercial Media History Digital Library for trade papers. The European portal for cultural heritage collections, Europeana offers a sizeable collection of newspapers from 20 European countries, while the International Coalition on Newspapers allows for a worldwide search for digitized newspaper titles in subscribed institutions. The most notable databases of Victorian print titles are Gale's "19th Century British Library Newspapers" and "19th Century UK Periodicals", The British Library's "The British Newspaper Archive" (a collaboration with findmypast) and ProQuest's "Periodicals Archive Online". For a more exhaustive list with a focus on U.S. American newspapers, see Barry Popik, "Digital Historical Newspapers: A Review of the Powerful New Research Tools", *Journal of English Linguistics*, vol. 32, no. 2 (June 2004): 114–123. For German-speaking countries, see Birgit Seiderer, "Die Digitalisierung von Zeitungen im deutschsprachigen Raum – ein Zustandsbericht", *Zeitschrift für Bibliothekswesen und Bibliographie*, vol. 58, nos. 3–4 (2010): 165–171.

563 Bob Nicholson, "The Digital Turn: Exploring the Methodological Possibilities of Digital Newspaper Archives", *Media History*, vol. 19, no. 1 (2013): 59–73, here 64.

those articles were received by readers and how much significance was ascribed to them.[564]

This is especially pertinent when images are reproduced alongside text, as Adrian Bingham points out: "The visual content – photographs, cartoons and sketches – is in particular danger of being lost with a reliance on keyword searching, and this is especially problematic for twentieth-century newspapers and publications where the visual content had such an impact."[565] Illustrations from newspapers and magazines were also frequently adapted (and in many cases pirated) for projection with the magic lantern, where they reached a wider – and not necessarily literate audience.[566]

Compared to the amount of digitized newspaper and magazine pages, the efforts in mass digitization of magic lantern slides are still in their infancy, although a growing number of individual collectors, archives and other heritage institutions are increasingly making digitized images available. The most notable is Lucerna – The Magic Lantern Web Resource, a relational database that links records for individual slide sets with information about accompanying readings, producers, distributors and exhibitors. The portal Europeana aggregates digitized images from European cultural heritage collections but does not currently allow users to filter specifically for magic lantern slides. With their combination of spoken words, music and projected images, works in the historical art of projection pose their own specific set of challenges when selected for digitization.[567] eLaterna Archive, a pilot project developed at the University of Trier, demonstrates the usefulness of digital facsimiles of lantern slides for comparative research.[568] Critical editions like the one of ORA PRO NOBIS (Bamforth) collate multiple versions and variants of individual slides and slide sets as they survived in private and public collections. High-resolution digital facsimiles of slides and related material are combined with editorial comments on the provenance and performance contexts. These

---

564 Adrian Bingham, "The Digitization of Newspaper Archives: Opportunities and Challenges for Historians", *Twentieth Century British History*, vol. 21, no. 2 (2010): 225–231, here 230. Similar concerns are expressed by Richard Abel, "The Pleasures and Perils of Big Data in Digitized Newspapers", *Film History*, vol. 25, nos. 1–2 (2013): 1–10, here 9.

565 Bingham, "Digitization", 230. Since early 2017, the British Newspaper Archive offers a search for pictures in selected titles like the *Illustrated Sporting and Dramatic News*, *The Sketch* or *The Graphic*. However, the images themselves were not indexed individually to make them searchable, instead the tool merely displays images found on the same page as the search term entered by the user.

566 One example for the importance of projected images for political campaigning is their role in the Irish question. Political cartoons where popular subjects: Lucerna – the Magic Lantern Web Resource lists at least two slide sets with reproductions from the *Freeman's Journal* and the *St Stephen's Review*. A set of 60 slides showing eviction scenes photographed between 1886 and 1889 was distributed by the well-known Irish slide manufacturer William Lawrence of Dublin. See Fintan Cullen, "Marketing National Sentiment: Lantern Slides of Evictions in Late Nineteenth-Century Ireland", *History Workshop Journal*, vol. 54, no. 1 (2002): 162–179, here 164–165.

567 For a conceptual discussion of digital editions of lantern slide series, see Ludwig Vogl-Bienek, "eLaterna – Digitale Editionen von Werken der historischen Projektionskunst", *editio. Internationales Jahrbuch für Editionswissenschaft*, vol. 32, no. 1 (November 2018): 104–118, here 109–117.

568 See subsection "eLaterna Archive" of eLaterna – Historical Art of Projection (https://elaterna.uni-trier.de/#/ea).

model editions also allow users to collocate two individual slides in a light box and to enlarge them to a level that exposes details in the glass or the binding which would be impossible to perceive with the naked eye on the analogue objects.

Practical issues relating to the digitization, storage and preservation of newspaper collections are continuously discussed within the librarian and archival community.[569] Editors of media historical resources like Martin Loiperdinger of the Importing Asta Nielsen Database and Eric Hoyt of the Media History Digital Library have also reflected on the presentation of digitized sources and the practice of digitization in general.[570] Scholarly users on the other side of the computer have been slower to question the basic assumptions and inherent limitations of digital tools. As historian of the press James Mussell argues, new digital tools for historic research call for a corresponding digital methodology: "[W]ithout developing corresponding methodological approaches in how to think about and use these resources, we remain trapped in methodologies shaped by our encounters with certain forms of printed objects in certain dusty rooms."[571] Historian Bob Nicholson echoes this perception when he calls for "robust methodological responses to digital archives" and asks researchers to "understand how newspapers are changed by digitisation".[572] This extends beyond the obvious difference between a paper copy of a newspaper and a digital image (often made from microfilm) of that paper: "By the time we view a digital archive, its contents have been through a complex process of transformation; the questions we can ask of a digital source are, in this sense, determined before we even login to the database."[573] Sarah Dellmann similarly points out that the specific properties of digital tools and environments will

---

569　See, e.g., Lorna Hughes, *Digitizing Collections: Strategic Issues for the Information Manager* (London: Facet Publishing, 2004) and recent publications of the Newspaper Section of the International Federation of Library Associations and Institutions (IFLA). From another perspective, humanities scholars as users of digital tools are also increasingly becoming the object of study, see Claire Warwick, "Studying Users in Digital Humanities", in Claire Warwick, Melissa Terras and Julianne Nyhan (ed.), *Digital Humanities in Practice* (London: Facet Publishing, 2012), 1–21, especially 2–9. At the same time, users are also asked to interact with scholarly digital resources by correcting faulty data or even producing their own digital editions. See Patrick Sahle, *Digitale Editionsformen. Zum Umgang mit der Überlieferung unter den Bedingungen des Medienwandels*, vol. 2, *Befunde, Theorie und Methodik* (Norderstedt: Books on Demand, 2013), 257–259.

570　Martin Loiperdinger, "Early Film Stars in Trade Journals and Newspapers: Data-Based Research on Global Distribution and Local Exhibition", in Daniel Biltereyst, Richard Maltby and Philippe Meers (ed.), *The Routledge Companion to New Cinema History* (London, New York: Routledge, 2019), 138–146, here 142–145, and Eric Hoyt et al., "*Variety's* Transformations: Digitizing and Analyzing the First 35 Years of the Canonical Trade Paper", in Daniel Biltereyst and Lies Van de Vijver (ed.), *Mapping Movie Magazines: Digitization, Periodicals and Cinema History* (Cham: Palgrave Macmillan, 2020), 17–38. Both Stephen Bottomore, "Scholarly Research, Then and Now", *Early Popular Visual Culture*, vol. 14, no. 4 (2016): 302–318, and Richard Abel, "The Pleasures and Perils of Big Data in Digitized Newspapers", *Film History*, vol. 25, nos. 1–2 (2013): 1–10 mainly reflect on the impact digitization has had on their own media historical research in the last decades.

571　James Mussell, "Ownership, Institutions, and Methodology", *Journal of Victorian Culture*, vol. 13, no. 1 (2008): 94–100, here 94.

572　Nicholson, "Digital Turn", 64.

573　Ibid., 65.

influence every aspect of a researcher's process, "from defining their research question to building their corpora to analysing and publishing the data".[574]

A digital source criticism widens the critical study of historical newspapers as sources to include the physical aspects and technological considerations specific to the digitization process and the search tools of digital collections. A broader perspective might also consider the economic aspects of digitization, evaluate how the results of large-scale digitization projects are made accessible to both scholars and the public, and address questions about sustainability and long-time data storage of such projects.[575]

4.2 Victorian Newspapers and Digitization

When discussing the research opportunities afforded by large amounts of digitized newspapers, it is helpful to consider the role of newspapers in British society in the tradition of source criticism in historic research. As historian Stephen Vella points out, any newspaper is more than a combination of printed words and can be studied from multiple angles: "It is at once a text, a record of historical events, a representation of society and a chronicle of contemporary opinions, aspirations and debates. A newspaper is also a business enterprise, a professional organization, a platform for advertisements and itself a commodity."[576] Newspapers have been used in historiography alongside other textual sources for more than a century.[577] As Ronald Zweig states, "[…] newspapers are often the only repository of details of events that are not recorded in other sorts of records. Easy and immediate access to these sorts of information is a boon for any historian."[578] However, newspapers are a selective representation of newsworthy events, not "neutral conduits of information, but rather gatekeepers and filterers of ideas".[579] It may seem trivial but should be kept in mind: Just because a media event is not reported in newspapers does not mean it did not take place (and vice versa!). Newspapers present an inherently subjective, filtered version of those events deemed relevant to either their readers, owners or advertisers: "Rather than simply report a reality 'out there', newspapers filter, frame and report news and analysis in a manner supportive of established power structures under whose authority they function, thus limiting the

---

574 Sarah Dellmann, "Analogue Objects Online. Epistemological Reflections on Digital Reproductions of Lantern Slides", *Early Popular Visual Culture*, vol. 17, nos. 3–4 (2019): 322–340, here 323.

575 See Melissa Terras, "Digitization and Digital Resources in the Humanities", in Warwick, Terras and Nyhan (ed.), *Digital Humanities in Practice*, 47–70.

576 Stephen Vella, "Newspapers", in Miriam Dobson and Benjamin Ziemann (ed.), *Reading Primary Sources: The Interpretation of Texts from Nineteenth- and Twentieth-Century History* (London, New York: Routledge, 2009), 192–208, here 193–194.

577 Gustav Wolf's *Einführung in das Studium der neueren Geschichte* published in Berlin in 1910 included an entire chapter on the press ("Das Zeitungswesen"), which identified as the main characteristics of contemporary newspapers the four factors of periodicity, topicality, variety and publicity.

578 Ronald Zweig, "Lessons from the Palestine Post Project", *Literary and Linguistic Computing*, vol. 13, no. 2 (June 1998): 89–95, here 94.

579 Vella, "Newspapers", 193.

bounds of debate and discussion accordingly."[580] These power structures are themselves subject to historical change. Throughout the 19th century, the influence of political powers on British newspapers steadily decreased as state control (in the form of taxes) was curtailed, while the importance of advertising increased:

> Advertisement revenue allowed the press to become increasingly independent of political control and market-oriented throughout the century. The newspapers representing rival political parties […] became less influential once editors realized that political involvement was to some extent a liability in pursuit of a large readership.[581]

Victorian readership grew constantly throughout the era but was also increasingly divided into reading segments by niche publications. As Aled Jones points out, Victorian newspapers before the 1850s aimed "broadly for a Whig or Tory readership", but after mid-century, most were "[…] targeted at very specific niche markets. Where once news had been broadcast, it was now very deliberately being narrowcast."[582] Finally by the 1870s, "the technologies of printing and distribution, and methods of news-gathering, had reached their peak, while virtually all fiscal and legislative restraints had been removed".[583] However, even after the decline of Chartist newspapers, Radical publications like *The Referee* or the socialist weekly *The Clarion* represented working-class political agendas alongside cartoons, sporting events and dramatic gossip.[584] By the 1880s, what Aled Jones has termed "the power of the press" to influence public opinion was considered so great that a journalist and historian of the press remarked: "[E]ven the humblest journals have done something to influence the public or local opinion, not only by their bare statements of facts, but by their modes of stating them, and by their few or many comments thereon."[585] Literary historian Kathyrn Sutherland also stresses the role newspapers played as both publishers of and commentators on Victorian literary culture:

> Part of the public record of society at any given time, the historic newspaper shared a passing moment with and influenced, often in profound ways, other products whose print trajectory was far different: essays, poems and fiction found a first audience in the newspaper or periodical press before being reprinted in single-author volumes; literary or other print works were reviewed in its pages or merely circulated at the same time.[586]

---

580 Ibid.

581 Matthew Rubery, "Journalism", in O'Gorman (ed.), *Companion to Victorian Culture*, 177–194, here 185–186.

582 Aled Jones, *Powers of the Press: Newspapers, Power and the Public in Nineteenth-Century England* (Aldershot, Hants: Scolar Press, 1996), 91.

583 Ibid., 64.

584 On *The Clarion*, see Eifler, *The Great Gun of the Lantern*, 67–68 and 94–95.

585 Henry Richard Fox Bourne, *English Newspapers. Chapters in the History of Journalism* (1887), quoted in Jones, *Powers of the Press*, 64.

586 Marilyn Deegan and Kathryn Sutherland, *Transferred Illusions: Digital Technology and the Forms of Print* (Farnham, Burlington: Ashgate, 2009), 51.

In George Sims's case, many of his ballads were first published in *The Referee* or other newspapers before they were reprinted and sold as collections of poems. And, as newspaper reports indicate, many of them were recited publicly and thus became part of the general discourse long before they ever appeared in book form.[587] The Victorian period saw an unprecedented "boom in the volume of affordable books, magazines and newspapers produced to satisfy the demands of the first mass reading public".[588] New titles are continuously added to the various indexes of Victorian periodicals. The third series of the *Waterloo Directory of English Newspapers and Periodicals: 1800–1900* published in 2009 lists more than 73,000 individual titles.[589] As Laurel Brake cautions: "Of these, the percentage digitized in the first decade of the twenty-first century is tiny, although in numbers, and from a basis of zero, some 400 digitized nineteenth-century serials may appear overwhelming to researchers."[590] Consulting paper copies – which libraries are increasingly restricting access to – and microform editions alongside digital resources can prevent researchers from getting trapped in a digital bubble: "The absence of the great majority of titles from the digital archive situates those we have as indicative, icebergs on a surface that constantly remind readers of the invisible dangers, and riches, in their immediate environs."[591] We run the danger of a digital canon that excludes a wide range of material and presents a false picture of the Victorian press: "The dialogic properties of digitized papers will be silenced if we deploy digital material alone and if the print archive does not remain accessible and consulted."[592] It becomes a key task of the researcher to fill in the gaps left by digitization and re-establish connections lost in the selection process:

> Newspapers often engage in elaborate and unfolding debates with one another playing with one another's words and consciously turning meanings around in competing narratives. Therefore, in order to understand a newspaper article, it is often essential to use the comparative method: to read the text alongside parallel

---

587　The first so-called Dagonet ballad, *Told to the Missionary*, was published in *The Referee* as early as 9 December 1877. One week later, *The Referee* printed a parody by another author of the paper titled *Told to the Milkman* that satirized Sims's use of coarse language. In May of 1878, London newspaper *The Era* reported on a variety evening entertainment of songs and recitations, hosted by Herbert Beerbohm Tree, who also recited "Mr. G.R. Sims's touching poem called 'Told Jo [sic!], the Missionary,' the Story of a Coster-monger and his Dog, which is sure to bring tears to the eyes of all who read or hear it". "Willis's Rooms", *The Era* (12 May 1878): 5. Later, the ballad was included in the first collection of Sims's ballads in 1879 and presented by well-known reciters throughout the 1880s.

588　Rubery, "Journalism", 177.

589　*The Waterloo Directory of English Newspapers & Periodicals: 1800–1900*, third series (North Waterloo Academic Press, 2009) (accessed 16 December 2020, http://www.victorianperiodicals.com/series3/index.asp).

590　Laurel Brake, "Half Full and Half Empty", Digital Forum, *Journal of Victorian Culture*, vol. 17, no. 2 (2012): 222–229, here 225.

591　Ibid. As Brake rightly reminds us, none of the material presented in digital newspaper collections is new, it has just been made more easily accessible and searchable; even if there are considerable financial and regional limits as to what can be accessed by whom.

592　Ibid. Similarly, Eric Hoyt of the Media History Digital Library argues that film historians have focused on a few canonical titles and points to the wider availability of digital material. See Eric Hoyt, "Lenses for Lantern: Data Mining, Visualization, and Excavating Film History's Neglected Sources", *Film History*, vol. 26, no. 2 (2014): 146–168.

articles in other newspapers as well as in comparison with what preceded it in its own newspaper.[593]

This raises the question of how and why periodicals are selected for digitization; especially for large-scale digitization projects by national libraries or other heritage institutions.[594] Newspapers are selected for digitization because of various criteria like their historical significance, copyright status and importance to a certain public.[595] As Laurel Brake points out, present-day ideology also plays a role: "Selection strategies have been varied, but they are similarly subject to current cultural values in the prioritized market of higher education: in the gender-conscious, secular, Anglo-American and post-colonial academy for example, religious titles are few while magazines for women feature." The availability of material that is physically suitable for digitization is equally important: while microfilms are generally cheaper to digitize and less fragile, paper copies provide better image results (even in colour) and more accurate OCR.[596] Conversely, OCR accuracy can be seriously compromised by fragile or inadequate source material. But these are not the only factors. For example, the British Newspaper Archive does not include national newspapers like the *Daily Mail* or *The Times*, which maintain their own (commercial) archives. This is mitigated by the fact that throughout the 19th century, as Andrew Hobbs demonstrates, non-metropolitan newspapers had a substantially larger circulation than these national newspapers: "The provincial press was the majority newspaper press, for more than a century."[597] Still, it is a noteworthy (if perhaps inevitable) omission. Also, as it is an ongoing effort, newly digitized newspapers are continuously added to the British Newspaper Archive. Fundamentally speaking, working with digital collections means to accept that not all data will be collected and that any definitive statement might have to be challenged when a new batch of material is added to a database.

The main resource for digital copies of historical newspapers used in this book is The British Newspaper Archive, a large-scale digitization project by the British Library in connection with findmypast that has digitized over 40 million individual pages to date either from paper copies or microfilm.[598] It offers facsimiles of newspaper pages that can be viewed as full-page, enlarged

---

593 Vella, "Newspapers", 200.

594 Brake, "Half Full", 225.

595 Ibid., 225–226. For other factors in the selection of newspapers and periodicals suitable for digitization, see 226–228.

596 See Kenning Arlitsch and John Herbert, "Microfilm, Paper, and OCR: Issues in Newspaper Digitization: The Utah Digital Newspapers Program", *Microform & Imaging Review*, vol. 33, no. 2 (2004): 59–67, here 65.

597 Andrew Hobbs, "When the Provincial Press Was the National Press (c.1836–1900)", *The International Journal of Regional and Local Studies*, vol. 5, no. 1 (Spring 2009): 16–43, here 17. Hobbs cautions historians to consider this when discussing the national vs. the local press: "More careful use of terms such as 'national' and 'local' in discussions of print culture would specify whether these terms apply to the place of production, to the circulation area, the content or merely editorial aspirations." Ibid., 38.

598 See The British Newspaper Archive: "About The British Newspaper Archive" (https://www.british-newspaperarchive.co.uk/help/about).

or navigated by individual articles. The search function highlights individual terms, combinations of words or entire phrases on the relevant pages and offers snippets of (uncorrected) OCR text.[599] As historian of the press Laurel Brake points out, in this form of data representation "the items – articles or even fragments of articles – are de-contextualized and effectively severed from the journals in which they appeared", which is not conducive to the traditional approach of source criticism:

> [N]ot because the information is not there if sought, but because in the face of 50 hits, the user is less prone to look at the nature of the newspaper in which hits occur. In assessing the significance of a hit, it is important to know the party politics, the price and the other contents of the paper in which the hit appears. Its position in the paper is often telling: is it a leader or tucked away in the back? These may be unwelcome diversions to the pursuer of hits.[600]

The list-display of search results also obscures notable differences between newspapers and levels their historical importance. Weeklies and dailies are lumped together, results from both small and large, national and regional papers are presented as equally 'relevant'. Newspaper articles, especially for smaller titles, were often provided by news agencies and syndicators and frequently reprinted or even pirated.[601] This means of course that the first hit of an OCR search is not necessarily the first or only time something was published. In the case of reconstructing the performance contexts of lantern slide series, these distinctions (between daily and weekly or national and regional newspapers) are less relevant, but if historical discourses or attitudes are investigated, they should be noted.

The database of the British Newspaper Archive allows for various browsing options (by place, time and newspaper title) but because of the enormous amount of material most users will probably opt for the various search functions which display results based on machine-readable OCR text. OCR stands for optical character recognition and, according to Tanner, Muñoz and Ros, "primarily facilitates searching, indexing and other means of structuring the user experience of online newspaper archives".[602] OCR software converts a digital image into machine-readable text and enables full-text searches of large collections. The efficiency of the OCR software thus directly shapes the types of results and texts available to researchers. As Tanner et al. found in their study of the "19th Century Newspaper Project", a smaller-scale digitization project by the British Library concluded in 2010, the accuracy for "significant words" – actual search terms, not the very common function words such as the, he, it

---

599   The search function and snippets are offered free of charge while full-page views are available through various direct subscription models or subscribing institutions.

600   Brake, "Half Full", 224.

601   On syndication and news networks, see Hobbs, "The Provincial Press", 36–37.

602   Simon Tanner, Trevor Muñoz and Pich Hemy Ros, "Measuring Mass Text Digitization Quality and Usefulness: Lessons Learned from Assessing the OCR Accuracy of the British Library's 19th Century Online Newspaper Archive", *D-Lib Magazine*, vol. 15, no. 7/8 (2009), (http://www.dlib.org/dlib/july09/munoz/07munoz.html).

– was almost 10 per cent lower than the "average word accuracy".[603] The British Newspaper Archive acknowledges that OCR texts can be compromised by a number of factors but does not provide any numbers on OCR accuracy at this point.

These remarks on the limitations of the British Newspaper Archive should not overshadow the responsibility of individual researchers to extract meaningful data from digital resources, i.e. produce good results (or as the old dictum goes "garbage in – garbage out"). In the context of this study, this meant optimizing the efficiency and limiting the number of results for search queries. The two most sensible strategies are by narrowing the time frame and the use of precise keywords. When searching for reviews or reactions to a particular ballad, newspaper article or book publication, the precise date of first publication (and a publication history that takes into account the various published versions of a work) can serve as a starting date for any search.[604] These dates are significant because they mark the exact time that a work entered public discourse as indicated by reactions to Sims's articles in other newspapers or public recitations of his ballads. These dates were ascertained from microfilm and paper copies held at the British Library – since neither paper had been digitized yet.[605]

Magic lantern events were frequently reported on both in local and regional British newspapers and in periodicals by religious and charitable organizations that made use of projected images. A shortcoming of newspaper reports on magic lantern performances is that they generally only include shows that took place in fixed-site venues. The common tradition of travelling fairground attractions will usually not be reflected in newspaper reports. The activities of travelling projection vans are often documented meticulously in the periodicals of welfare organizations like the Church Army.[606] Despite these limitations, newspaper reports can provide valuable information on the reception contexts. They usually feature a rundown of the programme, name the organizer and venue, mention the lecturer or speaker and people who sang, read or recited. And of course the operator who "manipulated the lantern" or "exhibited by the aid of a oxy-hydrogen lantern". According to these reports, the events usually concluded with a polite "vote of thanks" or "round of applause" for the participants by a usually "appreciative audience".[607] While reception

603 Tanner, Muñoz and Ros, "OCR Accuracy".

604 Different versions of the same published work were often aimed at different reading publics differentiated by place of residence, income, political persuasion, etc. and thus evoke different reactions. One of the aims of this study has been to establish the precise dates of first publication for those works that are discussed in it. This includes many of Sims's Dagonet ballads and his series of articles on the London poor *How the Poor Live* (1883). A (necessarily incomplete) list of the dates of first publication is given in Appendix A.

605 The British Newspaper Archive has added *The Referee* to their list of digitized newspaper titles in late May of 2018.

606 Torsten Gärtner estimates that the minimum number of projection services given by up to 68 Church Army mission vans between 1892 and 1914 amounts to 8,000 services. See Gärtner, "Church on Wheels", 138. Karen Eifler "cautiously" estimates that magic lantern projections by Church Army vans alone reached an audience of 1.5 million people and states that a more optimistic estimation would come closer to 17.5 million. Eifler, "Attraction and Instruction", 368.

607 Karen Eifler finds that reports about projection shows ("Projektionsaufführungen") in publications by

contexts as such (venue, programme) can be reconstructed with the information provided in these reports, the question remains if any meaningful conclusions about the nature and the reactions of historical audiences can be drawn. Even an explicit attribution like "the poor children" could refer to fairly different groups of people if the show took place in a large city or a small rural town. Still, some information on audiences can be inferred from the performance context and the reporting, if additional sources are consulted. For example, entertainments by the Band of Hope were usually aimed at children and young adults from working-class families. If, on the other hand, attendants were asked to donate for a charitable cause following the lantern show, a more affluent audience can be assumed. The make-up of audiences can also be guessed at by considering admission prices and the location of the venue in working-class or affluent neighbourhoods.

Without digital collections it would be impossible to collect reports on magic lantern events over such a long time period and variety of places with relative ease. By contrast, an extensive search in paper copies of *The Sunday School Chronicle* (1883–1900), *The Temperance Chronicle* (1891–1900) and the *Church Army Gazette* (1891–1895) yielded very disappointing results with a single mention of THE ROAD TO HEAVEN over the entire period and no mention of IN THE WORKHOUSE. Still, the search for digitized reports about magic lantern events where adaptations of Sims's works were shown proved challenging. His most popular ballad *In the Workhouse. Christmas Day* is problematic as a search term. The adaptation for the art of projection was simply titled IN THE WORKHOUSE and since the British Newspaper Archive ignores "stop words" like "in", "the" and "to", a search for that phrase (or rather, effectively, the term "workhouse") yielded well over half a million results between 1890 and 1914.[608] Here, the terms "Sims" and "lantern" were added to narrow the number of search results and the longer phrases "Christmas Day in the Workhouse" and "In the Workhouse Christmas Day" were used alternatively – even if this decision drastically lowered the number of results. Compared to the systematic search conducted with the title "road to heaven" between the years 1883 and 1914, not surprisingly, this search yielded fewer results and the analysis is thus focused more on a qualitative interpretation of individual performance contexts and performers. By contrast, reviewing the roughly 3,000 search results for the phrase "road to heaven" revealed that illustrated recitals of the ballad and traditional recitations ran in parallel (with the latter outweighing the former) over the entire period. The research questions that can be asked and answered through the use of digital collections will thus differ widely depending on the factors outlined above.

religious and welfare organizations follow the same pattern as newspaper reports but provide more details on physical crowd reactions and exclamations that stress the effectiveness of projected images for their respective causes. See Eifler, *The Great Gun of the Lantern*, 101–107.

608   That number has since climbed to more than 1.7 million results as of March 2021. For "stop words", see The British Newspaper Archive: "Search Tips" (http://www.britishnewspaperarchive. co.uk/content/help).

5

Case Studies

The following case studies highlight different aspects of three popular poverty works by George R. Sims and their adaptations. The first one analyses the authenticating strategies and interplay between text and images in his series of articles *How the Poor Live*. Their effectiveness is demonstrated by reactions from readers in letters to the editor of the *Pictorial World* and the reception contexts for various lantern slide series based on the work. The second takes Sims's most famous ballad *In the Workhouse. Christmas Day* as an example for the changing meaning attributed to depictions of poverty over time. A detailed analysis of two adaptations, one for the art of projection (IN THE WORKHOUSE, Bamforth, 1890) and one for the cinema (CHRISTMAS DAY IN THE WORKHOUSE, G.B. Samuelson, 1914), shows how these adaptations were shaped by their specific production and distribution contexts. The third case study presents another ballad, *The Road to Heaven*, as an example of the interplay between authentic and picturesque aspects in popular depictions of poverty. Common motifs in George Sims's ballads and authenticating strategies are considered alongside pictorial influences from other visual media on the life model adaptations. That section also illustrates the potential offered by comparative analysis of lantern slide series for the study of the historical art of projection.

5.1 Into Poor Homes – *How the Poor Live* (1883)

Publication History

Like Henry Mayhew's *London Labour and the London Poor*, *How the Poor Live* was first published as a series of newspaper articles and later reissued in two different book editions. The series of articles written by George R. Sims and illustrated by Frederick Barnard was originally published in the London paper the *Pictorial World* between June and August of 1883.[609] First published in 1874 and renowned for its illustrations, the *Pictorial World* cost sixpence and was published weekly with a circulation of around 40,000 copies in 1883.[610] Gilbert and Harvey Dalziel had bought the paper in June of 1882 but were forced to wind up the Pictorial Printing and Publishing Company in July of 1883 after their efforts to increase circulation of the paper had bankrupted the company

---

609   *Pictorial World*, vol. 2, no. 40 (2 June 1883) through vol. 3, no. 52 (25 August 1883).

610   See *St James's Gazette* (25 April 1883): 2 for details about the Pictorial Printing and Publishing Company.

121

instead.[611] When Gilbert Dalziel commissioned him to write *How the Poor Live*, Sims was best known for his successful melodrama *The Lights o' London* (1881) and his popular Dagonet Ballads. Sims's contributions to the *Pictorial World* marked his first foray into investigative journalism, even though it was reminiscent of his fictionalized stories of London life collected in *The Social Kaleidoscope* (1881).[612] Frederick Barnard, the artist who accompanied Sims, had made a name for himself both as a painter and an illustrator for the *Household Edition* of *The Works of Charles Dickens* (1871–1879) and in the previous year had illustrated Walter Besant's best-selling East End novel *All Sorts and Conditions of Men*.[613] Sims had apparently conducted his research for *How the Poor Live* in April of 1883 when he alluded to the upcoming publication in his column in *The Referee*:

> I have just completed a house-to-house visitation of certain one-room districts of the East. I have been where policemen are unknown and the sanitary inspector would be as strange a visitor as the Archbishop of Canterbury. I have seen with my own eyes a state of things which would disgrace a cannibal commune. Whether, when I tell my tale, it will fall on attentive ears has yet to be seen, but I fancy that at last the public attention is fully aroused to an evil to which I have never ceased to draw attention since I first had the honour of signing myself DAGONET.[614]

The first article of the series appeared in the *Pictorial World* on 2 June 1883 with an announcement by the editor. The series was brought to a close on 25 August when it was announced that the paper had "changed hands" and that the *How the Poor Live* Fund, established in response to the series at the beginning of July, was to be discontinued as well.[615] It is unclear if Sims and Barnard originally

---

611 See "High Court of Justice. Chancery Division. The Pictorial Printing and Publishing Company", *London Evening Standard* (30 July 1883): 2.

612 A recurring theme in the analysis of Sims's (and indeed many Victorian) works is the difficulty of distinguishing neatly between fictional and non-fictional writing, a distinction that is necessarily ahistoric and artificial. Contemporary readers and audiences were used and even expected narrative elements and sensational descriptions in journalistic pieces like *How the Poor Live* just as much as they appreciated the realism of the street scenes in Sims's melodrama *The Lights o' London*. In his introduction to the second series of *The Social Kaleidoscope*, Sims himself repeatedly blurred the lines: "There shall be no picture found in the gallery which is not painted from life, – in which the figures are not drawn from living, breathing models. […] I may slightly alter the surroundings, put a year or two on to their ages, change the colour of their eyes, and move them, say, from Camden Town to Camberwall; but with these trifling exceptions the descriptions of the changing figures in the 'Social Kaleidoscope' are the truth, the whole truth, and nothing but the truth." Sims, *Social Kaleidoscope*, iii–iv.

613 For a list of the individual works in the Household Edition illustrated by Barnard, see The Victorian Web: Philip Allingham and Chris Louttit, "The Illustrators of the Household Edition of the *Works of Charles Dickens* (22 vols, 1871–1879)", (accessed on 13 December 2020, http://www.victorian-web.org/art/illustration/barnard/household. html).

614 Dagonet, "Mustard and Cress", *The Referee* (15 April 1883): 7. It is not clear from that passage whether Barnard already accompanied Sims on this "visitation" or if they undertook a second slum tour together. In another column later that year, Sims stated the following: "I have received from Messrs. Chatto and Windus an announcement that they will publish early in the week a shilling volume, entitled *How the Poor Live*, written by George R. Sims, and illustrated by Mr. Frederick Barnard, the artist who accompanied the author on his journey through outcast London in the spring of the present year." Dagonet, "Mustard and Cress", *The Referee* (11 November 1883): 7.

615 See *Pictorial World* (23 August 1883): 182.

intended to continue the series as the London correspondent of two provincial papers suggested: "When *How the Poor Live*, a series of papers by Mr. George R. Sims, illustrated by Mr. Frederick Barnard, ceased to appear in the *Pictorial World*, owing to a change in the proprietorship of that journal, author and artist had by no means finished their appointed task."[616] Sims himself makes no mention of such plans but since both his and Barnard's connection with the *Pictorial World* were established through their personal acquaintance with the Brothers Dalziel it seems possible. In an undated letter from Barnard to Sims the former asks "Who are the proprietors of the *Pictorial World* our magic lantern friend speaks of?", which suggests that their connection with the paper was indeed severed when the ownership changed hands.[617]

As early as December 1883, *How the Poor Live* (including all 60 of Barnard's illustrations) was reissued as a shilling book by the London publisher Chatto & Windus with the *Pall Mall Gazette* reporting that 60,000 copies had been printed.[618] It included a short preface by Sims, who thanked Frederick Barnard, "the eminent artist, who [...] accompanied me on a painful journey", and assured readers that he had chosen, "all circumstances considered, to let the work stand in its original form, and have in no way added to it or altered it".[619] Sims also stressed the influence of the series on the enormously popular pamphlet *The Bitter Cry of Outcast London*, which had appeared in October 1883 shortly after *How the Poor Live* and had caused even more of a sensation.[620] Sims's assertion that he had "the permission of the author of *The Bitter Cry of Outcast London* to say that from these articles he derived the greatest assistance while compiling his now famous pamphlet" was clearly intended to boost book sales.[621]

Between 19 November 1887 and 11 February 1888, the illustrated comic weekly *Ally Sloper's Half Holiday* re-serialized Sims's articles and Barnard's illustrations as a supplement.[622] According to historian Peter Bailey, *Ally Sloper's Half-Holiday* "stood in a clear line of inspirational descent from *Punch*", but at the cost of one penny it was "clearly aimed at a more numerous lower class readership".[623] It was founded by Gilbert Dalziel, who had previously been one of the proprietors of the *Pictorial World* and had originally commis-

---

616   "Our London Correspondent", *Morpeth Herald* (29 December 1883): 5, and *Walsall Advertiser* (29 December 1883): 2.

617   See Appendix D for a transcript of the letter.

618   *Pall Mall Gazette* (6 December 1883): 6. The book was also distributed in Ireland by M. H. Gill & Son of Dublin. See *Freeman's Journal* (11 December 1883): 8.

619   George R. Sims, "Preface", *How the Poor Live* (London: Chatto & Windus, 1883).

620   The penny pamphlet was published by the London Congregational Union, the author is assumed to be the Reverend Andrew Mearns. See Wohl, *Eternal Slum*, 201. For a longer discussion, see Anthony Wohl, "The Bitter Cry of Outcast London", *International Review of Social History*, vol. 13, no. 2 (1968): 189–245.

621   Sims, *How the Poor Live* (1883), 4.

622   See Donovan and Rubery, *Secret Commissions*, 151.

623   Peter Bailey, "*Ally Sloper's Half-Holiday*: Comic Art in the 1880s", *History Workshop Journal*, vol. 16, no. 1 (October 1983): 4–32, here 7.

sioned Sims and Barnard to produce *How the Poor Live*.[624] Lastly, in June of 1889, Chatto & Windus issued a reprint of *How the Poor Live* together with Sims's letters about *Horrible London* for the price of one shilling.[625] The preface was almost the same as in the previous edition by Chatto & Windus, slightly amended to reflect the inclusion of *Horrible London* in the latter volume: "The papers which form this volume appeared originally in *The Pictorial World* and *The Daily News*."[626] Sims repeated his assertion that he had "in no way added to it or altered" the work – but that is not true. He (or someone else) most certainly edited the text in between the two editions. A small but notable difference is that references to the *Pictorial World* as the original means of publication were removed from the text (but not the preface). Thus "the nameless abominations which could only be set forth were we contributing to the *Lancet* instead of the *Pictorial World*" were amended to "the nameless abominations which could only be set forth were we contributing to the *Lancet* instead of writing a book".[627] And in the final chapter a reference to the "many letters which have appeared in the *Pictorial World*, and which have reached us privately" was changed to "the many letters which have appeared in the newspapers, and which have reached me privately".[628] Sims's use of the singular in the second quotation is the result of a more fundamental difference between both editions: Frederick Barnard's illustrations were not included in the 1889 edition and his contribution was not acknowledged in the preface anymore.[629] Any direct references to his sketches in the text were quietly removed or amended to account for the fact. In most cases, sentences which asked readers to consider a specific sketch were dropped from the later edition. In others, whole paragraphs were reformulated to account for the 'missing' images. This difference is especially relevant considering that researchers frequently quote from the 1889 edition when citing *How the Poor Live*; even if they give 1883 as the original date of the publication. Scholars should be aware that the two editions are fundamentally different not only because Barnard's contribution is missing but also because Sims's earlier text relied heavily on

---

624 See Sims, *My Life*, 136. Dalziel possibly still held partial copyright for Barnard's illustrations and might have sought to boost sales of *Ally Sloper* with the supplement.

625 Sims had teased his readers with possible future revelations: "Some of the terrible sights which we have seen we have too much respect for the readers' feelings to reproduce." Sims, *How the Poor Live* (1883), 42. He claimed that the "history of Horrible London has yet to be written" but that such "work is for stronger hands than mine to do". Ibid., 42–43. Sims being Sims, he proceeded to write the history of *Horrible London* himself only a few months later – possibly in response to the success of the drastic revelations in *The Bitter Cry of Outcast London*. Five articles were published in the liberal London paper the *London Daily News* between 8 November and 7 December 1883 and discussed at length in letters sent to the editors of the *London Daily News,* mentioned in sermons and even in several Welsh newspapers.

626 George R. Sims, "Preface", *How the Poor Live and Horrible London* (London: Chatto & Windus, 1889).

627 Sims, *How the Poor Live* (1883), 29, and Sims, *How the Poor Live* (1889), 45 respectively.

628 Sims, *How the Poor Live* (1883), 61, and Sims, *How the Poor Live* (1889), 104 respectively.

629 One of Barnard's illustration, "An East-End 'Masher'", was used as the frontispiece. It is unclear why the edition did not include Barnard's sketches. The fact that references to the *Pictorial World* were removed suggests issues between the publisher and the owners of the copyright but the higher printing costs for an illustrated work might also have been the cause.

Fig. 14: Frederick Barnard - *The Water Butt*, from George Robert Sims, *How the Poor Live* (1883), Public domain, Staatsbibliothek zu Berlin, BiblioCopy.

those pictures as a means to illustrate and authenticate his words. For example, his remarks on the deficient water supply of overcrowded districts were supported by a small sketch subtitled "The Water Butt".

Sims suggested that the difficulties of maintaining cleanliness in the slums could be appreciated "from the contemplation of this butt, sketched in the back yard of a house containing over ninety people".[630] That the water supply drawn from such a small barrel is wholly inadequate for such a densely populated house is obvious to the reader without further remarks. In the 1889 edition however, that passage was changed to the following:

"The difficulties of attaining that cleanliness which we are told is next to godliness may be imagined from a description of a water-butt which we found in the back-yard of a house containing over ninety people."[631] The "description" Sims speaks of is notably missing. The reader is now asked to trust Sims's words without visual proof instead of forming his own judgement from the display of Barnard's drawing. The dynamic interplay between words, images and *word-images* characteristic of Sims's writing is also necessarily disrupted in the 1889 edition. Consider for example Sims's description of "A 'B' meeting", where parents whose children did not regularly attend school had to explain their absences to the School Board. The 1883 edition includes a sketch by Barnard that Sims was obviously looking at when composing the explanatory text; here Sims's words authenticate the image and imbue it with meaning:

> You will easily recognise the president of the meeting, with the book before him, in which the cases to be heard are fully entered up. [...] The gentlemen standing round the room are the School Board officers of the different divisions in the

---

630 Sims, *How the Poor Live* (1883), 39.

631 Sims, *How the Poor Live* (1889), 64.

district. [...] Somewhere or other in the scene the artist has, I perceive, depicted 'us.' Where, I leave the reader to discover.[632]

Sims and Barnard are shown on the far right of the picture, Sims is facing the scene but Barnard has his back half-turned to hide a sketch-book that he is drawing in with one hand. Sims explains the peculiar pose in the accompanying text:

> We are accepted by the parents who come and go as part and parcel of the 'Inquisition,' and some care is necessary in executing our task, for this class is very great on the rights of property; and more than one energetic dame, if she knew her face was being 'scratched' by an unauthorised interloper, would literally return the compliment.[633]

Here like in several other instances, Barnard apparently took his sketches on the spot without permission of those he chose to depict and he and Sims presented themselves as somehow connected to the School Board.[634] A precaution, as Sims had argued in the first chapter, against violent reactions from their objects of study. Since the 1889 edition did not include the sketch of the 'B' meeting that Sims was describing and explaining in the text, the entire passage had to be amended:

> The president of the meeting sits with the book before him, in which the cases to be heard are fully entered up. [...] Standing round the room are the School Board officers of the different divisions in the district. [...] Somewhere or other in the scene my friend and I stand. We are accepted by the parents who come and go as part and parcel of the 'Inquisition,' and some care is necessary in executing our descriptive task, for this class is very great on the rights of property; and more than one energetic dame, if she knew she was being 'noted' by an unauthorized interloper, would return the compliment with interest.[635]

The difference is small but noteworthy. Instead of showing and explaining the meeting (and their role in it) to the reader in words and image, Sims only describes the make-up of the scene but provides no details as to how it looks. Sims necessarily shifts the paradigm of representation from the visual to the verbal: their task becomes descriptive and, the pun now lost, a woman might object to being *noted* by Sims instead of being *scratched* by Barnard. Compare this to a passage from the first chapter where Sims paints a vivid picture of a little girl in the attic, left alone to care for her sibling. Here Sims's description could stand on its own but in combination with Barnard's sketch of the "Little Sentinel", text and image reinforce and authenticate one another:

> The attic is almost bare; in a broken fireplace are some smouldering embers, a log of wood lies in front like a fender. There is a broken chair trying to steady itself

---

632 Sims, *How the Poor Live* (1883), 20.

633 Ibid.

634 This clearly distinguishes the poor persons depicted in *How the Poor Live* from those making their living on the streets portrayed in Mayhew's *London Labour and the London Poor* and Thomson's *Street Life in London*, who had to pose for the camera when their pictures were being taken. The possibility of a more natural depiction of people in their surroundings was a distinct advantage of sketching over photography as the means of depicting the homes of the poor.

635 Sims, *How the Poor Live* (1889), 30.

Fig. 15: Frederick Barnard - *A "B" Meeting*, from George Robert Sims, *How the Poor Live* (1883), Public domain, Staatsbibliothek zu Berlin, BiblioCopy.

Fig. 16: Frederick Barnard - *The Little Sentinel*, from George Robert Sims, *How the Poor Live* (1883), Public domain, Staatsbibliothek zu Berlin, BiblioCopy.

against a wall black with the dirt of ages. In one corner, on a shelf, is a battered saucepan and a piece of dry bread. On the scrap of mantel still remaining embedded in the wall, is a rag; on a bit of cord hung across the room are more rags – garments of some sort, possibly; a broken flower-pot props open a crazy window-frame, possibly to let the smoke out, or in – looking at the chimney-pots below, it is difficult to say which; and at one side of the room is a sack of Heaven knows what – it is a dirty, filthy sack, greasy and black and evil looking. I cannot guess what was in it if I tried, but what was on it was a little child – a neglected, ragged, grimed, and bare-legged little baby girl of four. There she sat, in the bare squalid room, perched on the sack, erect, motionless, expressionless, on duty. She was 'a little sentinel,' left to guard a baby that lay asleep on the bare boards behind her, its head on its arm, the ragged remains of what had been a shawl flung over its legs.[636]

Paradoxically, Sims's detailed description of every item in the attic – as an observer would register them by looking around the space – highlights the emptiness of a room stripped of anything but the bare necessities. Not surprisingly, the image of the little girl in her destitute situation was frequently referenced in contemporary reviews and has become one of the most emblematic Victorian representations of poor homes. Her image is the frontispiece of Donovan and Rubery's *Anthology of Victorian Investigative Journalism* (2012) – one of several modern anthologies that have included Sims's articles or selections thereof.[637]

Scholarly Responses

Excerpts from *How the Poor Live* have repeatedly been anthologized, most notably in Peter Keating's foundational collection *Into Unknown England, 1866–1913: Selections from the Social Explorers* (1976).[638] More recently, shorter excerpts were included in John Marriott and Masaie Matsumura's monumental multi-volume collection of writings on *The Metropolitan Poor: Semifactual Accounts, 1795–1910* (1999).[639] The series is also cited frequently in urban studies as an important contribution to debates on overcrowding and working-class habitation in the 1880s. Social historians, especially those studying poverty, mostly discuss *How the Poor Live* in conjunction with *The Bitter Cry of Outcast London*, which is considered to have had more of an impact. However, historian Geoff Ginn's assertion that both "have been well-studied and do not

---

636   Sims, *How the Poor Live* (1883), 9.

637   See Donovan and Rubery, *Secret Commissions*, 149–158. Notably, in line with their focus on journalism, the editors reprint a transcript of the first chapter from the *Pictorial World* not from one of the subsequent editions.

638   See Keating, *Into Unknown England*, 65–90. Keating's selections are taken from the 1889 Chatto & Windus edition. He reprints the first chapter in its entirety and includes longer passages from Chapter III ("furnished rooms"), Chapters VI and VII ("pigging with their relations") and Chapter XIII ("legislation wanted not almsgiving").

639   John Marriott and Masaie Matsumura (ed.), *The Metropolitan Poor. Semifactual Accounts, 1795–1910*, vol. 3.: *People of the Abyss, 1885–1910* (London: Pickering & Chatto, 1999), 125–135. The excerpts consist of pp. 1–10 of the 1889 Chatto & Windus edition. The editors also include passages from Sims's *Horrible London, The Black Stain* and *Off the Beaten Track*.

require re-examination" is puzzling.[640] Historian Harold James Dyos only mentions Sims in passing in his survey of secondary sources about "The Slums of Victorian London" and contends:

> *How the Poor Live* and *Horrible London*, somewhat overdramatized though that the volume appears now, stimulated wide interest in the whole question of what should be done about the slums, and was the germ of the idea that presently erupted as *The Bitter Cry of Outcast London*.[641]

Similarly, historian Gertrude Himmelfarb argues that while Sims's articles created "a stir" when they were published, they were "overshadowed four months later by *The Bitter Cry of Outcast London*".[642] Neither of them discuss Barnard's illustrations. The most detailed analysis of *How the Poor Live* remain the passages devoted to it in historian Anthony Wohl's study on housing and social policy in London, *The Eternal Slum* (1977), in which Wohl even reprinted several of Barnard's sketches.[643] He acknowledges the impact of Sims's articles, which "heralded an awakening of press interest in the housing problem" and "struck home as nothing else had".[644] Wohl stresses Sims's "photographic and sensational descriptions", which "marked a new type of popular reform journalism" but posits that unlike *The Bitter Cry*, "Sims's writings did not make a lasting impression upon public opinion".[645] I will disprove both parts of that claim. That the articles *did* make an impression upon public opinion is obvious even from Wohl's own review of press reactions to the series:

> They caused such a stir that the *Daily News* began two regular columns, 'Homes of the London Poor' and 'Evenings with the Poor', besides a regular correspondence page devoted exclusively to housing matters. [...] Other newspapers rushed to join the bandwagon of housing reform, either by giving Sims's articles prominent coverage in their 'From our Contemporaries' or 'Public Opinion of the Day' Columns, or by presenting their own investigations and exposés.[646]

A broader review of press and reader reactions to *How the Poor Live* shows that the *Pictorial World* clearly intended to draw a national audience for the series. During the run of the series in June and July of 1883, ads with the same wording were published – often weekly or even daily – in local and regional papers across the British Isles (including Scotland and Guernsey):

> The Series of Articles *How the Poor Live* by George R. Sims, Illustrated by Frederick Barnard, Now Appearing in the *Pictorial World*, Should be read by all those who

---

640   See Ginn, "Urban Description and Social Reform", 10.

641   Harold James Dyos, "The Slums of Victorian London", *Victorian Studies*, vol. 11, no. 1 (1967): 5–40, here 19.

642   Gertrude Himmelfarb, *Poverty and Compassion: The Moral Imagination of the Late Victorians* (New York: Alfred A. Knopf, 1991), 58–59. It should be noted that Himmelfarb quotes only from the 1889 edition and does not mention Barnard's illustrations at all.

643   Wohl, *Eternal Slum*, 201–205. Most of the arguments were developed in Wohl's earlier essay "*The Bitter Cry of Outcast London*", where *How the Poor Live* is discussed on pp. 202–204.

644   Wohl, *Eternal Slum*, 201.

645   Ibid., 205.

646   Ibid., 201–202.

have at heart the interests of their fellow men, as they show, in a powerful, graphic, and truthful manner, the hardships and privations endured by the London poor.[647]

The sheer number of ads and the broad targeting of regional markets suggest that a claim made after the Pictorial Printing and Publishing Company (which owned the *Pictorial World*) was wound up in late July was not entirely unsubstantiated. A correspondent for the *Liverpool Mercury* had suggested that *How the Poor Live* was a last-ditch effort to save the ailing paper:

> The Pictorial World Company has been wound up, and, after gallant struggle, one of our illustrated journals seems doomed to disappear. […] Latterly the *Pictorial World* has published a number of papers by Mr. George R. Sims, entitled *How the Poor Live*, and illustrated by Mr. Barnard. These ought to have been popular, for both writer and artist were the fittest that could be employed on such work. Nobody knows the poor better than Mr. Sims, and Mr. Barnard has long been famous for his pictures of London life. But apparently this idea came too late to save the company.[648]

That *How the Poor Live* still reached a national audience can be gauged from the numerous letters to the editor which were printed in the *Pictorial World* in response to the articles. The section "Correspondence. To the Editor of the *Pictorial World*" was filled week after week with contributions from readers across the country both from larger centres (e.g., London, Plymouth, Birmingham, Edinburgh) and smaller cities and villages (e.g., Barnstaple, Devon; Loxwood, Sussex), who lauded Sims and Barnard for their efforts and offered their own suggestions to ameliorate the plight of the poor.

That the impression made by *How the Poor Live* on public opinion was "long lasting" can be inferred first from reactions printed in other newspapers and secondly from the numerous magic lantern lectures given on the subject years after the series was first published. In late May and early June of 1883, announcements for *How the Poor Live* – some with quotes from the first chapter – appeared in the larger London papers *Pall Mall Gazette* and *Morning Post* but also in smaller regional papers like the *Royal Cornwall Gazette*, the *Bury and Norwich Post* and the *Framlingham Weekly News* in Suffolk.[649] Excerpts from the first chapter of the series (usually the touching story of the 'little sentinel') were also reprinted in regional English papers like the *Reading Mercury* and even local Welsh newspapers like the *Rhyl Record and Advertiser* and the *North Wales Chronicle*.[650] Following the success of the pamphlet *The Bitter Cry of Outcast London* in October of 1883, George Sims published a series of letters in the *London Daily News* between 8 November and 7 December 1883 and Chatto &

---

647 Similar advertisements appeared between June and July of 1883 in the *Canterbury Journal*; *Kentish Times and Farmers' Gazette*; *Leighton Buzzard Observer and Linslade Gazette*; *Falkirk Herald*, Scotland; *Whitstable Times and Herne Bay Herald*; *Hartlepool Northern Daily Mail*; *Buckingham Advertiser and Free Press*; *Lichfield Mercury*; *Hastings and St Leonards Observer*; *Fife Herald*, Scotland; *Cornishman*; *The Star*, Guernsey.

648 "Our London Correspondence", *Liverpool Mercury* (30 July 1883): 5.

649 *Pall Mall Gazette* (31 May 1883): 16; *Morning Post* (7 June 1883): 6; *Royal Cornwall Gazette* (1 June 1883): 5; *Bury and Norwich Post* (19 June 1883): 8; *Framlingham Weekly News* (2 June 1883): 4.

650 *Reading Mercury* (9 June 1883): 8; *Rhyl Record and Advertiser* (2 June 1883): 4; *North Wales Chronicle* (9 June 1883): 7.

Windus announced their publication of a shilling volume of *How the Poor Live* in early November of the same year. Even if Sims does not explicitly refer to *The Bitter Cry*, he clearly had it in mind when he wrote in the first letter:

> The housing of the poor has long been a smouldering question, dozens of willing hands have sought to fan it into a flame, but hitherto with small results. At the last moment a little pamphlet laid modestly on the dying embers has done what all the bellows-blowing of the Press failed to accomplish, and the smouldering question has become a brightly-burning one.[651]

Sims's letters on *Horrible London* were written in the same authentic style as *How the Poor Live*, the editors of the *London Daily News* assuring their readers that the articles were "full of pain because they are full of truth".[652] They functioned as a sequel of sorts to *How the Poor Live*, Sims again drawing information from his slum visits earlier in the year, and were quoted widely in the daily press.

In February of 1884 a Royal Commission was established to investigate the Housing of the Working Classes, which eventually led to legislative action with the Housing Act of 1885.[653] *The Graphic* suggested that it was the result of the "public interest which was roused last autumn in the condition of the London poor by *The Bitter Cry of Outcast London* which had followed Mr. Sims's *How the Poor Live*".[654] George Sims repeatedly commented on the investigations of the commission in his column for *The Referee* and even appeared as a witness – the only journalist to receive that distinction.[655]

"How the Poor Live" quickly became a catchphrase in discussions of the social question but could also be used as a slogan to attract audiences. In mid-September 1883, several newspapers reported on a hoax perpetrated in Bedford, Bedfordshire, where a man and a woman "of an evidently professional cut" had "placarded the town with bills", arranged for a band and sold tickets for an entertainment entitled *How the Poor Live*, then failed to show up at the venue.[656] And from mid-December to January 1884, a Juvenile Fine Art Exhibition at Portland Hall in London's Regent Street featured not only children's toys and games but also a "Visit of 'Horrible London' to the West End. Illustrating 'How the Poor Live'", which consisted of "children and others from the East-end of

---

651 *London Daily News* (8 November 1883): 5.

652 *London Daily News* (14 November 1883): 4. Still, the full extent of "Horrible London" apparently could not be described: "Ghastly indeed are some of the descriptions Mr. Sims gives in our columns to-day; and he tells us truly that he could not disclose all the truth. One hardly knows which is more shocking, the revelation or the necessary refusal to reveal still further; but the shock in either case is one of which the public seems to have stood sadly in need." Ibid.

653 See Himmelfarb, *Poverty and Compassion*, 65–67, and Wohl, "Bitter Cry", 229–234.

654 *The Graphic* (5 July 1884): 22. For an international contemporary reaction to both texts, see the review article "Eene beweging tot verbetering van arbeiderswoningen in Engeland" by Johannes Beelaerts van Blokland in the Dutch journal *De Economist*, vol. 34, no. 1 (1885): 536–544.

655 See Wohl, "Bitter Cry", 203.

656 *Portsmouth Evening News* (14 September 1883): 4.

London, engaged in their regular occupation"; making match boxes, shirts and trousers.[657]

Authenticating Strategies

Literary historian Peter Keating famously coined the term "social explorers" to refer to the writers involved in the study of poverty and the state of Victorian society in the 19th and early 20th century: "Acting as representatives of upper- or middle-class life, they cast themselves as 'explorers', entering, for the good of society as a whole, a world inhabited by the poor and destitute."[658] Literary historian Tanushree Ghosh further defines the genre as "an assorted mix of parliamentary reports, popular journalism, and fictional pieces in literary periodicals, all tackling the issues of urban poverty and the condition of the lower classes with ostensibly reformist intent".[659] Keating's anthology *Into Unknown England, 1866–1913, Selections from the Social Explorers* (1976) includes excerpts from James Greenwood's *A Night in A Workhouse*, Sims's *How the Poor Live* and Mearns's *The Bitter Cry of Outcast London*. In his introduction Keating identifies a common mindset shared by the "explorers" which manifests itself in calls for political reform, a desire to shine a light on hidden poverty and a suspension of their own moral judgement in favour of representing the 'true' lives of the poor. Their reports were frequently written in the style of trave-logues, their explorations of "Darkest England" paralleling Stanley's discover-ies in "darkest Africa".[660] George Sims expressly refers to such illustrated travel volumes, "eagerly studied by the stay-at-home public, anxious to know some-thing of the world in which they live", as a model for their own "journey with pen and pencil into a region which lies at our own doors".[661] The explorers thus cast themselves as experts on a 'region' and 'people' that had remained hidden to the majority of their middle and upper-class readers:

> Sewers, drains, street cleaning, cesspools, cemeteries, water supply, all occupied more public attention, and were better described and therefore better known than the interior domestic arrangements of the poor. Until the revelations of the early 1880s few writers bothered to take their readers out of the slum streets and into the houses of the working classes.[662]

In his study *The other empire: Metropolis, India and progress in the colonial imagination* (2003), historian John Marriot found "distinct homologies between the dis-cursive appropriation of the poor and of colonial subjects during the long

---

657 Advertisement in the *Morning Post* (15 December 1883): 1. The "special section" devoted to "horrible London" also put on display "three poor widows, with families varying from two to six, making and finishing trousers" and proceeds apparently went to London children's hospitals. See *St. James's Gazette* (18 December 1883): 8.

658 Keating, "Preface", in Keating (ed.), *Into Unknown England*, 9–10, here 9.

659 Ghosh, "Liberal Guilt", 93. See ibid., 94–95 for a succinct overview of scholarly responses to the genre of 'social exploration'.

660 General Booth quoted in Keating, "Introduction", in Keating (ed.), *Into Unknown England*, 11–32, here 14.

661 Sims, *How the Poor Live* (1883), 5.

662 Wohl, "Bitter Cry", 192.

nineteenth century, suggesting that the London poor were an object of imperial and not merely domestic concern".[663] Sociologist Rolf Lindner has similarly pointed out that the social explorers and those exploring the 'unknown' continents of Asia and Africa shared a similar mindset:

> Both are connected by an 'imperial drive', according to Edward Said, to fill in the blind spots on the map. By making accessible the 'black continent' *at home* and locating the 'savages of civilization' – 'its own pygmies', as Salvation Army founder William Booth called the inhabitants of London's impenetrable 'jungle' – this type of social exploration potentially enables the colonization of its subjects.[664]

In *How the Poor Live,* this manifests itself in the use of racialized language to describe the poor and their 'peculiar customs' and in the description of various efforts to civilize "the wild races".[665] When discussing the latter, Sims separates the poor into two distinct groups. On the one hand, those so accustomed to moral decay and filth as to be incorrigible, associated with drunkenness, prostitution and crime. And, on the other hand, those among the poor, who could still be reached through missionary activity or state intervention: young, clean, eager to learn and in Sims's case often female:

> The old people born and bred in filth won't live out of it. If you gave some of the slumites Buckingham Palace they would make it a pigsty in a fortnight. These people are irreclaimable, but they will die out, and the new race can be worked for with hope and with a certainty of success.[666]

As historian Gareth Stedman Jones has pointed out, this marked a shift in attitudes towards poverty, away from the demoralization theories of the 1860s and 1870s, which had focused on pauperism as an "act of will", towards a theory of degeneration, which considered chronic poverty "the result of long exposure to the degenerating conditions of city life", and found that the "ultimate causes of their poverty were neither economic nor moral but biological and ecological […] the product of generations of decaying slum life".[667] In *How the Poor Live,* Sims stressed both the vital importance of educating poor children to better their lives as well as the corrupting influence that the current housing conditions had on the honest poor. Sims frequently played into fears of revolution and contamination to agitate for political reform:

> For very shame England must do something, nay, for self-preservation, which is the most powerful of all human motives. This mighty mob of famished, diseased, and filthy helots is getting dangerous, physically, morally, politically dangerous. The barriers that have kept it back are rotten and giving way, and it may do the State a mischief if it [is] not looked to in time. Its fevers and its filth may spread to the homes of the wealthy; its lawless armies may sally forth and give us a taste of the lesson the mob has tried to teach now and again in Paris, when long years of neglect have done their work.[668]

---

663   Marriott, *Other Empire*, 7.

664   Lindner, *Walks on the Wild Side*, 14. Translated from the German by the author.

665   Sims, *How the Poor Live* (1883), 5.

666   Ibid., 29.

667   Stedman Jones, *Outcast London*, 290 and 287.

The language of social exploration permeates both Sims's characterization of himself and his illustrator Barnard and of the "wild races who inhabit" the "dark continent that is within easy walking distance of the General Post Office".[669] Sims explicitly refers to the familiar genre of travel literature, which was both commercially successful and familiar to his readers. He assures them that the lives of the poor in their midst are just as interesting as "those newly-explored lands which engage the attention of the Royal Geographical Society".[670] As Peter Keating points out, these parallels also invoked the familiar theme of telescopic philanthropy, as authors contrasted "the moral fervour aroused by the plight of the foreign and distant poor with that of the poor at home" to plead for greater state efforts in abating abject poverty.[671] Sims explicitly draws the comparison in the final chapter: "Now, is it too much to ask that in the intervals of civilizing the Zulu and improving the condition of the Egyptian fellah the Government will turn its attention to the poor of London and see if in its wisdom it cannot devise a scheme to remedy this terrible state of things?"[672]

The serial format of *How the Poor Live* meant that each new instalment in the *Pictorial World* had to re-engage the newspaper's readership, which is why the travel metaphor is used repeatedly at the beginning of new chapters. It also becomes evident in Sims's recurrence to the familiar tropes of foreign exploration – dangerous discoveries and threatening natives: "Our knock has alarmed the neighbourhood. Who are we? The police? No. Who are we? Now they recognise one of our number – our guide – with a growl. He and we with him can pass without let or hindrance where it would be dangerous for a policeman to go."[673] A later chapter ironically inverts that trope when Sims and his companion visit an East-End music hall in disguise but are instantly recognized and ridiculed as intruders:

> All this vast audience was purely local. Our advent, though our attire was a special get-up for the occasion, attracted instant attention, and the cry of 'Hottentots' went round. 'Hottentots' is the playful way in this district of designating a stranger, that is to say, a stranger, come from the West.[674]

668 Sims, *How the Poor Live* (1883), 28–29.

669 Ibid., 5. Sims's use of the term "wild races" recalls Henry Mayhew's "wandering tribes" and "nomadic races of England". But where Mayhew believed in a biological foundation for different social stations, Sims saw poverty more as a result of adverse circumstances and even made fun of the popular notion of 'survival of the fittest': "Most chairs are born with four legs, but the chairs one meets with here are a two-legged race – a four-legged chair is a *rara avis*, and when found should be made a note of. The tables, too, are of a type indigenous to the spot. The survival of the fittest does not obtain in these districts in the matter of tables. The most positively unfit are common, very common objects. What has become of the fittest I hesitate to conjecture. Possibly they have run away. I am quite sure that a table with legs would make use of them to escape from such surroundings." Ibid., 14.

670 Ibid., 5.

671 Keating, "Introduction", 19.

672 Sims, *How the Poor Live* (1883), 63.

673 Ibid., 6.

674 Ibid., 52.

Unlike other social explorers like James Greenwood, 'The Amateur Casual', who used disguise as a means to infiltrate and investigate poor spaces, Sims and Barnard usually pretended to be connected with the School Board to investigate the homes of the poor: "We are supposed to be on business connected with the School Board, and we are armed with a password which the worst of these outcasts have grown at last sulkily to acknowledge."[675] That Sims directly referred to the circumstances of their slum visits and frequently acknowledged the difficulties he and Barnard encountered lends additional authenticity to his reports – even if the actual details remain vague. One chapter is devoted to the entertainments of the poor and "accordingly it is a Saturday night we select to take a trip once more through the streets of the unfashionable quarters".[676] Sims proceeds to describe the various amusements they encounter on the streets in "the heart of a thickly-populated district", the food-stalls, target shooting and the public-houses filled to the brim with drinking customers, but when they spot an impromptu gambling stand, "presided over by a villainous-looking Jew", their curious stares are returned in kind:

> What the game was we could not stay long enough to study, for our approach was signalled by scouts, and as we came close to the crowd it dispersed as if by magic, and the gentleman with the board produced from his pocket a quantity of coughdrops, and flung them upon the board, bawling aloud, 'Six a penny, six a penny!' in a manner intended to convince us that this was his occupation. Possibly we were mistaken for plain clothes policemen; at any rate, we were followed and watched for fully a hundred yards.[677]

In this instance the poor refuse to become an object of study, in others Sims stresses the impossibility to faithfully depict in drawings what they witnessed with their own eyes: "The sketch herewith, taken by the light of successive vestas, fails to give the grim horror of that awful staircase. The surroundings, the ruin, the decay, and the dirt, cannot be reproduced."[678] And in a later chapter, he hints at sights too unsettling to describe: "[R]otten floors, oozing walls, broken windows, crazy staircases, tile-less roofs, and in and around the dwelling-place of hundreds of honest citizens the nameless abominations which could only be set forth were we contributing to the *Lancet* instead of the *Pictorial World*."[679] It was a familiar claim and "under the guise of delicacy", it provided "a convenient way to titillate and excite his readers", as Anthony Wohl has pointed out.[680] Literary historian Carol Bernstein calls this trope "the

---

675   Ibid., 6. On the meaning of disguise for the social explorers, see Keating, "Introduction", 17–18.

676   Sims, *How the Poor Live* (1883), 49.

677   Ibid., 52. Casual racism and occasional antisemitism reappear throughout Sims's articles, but as John Marriott points out: "[W]hile Sims's arguments were replete with racist characterizations of 'savage tribes' which commanded the attention of much missionary activity, and references to the 'quaint sayings and peculiar wit of the nigger breed', the metropolitan poor are not thought as a race apart; indeed, the poor are entitled along with the rest of British society to participate in the benefits of empire [...]." Marriott, *Other Empire*, 173.

678   Sims, *How the Poor Live* (1883), 7.

679   Ibid., 29.

680   Wohl, *Eternal Slum*, 203.

convention of the indescribable, through which whatever offends or horrifies may be signified but neither named nor described".[681] Bernstein cautions that this can quickly turn the unspoken into the unspeakable: "But while it may authenticate their claims not to step outside the bounds of civilized discourse, no matter how uncivilized the subject, it may also place that subject beyond the limits of representational language."[682] Throughout *How the Poor Live*, seeing and witnessing (not writing and sketching) are established as the only means to truly comprehend the 'reality' of poverty:

> This short and hurried sketch of life in the Docks is necessarily incomplete. It's one great feature connected with the subject of these articles my readers can see for themselves at any time they like to take a long walk in the very early morning. No one who does not see the vast crowd can appreciate the character and pathetic elements it contains. I cannot write them with my pen, nor can my collaborator draw them with his pencil.[683]

This rhetorical device renders Sims's vivid descriptions of "narrow dirty passages", "squalid tumble-down houses" and "awful staircases" even more effective when he claims to only make the reader see exactly what he has seen for himself: "I do not imagine for one moment that I have seen, or that I am likely to see, the worst phases of the evil which has become one of the burning questions of the hour. But what I have written about I have in every case seen with my own eyes, and in no case have I exaggerated [....]."[684] The act of seeing thus becomes part of the narrative according to media historian Helen Groth:

> This concept of 'making' the reader see the details of actual streets, houses, rooms, and figures through the vivid descriptive force of narrative technique implicitly blurs the ontological distinction between the illusion of the real and the reality it represents. Fiction's illusion of the real is just as, if not more real, than the streets, houses, rooms, and figures it represents precisely because it makes the act of perception an integral part of the narrative sequence.[685]

Sims's own authority as an eyewitness is also established in relation to his illustrator Frederick Barnard, "an artist who has not hitherto studied 'character' on ground where I have had many wanderings".[686] And like Henry Mayhew, who correlated wage statistics and first-hand interviews with workers, Sims supported his claims with quotations from official sources like reports from the sanitary inspector for Whitechapel, Dr Liddle, and direct quotes from the poor. In one chapter, Sims asks his readers to accompany him to a 'B' meeting, "held under the auspices of the School Board, to hear the reasons parents may

---

681 Carol Bernstein, *The Celebration of Scandal: Toward the Sublime in Victorian Urban Fiction* (University Park, Pa.: The Pennsylvania State University Press, 1991), 19.

682 Ibid.

683 Sims, *How the Poor Live* (1883), 60.

684 Ibid., 37.

685 Groth, "Social Kaleidoscope", 94. Similarly, film historian Brian McFarlane observes a tendency in late Victorian novels to put "a stress on showing rather than on telling" and to reduce "the element of authorial intervention in its more overt manifestations". Brian McFarlane, *Novel to Film: An Introduction to the Theory of Adaptation* (Oxford: Clarendon Press, 1996), 4.

686 Sims, *How the Poor Live* (1883), 6.

have to give why they should not be summoned to appear before a magistrate for neglecting to send their children to school".[687] As Sims points out, Frederick Barnard and he himself again pretended to be members of the School Board in order to observe the meeting and sketch the parents and children without their knowledge. To authenticate his description, Sims quotes "a few statistics gleaned from the papers which I turn over on the chairman's desk by his kind permission" and includes long direct quotes from the parents asked to appear before the board, all given in carefully transcribed colloquial speech:

> Here is a lady who very much objects to being summoned.
> 'What bizerness 'as he to summings me,' she says, pointing to the officer, 'just cus my boy ain't bin fur a week? He's 'arsh and harbitury, that's what he is. 'Arsh and harbitury. D'ye think I ain't got anything to do without a-trapesin' down here a-losin' my work. I tell ye what it is –'.[688]

The correspondence published in response to *How the Poor Live* in the *Pictorial World* frequently corroborated Sims's descriptions. In response to the afore-mentioned chapter, one reader, who claimed he was a member of a 'B' Committee of a large town in an agricultural district, offered "my best thanks to Messrs. Sims and Barnard, for their admirable description of the proceed-ings of a 'B' Committee, which I can testify is strictly true to fact, neither 'over-coloured' nor 'exaggerated'".[689] Another means for George Sims to reaffirm the truthfulness of his depictions was to repeatedly renounce the picturesque mode of depicting the poor. Sims cautioned his readers that they should not expect to gain pleasure from reading his articles:

> [I]n a truthful account of *How the Poor Live* there can be but little to attract those who read for pleasure only. Rags – that is to say, the rags of our cold, sunless clime – are never picturesque; squalor and misery can only be made tolerable by the touch of the romancist [sic] – and here I dare not romance.[690]

Even if this truthfulness and the resulting lack of picturesqueness might diminish their appeal:

> The difficulty of getting that element of picturesqueness into these Chapters which is so essential to success with a large class of English readers, becomes more and more apparent as I and my travelling companion explore region after region where the poor are hidden away to live as best they can.[691]

The monotony of the slums, he argued, does not lend itself to pretty pictures (unlike the picturesque poverty of the countryside): "The story of one slum is the story of another, and all are unrelieved by the smallest patch of that colour which lends a charm to pictures of our poorest peasantry."[692] However, the beautiful and picturesque enter the series in that same chapter, when Sims and

---

687 Ibid., 19.

688 Ibid., 21.

689 "Correspondence", *Pictorial World* (7 July 1883): 19.

690 Sims, *How the Poor Live* (1883), 28.

691 Ibid., 29.

692 Ibid.

Barnard describe the clean and well-mannered children who attend a school, "recruited from such homes as we have familiarised you with in previous chapters".[693] Interestingly, the sad stories and touching sketches of the children are used to promote a charity that Sims personally vouches for; "[…] an excellent society, which provides dinners for poor Board School children, has done much to alleviate this painful state of things. A starving body, a famished child: there is no fear of imposture here […]."[694] One pair of children in particular appeals to both the writer and his illustrator: "They are a pretty pair as they toddle out hand in hand, and they form a pleasant picture in this brief sketch of the little scholars who come daily from the garrets and cellars of the slums to get that 'little learning' which in their cases is surely the reverse of a 'dangerous thing'."[695] The dominant mode of depicting poverty in *How the Poor Live* was, however, the authentic which is confirmed by the letters from readers of the *Pictorial World* printed during the run of the series and discussed in the following section.

Modes of Reception

Numerous letters to the editor (typically called 'Correspondence') document reactions to *How the Poor Live* and give some indication of the mode of reception and of how the texts and images of the series were understood by readers.[696] The first two letters appeared together with the fourth chapter of the series on 23 June 1883, although the editor of the *Pictorial World* noted that they were merely "samples of many we have received upon this subject".[697] One writer claimed that he had lived in London for 43 years and "penetrated into many deplorable places", so he could "vouch for the accuracy of your two contributors".[698] Initially, others were less swayed by Sims's articles, as the editor noted: "[T]here are many correspondents who do not hesitate to say that our statements are 'exaggerated', 'over coloured', 'ultra sensational'." But he was quick to dismiss them: "But to all these objectors we say emphatically that the statements made by Mr. Sims and the drawings by Mr. Barnard are strictly true to fact and not in the least exaggerated; the difficulty is to reproduce things as they are."[699] The letters chosen for publication in the following weeks, perhaps not surprisingly, confirmed his claim. Many correspondents testified to the truthfulness of Sims's descriptions, often from their own experiences in

---

693 Ibid., 30.

694 Ibid., 32. It is the only occasion throughout the series that Sims directly recommends a charity, since he is often critical of indistinct almsgiving: "There are in London scores and scores of men and women who live by getting up bogus charities and sham schemes for the relief of the poor." Ibid., 61. This particular charity was probably the *Referee* Children's Dinner Fund which Sims himself had founded together with a Mrs Burgwin from Orange Street School in Southwark in the early 1880s.

695 Ibid., 33.

696 This section focuses on reactions published directly in response to *How the Poor Live* in the *Pictorial World*, for responses in other newspapers, see above.

697 "Correspondence", *Pictorial World* (23 June 1883): 698.

698 Ibid.

699 Ibid.

Fig. 17: Frederick Barnard - *A Pretty Pair*, from George Robert Sims, *How the Poor Live* (1883), Public domain, Staatsbibliothek zu Berlin, BiblioCopy.

London and elsewhere. One who called himself "a worker in Southwark" stated: "Having been for some years associated with the work carried on by the Sisters of St. John the Baptist, in All Hallows, Southwark, I can testify from personal experience to the truthfulness and accuracy of the descriptions given in these Papers."[700] A temperance reformer from Plymouth thanked Sims for his "vivid word-pictures", and explained that "readers who are used to frequent the habitations of their less prosperous fellow-creatures, even in other towns and cities, know well that his accounts are not exaggerated; that they, too often, could find parallel cases in their own experience".[701] A third contributor, who gave his full name as James Stanley Little, wrote that he had "seen much of the misery Mr. Sims so ably describes" and thus "unhesitatingly believe[d] every word of it".[702]

Other readers expressed their strong reactions to the series, which they clearly accepted as authentic, one stating that he was "much shocked by the miseries set forth in your paper", another that he was "astonished and horrified".[703] "An Englishwoman" wrote that the "abuses and misfortunes so ably exposed in your illustrated journal" would surely be read "with mixed feelings of shame and sorrow"; and a C.H.L. stated that Sims's sketches were "much needed, and calculated to arouse popular feeling on the subject", hoping they would "do as much good as some of Dickens's works did in reforming abuses of the nature they refer to".[704] Correspondents also repeatedly praised both Sims and Barnard and the *Pictorial World* for bringing the living conditions of the poor to

---

700   "Correspondence", *Pictorial World* (11 August 1883): 146.

701   Ibid.

702   "Correspondence", *Pictorial World* (30 June 1883): 723.

703   Ibid. and "Correspondence", *Pictorial World* (28 July 1883): 98.

704   Ibid. and "Correspondence", *Pictorial World* (21 July 1883): 74.

public attention and often included their own suggestions and schemes to ameliorate their plight.

Judging from the correspondence published in *The Pictorial World* in response to *How the Poor Live* and from reports in other newspapers, the series also motivated many middle- and upper-class readers to take action directly. Perhaps the most immediate response came from a reader who enclosed 10 shillings with his letter and asked if Sims and Barnard "would kindly leave a shilling in some of the poor dwellings they visit".[705] The first contribution printed in the "Correspondence" section in response to *How the Poor Live* was by a correspondent who called himself Ivan and suggested that a "philanthropic fund" should be started by the journal to "in some measure relieve and humanise these images of God".[706] After other contributors agreed with the sentiment, the *Pictorial World* was quick to announce that the proprietors had "decided to start a Fund for the Relief of the Poor, to be entitled the 'How the Poor Live' Fund", which was established in "answer to numerous requests from Subscribers and the Public generally".[707] Subscribers to the fund were acknowledged weekly in the paper and by the close of the series had contributed more than 38 pounds in total to the fund. However, the *Pictorial World* announced that it "changed hands" on 25 August and the new proprietors decided to discontinue the fund and hand the money to a chartered accountant, "who will deal with it in the manner best calculated to carry out the wishes of the subscribers".[708]

In the final chapter of the series, which appeared in the same issue, George Sims also commented on "the many letters which have appeared in the *Pictorial World*, and which have reached us privately".[709] He welcomed the "very earnest desire among the writers to do something for the people on whose behalf we have appealed to their sympathy", but cautioned: "I have been grievously misunderstood if anything I have said has led to the belief that all Englishmen have to do to help the denizens of the slums and alleys is to put their hands in and pull out a sovereign or a shilling. It is legislation that is wanted, not almsgiving."[710] He urged readers instead to pressure lawmakers for reform and "to raise their voices and give strength to the cry which is going up at last for a rigid and searching inquiry into the conditions under which the Poor of this vast city live".[711] One reader must have taken his words to heart. In December of 1883, the *Manchester Courier* reprinted a letter sent to Prime Minister William

---

705 "Correspondence", *Pictorial World* (30 June 1883): 723.

706 "Correspondence", *Pictorial World* (23 June 1883): 698.

707 *Pictorial World* (7 July 1883): 22.

708 "'How the Poor Live' Fund", *Pictorial World* (25 August 1883): 202.

709 Sims, *How the Poor Live* (1883), 61.

710 Ibid.

711 Ibid., 64.

Gladstone. The unnamed author, who identified himself as a Liberal, quoted directly from *How The Poor Live* and respectfully urged Gladstone to "rouse such indignation as will make a clean sweep of the heartless, grasping oppressors of the poor, whose systematic neglect of their duty has brought about the horrible state of things depicted by Mr. Sims, and render its continuance for ever impossible".[712] And in August of 1884, the same newspaper reported on discussions about various schemes for settlements in the East End of London held at Oxford University and stated: "The treatise of Mr. Sims on *How the Poor Live* even if somewhat theatrically conceived and the clever novel of Mr. Besant entitled *All Sorts and Conditions of Men*, have largely helped to arouse a widespread feeling that it was high time to be up and doing."[713] That a Royal Commission on the Housing of the Working Classes was announced in early March of 1884 and that George Sims was asked to appear as a witness also testifies to the fact that *How the Poor Live* had some influence in the political sphere.

Lantern Slide Series

How the Poor Live was released as a shilling book in December of 1883 and adapted as a magic lantern lecture shortly thereafter. The combination of words and illustrations lent itself to the genre of the illustrated lecture, where pictures were thrown upon a screen by an operator to illustrate a subject explained by a lecturer. George Sims's words and Frederick Barnard's images were also used separately – both for considerations of copyright and to match the demands of individual lecturers, who stressed particular aspects of the series, e.g., the evil of drink or the need for missionary work in London's slums.

Frederick Barnard drew a total of 60 illustrations for *How the Poor Live*, mostly sketches of poor homes and individual 'slum characters' taken on the spot and often without their consent if Sims's descriptions are to be believed: "We didn't get much out of our J.L. Toole except his portrait, and that was taken entirely without his permission, and is herewith presented gratis to our readers."[714] As Sims explains, Barnard's small sketches (less than four inches wide) were often taken under adverse circumstances, with poor lighting and the need to hide the sketch-book from unwilling subjects posing particular challenges.[715] The original sketches were later completed with black ink and Barnard kept at least one (called the "portly gentleman") in his personal book of sketches. The isolated figures before a white background were well-suited for photographic

---

712   *Manchester Courier and Lancashire General Advertiser* (29 December 1883): 5. The paper also published a short reply sent by Gladstone's secretary, who acknowledged that the letter was received, and that Gladstone could "only say that the Government are sensible of the importance of dealing with the difficult questions of the housing of the poor". Ibid.

713   *Manchester Courier and Lancashire General Advertiser* (16 August 1884): 5. The article mentions a speech by Octavia Hill but does not name the leaders of the movement. They could have included Henrietta and Samuel Barnett who went on to establish the Toynbee Hall settlement in Tower Hamlets.

714   Sims, *How the Poor Live* (1883), 38.

715   Ibid., 7 and 20.

Fig. 18: Frederick Barnard - *Mrs. O'Flannigan*, from George Robert Sims, *How the Poor Live* (1883), Public domain, Staatsbibliothek zu Berlin, BiblioCopy.

reproduction and projection and required no colouring – although at least one example of a coloured reproduction survives in my personal collection of lantern slides.[716]

Apart from these smaller sketches, Frederick Barnard also produced several full-page illustrations for *How the Poor Live*. Here, the private spaces of the poor are depicted in quiet scenes of misery set in decrepit interiors peopled only by individuals or small groups ("A Domestic Tragedy", "The Watery Nest"). In contrast, depictions of public spaces show larger groups of people as in the busy street scenes ("Go it, Sal!", "'Ere Y' Are; Three Shots a Penny!") that recall Barnard's well-known 1876 painting *Saturday Night in the East End*.[717] And the disorderly crowds shown drinking in the public house ("A Roaring Trade") and peering in the music hall ("A Critical Audience") even threaten to overflow the boundaries of the bar and balcony that barely manage to contain them.

716 The lantern slide in question is slide number 8, "Mrs O'Flanaghan" (the original drawing was titled "Mrs. O'Flannigan"), and was acquired from a collector's assortment of individual slides – not preserved as part of a set.

717 The original oil painting was lost, a journalist who saw it exhibited described it as follows: "Here we have presented life among the very poor – the poor enjoying themselves in their own way after the week's work is over, and which is not always the right way – and the poor doing their shopping at huckster's stalls and booths, where everything is low priced. […] the whole work is dark, and a great deal of very good drawing and composition may be easily passed without notice." "The Arts Association Exhibition", *Newcastle Courant* (26 September 1879): 6.

Fig. 19: "Mrs. O'Flanaghan" [sic], Slide 8 of OUTCAST LONDON: OR, HOW THE POOR LIVE (York & Son, in or before 1884, 40 slides), Lydia Jakobs Collection.

All of these larger images and many of Barnard's smaller sketches were included in a set of 40 photographic lantern slides called OUTCAST LONDON: OR, HOW THE POOR LIVE produced by the London-based manufacturer York & Son.[718] While the title suggests a relation to Andrew Mearns's pamphlet of the same name, the individual slide titles frequently match the captions of Frederick Barnard's illustrations for *How the Poor Live*. In total, roughly half of the 40 slide titles are identical to those in the captions but they are presented in a different order. Other slide titles can be matched to Sims's description of certain images and only two could not be matched easily to any of Barnard's illustrations.[719] George Sims's text was not mentioned in the catalogue and no

---

718   See *Catalogue of Lantern Slides* (London: York & Son, after 1901), 117.

719   For a list of the individual slides in the set, see the Lucerna record for OUTCAST LONDON (http://lucerna.exeter. ac.uk/set/index.php?id=3002943).

Fig. 20: Frederick Barnard - *A Domestic Tragedy*, from George Robert Sims, *How the Poor Live* (1883),
Public domain, Staatsbibliothek zu Berlin, BiblioCopy.

Fig. 21: Frederick Barnard - *"Ere Y' Are; Three Shots a Penny! Now's Yer Chance!!!"*, from George
Robert Sims, *How the Poor Live* (1883),
Public domain, Staatsbibliothek zu Berlin, BiblioCopy.

Fig. 22: Frederick Barnard - *A Roaring Trade*, from George Robert Sims, *How the Poor Live* (1883), Public domain, Staatsbibliothek zu Berlin, BiblioCopy.

Fig. 23: Frederick Barnard - *A Critical Audience on the Question of "Step-Dancing"*, from George Robert Sims, *How the Poor Live* (1883), Public domain, Staatsbibliothek zu Berlin, BiblioCopy.

accompanying reading was offered for lecturers. The set was listed in catalogues of a number of different retailing firms and organizations who offered it for sale and hire in England (E. G. Wood, UK Band of Hope Union), Northern Ireland (W. Erskine Mayne), the United States of America (McIntosh Stereopticon Company) and the Netherlands (Ivens & Co).[720]

In December of 1883, George Sims gave Captain Evatt Acklom "permission to utilise his work, *How the Poor Live*, as the basis of a lecture", which Acklom intended to "produce during his present country tour, and bring it to London" in May or June of 1884.[721] Acklom was interested in the question of the housing of the poor and contributed to the discussions following the publication of *How the Poor Live*. On 1 December 1883, the *London Daily News* published a letter by Acklom among their correspondence in which he commended George Sims for his "admirable work" that called "attention to the gross neglect of their interests by the State" and outlined his own scheme for model dwellings.[722] In January and February of 1884, Acklom filled large venues in both Liverpool and London for several nights in a row with his lecture, "founded on incidents narrated in George R. Sims's book" and accompanied by "enlarged copies of Mr. F. Barnard's drawings".[723] In Liverpool, Acklom gave his lecture on several evenings during two weeks at the Bijou Opera house and combined it with "several dramatic recitations from various authors".[724] During the lecture Acklom "freely quoted" George Sims's writings which he "interspersed with expressive observations of his own" ranging from his opinions on emigration to the absolute necessity of temperance while a Mr T. W. Hoare exhibited the "pictorial illustrations of wretched life in London", which included the "'appy Dossers'" and "The Crèche".[725] Acklom returned to London in mid-February when papers announced that he would lecture and recite for five nights at the Portland Institute, a West-End club with admission prices between sixpence and two shillings.[726] With his lectures on *How the Poor Live* Acklom deviated markedly from his usual repertoire of dramatic recitals. From remarks he made during one of his performances in Liverpool, it seems clear that Acklom was by no means a political radical but simply intended to educate the public on the hidden misery of the London poor and argue for political reforms:

> He said unhesitatingly that the dens of iniquity, disease, and filth he had described must be cleared off the face of the earth at the cost of the nation and not of the

---

720   See ibid. and *Belfast News-Letter* (30 October 1884): 4 for Erskine Mayne.

721   *Morning Post* (31 December 1883): 2. Tour dates can be found in *The Era* (8 December 1883): 16 although they could not be confirmed.

722   "The London Poor", *London Daily News* (1 December 1883): 6.

723   *Liverpool Mercury* (5 January 1884): 5.

724   "How the Poor Live", *Liverpool Mercury* (8 January 1884): 6.

725   Ibid.

726   See *Morning Post* (18 February 1884): 1, and *Pall Mall Gazette* (9 February 1884): 6. On Sundays, the Portland Institute was apparently open for working men and women free of charge and offered music and books as means of entertainment. See *Lloyd's Weekly Newspaper* (10 February 1884): 10.

parish, for they were not only a danger to the physical and moral well-being of the nation, but a disgrace to Christianity and civilisation.[727]

Other lecture sets which contained photographic reproductions of Frederick Barnard's drawings or referred to George Sims's writings were also released in 1884 and remained in constant circulation on the British Isles (and in New Zealand) throughout the 1880s and 1890s. Newspaper reports refer most frequently to series called either OUTCAST LONDON or HOW THE POOR LIVE, probably the set of 40 slides produced by York & Son. Newspaper reports also frequently mention a set of around 50 slides called HOW THE POOR LIVE IN LONDON. As one report notes, the slides showed "sketches [...] for the most part drawn from real life" and another states that "selections from Sims's writings" were read to illustrate the slides. It is safe to conclude that this set also featured reproductions of Barnard's drawings.[728]

Between April 1884 and May of 1908, over 70 newspaper items either announced a magic lantern event that was to include HOW THE POOR LIVE or reported on a previous event that had featured the series. In several cases organizations like the Band of Hope Union reported on lecture tours with shows in multiple towns.[729] The shows were performed mainly but not exclusively during the lantern season between October and March. They were predominantly given in connection with religious organizations or individuals and frequently took place in small towns in England, Scotland, Wales and on the island of Guernsey.[730] Most reviews mention both a lecturer (usually a Reverend) and an operator by last name and the early reports in particular refer to the apparatus used for projection as "oxy-hydrogen triple lantern", "biunial oxy-hydrogen lantern", "triunial lantern" and even "a pair of powerful oxyhydrogen lanterns", which suggests a sophisticated performance. More often, reports simply state that a lecture was accompanied by "dissolving views" or by "lantern views" or, conversely, that "connective" or "descriptive readings" were given during a "magic lantern entertainment". According to the newspaper reports, the images taken from *How the Poor Live* were the principal or even the only type of lantern slides that were shown at most events, although they were often combined with singing and music or part of religious services. In

---

727 "How the Poor Live", *Liverpool Mercury* (8 January 1884): 6.

728 *Exeter and Plymouth Gazette* (23 February 1886): 2, and *Cheshire Observer* (21 March 1891): 3. Other variations and similar titles probably related to *How the Poor Live* appeared in individual reports on magic lantern events and include "Horrible London; or How the Poor Live", "The homes and haunts of the heavy laden, or the bitter cry of outcast London" and "Darkest London; or how the poor live".

729 Based on the evaluation of repeated search queries with the phrases "how the poor live", "how the poor live" + lantern and "outcast london" in the British Newspaper Archive between July 2014 and January 2016 and in the "Newspaper" section of the Papers Past database of the National Library of New Zealand.

730 Individual events were also reported from large cities like London and Edinburgh and towns like Northampton, Middlesbrough, Exeter and Burnley. This does not necessarily mean that there were fewer lantern shows in large towns but mainly that lantern entertainments were considered more newsworthy in provincial newspapers.

some cases, however, the images were combined with pictures of London sights or landscape slides or followed by recitations or comic slides which would be considered a more typical lantern show programme for the period.

Audience numbers were only rarely given, although most reports refer to crowded rooms and a "large audience" or a "good audience" (only one report expressly refers to attendance as "very small" and that was for a lecture given on New Year's Eve) so it is safe to assume that these lantern entertainments were generally met with great interest. The concrete numbers of attendance given for indoor performances range from 90 mothers invited to a school-room to a veritable crowd of 800 persons gathered in a church, which incidentally were also the two most common types of venues mentioned. The latter event was held in a Baptist Church in Middlesbrough, already a town of more than 50,000 inhabitants at the time, and "about fifty dissolving views" were projected on a "large sheet, each picture being twenty feet diameter, and excellent effects were produced by the powerful lantern" operated by the owner, a Mr Goldston from London.[731] There is no direct reference to George Sims's words in the description of the event but the lecturer, a Reverend W. Whale, spoke at length about local relief efforts for the poor and those out of work, including a Relief Committee which provided regular dinners for children. His statement that not all those living in poverty were drunkards and that "many a sober man had known want this winter" mirrored Sims's own opinion on the relation between alcoholism and poverty.[732] The audience was probably a mixed one of both working people and better-off patrons since the lecturer addressed them directly when he "spoke a hopeful word of good cheer to those who were still out of work or on short time and low wages" but also noted that "individual kindness by the more highly favoured, congregational and social benevolence" helped alleviate the destitution.[733] Also, there was no collection or admission fee for the lecture so the audience was not necessarily expected to be able to give money themselves. This was not always the case, in fact quite frequently the proceeds of lantern shows given by religious organizations were added to their funds or collections were made to contribute to them. One example is the Church Pastoral Aid Society, a home mission society that raised money for the Church of England. Between 1885 and 1895 the society gave multiple lectures on HOW THE POOR LIVE to bolster their funds, which were used for evangelistic work and religious teaching in the East End of London (mainly Spitalfields).[734] Temperance organizations like the Band of Hope Union, the Church of England Temperance Society or the Total Abstinence Society also showed the pictures of OUTCAST LONDON both as a deterrent example of the effects of alcoholism, probably with drawings like *Mrs O'Flannigan* (see Fig.

---

731 *Daily Gazette for Middlesbrough* (22 January 1885): 4.

732 Ibid.

733 Ibid.

734 See "Church Pastoral Aid Society", *Sheffield Daily Telegraph* (30 March 1886): 6.

18) and *A Roaring Trade* (see Fig. 22) that motivated audiences to sign the pledge or to contribute financially to their cause, and as part of healthy entertainments offered to poor children.[735]

A wholly different use of projected images from HOW THE POOR LIVE is described in the *Palace Journal*, the weekly newspaper of the People's Palace, an institution which aimed to provide education and entertainment for East End communities. One article considered the usefulness of the magic lantern "for teaching and pleasing the people" and described a large outdoor projection given in London for the occasion of a visit from the German Emperor and Empress in July of 1891.[736] A Mr Melville of the Polytechnic projected "G.R. Sims's *How the poor live*" on a large screen erected on a moored barge in the River Thames. The images were "interspersed with statistical slides" on the subjects of national poverty and crime and during three hours "some 3,000 persons witnessed the novel display from the Embankment".[737] The Prince of Wales, who accompanied the German dignitaries, had headed the Royal Commission on the Housing of the Working Classes in 1884 and was committed to the issue of housing reform, which might explain why Barnard's images were selected for the experiment (that they are attributed to Sims was likely due to his prominence as a public figure).

While the reception contexts vary, they clearly show that the images from *How the Poor Live* were presented as realistic representations of the lives of the London poor, one report expressly stating that they were "all drawn from life so that their absolute faithfulness might be depended on".[738] The fact that they were frequently used to raise money for various causes like missionary work, temperance activities or local causes like that of a "sick and distressed parishioner" in Newtown, Chester, also testify to that fact.[739]

The *How the Poor Live* series spanned thirteen newspaper articles, all between two and three pages long and each illustrated with three or four drawings by Frederick Barnard, taken on the spot, as George Sims assured his readers. What distinguished *How the Poor Live* from many other works about the London poor and made it a significant stepping stone towards housing legislation were

---

735 Magic lantern lectures and entertainments were used purposefully by many temperance organizations and many had their own apparatuses and stock of slides for hire. Regional branches also had their own equipment for projection. The Seagoe Temperance Association in Northern Ireland reported that they had recently acquired their own magic lanterns for use at their meetings. See "Seagoe Temperance Association", *Sheffield Evening Telegraph* (15 November 1890): 7. And at their annual meeting, the Sussex Band of Hope Union reported on a series of lectures given in various towns in Sussex and also announced the purchase of three sets of slides on "Analyses of Foods and Drinks" available to speakers on application. See "Sussex Band of Hope Union. Annual Meeting at Lewes", *Sussex Agricultural Express* (2 May 1908): 5.

736 "A Magic Lantern Mission at Mile End", *Palace Journal*, vol. 8, no. 198 (28 August 1891): 130.

737 Ibid.

738 "Missionary Meetings", *Alnwick Mercury* (12 October 1889): 8

739 "Christ Church, Newtown", *Cheshire Observer* (3 April 1886): 8.

Sims's forays directly into the homes of the poor made in conjunction with a School Board officer.[740] Sanitary reports and investigative reporting alike had already brought the foul odours, dirty water and unsanitary conditions of slum life in the metropolis to the attention of the public. But the personal stories of the individual men, women and children who lived and worked there led many correspondents to remark how shocked they were by these conditions. Combined with Frederick Barnard's sketches, Sims's reportages presented shocking images of poor and decrepit dwellings and sweated labour combined with a vigorous condemnation of the high rents the poor were expected to pay for unsanitary and unfit housing. Sims described instances of children being left alone to care for their siblings for hours on end ("The little sentinel") and quoted newspaper reports about corpses being left in the family rooms for days because they couldn't afford the funeral.[741] Later chapters focused less on the homes of the poor and more on their livelihood and work, like the efforts of day labourers to secure a day's work at the West India Docks described in Chapter XII.

Sims and Barnard conducted their "explorations" during the day when those not sick or forced to work from their rooms were out looking for work and the School Board officers were looking for children absent from school. In his testimony before the Royal Commission, Sims described his research method as follows: "Did you find much overcrowding in the districts which you visited? – I knew of it; but should not find it so much on account of the hour at which I went, when the children were at school. I used to go and see the children at school, and then go back to the house from which I ascertained they came."[742] From his own charitable work, Sims was familiar in particular with one school in Southwark's Orange Street and he often used children – generally considered both authentic and deserving poor who were undeserving of their fate – to appeal to the sympathies of his readers and express hope that they at least could be "salvaged" through education. Sims also agitated for political reforms to prevent overcrowding and balance rents but his suggestions remained vague. Still, his warnings about a "mighty mob of famished, diseased, and filthy helots" and the suggestion that the honest, working poor and their children were forced to herd with criminals and were bound to be corrupted by them aimed to rouse his fellow Londoners into action.

---

740   Sims had met School Board officer Arthur B. Moss when he gave a lecture about "The Poetical Side of Poverty" at a Radical club in Southwark in 1880. See Sims, *My Life*, 135–136.

741   Sims includes verbatim quotes from a report by the Medical Officer of Health of Whitechapel, a Dr Liddle, about several cases of corpses being kept in one-roomed homes, sometimes for more than two weeks after their deaths. Sims played into upper class fears of contamination as a means to justify his graphic descriptions: "Note the fact that in the first the child has died of scarlet fever, and that tailoring work is going on around it – work which when finished will be carried, in all human probability, with the germs of disease in it to the homes of well-to-do and prosperous people – a class which too frequently objects to be worried with revelations of the miseries of the masses." Sims, *How the Poor Live* (1889), 61.

742   Sims quoted in *First Report of Her Majesty's Commissioners*, 183.

George Sims framed his articles as colourful reports from "Poor Man's Land" through the use of the familiar tropes of social exploration. But he also included official documents and cited reports by sanitary officers to support his claims. The use of direct quotes and carefully observed lower class vernacular lend additional credibility to his writing. Lastly, he proposed to function as an impartial eyewitness, who only censored himself so as not to offend the sensibilities of his readers. Between the first publication in 1883 and the reprint in 1889, the mode of reception notably shifted. The editor of the *Pictorial World* had initially framed the series as authentic reporting, which would inform readers truthfully on *How the Poor Live*:

> I have been favoured with a sight of some of these Papers and from a personal acquaintance with many poverty-stricken districts of London, can say without much fear of contradiction, that his pictures are true reproductions of life as it is to be met with in the slums and alleys and courts of this mighty and magnificent London of ours.[743]

Fittingly, Sims's articles and Barnard's sketches were repeatedly described as shocking revelations and readers called both for legislative action and immediate relief for the poor. Letters to the editor of the *Pictorial World* mostly confirmed what Sims and Barnard reported and many readers expressed sadness and shock at what they read. Some offered money and assistance or brought attention to various schemes to ameliorate the plight of the poor either in London or other large cities. Similarly, when *How the Poor Live* was reprinted in *Ally Sloper's Half-Holiday* in 1887 and 1888, the paper included "appeals for the Ally Sloper Relief Fund" and a review noted that the articles afforded "the reading public generally an opportunity of forming their own opinion on the deplorable state of things which unfortunately exist in our very midst".[744]

An ad for the shilling volume by Chatto & Windus in December 1883 had quoted the *London Daily News* to stress the accuracy of their observations: "Mr. Barnard's sketches appropriately accompany Mr. Sims's descriptions; and, terrible as both are, there is every reason to believe that they are by no means exaggerated."[745] Conversely, by 1889, the same publisher advertised the book edition with praise from *The Scotsman* as "[a] very interesting, and indeed, entertaining book".[746] And a short review in the *Morning Post* noted that "the seamy side of existence in the rookeries of the greatest city in the world is vividly portrayed" and that "the general tone of the tale which the author has to tell is extremely pathetic".[747] The focus had shifted from the content of the piece to its style of description – from revelations on how the poor live to revelations by Mr Sims.

743 W.P., "Notes of the Week", *The Pictorial World* (2 June 1883): 591.

744 *Lincolnshire Chronicle* (25 November 1887): 3.

745 "Chatto & Windus's New Books", *The Athenaeum* (1 December 1883): 691.

746 *Pall Mall Gazette* (21 June 1889): 3.

747 *Morning Post* (8 June 1889): 3.

5.2 Angry Old Man – *In the Workhouse. Christmas Day* (1877)

In the Workhouse. Christmas Day is doubtlessly George Sims's most famous ballad and, according to Joss Marsh and David Francis, "the only Sims ballad which has permanently entered the lexicon of British poetry".[748] In 21 stanzas of eight verses, Sims tells the story of a workhouse inmate who is reminded of his wife's tragic fate during the annual Christmas dinner for the paupers. She starved to death on the previous Christmas Day after she refused to enter the workhouse for fear of being separated from her husband who was denied out-relief by the workhouse guardians.[749] *In the Workhouse. Christmas Day* was first published under that title in *The Referee* on 23 December 1877.[750] It was only the second ballad published under George Sims's pen-name Dagonet in the Radical weekly newspaper. The first, *Told to the Missionary*, had been published two weeks earlier.[751] The ballad was reprinted in newspapers in England and Wales throughout the 1880s, usually as a topical piece in December or January.[752] It was also included with minor amendments in various contemporaneous collections of Sims's poems like *The Dagonet Ballads* (1879), *Ballads and Poems* (1883) and *The Dagonet Reciter* (1888).[753] And in the 20th century, it formed part of anthologies like Arthur Calder-Marshall's edition of Sims's poems *Prepare to Shed Them Now* (1986) and Michael Turner's collection of *Victorian Parlour Poetry* (1992).[754] The earnest pathos of the piece quickly lent itself to both spoken and written parodies which remained popular well into the past century: "Later, its opening line, somewhat inaccurately rendered, became a national catch-phrase and humorous and bawdy versions of the poem

---

748   Marsh and Francis, "Poetry of Poverty", 78.

749   Relief provided to poor persons (especially able-bodied individuals) not living in the workhouse was reduced significantly following the Poor Law reforms of 1834. Proponents of the law claimed that if poor relief was distributed indiscriminately, it rendered recipients permanently dependent on these subsidies, effectively pauperizing them. See Ashforth, "Urban Poor Law", 129. It was also seen as an additional burden on ratepayers. From the 1870s onward, a growing number of poor relief recipients were required to live in workhouses in order to receive food and shelter, while "numbers of out relief fell sharply in the last quarter of the century". Rose, "Disappearing Pauper", 63.

750   Dagonet, "In the Workhouse. Christmas Day", *The Referee* (23 December 1887): 5.

751   Dagonet, "Told to the Missionary", *The Referee* (9 December 1877): 5. The dramatic story told to said missionary by an old coster about his faithful dog who once saved him from drowning in the Thames was later adapted for the magic lantern as TOLD TO THE MISSIONARY (Bamforth, 1889, 4 slides).

752   See, e.g., *Tamworth Herald* (15 January 1881): 8; *Y Genedl Gymreig* (17 January 1883): 3; *North Wales Chronicle* (25 December 1886): 7; *Cornish Telegraph* (29 December 1887): 7; *Sheffield Weekly Telegraph*, no. 1442 (7 December 1889): 776; *Bridport News* (3 January 1890): 8.

753   Apart from some changes in the punctuation, in the third stanza "their bellies" was replaced with "their stomachs" while in the eleventh stanza, "the woman who loved me" was changed to "the woman who'd loved me". Compare Dagonet, "In the Workhouse. Christmas Day", *The Referee* (23 December 1877): 5 with George R. Sims, "In the Workhouse. Christmas Day", *The Dagonet Ballads. Chiefly from the Referee* (London: E.J. Francis, 1879), 8–15. See also George R. Sims, "In the Workhouse. Christmas Day", *Ballads and Poems* (London: J.P. Fuller, 1883), 8–15, and George R. Sims, "In the Workhouse. Christmas Day", *The Dagonet Reciter*, 78–83.

754   Calder-Marshall (ed.), *Prepare to Shed Them Now*, 63–70; Michael R. Turner (ed.), *Victorian Parlour Poetry: An Annotated Anthology* (New York: Dover Publications, 1992), 203–208.

are still in circulation today [...]."[755] Literary historian Peter Keating has called this retranslation of the literary ballad into the oral tradition "a classic example of genuine working-class response to superimposed middle-class sentiment".[756] Sims's *In the Workhouse* combines lyric, epic and dramatic elements, as is typical of the ballad form. The double quatrain (i.e. ballad) stanzas and *abcb edfd* rhyme scheme give the ballad a rhythmic drive towards the finish that is characteristic of Sims's Victorian reinterpretation of the medieval ballad form.[757] In the first five stanzas, a narrative voice introduces the setting and main characters of the ballad including the protagonist, whose subsequent monologue accounts for two thirds of the poem. The initial authorial description of a festive workhouse ("the cold, bare walls are bright / With garlands of green and holly" st. 1, v. 2–4) quickly turns into a condemnation of the visiting guardians and their ladies, who "have come in their furs and wrappers to watch their charges feast / To smile and be condescending" (st. 2, v. 1 + 3–4), which sets the tone for the old pauper's diatribe.[758] With this direct criticism of the ratepayers in an authorial voice, George Sims establishes a distance between these fictional benefactors and his better-off readers (or listeners). According to Arthur Calder-Marshall, this allows for a cathartic experience: "The well-to-do readers, or audience, might not immediately identify themselves with the paupers sitting at their tables. But they dissociated themselves from the 'guardians and their ladies' [...]."[759] To further this alienation, the representatives of the workhouse are not presented as individuals but merely described with the unspecified "they": "I came to the parish, craving / Bread for a starving wife [...] And what do you think they told me / Mocking my awful grief? / That 'the house' was open to us / But they wouldn't give 'out relief'" (st. 11, v. 1–2 + 5–8).

At first, the direct speech of the old pauper's monologue is interrupted by a trenchant description of the reactions from the present gentlefolk – "Then the ladies clutched their husbands / Thinking the man would die / Struck by a bolt, or something / By the outraged One on high" st. 4, v. 4–8) – and the interjections of the workhouse master, who attempts to silence his insolent charge: "'He's drunk!' said the workhouse master, 'Or else he's mad and raves'." (st. 6, v. 3–4) This interplay of action and dialogue can be considered the dramatic element of the ballad, which culminates in the old man's angry

---

755 Longmate, *The Workhouse*, 223–224. They were also popular among English-speaking soldiers during the First and Second World War. See John Brophy, *The Long Trail. Soldiers' Songs and Slang 1914–1918* (Freeport: Books for Libraries Press, 1972), 56, and Brian Murdoch, *Fighting Songs and Warring Words: Popular Lyrics of Two World Wars* (London: Routledge, 1990), 79.

756 Keating, *The Working Classes*, 39.

757 See Marsh and Francis, "Poetry of Poverty", 67–68.

758 These and all subsequent quotations with stanza and verse numbers are taken from the version of *In the Workhouse. Christmas Day* published in *The Referee* (23 December 1877): 5. For easier legibility, verse breaks are indicated by slashes, which replace the commas and full stops of the original text. Exclamation marks and question marks are reproduced as they appear in the original.

759 Calder-Marshall, "Introduction", 37.

outcry: "Keep your hands off me, curse you! / Hear me right out to the end / You came to see how paupers / The season of Christmas spend / You came here to watch us feeding / As they watch the captured beast / Hear why a penniless pauper / Spits on your paltry feast" (st. 8, v. 1–8). In the fourteen stanzas that follow, the protagonist John relates the tragic fate of his wife Nancy who starved alone in their "filthy den" (st. 10, v. 2) as he was twice refused food from the same workhouse that is now offering him a sumptuous Christmas feast. His monologue reaches a climax with the angry condemnation of the workhouse guardians in the penultimate stanza:

> Yes, there, in a land of plenty / Lay a loving woman dead /
> Cruelly starved and murdered / for a loaf of the parish bread /
> At yonder gate, last Christmas / I craved for a human life
> You, who would feed us paupers / *What of my murdered wife!*[760]

How could a pauper speak out in such drastic terms against the welfare system maintaining him, even call its representatives murderers, yet remain a sympathetic character who readers might identify with? To that end, George Sims employed a number of simple yet effective narrative devices. John is depicted as the victim of adverse if unspecified circumstances and did not become poor through any fault of his own. This separates him from those who had supposedly ended up poor through their own immorality or lack of ambition and were therefore considered undeserving of charity or empathy.[761] He bears the hallmarks of a deserving poor character, morally upright and not prone to alcoholism and its adjacent sins: "'Not drunk or mad,' cried the pauper / 'But only a haunted beast'" (st. 6, v. 5–6). He refuses to steal ("And the bakers' shops were open / Tempting a man to thieve / But I clenched my fists together" st. 12, v. 3–5) and in his despair resorts only to wresting food from a stray dog. John is presented as a loving husband, caring for his dying wife ("All through that eve I watched her / Holding her hand in mine / Praying the Lord and weeping" st. 14, v. 1–3), who was once a respected businessman ("For ere the ruin came / I held up my head as a trader / And I bore a spotless name" st. 10, v. 6–8). Until that night, when the situation has become impossible to bear, he had not even sought relief from the parish: "I had never been to the parish / I came to the parish then / I swallowed my pride in coming" (st. 10, v. 3–5). Before these details are revealed, the protagonist is already presented as distinct from the other workhouse inmates in the narrative description. The first stanza introduces them as one uniform group: "For with clean-washed hands and faces / In a long and hungry line / The paupers sit at the table / For this is the hour they dine" (st. 1, v. 4–8). But while the other paupers are quietly eating

---

760 St. 20, v. 1–8. Original emphasis.

761 This distinction between deserving and undeserving poor manifested itself materially in the founding of the Charity Organization Society (C.O.S.) in 1868. The C.O.S. was to function as a "clearing house for all applicants for charitable relief". Rose, "Disappearing Pauper", 63. Charities were supposed to refer applicants for relief to their respective C.O.S. branch which would send a trained visitor to assess the needs of the applicant and his family and refer them to a suitable charity. However, if the applicant was found to be a member of the 'undeserving poor' no private aid was supposed to be distributed and they were to be sent to the workhouse instead.

their dinners ("Oh, the paupers are meek and lowly / With their 'Thank'ee kindly, mum's!'" st. 3, v. 1–2), John is unable to contain his rage and grief which eventually bursts out: "But one of the old men mutters / And pushes his plate aside / 'Great God!' he cries, 'but it chokes me! / For this is the day she died!'" (st. 3, v. 5–8). While they are only concerned with filling their stomachs ("So long as they fill their bellies / What matter it whence it comes" st. 3, v. 3–4), John refuses to eat "the food of villains" (st. 5, v. 7) and accept their condescension and complacency:

> Do you think I will take your bounty / And let you smile and think
> You're doing a noble action / With the parish's meat and drink?
> Where is my wife, you traitors – / The poor old wife you slew?
> Yes, by the God above me / My Nance was killed by you![762]

Neither the despondent, silent paupers nor the condescending, silent benefactors invite the listener's identification, which leaves only the old man. This is reinforced by his use of standard English, a deviation from Sims's ballad formula, which frequently relied on "authentically observed lower-class speech as a deliberate alienating device" and authenticating strategy.[763] In *In the Workhouse*, the protagonist's previous life as a respectable shopkeeper thus not only establishes him as a deserving poor character but also justifies the lack of a dialect or accent.[764] This leads literary historian Jacqueline Bratton to conclude that it is "[t]he only ballad in which the main speaker is given the listener's undivided personal identification".[765] It can also be considered, as Joss Marsh and David Francis have remarked, Sims's "most famous, most angry ballad".[766] Unlike many religious and temperance writings of the time, *In the Workhouse* offers neither religious conversion nor abstinence from alcohol as solutions to the problem of poverty. John's wife Nancy is morally pure (and mostly suffering in silence) but dies a miserable, lonely death in a small garret, her only consolation delirious memories of their home in Devon. This, according to Bratton, is another deviation from Sims's usual narrative pattern:

> His chief narrative device for neutralising the pain and injustice he describes is the importation of a directly religious solution: justice and happiness in Heaven are overtly offered as a redress for suffering on earth, both in order to calm the conscience, and as a reason the sufferers might be expected to accept for not rising up in their own defence.[767]

---

762 St. 9, v. 1–8.

763 Bratton, *Victorian Popular Ballad*, 124.

764 This is referenced indirectly when the protagonists's wife, Nancy, delirious and half-starved starts to ramble in her native Devon accent: "And her lips were parched and parted, and her reason came and went / For she raved of our home in Devon, where our happiest years were spent / And the accents, long forgotten, came back to the tongue once more / For she talked like the country lassie I wooed by the Devon shore." St. 15, v. 5–8 and st. 16, v. 1–4.

765 Bratton, *Victorian Popular Ballad*, 123.

766 Marsh and Francis, "Poetry of Poverty", 74.

767 Bratton, *Victorian Popular Ballad*, 125–126.

There is no mention of heaven in the ballad. On the contrary, John speaks of the "dank, unhallowed graves" (st. 6, v. 2) from which victims of the workhouse and its guardians "cry for vengeance" (st. 6, v. 1).

The Workhouse in Works by George R. Sims

Sims's rendition of the workhouse on Christmas is notably at odds with a concurrent trend in newspaper and magazine coverage that stressed Christian benevolence and private almsgiving at that time of the year, according to historian Michael Rose:

> At Christmas time, attention might be focussed on the workhouse in a rather sticky, sentimental fashion. Local newspapers would report the serving of a Christmas dinner or the erection of a Christmas tree, often paid for by the guardians themselves since poor law forbade such frivolities.[768]

The tone of *In the Workhouse* is unusually harsh compared to George Sims's later ballads, but he continued to raise the spectre of the workhouse in his prose writings and poems. The short sketch, *A Pair of Boots* from his collection of stories about pawnbrokers *Three Brass Balls* (1880) features a similar pair of poor characters with a passive, suffering woman and her devoted husband.[769] Jack, a silverer affected by mercury poisoning, and his wife Nelly who is wholly dependent on him after she was blinded in an accident at the fireworks factory. They are displaced when their overcrowded building is demolished to make room for a model lodging house. Unwilling to go to the workhouse, they struggle to find shelter for the night. Jack pawns his shoes but the nearest lodging house has also been torn down. As he lies down, exhausted from the cold and shivers, Nelly goes looking for help and hits her head. She wakes up, calmed and cared for in a hospital while her husband freezes to death in the ruins. At the end, Nelly is left to tramp from casual ward to casual ward, "[…] a poor sightless, ragged creature who once called the dead man husband. No loving hand leads her footsteps now; the last ray of light has flickered out from the eternal darkness of her life."[770] In the authorial description, the homelessness and death of the protagonists is framed as a direct consequence of political action (The Artisans' Dwellings Act) and not merely blamed on a lack of compassion.[771]

The workhouse also appears frequently in Sims's ballads – in particular those selected for magic lantern slide adaptations. In *The Street Tumblers* (1882) a family of artists making a living in the streets by performing tricks is without

---

768 Rose, "Disappearing Pauper", 66.

769 First published as serialized articles in *The Weekly Dispatch* from February 1880 and published in book form by John P. Fuller by September of that year. See *The Referee* (19 September 1880): 8 for an advertisement by J.P. Fuller for various books by George R. Sims.

770 George R. Sims, *Three Brass Balls* (London: J.P. Fuller, 1880), 156.

771 In May of 1880, George Sims discussed the impact of the Artisans' Dwellings Act at a public lecture in a Radical Club in Whitechapel, which also included a recitation of *In the Workhouse. Christmas Day.*

the means of subsistence after the father injures his leg and cannot perform.[772] They initially choose not to enter a workhouse or seek temporary shelter in a casual ward even as the situation becomes dire. Unable to continue tramping or earn any money, the family is left with no choice but to "go to the workhouse for the sake of a meal and bed" (st. 5, v. 6). Ultimately, the child and husband get better and the mother is taught to appreciate her fate and station after observing the sudden death of a rich woman's child: "Then its eyes looked up so sweetly, like an angel's, into mine / And I thanked the God of Mercy for a blessing so divine / For I had my babe – my darlin' – what matter the workhouse bed?" (st. 13, v. 5–7). The ballad is told entirely in direct speech and from the mother's perspective, who defends their dangerous occupation and itinerant lifestyle ("We're happy we three together as we roam from place to place / We should die pent up in cities, for we come of a gipsy race" st. 2, v. 7–8) to a critical but silent interlocutor. The family of street tumblers are presented as deserving poor characters, willing but unable to work, brought to the workhouse reluctantly and out of sheer necessity. The woman clearly distinguishes her family from the other inmates, an anonymous, threatening group of lazy outcasts: "It's only folks like ourselves, ma'am, as can tell what artists feels / When they're treated like common loafers that tramps and cadges and steals / It seemed to us like a prison, with all them heartless rules" (st. 6, v. 1–3).

In another ballad centred around a woman protagonist, *One Winter Night* (1880), a similar distinction is made in the authorial description between the willing inmates of a casual ward ("the refuse of the town") and those driven there by need ("the wounded in life's battle"):

> Ragged, wretched, worn and weary / Come the casuals, creeping in,
> Where the Parish nightly shelters / Shame and sorrow, sloth and sin;
> Where the wounded in life's battle / Pushed aside and trodden down.
> Share the Poor Law's tender mercy / With the refuse of the town.[773]

One Winter Night tells the story of a poor widow forced to tramp from workhouse to workhouse with her small baby. She is initially characterized as a deserving vagrant, thrust into a helpless situation by the death of her husband ("Rent and ragged are her garments / Pinched and pallid is her face / She is tramping from the workhouse / To her distant native place" st. 8, v. 1–4). This separates her from the ordinary vagrants, who were generally accused of refusing to accept regular work, travelling across the country from casual ward to casual ward instead.[774] After a short rest in a village church, she is caught in a snowstorm and remembers the soothing words of the parson: "When your

---

772 George R. Sims, "The Street Tumblers", *The Lifeboat and Other Poems*, 49–58. On other depictions of child acrobats in Sims's theatrical works and their social context, see Crozier, *Notions of Childhood*, 100–105.

773 St. 1, v. 1–8. George R. Sims, "One Winter Night", *Ballads of Babylon*, 12–18, here 12. The ballad was first published in *The Referee* (18 January 1880): 8.

774 Casual wards provided nightly shelter to itinerant and vagrant paupers, earning them the disparaging nickname "pauper's hotels" in the 1830s. Following the Poor Law reforms of 1834, inmates of casual wards were required to perform several hours of hard work before being released the next day. See Longmate, *The Workhouse*, 232–233.

Fig. 24: Slide 8 of ONE WINTER NIGHT (Bamforth, 1891, 9 slides),
Cinémathèque française Collection, reproduced with permission.

cherished darlings die / Think how warm within God's bosom / In that happy land they lie" (st. 10, v. 2–4). Desperate and freezing, she lets her starving child die in the snow, is found, arrested and sentenced to death but mercifully dies in her cell. The lantern slide adaptation ONE WINTER NIGHT by Bamforth (1891, 9 slides) leans heavily into the picturesque in its illustration of the poor mother and her child in the snow.

Not all of Sims's ballads featuring workhouses end tragically, and death is not always the price characters pay for refusing to live in it. The eponymous ballad of his collection of poems *The Land of Gold* (1888) is one example.[775] When a woman abandoned by her gambling husband falls ill and is unable to pay rent for herself and her two children, the landlord sends for the parish. "The woman must go to the workhouse, and the young 'uns to the schools / Outdoor relief? Oh, nonsense! – besides it's against the rules" (st. 1, v. 1–2) is the verdict. The woman, Elizabeth Roy, has no choice but the young boy and girl hide from the workhouse officer and run away, dreading "their pauper fate" (st. 3, v. 3). They sneak aboard a ship to Australia, the "Land of Gold / Where you pick up the yellow nuggets as big as your hand can hold" (st. 9, v. 5–6). Through happy coincidences, the two are reunited with their father who made an unexpected

---

775   The ballad was first published in *The Referee* (26 December 1886): 5. In 1890 the slide manufacturer Bamforth produced an adaptation for the magic lantern (16 slides).

fortune working in the mines. The three of them are able to return trium-phantly to England and release Elizabeth from the workhouse to live happily ever after: "Peep through the hedge and see / The dear old home and the garden, just as they used to be / And a happy wife and husband, smiling the smile of old / As the children tell the story of their trip to the Land of Gold" (st. 19, v. 5–8).

In these ballads, the workhouse acts both as a backdrop (figurative and later literal) or location for the main story, when the protagonist is or reluctantly becomes a workhouse inmate. It also functions as a symbol of the failed Poor Law; a place of cruel rules and indignities levelled indiscriminately against honest itinerant performers or the innocent families of absent men and against those dubbed "the refuse of the town" by Sims. The provision separating families and old couples upon entry into the workhouse is condemned from a personalized perspective provided by individual poor characters, "a number claiming a name and the right to tragedy", as Joss Marsh and David Francis put it.[776]

The Workhouse in Journalism and Literature

Sims's writings were preceded by famous descriptions of workhouse life in literature and first-hand reports by journalists and social explorers. The first journalist to attempt such an undercover report was James Greenwood, who published his series of articles titled "A Night in a Workhouse" in the *Pall Mall Gazette* in 1866.[777] Greenwood assumed an alias and dressed in ragged clothes in order to be admitted overnight into the casual ward of the Lambeth workhouse. Casual or vagrant wards had been established in London work-houses following the Metropolitan Houseless Poor Act of 1864, which "obliged guardians of the poor to provide food and lodging for all 'destitute wayfarers, wanderers, and foundlings' regardless of their character and place of settlement".[778] These vagrant poor could not (on account of their settle-ment) or did not want to be permanently admitted into the workhouse but, like regular inmates, were required to work for their bed and two meals. They usually left after one or two days, often to find the next workhouse.[779] Green-wood's retelling of his night in the casual ward became an instant sensation: "The series sold by the thousands in penny broadsides for the poor and in shilling pamphlets for the well-to-do [...]."[780] His vivid description of the

776 Marsh and Francis, "Poetry of Poverty", 75.

777 See Koven, *Slumming*, 26–87, and Longmate, *The Workhouse*, 240–241. In 1874 Greenwood, acting as a regular journalist, embarked on another tour of London's workhouses to inquire into the payment of the work. See Schmandt, *Armenhaus und Obdachlosenasyl*, 106.

778 Koven, *Slumming*, 33.

779 See Higginbotham, *The Workhouse Cookbook,* 105. Following *A Night*, a ticketing system controlled by the local police force made sure that each applicant received a permit and separated the deserving poor from the undeserving vagrants. See Koven, *Slumming*, 49.

780 Ibid., 26.

humiliating bathing ritual each inmate was subjected to provided readers with a voyeuristic sensation emblematic of the entire report:

> [I] followed Daddy into another apartment where were ranged three great baths, each one containing a liquid so disgustingly like weak mutton broth that my worst apprehensions crowded back. 'Come on, there's a dry place to stand on up at this end,' said Daddy, kindly. 'Take off your clothes, tie 'em up in your hank'sher, and I'll lock 'em up till the morning.' Accordingly, I took off my coat and waistcoat, and was about to tie them together when Daddy cried, 'That ain't enough, I mean *everything*.' 'Not my shirt, Sir, I suppose?' 'Yes, shirt and all; but there, I'll lend you a shirt,' said Daddy. [...] With a fortitude for which I hope some day to be rewarded, I made up my bundle (boots and all), and the moment Daddy's face was turned away shut my eyes and plunged desperately into the mutton broth.[781]

For regular workhouse inmates, the required bathing and workhouse uniforms which replaced their own clothing upon entry marked the beginning of a life dominated by strict rules and deprivations:

> Families were separated, the men going to one ward, the women to another and children to a third, perhaps to await transfer to a separate institution. They slept in bare dormitories, roused and ordered to bed early. Their day was carefully timetabled, with periods of hard unpleasant work, stone breaking or oakum picking, for those able to perform it. They were fed institutional food at regular hours in carefully weighed and calculated amounts.[782]

For Greenwood, "the amateur casual", the bath was followed by a single restless night. Yet, as historian Seth Koven points out, Greenwood's description of the nightly sights and sounds caused quite a stir. He made suggestive allusions to alleged immorality (i.e. homosexual acts) taking place among the overnight casuals: "According to Greenwood, public authorities were using public money to create the conditions that encouraged the most vicious male members of the metropolitan underclass to engage in sodomy."[783] In that context, it is interesting to note that Gustave Doré's houseless poor forced to take a bath to be admitted into an overnight charity shelter are depicted as surprisingly muscular and their well-formed naked bodies are presented to the viewer in a weirdly homoerotic scenario. A depiction that is completely at odds with Blanchard Jerrold's textual description of the forced bath:

> Young and old are here – houseless, and with babes to carry forth to-morrow into the east wind and the sleet. This story is told by the coughs that cackle like a distant running fire of musketry – all over the establishment. No wonder that many of them dread the bath upon their feeble, feverish limbs: and with chests torn to rags as many of them must be.[784]

His comment reveals the problematic nature of Greenwood's disguise. For him the bath is a matter of shame and disgust, for those actually waiting for admission it might be life-threatening. Greenwood obviously makes no ex-

---

781 [James Greenwood], "A Night in a Workhouse", *Pall Mall Gazette* (12 January 1866): 9–10, here 10.

782 Rose, "Disappearing Pauper", 66.

783 Koven, *Slumming*, 27.

784 Doré and Jerrold, *London*, 143–144.

plicit reference to any sexual acts; however, his vague phrasing and ambiguous hints lend credibility to Koven's theory. As Koven notes, the following passage "must have tested the limits of permissible expression in the daily press of the 1860s": "For several minutes there was such a storm of oaths, threats, and taunts – such a deluge of foul words raged in the room – that I could not help thinking of the fate of Sodom; as, indeed, I did several times during the night."[785] By comparison, George Sims's description of the location in *In the Workhouse. Christmas Day* appears very matter-of-fact. Apart from mentions of Christmas decorations in the first stanza, neither the authorial voice nor the protagonist in his monologue offer any details about the actual workhouse building or life inside it. Perhaps this was superfluous as the mere mention of "the house" was enough to spur readers' imaginations. Only Nancy's reaction to her husband's suggestion to enter the workhouse might hint at the "unspeakable horrors" supposedly taking place there: "Then I told her the house was open / She had heard of the ways of *that* / For her bloodless cheeks went crimson / and up in her rags she sat."[786] Her blushing and her violent bodily reaction (here is a half-starved woman suddenly sitting up) could signal her moral repulsion to the corrupting influence of the workhouse but can just as easily be read as a general repudiation of the humiliating experience and fear of being separated from her long-time companion.

The most famous Victorian description of workhouse life, however, appears in Charles Dickens's novel *Oliver Twist: or the Parish Boy's Progress*, first published in monthly instalments in *Bentley's Miscellany* magazine (1837–1839) and in three volumes (1838) illustrated by George Cruikshank. Dickens paints a bleak picture of the conditions in parish workhouses marked by neglect and violence within the institution and hypocrisy and cynicism of those responsible.[787] Throughout the course of the novel, the protagonist, orphaned at birth and raised in a children's farm and workhouse, is

> [...] neglected, exploited, threatened with being devoured, maligned, threatened with being hanged, drawn, and quartered; he is starved, caned, and flogged before an audience of paupers, solitarily confined in the dark for days, kicked and cursed, sent to work in an undertaker's, fed on animal scraps, taunted, and forced to sleep with coffins.[788]

Dickens was especially critical of the Poor Law Commissioners and the mindset behind the New Poor Law after he had followed the parliamentary discussions as a gallery reporter.[789] The following passage from *Oliver Twist* is

---

785 Koven, *Slumming*, 43, and [Greenwood], "A Night in a Workhouse", *Pall Mall Gazette* (13 January 1866): 10.

786 St. 13, v. 1–4, original emphasis.

787 Richardson argues convincingly that Dickens drew on first-hand observations of the Cleveland Street Workhouse as inspiration even if he himself was never an inmate. See Richardson, *Dickens*, 2–3, 15–16 and 178–179.

788 Ibid., 235.

789 Ibid., 233–234.

his satirical condemnation of the reasoning behind the principle of less eligibility as embodied by the deterrent workhouse:

> The members of this board were very sage, deep, philosophical men; and when they came to turn their attention to the workhouse, they found out at once, what ordinary folks would never have discovered – the poor people liked it! It was a regular place of public entertainment for the poorer classes; a tavern where there was nothing to pay; a public breakfast, dinner, tea, and supper all the year round; a brick and mortar elysium, where it was all play and no work. 'Oho!' said the board, looking very knowing; 'we are the fellows to set this to rights; we'll stop it all, in no time.' So, they established the rule, that all poor people should have the alternative (for they would compel nobody, not they,) of being starved by a gradual process in the house, or by a quick one out of it.[790]

For a later journalistic piece, *A Walk in a Workhouse* (1850), Dickens inspected a London workhouse and to his surprise, "found the pauper children in this workhouse looking robust and well, and apparently the objects of very great care".[791] One inmate, an old pauper, when asked about the quality of life bemoaned only the small amount of bread to go with the tea. Dickens was critical of the fact that old, young, sick, healthy, mentally stable and unstable people were all housed under the same roof. He also emphasized the dull monotony of workhouse life and concluded that poor children attempting to learn a trade or adult inmates who desired "better board and lodging" would be best advised to smash a workhouse window in the hopes of being "promoted" to prison: "[W]e have come to this absurd, this dangerous, this monstrous pass, that the dishonest felon is, in respect of cleanliness, order, diet, and accommodation, better provided for, and taken care of, than the honest pauper."[792] George Sims repeated the idea that criminals were treated better than workhouse inmates more than 30 years later in his "Mustard and Cress" column in *The Referee* after the paper had published the food rations of a London workhouse. Sims sarcastically advised: "There now, if you haven't a roof over your head, and you want to be really comfortable, don't attempt the workhouse; prig a young lady's purse out of one of those nice convenient back pockets, and then you'll go to quod and enjoy yourself."[793]

These and other accounts of workhouse life, corroborated by newspaper reports on various workhouse scandals, created a cultural context in which Sims could assume that John and Nancy's refusal to accept the rules of the workhouse in return for food and shelter would be met with sympathy from his readers, while the inhumane treatment of a deserving poor couple by the guardians would be strongly condemned. The fact that a case such as theirs would have required authorities to grant out-relief and that old couples were allowed joint living quarters (if available) did not undermine the central

---

790 Charles Dickens, *The Adventures of Oliver Twist* (London: Chapman and Hall, 1866), 11.

791 Charles Dickens, "A Walk in a Workhouse", *Household Words*, vol. 1, no. 9 (25 May 1850): 204–207, here 205.

792 Ibid., 205 and 206.

793 Dagonet, "Mustard and Cress", *The Referee* (24 April 1881): 7.

message of the ballad: Here was a system that valued its principles (and the money of ratepayers) more than the lives of innocent and deserving poor people.

Lantern Slide Series IN THE WORKHOUSE *(Bamforth, 1890)*

In the Workhouse. Christmas Day was adapted for the magic lantern by the British lantern slide manufacturer Bamforth of Holmfirth, Yorkshire. Four photographs were registered for copyright in July of 1890 and the full set containing nine slides appeared in catalogues of the UK Band of Hope Union and the Church of England Temperance Society (C.E.T.S) shortly thereafter.[794] The life model set was also distributed by slide retailers and producers Riley Brothers of Bradford as well as Walter Tyler and J. Theobald & Co. of London.[795] IN THE WORKHOUSE was one of six adaptations of George Sims's popular ballads produced by Bamforth in 1890. With four adaptations produced in the previous year and another one (THE ROAD TO HEAVEN) produced before 1888, this early period accounts for half of the 21 Sims adaptations produced by the Holmfirth manufacturer until 1909.[796] The series provides a good example of the production processes and the pictorial conventions of Bamforth's life model slides.[797] Before he began producing lantern slides in his specially outfitted studio in the mid-1880s, James Bamforth ran his own photographic studio in Holmfirth from 1870.[798] In the late 1890s, the company briefly ventured into film-making together with their business partners Riley Brothers of Bradford and in the early 1900s, Bamforth began producing picture postcards as a successful offshoot of their lantern slide business.[799] Several photographs from their first life model set were registered for copyright in September of 1886 and as their annual production increased rapidly by 1902

---

794 See *Complete Catalogue of Lantern Slides, Dissolving Views, Magic Lanterns etc.* (London: UK Band of Hope Union, 1891), Section C, 43, and the list of "new lecture and reading sets for 1890–1" of the Church of England Temperance Society, quoted in William Thomas Stead, "A Magic Lantern Mission", *Review of Reviews*, vol. 2, no. 12 (December 1890): 561–567, here 564–565.

795 See Lucerna record for IN THE WORKHOUSE (http://lucerna.exeter.ac.uk/set/ index.php?id=3000606), and *J. Theobald and Company's Extra Special Illustrated Catalogue*, 144.

796 Several slide series were updated and released as new versions. See Richard Crangle's analysis of the 1908 Bamforth catalogue. Crangle, *Hybrid Texts*, Appendix D, 246–295.

797 The following applies to a lesser extent to the Bamforth song slides which became popular in the 1900 and 1910s. Judging from more than 170 song sets with digital reproductions of slides included on the DVD *The Illustrated Bamforth Slide Catalogue*, compiled by Richard Crangle and Robert MacDonald (London: The Magic Lantern Society, 2009), the number of outdoor scenes appears to grow markedly while characters are more frequently posed towards the camera and not always shown from head to toe. Close-ups of isolated objects and specific body parts referenced in the lyrics (rings, hands, books) appear to be a novel feature.

798 See Crangle, "Zweidimensionales Leben", 34, note 1.

799 See Allan T. Sutherland, "The Yorkshire Pioneers", *Sight and Sound*, vol. 46, no. 1 (1977): 48–51, here 50, and McMillan, "James Bamforth", 12. Bamforth briefly took up film production again in 1914 before abandoning it altogether. On Bamforth's film and postcard activities, see also Richard Brown, "Film and Postcards – Cross Media Symbiosis in Early Bamforth Films", in Vanessa Toulmin and Simon Popple (ed.), *Visual Delights – Two: Exhibition and Reception* (Eastleigh: John Libbey, 2005), 236–252.

Bamforth could credibly claim to be the "Largest producer of Life Model Slides in the World".[800]

James Bamforth had apprenticed with his father, a painter and decorator.[801] Combined with his practical experience as a portrait photographer, this perhaps uniquely qualified him to produce life model slides. He was able to paint the large canvasses that served as backgrounds for the photographs himself (as he was happy to demonstrate to reporters), was familiar with posing live models in a studio setting and knew how to dress a scene using props. These aspects correspond to the three basic elements of Bamforth's life model slide composition identified by Richard Crangle:

> These were: location (the attempt to establish a realistic physical space, either a counterfeit using quasi-theatrical or other scenery, or less often a 'real' location); props (attempting to create or reinforce a physical or social location through the presence of material objects, either by association or by attaching a kind of iconic status to the objects); and characters (almost always human figures, positioned singly or in groups in relation to the location and props to represent social situations).[802]

The pictorial conventions of Bamforth's life model slides were also heavily influenced by James Bamforth's efforts to economize production costs.[803] The entire slide manufacture at Bamforth from the planning of new motifs, the set design, scene-painting and taking of the photographs to the formatting and fitting of the slides for shipping was conducted on site.[804] This has lead Robert McMillan to conclude: "Bamforth's were in fact a highly efficient and competitive business, running as an organised assembly line in which cheapness, speed of response to the market, speed of production and the cutting of costs

---

800   See Vogl-Bienek, *Lichtspiele*, 244, and Alfred Saunders, "Prominent Men in the Lantern World: New Series, No. 1. Mr James Bamforth, of Holmfirth, Yorkshire", *The Optical Magic Lantern Journal*, vol. 13, no. 151 (October 1902): 7–9, here 7.

801   See Vogl-Bienek, *Lichtspiele*, 247–248.

802   Crangle, *Hybrid Texts*, 140.

803   In 1899, James Bamforth claimed that after returning to Holmfirth from an unsuccessful attempt to make it in London, "he set up business on a capital of 8d". Harwood Brierly, "Among Life-Models", *Newcastle Courant* (18 November 1899): 2. He was most probably referring to his original photographic practice, but his thriftiness was also apparent in the way he conducted his slide-making business.

804   The premises and slide production at Holmfirth are described extensively in contemporary portraits of the company in trade journals, see, e.g., Saunders, "Prominent Men", 7–9; Reynolds, "Sentiment to Order", 337–343; "Life Model Studies. No. I – A Peep Behind Some Scenes", *The Photogram* (February 1899): 46–48, and "Life Model Studies. No. II – The Models Themselves", *The Photogram* (February 1899): 76–78. See also Ludwig Vogl-Bienek's exhaustive description of Bamforth's slide manufacture, which also includes letters and interviews with former Bamforth models recorded in the 1960s in *Lichtspiele*, 242–269. Slide production at York & Son, the other major manufacturer of life model slides, appears to have followed similar patterns and is described in detail by David Henry, "York & Son: Part 1", *The New Magic Lantern Journal*, vol. 3, no. 1 (February 1984): 12–17, and "York & Son: Part 2", *The New Magic Lantern Journal*, vol. 3, no. 2 (December 1984): 13–18, as well as Ine van Dooren, *Devices and Desires*, 25–29 with reference to articles that appeared in the trade press and photographic magazines.

were all-important."[805] Most photographs of outdoor scenes were taken inside the studios or on the firms' own grounds and for railway scenes James Bamforth could rely on "the officials at the local station [who] have obliged by putting a train by the platform and allowing a crowd to be posed".[806] The delicate task of colouring the black and white slides, at least according to one article, was conducted "by piece-work at the young worker's own homes in the little town below", which was cheaper than paying regular salaries and maintaining a proper workshop for that purpose on the studio grounds.[807] James Bamforth stated that his painting of the large background canvasses or cloths (10 by 14 or 10 by 16 feet, painted on both sides) for the photo shoots was a cost and time-saving measure: "'In fact I can never see,' he says, 'how there can be any profit made out of the work when backgrounds have to be paid for at the usual price'."[808] The storage and frequent reuse of the painted backgrounds for different slide sets was another means of economizing slide production. For the slide series IN THE WORKHOUSE (Bamforth, 1890, 9 slides) four different backgrounds were used to represent the different locations of the narrative: the workhouse, a London backstreet, the workhouse gate and the poor couple's small garret. In the first four slides, what appears to be a plain background sheet decorated with religious mottoes and greens and holly is used to establish a workhouse interior on Christmas Day that closely follows George Sims's description in the ballad ("the cold, bare walls are bright / With garlands of green and holly" st. 1, v. 2–3).

The paper mottoes were also reused, either to decorate bedroom walls as in NELLIE'S PRAYER (1890, slide 10) and THE LOST CHILD (1890, slide 23), or, adorned with garlands of holly, to signal that a story was set at Christmastime in THE ROAD TO HEAVEN (1887, slides 1 and 7) and THE NEWSBOY'S DEBT (1887, slide 6). The fifth slide of IN THE WORKHOUSE depicts the protagonist alone in front of the workhouse gate, his back facing the camera. The painted background shows one corner of a two-story building surrounded by a metal fence, a single lamp hanging over the entrance. The same painted backdrop, photographed from a slightly different angle and coloured differently, was used to depict workhouse entrances in two other Sims adaptations produced by Bamforth in the same year, THE STREET TUMBLERS (slide 6) and THE LAND OF GOLD (slide 15). An 1819 engraving of the outside of the City of London workhouse depicts a similar multi-story building with parallel rows of rectan-

---

805 McMillan, "James Bamforth", 14. Other cost saving measures taken by James Bamforth not directly related to the visual composition of the slides were the buying of chemicals in bulk and the use of a proper spring to supply the studio's darkrooms and dodge the local water rate. Presumably, this was some time after the Lighting and Water Supply Committee of the Holmfirth Board decided to charge James Bamforth ten shillings a year to supply his "photographic studio in Town Gate" in July of 1886. See "Holmfirth Local Board", *Huddersfield Chronicle* (22 July 1886): 4.

806 Reynolds, "Sentiment to Order", 342.

807 Brierly, "Among Life-Models", 2. Conversely, in his description of the firm's grounds for the *Optical Magic Lantern Journal*, Alfred Saunders referred to "the house, portion of which is set aside for painting slides", so the practice might have changed over time. Saunders, "Prominent Men", 8.

808 Reynolds, "Sentiment to Order", 343, and *The Photogram* (February 1899): 48.

Fig. 25: Slide 1 of IN THE WORKHOUSE (Bamforth, 1890, 9 slides), Philip and Rosemary Banham Collection, reproduced with permission.

Fig. 26: Slide 5 of IN THE WORKHOUSE (Bamforth, 1890, 9 slides), Philip and Rosemary Banham Collection, reproduced with permission.

Fig. 27: *The London Workhouse: view of the street façade*, engraving by Thomas Dale after Robert Blemmel Schnebbelie (1819), Wellcome Collection, Public Domain Mark.

gular windows and a lamp hanging over the front door. Such a building would have been a familiar sight to contemporary audiences and easily recognizable as a workhouse even without the accompanying verses.

The next slide shows the protagonist alone on a snowy street ("Back, through the filthy by-lanes! / Back, through the trampled slush" st. 18, v. 1–2), posed in front of a different painted background, a generic street corner with a narrow passageway at the back. The seamless colouring of foreground and background combined with the perspective drawing on the right side of the canvas is meant to create the illusion of three-dimensional depth. The background was also reused with added details, different colouring and a modified camera perspective for another Sims adaptation produced in 1890 (THE MATRON'S STORY, slides 5 and 9). It is difficult to gauge whether a contemporary audience that only saw the images on a screen and in succession (not as reproductions side

Fig. 28: Slide 6 of IN THE WORKHOUSE (Bamforth, 1890, 9 slides), Philip and Rosemary Banham Collection, reproduced with permission.

by side) would have become aware of the frequent reuse of backgrounds across slide sets and what the effect would have been.[809] But, as Richard Crangle rightly points out, "the repetition of backgrounds, generating in an audience at worst a sense of artificiality leading to a loss of realism, or at best a sense of familiarity enhancing realism, is and was an integral part of the Life Model mode of representation."[810]

The importance of props and accessories for the life model mode of representation (and possibly to mask the frequent reuse of backgrounds) becomes apparent by comparing IN THE WORKHOUSE with yet another Sims adaptation produced by Bamforth in 1890. Slides 7 through 9 were photographed in front of a background sheet that showed a simple back wall with a small window and wooden ceiling panel. Here as in other life model sets, the slanted ceiling functioned as a shorthand to indicate that the inhabitants could only afford to live in a small garret under the roof. The sparse furnishings with only a single chair, a bed and a dresser as well as the bare window and walls likewise signalled the old couple's destitute poverty. A slide for the adaptation of Sims's ballad *Nellie's Prayer* utilized the same painted backdrop and dresser but additional

---

809   See Crangle, *Hybrid Texts*, 142–143.

810   Ibid., 143.

Fig. 29: Slide 5 of THE MATRON'S STORY (Bamforth, 1890, 12 slides),
Ray and Pat Gilbert Collection, reproduced with permission.

furniture and details like a carpet, chair covers, a washstand and pitcher to represent a poor but respectable household.[811] Backgrounds were also frequently repeated within a single slide set; sometimes to signal the return of the narrative to a previously established location, sometimes to mark the passage of time. In at least one variant of slide 9 of IN THE WORKHOUSE, the backdrop and walls were coloured in a much darker shade (a deep blue) compared with the two previous images of the room. This indicated the time that had passed between the events depicted on both slides (as the protagonist returned once more to the workhouse, off-screen) and fit the character's description of the scene: "For there in the silv'ry moonlight / My Nance lay, cold and still" (st. 18, v. 7–8). This supports Richard Crangle's contention that, "[i]n the case of reuse within a slide set there is therefore a distinction (which is not always straightforward) to be drawn between recycling of backgrounds for expediency of production and reuse for narrative or representational effect."[812] Narrative effects could also be achieved by the repetition of slides during projection of a set to present a frame narrative or mark the beginning and end of a flashback.[813]

---

811 According to Richard Crangle, in temperance sets like THE DRINK FIEND (Bamforth, 1893, 15 slides), "the gradual disappearance of furnishings and objects from a room in successive images is used to reinforce the narrative of a decline into drunken poverty". Ibid., 144.

812 Ibid., 142.

Fig. 30: Slide 7 of IN THE WORKHOUSE (Bamforth, 1890, 9 slides),
Philip and Rosemary Banham Collection, reproduced with permission.

Fig. 31: Slide 4 of NELLIE'S PRAYER (Bamforth, 1890, 13 slides),
David Evans Collection, reproduced with permission.

Fig. 32: Slide 9 of IN THE WORKHOUSE (Bamforth, 1890, 9 slides),
Philip and Rosemary Banham Collection, reproduced with permission.

This was the case for IN THE WORKHOUSE where the third slide, showing the protagonist at the workhouse dinner as he begins his wife's story, is repeated as the final projected image, returning the narrative from the image of Nancy's deathbed to John's outburst in the present time and place.

Another factor that was both central to the compositional effect of life model slides and allowed manufacturers to cut expenses, were the live models themselves. Both Bamforth and York & Son frequently used their family members as models or even posed for the photographs themselves.[814] James Bamforth acted as the protagonist for IN THE WORKHOUSE while his wife Martha posed as one of the ladies visiting the paupers' Christmas dinner. According to James Bamforth, a position within the staged scenarios allowed him to direct his models more effectively than he could from behind the camera: "For instance, in the picture called THE MAN HUNT, [another Sims ballad] I took the part of the baker myself. The man who represented the thief was a very poor actor,

813 As George Sims often constructed his ballads around a principal character who relates his or her story to a silent interlocutor, many lantern slide adaptations utilized a framing device where those slides depicting the narrative action in different locations were preceded and followed by two or more slides depicting the story-telling situation in one location. Examples include THE ROAD TO HEAVEN (Bamforth, several versions; York & Son), TOLD TO THE MISSIONARY (Bamforth, 1889, 4 slides), THE MATRON'S STORY (Bamforth, 1890, 12 slides), THE OLD ACTOR'S STORY (Bamforth, 1899, 26 slides) and THE STREET TUMBLERS (Bamforth, 1890, 10 slides).

814 For York & Son, see van Dooren, *Devices and Desires*, 28.

but I gave him a sudden shake and had the photograph taken before he had time to alter the position."[815]

Most of the seven Bamforth children also appeared as models and later took on various roles in the slide production, with Edwin Bamforth acting as managing director of the company responsible for day-to-day business.[816] For any roles the Bamforth family or their employees could not fill, Bamforth recruited local townspeople to pose for the slides instead of hiring professional actors.[817] Apart from being cheaper, this could lend additional authenticity to a character and set if specific roles were filled by their Holmfirth counterparts:

> For example, if a scene in a grocer's shop is needed, the local grocer's aid is invoked both for the loan of articles to stock the dummy shop and also for the services of a shopman. This individual, being amid familiar surroundings, acts as he would at his daily work, and so his pose is entirely free from anything 'stagey' or artificial.[818]

James Bamforth was clearly proud of his ability to adequately direct his amateur models and of what he considered the realistic impression of his life model slides:

> The very personality of his sitters forced him to choose homely stories as his themes, and the very nature of the stories with the unaffected naturalness of the figures in the illustrations has endeared his life-model sets to millions of children and of 'the masses.' These critics are strong realists with no great amount of 'art' prejudice, hence they at once recognise a 'real' policeman, and like him much better than the policeman of the opera stage or the artist's studio.[819]

This verisimilitude was also achieved through the way the models were positioned and the poses they assumed. As Richard Crangle points out, the main characters of a given story often "used versions of melodramatic theatrical gesture conventions (facial, body and especially arm positions indicating emotions and inter-character relationships)".[820] These familiar, exaggerated poses rendered the slides easily legible as in the case of IN THE WORKHOUSE, where the old man's dramatic pose – his head thrown back, his hands covering his eyes – clearly communicates his despair at the sight of his dead wife (see Fig. 32). This was presumably heightened by a reciter's dramatic rendering of the accompanying verses: "I knew on those lips all bloodless / My name had been the last; She'd called for her absent husband / O God! had I but known! / Had called in vain, and in anguish / Had died in that den – *alone*."[821] By contrast, the pictorial composition of the four slides depicting the pauper among a group

---

815 Reynolds, "Sentiment to Order", 341.

816 See Lucerna record for Edwin Bamforth (http://lucerna.exeter.ac.uk/person/index. php?id=6002381), and comments by James Bamforth, quoted in Saunders, "Prominent Men", 9.

817 See Vogl-Bienek, *Lichtspiele*, 257. On the payment of Bamforth's child models, there is anecdotal evidence recorded in oral history interviews conducted in the 1960s. See ibid., 258–259.

818 Reynolds, "Sentiment to Order", 340–341.

819 *The Photogram* (February 1899): 76.

820 Crangle, *Hybrid Texts*, 150.

821 St. 19, v. 3–8, original emphasis.

Fig. 33: Slide 2 of IN THE WORKHOUSE (Bamforth, 1890, 9 slides),
Philip and Rosemary Banham Collection, reproduced with permission.

of workhouse inmates at their Christmas dinner, presided over by the "guardians and their ladies" (st. 2, v. 1), is rather static and avoids overly dramatic poses
(see Fig. 25). This matches Ine van Dooren's observations on the arrangement
of persons in life model slides:

> They are nearly always posed in the foreground, emphasizing a flatness and
> frontality. Positioned alongside one another, or when they do sit or stand behind
> each other it is never in such a way that one character obscures the other from
> view. The action is often centred or at least staged in such a way that it is
> immediately clear where the main focus of attention is.[822]

The dramatic action begins with the old man's outburst in the second slide of
IN THE WORKHOUSE, indicated by his outstretched arms ("But one of the old
men mutters / And pushes his plate aside" st. 3, v. 5–6) and the attention now
paid to him by the characters around him. He occupies the centre space of the
image while two extras hovering on the borders of the frame appear to be about
to walk into the scene. The man on the left side moves further towards the
centre of the image from slide to slide, one arm held out as if to intervene. Such
"deliberately untheatrical" poses of secondary characters or extras, who appeared to be arrested in motion, were common to many Bamforth slides.[823]
The overall effect of this positioning, according to Richard Crangle,

---

822 Van Dooren, *Devices and Desires*, 33.

Fig. 34: Slide 4 of IN THE WORKHOUSE (Bamforth, 1890, 9 slides),
Philip and Rosemary Banham Collection, reproduced with permission.

> [...] appears to have been that of the camera being present at an event which was
> occurring anyway. Characters were arranged to simulate instantaneously-arrested
> stages of everyday movement and situations into which the camera happened to
> have intruded, rather than situations created with only their framing and visual
> status in mind [...].[824]

This effect was also achieved by deliberately posing characters with their backs
turned towards the camera, as in slide 4 of IN THE WORKHOUSE. All the
characters in the foreground are now fully turned to witness the brawl between
the workhouse master and the old pauper. This also serves to highlight the
dramatic action as the characters in the background are equally focused on the
pair. It is interesting to note that the old man is shown raising his arm in two
subsequent slides as if about to strike the workhouse master who fends of his
attack with both hands in the second one. This shifts the dynamics of the
conflict suggested by the verses "I care not a curse for the guardians / And I
won't be dragged away" (st. 7, v. 1–2) and "I'll tell you the rest in a whisper / I
swear I won't shout again / Keep your hands off me, curse you! Hear me right
out to the end" (st. 7, v. 7–8 and st. 8, v. 1–2). It presents the subdued pauper
of the ballad as more aggressive. Here, the need for easily identifiable poses
and effective visual storytelling of the life model genre trumped its claim to
realism: such aggressive behaviour by an inmate towards the workhouse staff

---

823 Crangle, *Hybrid Texts*, 145.

824 Ibid., 146.

would have been heavily sanctioned.[825] In summary, the adaptation of IN THE WORKHOUSE closely follows the textual descriptions of the ballad which is transposed to the magic lantern according to the conventions of the life model slide genre and the production conditions of the Bamforth studio. The staging of the models aims to evoke an everyday situation caught on camera while their exaggerated gestures and poses clearly convey the characters' emotions and motivations. Decorations and props are only sparsely used (as befits the text of the ballad). In line with the realistic decorations, no projection or slide effects are used to illustrate the protagonist's flashback or his wife's delirious memories of their Devon home. A cinematic version of such an effect was however utilized for the film version which will be discussed in the following section.

CHRISTMAS DAY IN THE WORKHOUSE *(George Berthold Samuelson, 1914)*

In autumn of 1914, shortly after the outbreak of the First World War, CHRISTMAS DAY IN THE WORKHOUSE (1,000 ft) was one of the first films produced by the Samuelson Film Manufacturing Company. Directed by George Pearson from a scenario by Harry Engholm it starred resident Samuelson actor Fred Paul. The latter two had already collaborated on an adaptation of Sims's play *The Lights o' London* produced by The Magnet Film Company earlier in the same year. Producer George Berthold ("Bertie") Samuelson had run a profitable film renting company in Birmingham (the Royal Film Agency) and entered film production in late 1913 with the monumental and commercially successful SIXTY YEARS A QUEEN made with co-producer William Barker.[826] The profits allowed Samuelson to start his own production company, for which he recruited Pearson from Pathé and acquired Worton Hall, located in the countryside near London, to serve as the production's studio grounds.[827] Filming in the new glass studio began in July of 1914 with the completion of the Sherlock Holmes story A STUDY IN SCARLET. The Samuelson Company was touted as an All-British effort in the trade press and initially focused on adaptations of notable British authors and topical productions about British war heroes (THE LIFE OF LORD ROBERTS). As George Pearson noted in his autobiography, Samuelson was quick to begin and then postpone film projects that struck his fancy depending on current events.[828] Pearson was in the middle of directing "a tale of boyish heroism" called A SON OF FRANCE starring child actor Gerald Royston, when Samuelson intervened yet again:

---

825   The General Workhouse Regulations of 1842 specified the following punishments for such misbehaviour: "Refractory behaviour also referred to more serious or repeated offenses, including reviling a member of the workhouse staff, assaulting another person, damaging property, being drunk, and acting or writing in an indecent manner. Punishments were more severe, and the workhouse master was empowered to confine paupers for up to 24 hours, and impose a reduction in diet. Serious and more persistent offenders could be prosecuted and magistrates could impose prison sentences of up to 21 days' hard labour." Green, "Pauper Protests", 140–141.

826   See Gabriel Sivan, "George Berthold Samuelson (1889–1947): Britain's Jewish Film Pioneer", *Jewish Historical Studies*, vol. 44 (2012): 201–229, here 205–206.

827   Ibid., 208.

828   See George Pearson, *Flashback: The Autobiography of a British Filmmaker* (London: George Allen & Unwin, 1957), 46.

> We set to work, but halfway through were asked to sandwich in a short film Samuelson had promised the film-renters, *Xmas Day in the Workhouse*, based on a ballad by George R. Sims. Paul played a saddened old inmate who had known better times. We made it in three days, and hoping for the best, took up the threads of the French film again.[829]

The quality of the production apparently did not suffer from this brevity. One reviewer noted "the setting and photography is superb" and especially praised the falling snow effect as "about the best of this description we have seen".[830] Another was impressed by the extras used in the workhouse scenes: "The producer, with a true regard for the fitness of things, has engaged as 'extras' a number of striking types of humanity who lend an effective background to the tragic figure of the leading actor."[831] The film made good use of Worton Hall's varied indoor and outdoor filming locations with scenes photographed in more than six different settings (the workhouse gate, the workhouse door, the workhouse dining hall, the old couple's room, a street corner with a baker's shop, and – in a superimposition – the Devon countryside). Unfortunately, the above is all that Pearson had to say about the filming of CHRISTMAS DAY IN THE WORKHOUSE, but his comment is worth examining in some detail since it hints at some of the peculiarities of the British film market of the 1910s and its production, hiring and exhibition practices.

The first fixed-site cinemas in Britain appeared in 1906 (small storefront venues, converted theatres and penny gaffs). Before that, travelling showpeople and multi-purpose buildings like music halls or theatres had provided the primary exhibition contexts for cinematographic images.[832] The first purpose-built cinemas that could house more than a couple of hundred people were only constructed in 1909.[833] However, this was followed by a veritable "cinema boom" so that by 1914 there were 4,000 cinemas across Britain, which on average were "bigger and more elaborate and luxurious" than their international counterparts.[834] Film exhibitors thus faced strong competition in their districts and attempted to attract regular audiences with bi-weekly programme

---

829 Ibid.

830 "Christmas Day in the Workhouse", *The Cinema News and Property Gazette*, vol. 7, no. 108 (5 November 1914): 56.

831 "The Pick of the Programmes. What We Think of Them", *The Bioscope* (12 November 1914): 665.

832 See Gerben Bakker, *Entertainment Industrialised: The Emergence of the International Film Industry, 1890–1940* (Cambridge etc.: Cambridge University Press, 2008), 175.

833 See ibid., and Nicholas Hiley, "'At the Picture Palace': The British Cinema Audience, 1895–1920", in Christie (ed.), *Audiences*, 25–34, here 31–33.

834 Jon Burrows, *The British Cinema Boom, 1909-1914: A Commercial History* (London: Palgrave Macmillan, 2017), 2. Nicholas Hiley attributes the boom to a "radical shift of investment in the entertainment industry" that was accelerated by the 1909 Cinematograph Act, which tightened the controls on film exhibition but made it easier to obtain licenses to open cinemas if regulations were met. Hiley, "British Cinema Audience", 27. Economic historian Gerben Bakker provides the following numbers for London alone: "By 1911, London counted 94 cinemas, with a total of 55,000 seats, and an average of around 600 seats. This was a huge number, especially when compared with the theatres and music halls, which had already been around freely for over half a century: in the same year London counted 54 theatres and 50 music halls, with 140,000 seats in total." Bakker, *Entertainment Industrialised*, 176.

changes and by obtaining copies of popular films as quickly as possible.[835] Until 1915 Britain did not impose any tariffs on film imports which were traded more or less freely on an open market system that determined the types of films shown in British cinemas.[836] As a commentator for the *Moving Picture World* noted in 1914:

> As Great Britain is wanting in the advantage of a ready and reliable domestic source of supply, it naturally has become an international dumping ground for the film output of the world. Every reel of film made on the face of the earth ultimately is tagged and placed on the bargain counter of this 'free for all' market.[837]

As cinema historian Jon Burrows shows, in 1911 British film production was still "very much a fragmented cottage industry" with the "collective national output of fiction films" falling short of the films released in Britain in that year by Pathé Frères alone.[838] Burrows quotes George Sims who in 1912 bemoaned the prevalence of foreign films in British cinemas:

> You may go night after night to the picture shows and see nothing but American, Italian, or French films. English policemen, English soldiers and sailors, Englishmen and Englishwoman, are conspicuous by their absence, and the dramas and comedies take place in foreign lands.[839]

Jon Burrows shows convincingly that the small number of British films that were longer than 900 ft and thus suitable for feature film status was another reason for the predominance of foreign material in British cinemas. As Burrows explains, "long before multiple-reel films were produced in numbers, it had become common practice to foreground particular films as star attractions on handbills and posters".[840] As a consequence, "the concept of the 'feature attraction' was already widely used in Britain in the years when films rarely exceeded one reel in length".[841] Despite a significant increase in production between 1910 and 1914 (from 400 to 800 fiction films), British filmmakers were far from being able to supply the ever growing number of exhibitors with material.[842] Throughout 1914 the number of British film titles released in Britain averaged less than 20 per cent of the market share.[843] This partially explains why new production companies like Samuelson Film or the Neptune Film Company were promoted specifically as All-British efforts.[844]

---

835 The rise of a large British film hiring industry beginning in late 1907 "allowed exhibitors to temporarily hire films for very short engagements". Burrows, *The British Cinema Boom*, 151.

836 See Kristin Thompson, *Exporting Entertainment: America in the World Film Market, 1907–1934* (London: British Film Institute, 1985), 30.

837 Harold Z. Levine, "An Analysis of the English Market", *The Moving Picture World* (5 September 1914): 1350.

838 Burrows, *The British Cinema Boom*, 169.

839 George Sims quoted in ibid., 153.

840 Ibid., 159.

841 Ibid.

842 See Hiley, "British Cinema Audience", 27.

843 See Burrows, *Legitimate Cinema*, 5.

844 See, e.g., "Samuelson Film Studio Opening", *The Era* (8 July 1914): 18.

The open market system also had a bearing on the relations between film renters and film exhibitors. Before 1911 there were rarely exclusive contracts between theatres and film renters, instead cinema owners selected their features from any of the local renting agents.[845] Renters in turn bought prints from production companies and "distributed them to as many theatres as they could".[846] This, however, quickly led to "saturation bookings" with the same new and popular films showing in several cinemas in one district at the same time, so that audiences were already familiar with new films before they had had sufficiently long runs to pay for themselves.[847] As Jon Burrows points out, excessive competition between film renters lead to a rapid price dropping for cheaper service options (older and used films), in some cases as little as five shillings per reel per week, while prices for the desired first-run movies and star features could rise to as much as 35 pounds per reel in some cases.[848] To counter this, film renters adopted the so-called "exclusive" principle, supplying prints of films they had acquired exclusively and for a limited time to only one cinema in a district.[849] Jon Burrows sums up the advantages of this distribution model:

> [I]t straightforwardly solved the problem of programme duplication at adjacent cinemas. It also protected renters from the excessive competition of the open-market system, and the higher prices paid to secure exclusive distribution rights for films were counterbalanced by higher rental charges, and the tightly circumscribed number of prints released for each exclusive title radically extended their trading lifespan.[850]

By 1914 almost 30 per cent of all footage released in Britain was rented to exhibitors on exclusive terms.[851] There were two distinct types of exclusive films supplied by film agencies. The "special" or "aristocratic" exclusives which were "chiefly defined by their exceptional lengths [upwards of five reels], high production costs and corresponding rental tariffs".[852] And a much larger number of "short" or "ordinary" exclusives that were cheaper and ran shorter

---

845   See Thompson, *Exporting Entertainment*, 29. As Andrew Shail notes, until late 1907 "exhibitors still routinely bought films outright from producers". Shail, "Cinematic Celebrity", 470. As production companies could now sell fewer prints of their films (and that at a standardized rate of four pence per foot), producing films became less lucrative and English manufacturers increasingly favored film renting over film production. See ibid.

846   Thompson, *Exporting Entertainment*, 29.

847   Ibid., 30.

848   Burrows, *The British Cinema Boom*, 157.

849   The first British exclusive film was an adaptation of a recent theatre production of Henry VIII produced by William Barker in February of 1911. Barker sold the hiring rights to only one renter and produced 20 prints so that "cinemas paid a large premium for the exclusive right to screen the film in their district, with the guarantee that local competitors would be temporarily barred from booking it". Ibid., 191. A very similar practice was taking root in Germany at the time, see Martin Loiperdinger, "AFGRUNDEN in Germany: Monopolfilm, Cinemagoing and the Emergence of the Film Star Asta Nielsen, 1910-11", in: Daniel Biltereyst, Richard Maltby and Philippe Meers (ed.): *Cinema, Audiences and Modernity. New Perspectives on European Cinema History* (London, New York: Routledge, 2012), 142–153

850   Burrows, *The British Cinema Boom*, 191.

851   See ibid., 199.

852   Ibid., 192.

(usually between two and four reels), which made them more suitable for the still popular varied theatre programmes and affordable for smaller cinemas.[853] If G.B. Samuelson had indeed promised the CHRISTMAS DAY subject to film renters, George Sims was still a famous name that could be advertised to attract patrons to the theatre. This made it ideally suited for the "short" exclusive distribution model, where prices for prints also decreased after the first weeks but less steeply, making them affordable for smaller cinemas yet still profitable for renters.

CHRISTMAS DAY IN THE WORKHOUSE was distributed exclusively by four different agencies in London and the South (Imperial Film), North Staffordshire (Star Exclusive Film), Northumberland and Durham (B.B. Pictures) and through Samuelson's own Royal Film Agency in the remainder of the British Isles.[854] The Globe Theatre, a purpose-built cinema in Coventry with 1,000 seats, advertised their new varied programme for the half-week beginning on 7 December 1914 with CHRISTMAS DAY IN THE WORKHOUSE appearing right below the headliner as an "exclusive drama".[855] That same week, the equally large Palace Theatre of Pictures and Varieties in Sunderland, a former live theatre building, featured two Samuelson exclusives, CHRISTMAS DAY IN THE WORKHOUSE ("A dramatic reproduction from the poem by Geo R. Sims") and A SON OF FRANCE ("A thrilling incident in the Great European War") and promoted them both with the slogan "to be seen only at the palace".[856] In its second week the film was being shown in the large King's Hall in Stourbridge, West Midlands, a converted cinema that offered seating for 1,500, and at the Cardiff Cinema, a concert hall with a 2,000-seat capacity.[857] By Christmas of 1914, now in its third week, CHRISTMAS DAY IN THE WORKHOUSE was showing at Wood's Picture Palace, a 200-seat ballroom on the first floor of the town hall building in Bilston, Wolverhampton.[858] But even well into 1915, film exhibitors in purpose-built cinemas like the White Hall Cinema in Derby and the Palace Picture Playhouse in Cheltenham and in multi-purpose venues like the Church Institute in Burnley (home to Messrs Andrews' Kinema) still prominently featured the film in their advertisements and touted it as "from the famous poem by George R. Sims" and as "G.R. Sim's [sic] powerful story".[859] Apart from Sims's popular appeal, CHRISTMAS DAY IN THE WORKHOUSE also

---

853 See ibid., 193–194.

854 See advertisement by Samuelson Film Company in the *Cinema News and Property Gazette*, vol. 7, no. 111 (26 November 1914): 67.

855 See for example advertisement in *Midland Daily Telegraph / Coventry Evening Telegraph* (8 December 1914): 1. This and all subsequent information about the cinema buildings and seating capacities cited from Cinema Treasures (www.cinematreasures.org).

856 *Sunderland Daily Echo and Shipping Gazette* (7 December 1914): 1.

857 "The Provinces. Stourbridge", *The Stage* (17 December 1914): 8, and *Western Mail* (12 December 1914): 6.

858 "The Provinces. Bilston", *The Stage* (24 December 1914): 4.

859 *Derby Daily Telegraph* (26 December 1914): 1, and *Burnley News* (16 January 1915): 1. See also advertisement in *Cheltenham Looker-On* (26 December 1914): 1.

held an additional seasonal value as a Christmas film. Christmas films were an established part of seasonal cinema programming while the holiday itself was an increasingly popular film subject. Christmas, with its "religious elements and magical figures", offered various possibilities for filmic attractions and transformations whereas familiar narratives of charity and almsgiving appealed to middle-class audiences.[860]

Adaptation and Recitation

Upon the release of CHRISTMAS DAY IN THE WORKHOUSE, reviewers for trade magazines remarked on the difficulty of adequately representing poetry in the silent film medium. The *Kinematograph and Lantern Weekly* lauded Samuelson's effort but was critical of the principle:

> The poem is well-compressed into the picture, which though like its subject, unrelievedly mournful, should have a topical value during the coming weeks. We hope, however, that the practice of filming popular poems, which is now enjoying a mild vogue, will not be carried too far. It is almost impossible to convey the meaning of the pictures without flashing the verses on the screen alternatively with them, and we fancy that the great mass of the public have now been educated out of this rather elementary form of entertainment.[861]

Although there were experiments with synchronized recitations – sometimes aided by mechanical sound systems – and specialized film lecturers or able theatre managers who explained the events as they unfolded on the screen, the majority of British cinemas were not equipped to present spoken words by 1914.[862] In addition, any live recitation to accompany the film would have required a skilled reciter to stretch the text of a 7-minute poem recital in order to fit the images of a 14-minute film and to match their words with the lip movements of the main actor.[863] On the question of cinematic adaptations of poetry, *The Bioscope* thus similarly cautioned: "There are more difficulties than appear upon the surface when it is desired that a popular poem should be translated into moving pictures. The producer is, indeed, faced with a task of by no means a light order in the matter of sub-titles alone," but found that in this case, "the lines are well and aptly inserted without becoming in any way tedious."[864] Less than half of the poem's 168 verses (76 in total) were presented in eighteen intertitles, while 92 lines were dropped, presumably to speed the

---

860 Mark Connelly, *Christmas: A Social History* (London and New York: I.B. Tauris, 1999), 159.

861 "A Mixed Program. At A Composite Trade Show", *Kinematograph and Lantern Weekly*, vol. 16, no. 393 (5 November 1914): 55.

862 Nicholas Hiley shows that due to the rapid growth of cinemas, the demand for film lecturers quickly outgrew the supply. See Hiley, "British Cinema Audience", 26–27.

863 These average times match those of modern reenactments of IN THE WORKHOUSE (Bamforth, 1890, 9 slides) and CHRISTMAS DAY IN THE WORKHOUSE (G.B. Samuelson, 1914) on the DVD *Screening the Poor* 1888-1914 (Munich: Edition Filmmuseum, 2011). They assume a film screening steadily at sixteen frames per second and a relatively continuous recitation to accompany the projected lantern images. Historically, this was not necessarily the case. As Nicholas Hiley points out managers of small cinemas in particular, "were tempted to accelerate the projection of long films to increase audience turnover". Hiley, "British Cinema Audiences", 30.

864 "The Pick of the Programmes. What We Think of Them", *The Bioscope* (12 November 1914): 665.

Fig. 35: Superimposition CHRISTMAS DAY IN THE WORKHOUSE (G. B. Samuelson, 1914),
DVD: *Lichtspiele und Soziale Frage / Screening the Poor 1888-1914*
(Munich: Edition Filmmuseum, 2011), reproduced with permission.

action along and because the poem was familiar enough to be understood
without them. Intertitles generally showed a single stanza of four verses but
occasionally only two or as many as eight verses were flashed on the screen
between individual scenes. This alternating between written words and moving images in a way reversed the familiar representational mode of recitations
accompanied by lantern slides, where a continuous verbal narration was
illustrated by mostly unmoving images on a screen.

Media historian Caroline Braun is right to point out that CHRISTMAS DAY IN
THE WORKHOUSE "stands in the *oral narrative tradition* of the magic lantern" and
that "the individual scenes' main function is to illustrate and not to narrate the
story – similar to the function of lantern slides".[865] This is true for the various
scenes illustrating the pauper's tragic story and where Bamforth's IN THE
WORKHOUSE had condensed the visual narration, the Samuelson film ex-
pounds the incidents of the ballad. The film shows John returning to the
workhouse gate twice only to be driven away forcefully, taking a loaf of bread
from a baker's window only to return it remorsefully seconds later and actually
fighting a mongrel in the street for a loaf of bread. Braun has shown how the
film emulated "familiar representational techniques and narrative patterns" of
life model slides, while the actors' "standardised interpretations of emotions
with overacted gestures of fear, dismay, anger, grief" followed familiar theatrical conventions.[866] The former is particularly apparent in a short scene in the
old couple's garret, when a vision of their former home in Devon materializes

865   Braun, "Early Christmas Films", 105.

866   See ibid., 103 and 108.

to a feverish Nancy. The effect is realized as a superimposition of a smaller circular image onto the dark space of the door in the upper-left corner of the frame in the familiar style of magic lantern dream sequences.[867] Several contemporaneous reviewers remarked on the faithfulness of the adaptation to Sims's ballad, one noting, "In all respects it has been faithfully rendered and gives us a vivid impression of this tragedy of pauperdom", while another claimed, "The poem admirably lends itself to the film, and it is very closely followed throughout the picture".[868] This is true for most of the filmic action. The ending, however, materially changes the tone of the original ballad. The dramatic climax of the film is prepared by the words "At yonder gate, last Christmas / I craved for a human life / You, who would feed us paupers / *What of my murdered wife!*" (st. 20, v. 4–8), shown as the last intertitle before John fights a dog for bread and returns home – only to find his wife already dead. For the resolution of John's flashback director George Pearson adopted a genuinely filmic device. After the image of John mourning the dead Nancy in their home is dissolved into that of John surrounded by the other workhouse inmates and the guardians, all characters in the frame appear to pause for one moment before breaking into movement to mark the return to the present time and setting; the workhouse on Christmas Day. After uttering the words "what of my murdered wife" John collapses on the floor, is found dead and quickly covered with a fur coat and flowers before the screen fades to black. Compared to the ending of the ballad, John's death assures that the story of the film is self-contained and offers a narrative resolution for the audience that could almost be considered a happy ending. As the reviews stated, "Finally, overcome by his memories and his woes, the pauper himself collapses on the floor, his spirit joining her he had loved so well", and, "His sufferings were told and at an end. He had joined the wife he loved so well".[869] In contrast, a dramatic recitation of the original poem ended with an angry and bitter old man – very much alive – who denied the workhouse guardians and thus the audience an easy return to their own complacency in the final stanza: "There, get ye gone to your dinners / Don't mind me in the least / Think of the happy paupers / Eating your Christmas feast / And when you recount their blessings / In your smug parochial way / Say what you did for me, too / Only last Christmas Day."[870]

---

867   It is interesting to note that the Bamforth adaptation IN THE WORKHOUSE (1890) did not use a superimposition or any other projected effect to realise either the protagonist's flashback or his wife's fever dream. This foregrounded the claim to realism of the images and the central narrative instead. Other Sims adaptations by Bamforth produced in the same year like NELLIE'S PRAYER or THE LAND OF GOLD make use of this device to depict dreams and visions respectively.

868   "A Mixed Program. At A Composite Trade Show", *Kinematograph and Lantern Weekly*, vol. 16, no. 393 (5 November 1914): 55, and "Christmas Day in the Workhouse", *Cinema News and Property Gazette*, vol. 7, no. 108 (5 November 5 1914): 56.

869   Ibid.

870   St. 21, v. 1–8.

Recitation, Elocution and Authenticity

George Sims repeatedly insisted that his ballads were never "put forward" as poetry but rather meant to be recited, indeed performed.[871] Public performances thus situate them within the long oral and communal tradition of medieval folk ballads.[872] As Joss Marsh and David Francis state: "Sims's ballads spoke directly to that oral tradition, in its new Victorian manifestation – recitation. Thus *Ostler Joe* scandalised America in 1886 not when it was read but when it was recited."[873] The variety of reception contexts that Sims's *In the Workhouse. Christmas Day* was read and recited in between 1877 and 1914 is both a testament to the popularity of the ballad and the ubiquity of recitation in Victorian culture.[874] It was performed by amateurs and professional reciters alike, recited during village concerts and elocutionary competitions, read aloud by clergymen and trade unionists, formed part of music hall acts and illustrated lectures, where recitations were accompanied by magic lantern slides and finally in 1914, it was adapted for the cinema screen. In this section, I will focus on recitations given in two distinct types of exhibition contexts that run in parallel throughout the late Victorian period and mark two sides of the spectrum between authentic and picturesque depictions of poverty. First on recitations or readings of *In the Workhouse. Christmas Day* given in political contexts surrounding discussions of the social question. Second on dramatic recitations given by professional reciters in entertainment contexts and as elocutionary exercises for amateurs.

George Sims's ballad could be read as political commentary in dramatic form as it showed the drastic consequences of current poor law legislation for a clearly deserving poor couple. Sims's pointed criticism of the current practice of out-relief thus lent itself to political agitation. In 1880 the Reverend Arthur Mursell, a nonconformist and travelling lecturer, read the ballad in its entirety as part of an address delivered to working men and women in the Birmingham Music Hall. Mursell argued for the need of reforming poor relief, as "it would appear to stand in need of some amendment amongst the poor, if the story which I am about to recite to you in rhyme be a true picture, or anything near

---

871   See Sims, *My Life*, 182. Fittingly, one ballad, *The Street Tumblers*, was published with the headline "Poem for Recitation" in the monthly review magazine *The Theatre* (January 1882): 36–38.

872   Jacqueline Bratton is careful to point out that the audiences for these 'modern' ballads were not necessarily familiar with the traditional ballads: "The great urban communities of the nineteenth century did not know them; but these were not a people without a culture, and the habit of singing and of verse did not die out with the old songs. The remnants of the old ballads were submerged, and subsumed, in a new upsurge of poetry and song which expresses the feeling and is the creation of the Victorian people." Bratton, *Victorian Popular Ballad*, 3.

873   Marsh and Francis, "Poetry of Poverty", 75.

874   As literary historian Peter Kirkpatrick points out, "The great influence of elocutionary practices throughout the nineteenth century on public entertainments such as lectures, recitals and music hall, in conjunction with an ever-expanding market for ballads and topical verse in newspapers, made the speaking of poetry very popular indeed." Peter Kirkpatrick, "Hunting the Wild Reciter: Elocution and the Art of Recitation", in Joy Damousi and Desley Deacon (ed.), *Talking and Listening in the Age of Modernity: Essays on the History of Sound* (Canberra: The Australian National University Press, 2007), 59–71, here 60.

it".[875] There is ample evidence that George Sims originally intended *In the Workhouse* as a political ballad meant to agitate against the injustices of the New Poor Law. It was first published in *The Referee*, a weekly paper that frequently combined coverage of sports and theatre events with topical commentary on politics and social issues like Christian charity or the living conditions inside London workhouses. Published weekly on Sundays and priced at one penny, the Radical paper clearly aimed for a broad readership, although contemporary critic Edward Salmon hesitated to call it a bona fide "working-man's paper": "*The Referee* cannot properly be called a working-man's paper, though many artisans and shop assistants look forward to its perusal on Sunday morning as regularly as they look forward to their breakfast."[876] In his autobiography George Sims referred to his political persuasion at the time as "still 'a bit of a Radical,' as the phrase went", who "accepted invitations to lecture on Sunday evenings at certain Radical clubs and for certain Radical societies".[877] One of these invitations was for a public lecture at the Tower Hamlets Radical Club in London in May of 1880, where Sims mused on "The Poetical Side of Poverty" and recited two of his own ballads, *Billy's Rose* and *In the Workhouse. Christmas Day*. According to one newspaper report, Sims mainly discussed politics relaying "the origin of the poor laws, and their effects at the present time" as well as the detrimental effects of the 1875 Artisans' Dwellings Act.[878] One audience member, turned newspaper columnist ten years later, remembered that "Mr. Sims, who only expected to meet a small and select party of members, found himself face to face with an excited crowd of enthusiasts, who accorded him a greeting more befitting a political hero than humble poet".[879] In such a context, a recitation of a story about the effects of the New Poor Law on an old couple told in a pauper's own words could certainly have been perceived as authentic.

George Sims was not the only reciter of *In the Workhouse. Christmas Day* with a political agenda. In fact, one of the first people to recite the ballad publicly (at least according to his own remembrances) was the trade unionist and labour representative Frederick Rogers:

> The simple vigour and picturesque description of the *Dagonet Ballads* made them immensely popular on the platforms of workmen's clubs, and I was probably one of the first to recite *Christmas Day in the Workhouse*, since I committed it to memory

---

875 Arthur Mursell, *Hard Lines. An Address Delivered in the Birmingham Music Hall, on Sunday, February 8ᵗʰ 1880* (Manchester, London: John Heywood, 1880), 74.

876 Edward Salmon, "What the Working Classes Read", *The Nineteenth Century: A Monthly Review*, vol. 20, no. 113 (July 1886): 108–117, here 111–112.

877 Sims, *My Life*, 135.

878 "Poverty", *Surrey Mirror* (15 May 1880): 5.

879 He was, however, less than impressed by Sims's abilities as a lecturer: "The fervour of the reception seemed to stagger 'Dagonet,' and although he succeeded in reciting (with the assistance of a prompter) two of his own pieces [...] with considerable effect, yet the lecture itself, which was a very brief affair, was somewhat a failure. This was, I believe, the first, last, and only occasion on which Mr. Sims publicly trod the boards." Philharmonic, "Musical Notes", *Western Times* (29 December 1890): 3.

and recited it at the Dublin Castle Club, in East London, within a week of its appearance in the *Referee*.[880]

Rogers, a bookbinder, newspaper contributor and "an outstanding example of a working-class autodidact", campaigned tirelessly for old-age pensions which were finally introduced in 1909. As Rogers noted, he believed that Sims's poem "had its influence in moulding and educating public opinion" on the matter.[881] Rogers also remembered encountering old and destitute poor persons who refused to enter the workhouse in the hopes of legislation that would spare them the humiliation, thus lending credibility to Sims's ballad: "Old men and women, 'poor human ruins tottering o'er the grave,' came to me, 'willing to starve a little longer rather than go into the workhouse' if I could tell them that Pensions would come next year."[882] Another example shows how the poem was directly connected with political agitation. On 10 December 1894 the *Bristol Mercury* printed a short notice about a Socialist meeting held on the previous evening at the local Shepherd's Hall.[883] The mixed programme included several Socialist and labour songs (*The Red Flag, Hail Dawn of Liberty*), musical performances and a recitation of Sims's poem followed by a lecture and discussion on old age pensions. Since *In the Workhouse. Christmas Day* was the only piece of poetry chosen for recitation it was obviously interpreted as supporting their cause. By the 1890s, *In the Workhouse. Christmas Day* had been adapted for the magic lantern and had now fully entered the political arena. While it was often used to campaign for old age pensions and against the cruelties of the workhouse, recitations in political contexts also offered opportunities for critics to refute the events of the poem. When the poem was recited at a Radical club in Leamington Spa, Warwickshire, one of the guardians of a nearby workhouse "pooh poohed the sentiments expressed therein" and was quick to assure the audience that "[s]uch things as described in the ballad may not happen at Warwick as long as he was guardian".[884] Around Christmas, newspapers routinely reported on the festive celebrations at their local workhouses. And even in 1910, more than 30 years after the ballad was first published, an account of "Christmas Day in the Workhouse" by "an inmate of

---

880 Frederick Rogers, *Labour, Life and Literature. Some Memories of Sixty Years* (London: Smith, Elder & Co, 1913), 137. Rogers also gave a lecture at that same club in October of 1882 on George Sims "as a public teacher", recorded in detail by *The Barnsbury Bohemian*, "A Sunday Night Lecture at a Working-Men's Club", *Islington Gazette* (31 October 1882): 2. It is notable that according to the report, Rogers praised Sims's *The Social Kaleidoscope* as "absolute facts, names and places altered, to be sure, but perfectly true as to the instance", and allowed that Sims "hates shams, and on every fitting occasion showed a loyalty to truth". By contrast, in his autobiography Rogers denied that Sims possessed "any knowledge of working-class life". While he saw "a foundation of truth in his most extreme utterances", Rogers admitted that, "it was not the truth so much as the denunciations that appealed to us in the 'seventies". Rogers, *Labour, Life and Literature*, 138. His perception of the verisimilitude of the piece had apparently changed over time.

881 David Rubinstein, "Rogers, Frederick (1846–1915)", *Oxford Dictionary of National Biography* (Oxford: Oxford University Press, 2004), (http://www.oxforddnb.com/view/article/37909).

882 Rogers, *Labour, Life and Literature*, 252–253.

883 "Socialist Meeting", *Bristol Mercury* (10 December 1894): 7.

884 O.P.Q., "Local Jottings", *Leamington Spa Courier* (22 January 1887): 3.

the infirmary" of the Hastings Workhouse still referenced Sims's poem and assured readers of the *Hastings and St Leonards Observer* that it "does not convey any idea of what transpires in any particular Workhouse, much less does it do so in regard to the Union infirmary in our own town".[885] The relevant question, however, is not whether Sims's description of an old man's Christmas Day in a workhouse matched the experiences of actual workhouse inmates, but why the poem enjoyed such unusual longevity and at the same time was repeatedly denounced as "a mischievous attempt to set the paupers against their betters" and as complete fiction.[886] Clearly, in specific exhibition contexts it could be perceived not necessarily as factual but nonetheless as *authentic*. In these contexts, the contents of the ballad and the question of its verisimilitude were of primary importance. From the 1880s and well into the 1910s, there was another type of exhibition context that favoured delivery above all else: public elocution and dramatic recitals.

Elocution refers to a practice of public speaking, taught in schools and by specialist teachers, described in manuals and subject to strong regulation. It was on the one hand essentially a gentrifying pursuit, "designed to recuperate the vitality of the spoken word from rural and rough working-class contexts by regulating and refining its 'performative excess' through principles, science, systematic study, standards of taste and criticism".[887] On the other hand, "the recitation of verse was seen as a useful skill for 'raising' and standardising pronunciation and thus, supposedly, helping to overcome social division".[888] The memorization and recitation of prose and verse thus formed part of the English school curriculum from the last quarter of the 19th century.[889] Young men and women displayed their skills by reciting during concerts or in elocutionary competitions. In February of 1889, the *Hampshire Telegraph* described in some detail the "annual gold medal championship competition in elocution" held in Landport (Portsmouth) by the Young Men's Christian Association.[890] The selections included no less than three ballads by George Sims (one, *The Road to Heaven*, even recited twice) with a Miss Amy Ham victorious among the "five lady competitors" with her recitation of *In the Workhouse. Christmas Day*. The judge, a professor of elocution, specified the hallmarks of a prize-worthy recitation. The variation of hand movements and voice inflection but decidedly not the audience response to the recited piece:

> In the course of his criticisms, the adjudicator condemned the exceedingly monotonous movement of the hands of most of the competitors, and also the monotony of their voices. He recognised the difficulty which had been created by

---

885 "Christmas Day in the Workhouse", *Hastings and St. Leonards Observer* (31 December 1910): 4.

886 Sims, *My Life*, 181.

887 Dwight Conquergood quoted in Kirkpatrick, "Wild Reciter", 60.

888 Ibid., 61.

889 See Catherine Robson, "Standing on the Burning Deck: Poetry, Performance, History", *PMLA / Publications of the Modern Language Association of America*, vol. 120, no. 1 (January 2005): 148–162, here 153.

890 "Elocutionary Competition", *Hampshire Telegraph and Sussex Chronicle* (16 February 1889): 5.

the selection of pieces, and held that no prize should be awarded to the reciter because he or she happened to have chosen a piece which pleased the audience.[891]

Dramatic recitations, sometimes illustrated with magic lantern slides, frequently formed part of varied concert programmes, religious evenings and temperance entertainments which combined the spoken verses with instrumental music and songs. On these occasions, amateur and professional reciters alike could rely on a familiar formula described by literary historian Jacqueline Bratton:

> The ingredients were a strong voice, and a magic lantern: the performer stood in strong spot-light or in dramatic silhouette, and a series of slides depicting scenes in the ballad were thrown on the wall or screen behind, while the artist delivered the ballad with all the dramatic gesturing and vocal acrobatics at his or her command.[892]

These events also allowed genteel audiences to indulge in emotional responses to the sentiment and pathos displayed on the stage and sometimes prompted them to donate to charitable causes. In October 1879 the *Musical World* reported on a "drawing-room entertainment" held on behalf of the Merchant Seamen's Orphan Asylum. The musical performances by amateurs were interspersed with "recitals at the hands of Mr H. Dacres Smith and Mr Arthur Wieland, the latter declaiming, with emphatic pathos, those powerful lyrics by Dagonet, *Christmas Day in the Workhouse*".[893]

On the stages of music and concert halls across the country, professional reciters (whether reading authors, stage actors or learned elocutionists) combined spoken poetry with recitations of prose works by both canonical and popular writers, sometimes combined with character sketches:[894] "Middle-class audiences who wouldn't dream of joining the throng 'Down at the Old Bull and Bush' could hear sensational, pathetic or comic verses performed in the parlour or concert hall."[895] Take for example the music hall act of a Miss Bertie Brandon, male impersonator. Miss Brandon started her career in London in the early 1880s and began touring the country's music halls and Palaces of Varieties (including engagements in Aberdeen, Glasgow and Swansea) with her male impersonation and recitations as a "serio comic". Her talents were repeatedly advertised in the theatrical newspaper *The Era* with reference to successful past engagements as "impersonator of male characters" and "versatile artist", who gave songs, sketches, recitations and danced in music halls all over the country in the 1880s and 1890s. In October of 1886 she appeared at the Gravesend Palace of Varieties as "a clever male impersonator, whose reciting of G.R. Sims's *Christmas Day in the Workhouse* brings down the

---

891   Ibid.

892   Bratton, *Victorian Popular Ballad*, 107.

893   "Merchant Seamen's Orphan Asylum", *Musical World*, vol. 57, no. 42 (18 October 1879): 664.

894   Kirkpatrick, "Wild Reciter", 59.

895   Ibid., 65.

house".[896] Tucked in between "a very amusing sketch" and an eccentric (male) dancer, I think it is safe to say that Miss Brandon's recitation of Sims's words did not necessarily seem "true to life" for her audience. On another occasion Miss Brandon, who dressed to thoroughly look like the characters she adopted, was presented with a silver bracelet "at the Star Music Hall, Liverpool, in recognition of her pathetic and artistic rendering of G.R. Sims's poem *Ostler Joe*".[897] Other performers specialized in recitations of Sims's works, with one J.W. Martin advertising in *The Era* and *The Stage* as a "New Dagonet Reciter", who "Looks like Sims, studies him, recites him, realises him".[898]

By 1914 when the film adaptation CHRISTMAS DAY IN THE WORKHOUSE was released, George Sims's ballad was still familiar to audiences from a variety of reception contexts but the 'events' of the poem were becoming less resonant. With the introduction of Old Age Pensions by the Liberal government in 1909 and a rudimentary system of unemployment and health insurance introduced under the National Insurance Act of 1911, workhouses (now referred to as poor law institutions) had lost much of their terror.[899] Social historian Mark Connelly notes: "As the question of poverty and ways in which to tackle it subtly changed during the Edwardian and Georgian period, film-makers could look back and turn the Victorian schemes into entertainment."[900] A reviewer for the *Kinematograph and Lantern Weekly* praised "the splendidly photographed scenes, which bring out in a realistic fashion the harshness of workhouse 'relief,' now largely mitigated".[901] But felt pressed to add: "'Dagonet' wrote this poem more than twenty [recte: thirty] years ago, when the 'Union' was only a less terrible fate than the gaol, and the regulations governing outdoor relief were callous and cruel to a degree."[902] Sims's radical (and, yes, sentimental) condemnation of Victorian poor relief had now been turned into "an ideal Christmas picture" suitable for "all patrons who enjoy a spell of

896   *The Era* (2 October 1886): 16.

897   "Presentation", *The* Era (14 April 1888): 16.

898   *The Era* (19 April 1890): 18, and *The Stage* (25 April 1890): 18.

899   See Brundage, *English Poor Laws*, 141–143. Brundage estimates that the combined effect of both measures lowered the number of recipients of poor relief (paupers) by almost 20 per cent between 1910 and 1913 with "both indoor and outdoor pauperism" in sharp decline after the outbreak of the First World War. However, all persons who had been on poor relief (apart from medical services) were initially exempt from receiving pensions, and from 1911 those who entered the workhouse remained ineligible for financial subsidies. See ibid., 142.

900   Connelly, *Christmas: A Social History*, 159.

901   "A Mixed Program. At A Composite Trade Show", *Kinematograph and Lantern Weekly*, vol. 16, no. 393 (5 November 1914): 55.

902   Ibid. From the 1870s, poor law guardians were increasingly discouraged from providing out-relief – even to deserving cases and even in times of growing unemployment – by the likes of the Poor Law Inspector for East London. See Longmate, *The Workhouse*, 257. By the late 1890s, aged poor persons in particular were treated much less harshly, the Conservative President of the Local Government Board affirming that "elderly people 'should not be urged to enter the workhouse at all'" and urging Boards of Guardians that "out-relief should be adequate to support an applicant". Ibid., 271.

lachrymation".[903] As Mark Connelly points out: "The poem [...] though designed to pull on the heart strings, also had a stinging message. By 1914 the sentimental side was clearly the most important."[904] By that time, George Sims himself had likewise abandoned his Radical tendencies and focused instead on *The Bitter Cry of the Middle Class* (1906) in a series of articles for *The Tribune* and argued that Socialism was in opposition to the fundamental principles of human nature in a pamphlet for the Anti-Socialist Union (1909).[905]

5.3 Death as Salvation – *The Road to Heaven* (1882)

The Road to Heaven was first published on Christmas Eve of 1882 in *The Referee*, the day of publication thus matched the setting for the dramatic incidents of the ballad.[906] Like *In the Workhouse. Christmas Day* it confronted readers with the sufferings of the poor and homeless on a day that celebrated the family and the home. The marriage of Queen Victoria to the German Prince Albert in 1840 had reinvigorated the Christian holiday in England: "The Prince introduced into England such long-established German customs as Christmas presents and Christmas trees, a process encouraged by *A Christmas Carol*, in 1843, and Christmas soon became everywhere a sacred rite."[907] Christmas was also a time to remember the plight of the poor and donate to charitable causes, even to visit workhouses at the annual dinner for the inmates. And throughout the 19th century it became a time to publish seasonal literature that emphasized middle-class values and the importance of Christian charity.[908] The commercial success of annuals published in December in the 1820s and 1830s, "conspicuous markers of status that could be displayed year-round as table books", continued with beautiful bound editions of serialized depictions of the poor in the 1870s.[909] Both Gustave Doré and Blanchard Jerrold's lavishly illustrated *London. A Pilgrimage* (1872) and the photographically illustrated *Street Life in London* (1877) by John Thomson and Adolphe Smith were advertised and sold as Christmas gift books from as early as November.

---

903 "Christmas Day in the Workhouse", *Cinema News and Property Gazette*, vol. 7, no. 108 (5 November 1914): 56, and "The Pick of the Programmes. What We Think of Them", *The Bioscope* (12 November 1914): 665.

904 Connelly, *Christmas: A Social History*, 160.

905 George R. Sims, *Socialism and Human Nature*, Anti-Socialist Tracts, no. 3 (London: Anti-Socialist Union Publication Department, 1909).

906 Dagonet, "The Road to Heaven. By Dagonet", *The Referee* (24 December 1882): 7.

907 Longmate, *The Workhouse*, 222.

908 See Tara Moore, "Starvation in Victorian Christmas Fiction", *Victorian Literature and Culture*, vol. 36, no. 2 (2008): 489–505, here 489. This type of seasonal programming centered around the Christian holiday also extended to other popular media like the theatre with its Christmas pantomimes, magic lantern performances and Christmas films at the cinema.

909 Ibid.

The Road to Heaven, *The Dagonet Ballads and Authenticity*

The Road to Heaven was the fourth Dagonet ballad published in *The Referee* in 1882. In the following years Sims reduced the number of ballads printed in the Sunday newspaper, eventually submitting only a single ballad per year in time for the Christmas week issue. Accordingly, there are various references to Christmas in *The Road to Heaven*. The hospital ward is decorated with "mistletoe green and holly, in honour of Christmas Day".[910] The unnamed narrator who finds the two homeless boys huddling from "a biting Christmas frost" (st. 5, v. 1) and notices them by way of a Christmas melody: "I fancied the seats were empty, but, as I passed along / Out of the darkness floated the words of a Christmas song."[911]

The Road to Heaven was divided into 24 stanzas of four verses each (some spread over five or six lines) and filled exactly one column alongside Sims's regular contribution in *The Referee*. It tells the story of a young street urchin who is looking for a way to heaven but only finds the cold water of the Thames and eventually dies in a children's hospital. It is told in the form of a monologue by a first-person narrator who relates the story of little Mike to one of the doctors at the hospital. In rather anti-climactic fashion, the ballad begins after the boy's death and then flashes back to the circumstances of his "dreadful fall" (st. 1, v. 4) into the river. The narrator claims to have stumbled upon Mike and another homeless boy in one of the stone recesses of London Bridge on Christmas Eve. Unseen by the two waifs, he overhears them talking about heaven which one describes as "that place where ye're dressed in white / And has golding 'arps to play on, and it's warm and jolly and bright".[912] The unnamed narrator then relates the children's tragic fates. One, Jack, is an orphan whose drunken grandmother sends him on the streets to earn a living by singing songs. The other, Mike, has two drunkard parents who send him out to beg with a bad leg. He asks his companion who goes to Sunday School about heaven and how to get there, and Jack points down "to where the cold Thames water surged muddy and thick and brown".[913] Moments later, according to the narrator, the boy seems to lose his balance and falls into the water beneath, hitting his head on the stonework of the bridge. The tragic story then seemingly turns into a tale of salvation: the boy is brought to the hospital where he regains consciousness long enough to comically mistake white-robed patients for angels and his elderly doctor for God. He believes he has found the way to heaven and can die happily, as the last stanza suggests: "This is the day

---

910 St. 20, v. 2, p. 65. This and all subsequent quotations from the ballad are given with stanza, verse and page numbers and taken from George R. Sims, "The Road to Heaven", *The Lifeboat and Other Poems*, 59–67.

911 St. 8, v. 1–2, p. 61.

912 St. 10, v. 3–4, p. 62.

913 St. 16, v. 2, p. 64. Their dialogue suggests that Mike had also attended some sort of religious teaching at a mission or school but didn't fully understand its meaning nor the core principles of Christian belief: "Is that what they mean by 'eaven, as the misshun coves talks about / Where the children's always happy and nobody kicks 'em out?" St. 11, v. 1–2, p. 62.

of scoffers, but who shall say that night / When Mike asked the road to heaven, that Jack didn't tell him right? / 'Twas the children's Jesus pointed the way to the kingdom come / For the poor little tired arab, the waif of a London slum".[914]

The Road to Heaven combines several typical elements of Sims's Dagonet ballads. A silent interlocutor who is the addressee of the story told by the narrator who accidentally found Mike and happened to witness his fall into the water. According to literary historian Jacqueline Bratton, these observers – and not the poor characters whose stories are told – become "the point of identification in the ballad".[915] An innocent and deserving poor character whose naïve ideas of heaven are heart-warming and whose accent "serves rather to mark him off as someone of a different class revealing himself, in his pathos and quaintness, to the perceptive and sympathetic listener, his superior".[916] A tragic child death, seemingly advertised as a satisfying resolution to the unbearable living situation with a drunken mother and father: "The favourite drawing-room ballad character is the innocent, usually suffering child, and the favoured ending is death and translation."[917] In this case, I would argue that the ending is ambiguous. Death as salvation for poor children who are morally pure and innocent is a common motif in waif stories and in Sims's ballads.[918] However, the narrator is purposefully vague on the actual circumstances of Mike's fall into the river, leaving the option that the boy might have committed suicide: "He leaned right over and cried / 'If them are the gates of 'eaven, how I'd like to be inside!' / He'd stood but a moment looking – how it happened I cannot tell / When he seemed to lose his balance, gave a short shrill cry, and fell."[919] Additionally, Mike does not actively seek or passively receive religious conversion of any kind before his death nor is his misconception that the hospital is actually heaven corrected. To resolve this ambiguity, the lantern slide

---

914   St. 24, v. 1–4, p. 67. Here, the Sunday scholar Jack is referred to as "the children's Jesus", however, he innocently but fairly explicitly suggests suicide as the way to heaven that Mike is looking for: "'That there's *one* road to 'eaven,' he said as he pointed down / To where the cold Thames water surged muddy and thick and brown / 'If we was to fall in there, Mike, we'd be dead: and right through there / Is the place where it's always sunshine, and the angels has crowns to wear'." St. 16, v. 1–4, p. 64, original emphasis.

915   Bratton, *Victorian Popular Ballad*, 123.

916   Ibid.

917   Ibid., 132.

918   See Anna Davin, "Waif Stories in Late Nineteenth-Century England", *History Workshop Journal*, no. 52 (Autumn 2001): 67–98, here 85.

919   St. 17, v. 3-4 through st. 18, v. 1-2, pp. 64-65. Sims explicitly describes a suicide by drowning in the ballad *Two Women*. He describes a midnight meeting for prostitutes with a preacher and mocks the missionary's methods. Later one of the women, misled by the preacher's words, commits suicide out of repentance: "A plunge in the midnight river, a cry on the chill night air / And the waters upon their bosom a pilgrim sister bear / She has laved the stain of the city from her soul in the river slime / She has sought for the promised haven through the door of a deadly crime." Sims, *Ballads and Poems*, 68. Depictions of female suicide – especially by drowning – were ubiquitous in Victorian London, one of the most popular being Thomas Hood's famous poem *The Bridge of Sighs* (1844). See L.J. Nicoletti, "Downward Mobility: Victorian Women, Suicide, and London's 'Bridge of Sighs'", *Literary London: Interdisciplinary Studies in the Representation of London*, vol. 2, no. 1 (March 2004), (accessed on 14 December 2020, http://literarylondon.org/ the-literary-london-journal/archive-of-the-literary-london-journal/issue-2-1/downward-mobility-victorian-women-suicide-and-londons-bridge-of-sighs/).

manufacturer Bamforth even issued an alternative reading to accompany their adaptation of the ballad.

Arthur Calder-Marshall acknowledges that the ending is ambiguous in his introduction to Sims's ballads but interprets that as well-hidden irony: "Sims, no doubt, intended an irony, that Mike would be better dead than he could ever hope to be alive. But those who wished reassurance could believe that the cripple boy was compensated by eternal bliss."[920] While Jacqueline Bratton considers such an ending a "sentimentally and socially satisfying solution to a problem which admitted of no easy remedy".[921] Although Sims was capable of biting irony with regards to the lives and deaths of the poor, he repeated the idea that poor innocent children might be better off dead than being corrupted by a life of destitute poverty in his *How The Poor Live* series:

> Passing from cot to cot, and hearing the histories of the little ones lying there so clean, and, in spite of their suffering, so happy, one is inclined to think that the charity is a mistake – that to nurse these children back to health only to send them again to their wretched homes is a species of refined cruelty. It were better in dozens of cases that the children were left to die now, while they are young and innocent, than that death should be wrestled with and its prize torn from it only to be cast back into a state of existence which is worse than death.[922]

In the same chapter Sims insisted that hospitals are "the greatest blessing of the poor" and likened them to heaven in comparison with the homes of the poor:

> The hospitals are the heavens-upon-earth of the poor. I have heard little children – their poor pinched faces wrinkled with pain – murmur that they didn't mind it, because if they had been well they would never have come to 'the beautiful place'. Beautiful, indeed, by contrast with their wretched homes are the clean wards, the comfortable beds, and the kind faces of the nurses. Step across from the home of a sick child in the slums of the Borough to the Evelina Hospital, and it is like passing from the infernal regions to Paradise.[923]

Another aspect that speaks against an ironic use of Mike's death can be found within Sims's "Mustard and Cress" column published on the same day and the same page as the *Road to Heaven* in *The Referee*. Apart from his usual snarky commentary on the politics and London gossip of the day, Sims also writes about a visit to a school for poor children in the district of Southwark two days earlier.[924] Sims is deeply moved when he learns that a girl who fails to claim her prize has recently died of starvation:

> It was painful at times, when a little doll was held up and a girl's name called out, to hear, 'She's gone into the workus, sir, with 'er father,' and to be told, as a little petticoat remained unclaimed, that the little lass who was to have worn it this

---

920   Calder-Marshall, "Introduction", 42.

921   Bratton, *Victorian Popular Ballad*, 126.

922   Sims, *How the Poor Live* (1889), 56.

923   Ibid., 55.

924   Dagonet, "Mustard and Cress", *The Referee* (24 December 1882): 7. The visit is also described in the *South London Press* (23 December 1882): 12. Apart from Christmas gift-giving, Sims took pupils of the school on excursions to the countryside during the summer months.

> Christmas time lay dead in the garret from which, all the bitter winter through, she had trudged bravely, half clad and wholly starved, the gentlest child in all the class.[925]

Sims frequently wrote his ballads just in time for Sunday publication – and thus presumably under the impression of the day's events – as he himself admitted in his autobiography: "I generally wrote them on the Friday night, posted them about 3 A.M., and went to the office on Saturday afternoon to correct the proof."[926] It thus seems more likely that *The Road to Heaven* meant to offer comfort at the thought of a happier afterlife to those confronted with a child's death than an ironic mockery of such a belief.

The Road to Heaven was reprinted in regional newspapers in Scotland and England with reference to Dagonet (Sims's *nom de plume*) and *The Referee* in late December of 1882 and in June of 1883.[927] It was also included in the third collection of Sims's ballads published as *The Lifeboat and Other Poems* in March of 1883. The only change made to the verses from *The Referee* is in stanza 18, verse 4 where the original "With a thud on the parapet under; then splash in the Thames went Mike" was amended to the more precise "With a thud on the stonework under; then splash in the Thames went Mike". *The Graphic* offered a short review of the volume, praising Sims's verses for the strong reactions they could illicit from readers: "It must be a very cold-blooded person who could read without emotion such pieces as *Nellie's Prayer, Ticket-o'-Leave*, or above all, *The Road to Heaven*."[928] The weekly London paper also recommended the ballads for recitation – provided performers could keep their emotions in check: "In short, if public readers have their own feelings well under control, and can be sure of getting through a piece without publicly crying, there is a mine of wealth for them there."[929] In his autobiography, George Sims stressed the performative power of his Dagonet ballads, noting that they "were never put forward by me as poetry" but rather "intended for reciters who wanted something dramatic".[930] And indeed as early as January 1883, public recitations of *The Road to Heaven* formed part of religious and varied entertainments, often combined with songs and musical performances. Fittingly the ballad was also included in a selection of popular pieces in prose and verse selected specifically for recitations and readings by Sims himself and published as *The Dagonet Reciter and Reader* in late November of 1888 – right in

---

925 Ibid.

926 Sims, *My Life*, 182. Joss Marsh and David Francis argue that this peculiar writing process also manifests itself in the tone of the ballads: "All have an uninhibited, late-night feel. And indeed they were written in the small hours, in the smoke-filled rooms of the club, well lubricated with booze, with self-censorship at a dead-of-night low." Marsh and Francis, "Poetry of Poverty", 69–70.

927 *Scottish Aberdeen Weekly Journal*, no. 7042 (30 December 1882): 6, *Leeds Times* (30 December 1882): 6; *Fife Free Press, & Kirkcaldy Guardian* (2 June 1883): 6.

928 "Recent Poetry and Verse", *The Graphic* (31 March 1883): 339.

929 Ibid.

930 Sims, *My Life*, 182.

time for Christmas purchase.[931] In the 20th century, Arthur Calder-Marshall included *The Road to Heaven* in his 1968 anthology of Sims's poems titled *Prepare to Shed Them Now*.[932] In his introduction, Calder-Marshall breaks down Sims's successful ballad formula as follows:

> Sims, as I have said, was not an originator but an adaptor. Though the field of his Ballads was English, the formula was American, taken from the *Pike County Ballads* of Colonel John Hay. It was a simple recipe. In colloquial language and heavily accented verse, a first person narrator told a melodramatic story, expressing often opinions which appeared almost blasphemous but which in fact robustly restated simple faith.[933]

Sims's use of colloquial language, frequently a cockney accent, serves a double function. It could authenticate the poor characters of his ballads, similar to Henry Mayhew's extensive transcription of his verbal interviews in *London Labour and the London Poor*.[934] Sims's accuracy in the observation of dialects was noted in a contemporary portrait in the *Idler* magazine: "I noticed how cleverly he could catch the nuances of accent: Hibernian, Cockney, Yankee, Boulevardiere – even the Cymric."[935] Similarly, Jacqueline Bratton who is otherwise quite critical of Sims acknowledges his "gift of convincing dialect and colloquial writing".[936] The use of lower-class speech and the dramatic incidents of Sims's ballads also offered opportunities for reciters to demonstrate their range: "[T]he uneducated speech can be quaint in itself, a chance for the reciter to display talent, and also excitingly racy; and its way of expressing pious sentiments in a rough, untutored manner can be made pathetic or heart-warming."[937] In *The Road to Heaven*, Sims alternates direct colloquial speech by the two poor children with the standard English of a narrator character who retells the boys' stories to a visitor at the hospital. This provides the ballad both with a narrative drive towards the eventual climax and highlights the poor characters' linguistic deviation from the standard. A prominent marker of their cockney dialect is the dropping of initial *h*-sounds, which becomes most notable in variations of the titular phrase: "'That there's *one* road to 'eaven,' he said, as he pointed down"; and "Which is the way to 'eaven? How d'ye get there, Jack?"[938] The protagonist's mispronunciation (at least from a middle-class standpoint) of "heaven" matches his untutored ideas about it. However, the two sentences he speaks towards the end of the ballad upon waking up in the

---

931 See *London Evening Standard* (24 November 1888): 4 for a publisher's advertisement.

932 Calder-Marshall, *Prepare to Shed Them Now*, 120–126. On Sims's ballads, see also Vogl-Bienek, *Lichtspiele*, 200–204.

933 Calder-Marshall, "Introduction", 29.

934 For the linguistic characteristics of cockney, the dialect attributed to London's working-class citizens, see Arthur Hughes, Peter Trudgill and Dominic Watt, *English Accents and Dialects: An Introduction to Social and Regional Varieties of English in the British Isles*, 4th edition (London: Hodder Arnold, 2005), 73–78.

935 Keating, "George R. Sims", 288.

936 Bratton, *Victorian Popular Ballad*, 127.

937 Ibid.

938 St. 16, v. 1 and st. 15, v. 3, p. 64.

hospital are suddenly devoid of cockney dialect: "'I'm in heaven,' he whispered faintly. 'Yes, Jack must have told me true?'"; and "Then to the kind old doctor, 'Please, are you God?' he said."[939] His use and *dis*use of lower-class speech thus marks the boy's integration into society and its middle-class values.[940]

Alternative Reading by Robert Craven

In 1887 the lantern slide producer Bamforth began the publication of their "short lantern readings" series.[941] These thin booklets of around 20 pages contained readings for select slide series, either reprinted from other published sources or composed specifically to accompany their own slides. They were available for sale or hire to lantern operators, organizations and showpeople. These readings had the distinct advantage of printed slide numbers within the text that indicated a slide change. For convenience, short titles (usually the respective lines from the readings) were also printed on small paper slips and glued to the paper binding of individual slides. As Ludwig Vogl-Bienek has pointed out, this was also a means to regulate the temporal sequencing of lantern performances and a step towards standardized performances.[942] Between 1887 and 1896 Bamforth published a total of 24 short lantern readings, half of which were filled with texts attributed to one sole author, a Robert Craven, C.M.[943] These were mostly stories that accompanied short series of comic slides with titles like THE FATAL SAUSAGE MACHINE (Bamforth, 1891, 7 slides) or A LADY'S ADVENTURE IN A NEW DRESS (Bamforth, 1893, 4 slides) and temperance stories like THE FOOL'S PENCE (Bamforth, 1880s, 8 slides) and THE DRINK FIEND (Bamforth, 1893, 15 slides).[944] Craven also wrote alternative readings for magic lantern adaptations of popular literature like Hans Christian

939   St. 22, v. 1 and st. 22, v. 4, p. 66.

940   For other examples of waif speech and its eventual disappearance in stories like Silas Hocking's *Her Benny* (1879), see Davin, "Waif Stories", 76–77.

941   The series was also distributed through their main retailer Riley Brothers of Bradford who also sent the booklets in their own wrappers.

942   See Ludwig Vogl-Bienek, "Die historische Projektionskunst: Eine offene geschichtliche Perspektive auf den Film als Aufführungsereignis", *KINtop – Jahrbuch zur Erforschung des frühen Films*, no. 3 (1994): 11–32, here 26–27. That lecturers modified these readings (and presumably slide sequences) to suit their own needs and specific audiences is evidenced by a copy of a reading for STREET-LIFE: OR THE PEOPLE WE MEET (Riley Brothers, in or after 1887) held at the Research Library of the British Film Institute. The text was modified with a pencil in several places to shorten long passages, update regional references (a stone breaker "Yorkshireman" becoming a "Durhamman") and even to advertise locally appropriate products: A reference to "Brown's Hair Restorer, or Smith's Dentifrice" is replaced with "Buckles' Hair Restorer and Laverack's Dentifrice".

943   The author was previously thought to be a Robert Martin Craven, born 1824 in Hull, Yorkshire, a medical professional and member of the Royal Colleges of Surgeons (M.R.C.S.) of England and Scotland. Craven was a prominent citizen of Hull and president of the Hull Literary and Philosophical Society from 1879. See "Mr. R.M. Craven Knighted", *Hull Daily Mail* (1 January 1896): 3. However, the actual author was a different Robert Craven born 1834 in Leeds, Yorkshire, who died in 1897, after which date there were no new contributions to the short lantern readings series by Robert Craven, C.M. This Robert Craven was a schoolmaster who moved around the country frequently and in 1872 published a small collection of poems titled *A Tale of a Story Without an End and Other Poems* and advertised as "by Robert Craven, C.M." in the *Yorkshire Post and Leeds Intelligencer* (25 July 1872): 1.

944   See the Lucerna entry for Robert Craven (http://lucerna.exeter.ac.uk/person/index.php?id=6001292).

Andersen's *The Little Match Girl* and Sims's ballad *The Road to Heaven*. The latter was published in the fourth instalment of the short lantern readings series in 1887 and – unlike Sims's original ballad – composed specifically to accompany the existing illustrations of the lantern slides.[945] The numbers of the slides that should be projected to match the paragraphs of the reading are printed in bold on the left-hand side of the text. Instructions to "Repeat [slide] 2" and "Repeat [slide] 1" are printed centred in between paragraphs. A total of 7 slides (two of them shown twice) are enumerated in the text. They correspond to the number of slides and the slide titles given in the Band of Hope Catalogue of 1891.[946]

Robert Craven's version of *The Road to Heaven* attempts to follow Sims's ballad both in narrative and style – with a few significant alterations. Like Sims's ballad, Craven's monologue begins with an unnamed narrator in a hospital who relates the story of Mike and his friend Jack to one of the doctors. And it ends with Mike mistaking the ward for heaven – the place he longed to find – and his doctor for God. Where Sims's rhymes give the ballad a distinct rhythm that drives the narrative forward, Craven's attempts at rhyming couplets occasionally sound clumsy: "I chanced to be down on the bridge that night / Watching the vessels, each one with its light / They looked something like a moving town / As they traversed the river up and down" or "And now and then in the course of the day / One or the other would fetch away / The pence that charity had to him thrown / With which their wretchedness they would drown".[947] The lower-class speech which Sims uses to authenticate and endear his poor protagonists to the reader is almost completely absent from Craven's poem. The first sentence by Jack's friend Mike, "And is it all true, Jack, that hymn what you sings / About them there harps with the golden strings?", is the most notable example.[948] Their family situations, however, are described in similar terms in both texts. Mike and Jack are sent into the London streets to earn money by begging (Mike with his crippled leg) and singing (Jack). The little money they make is poured into gin by their families (parents and grandmother), which leaves them half-starved and afraid to go home for fear

---

945 Robert Craven, "The Road to Heaven", *Short Lantern Readings*, series no. 4 (Holmfirth: Bamforth, 1887): 10–13. Pamphlets 1 through 12 are listed for purchase in *J. Theobald and Company's Extra Special Illustrated Catalogue of Magic Lanterns*, 123–124. Interestingly, for series no. 4, George R. Sims original poem is offered for an additional shilling instead of the version by Robert Craven.

946 The Band of Hope Catalogue (1891) lists two versions of THE ROAD TO HEAVEN. One by Bamforth with seven slides and reading by Robert Craven and one by York & Son with eight slides and reading by George R. Sims. A Bamforth version with six slides to accompany recitations of Sims's poem was partially registered for copyright at Stationers' Hall in 1888 and mentioned with slide titles in the 1891 *Catalogue of Photographic Lantern Transparencies and Apparatus* by Riley Brothers of Bradford. In the same year Bamforth also released a new version of the series with additional slides numbered 5a and 5b which showed the boy in the water. Most surviving versions of the Bamforth series appear to be hybrid versions of both made by collectors. The printed numbers on the slides provided by the publisher are thus frequently replaced by handwritten notes to account for added or missing slides in order to assemble a complete set. At least one complete version of the York & Son series survives in the Nicholas Hiley Collection while seven of eight slides are preserved in the Gwen Sebus Collection.

947 V. 27–30, p. 10 and v. 57–60, p. 11. Craven's poem is not separated into regular stanzas so these and all subsequent quotations are given with verses numbered consecutively and with page numbers.

948 V. 73–74, p. 11.

of physical abuse. Robert Craven stresses that despite this desperate situation, Jack does not resort to stealing and even invents a mother figure for him: "For Jack's integrity still was left / His mother had taught him some years before / That crime never bettered even the poor."[949] Sims also describes Mike's parents as violent drunkards: "He'd a drunken father and mother, who sent him out to beg / Though he'd just got over a fever, and was lame with a withered leg / He told how he daren't crawl homeward, because he had begged in vain / And his parents' brutal fury haunted his baby brain."[950]

Abusive and often alcoholic parents, destitute but morally pure children and eventual religious conversion were typical plot elements of the so-called waif stories.[951] The protagonists of these popular prose stories were usually poor children forced to lead their lives on the streets but managed to remain uncompromised by the vice and sin surrounding them – and thus remained deserving of empathy. Literary historian Anna Davin describes them as follows:

> The children who were their central figures were objects of pathos – desperately poor and without parental support, their parents dead, missing or deficient and perhaps brutal. In the course of the story these heroic children would encounter and be converted to evangelical Christianity.[952]

The agents of conversion are usually adults (or sometimes children) of a higher station like priests, doctors, nurses, Sunday school teachers or simply well-meaning older men who teach them about evangelical beliefs.[953] As Anna Davin notes, hospitals often play a vital role in the narrative of waif stories and frequently become the place of conversion. Waifs are subsequently able to escape their miserable living situation either through help from charitable adults, the intervention of long-lost relations or by death and translation to heaven.[954] Written mainly by religious middle-class women between the 1860s and 1890s, waif stories were aimed at child readers of all classes:

> The writers' purpose was clearly didactic, and their message, though primarily religious, was also social and political. They aimed to interest a wide range of readers: pupils in Board (state) and voluntary (church) schools and in Sunday Schools; young servants; the children of modest middle-class households; and also 'fine children' from well-to-do families. Actual waif children, of course, were the least likely to come upon these books, or indeed to be able to read them if they did.[955]

---

949 V. 46–48, p. 11.

950 St. 14, v. 1–4, p. 63.

951 The term "waif" was often used to refer to orphaned children and could also designate abandoned and found debris. On the use of the term in reference to street children, see Hugh Cunningham, *The Children of the Poor: Representations of Childhood since the Seventeenth Century* (Cambridge: Blackwell, 1991), 137.

952 Davin, "Waif Stories", 69.

953 The two pillars of evangelical belief were the personal relationship with God and the transformative power of religious conversion. See Elisabeth Jay, *The Religion of the Heart: Anglican Evangelicalism and the Nineteenth-Century Novel* (Oxford: Clarendon Press, 1979), 51–69.

954 See Davin, "Waif Stories", 80 and 85.

955 Ibid., 69.

As deserving poor characters, the child protagonists could function both as moral examples and objects of pity for better-off readers. Waif stories were also widely adopted by missionary and temperance organizations who distributed copies at their meetings.[956] They addressed two of their key concerns, the dangers of alcohol and the importance of religion, and it is hardly surprising that from the 1890s life model slide adaptations of texts like *Jessica's First Prayer*, *Her Benny* or *Christie's Old Organ* formed part of temperance entertainments and charitable events.[957] Robert Craven's poem is clearly indebted to this literary tradition and the missionary zeal and temperance message became much more prominent in his reworking of *The Road to Heaven* than in Sims's original. Right in the first stanza, the narrator declares that his mission in telling the sad story is to fight the demon of alcoholism and encourage others to join the movement: "I thought it might help in some humble way / The demon, that causes these horrors, to lay / And it may do the same to you very like / When you hear the story of poor crippled Mike."[958]

A key element of waif stories is the religious conversion of the waif characters as it sets up their eventual salvation and in some cases translation to heaven. Such a scene is patently missing from Sims's version of *The Road to Heaven* and there is nothing to indicate that Mike's misconception of the hospital ward as heaven and his old doctor as God is corrected by anyone before his death. In this context the seemingly innocuous question "This is the day of scoffers, but who shall say that night / When Mike asked the road to Heaven, that Jack didn't tell him right?" in the last stanza almost appears like a mockery of devout Christian beliefs (and writings).[959] In Robert Craven's version on the other hand, the old doctor is used as an agent in Mike's conversion. He gently corrects his wrongful belief that his fall into the river transported him directly to heaven and points him towards the true (and only) path to eternal life:

> Poor Mike saw at once the mistake he had made
> But the doctor such tact and compassion displayed
> He won the lad's confidence day by day
> And, seeing how fast he was fading away
> Corrected that portion of poor Jack's creed
> That through death alone the soul is freed
> But that to reach the realms of endless day
> *Our Saviour Christ is the only way.*[960]

956 Ibid., 71.

957 *Jessica's First Prayer* by Hesba Stretton (1867) was adapted by Bamforth in 1896. See also David Henry, "Jessica's First Prayer", in Dennis Crompton, David Henry and Stephen Herbert (ed.), *Magic Images: The Art of Hand-Painted and Photographic Lantern Slides* (London: The Magic Lantern Society, 1990), 54–59. *Her Benny* by Silas Hocking (1879) was adapted by Bamforth in 1889. *Christie's Old Organ* was written by Mrs Walton in 1874 and adapted by Bamforth in 1892.

958 V. 22–24, p. 10.

959 St. 24, v. 1–2, p. 67.

960 V. 135–142, p. 13, original emphasis.

Such a straightforward Evangelical message might have been aimed especially at those religious and temperance organizations that bought lantern slides from Bamforth (or their main distributor Riley Brothers) and appreciated suitable material both for moral edification and teetotal entertainments. A list of "new lecture and reading sets for 1890–1" from the Church of England Temperance Society contains two versions of THE ROAD TO HEAVEN slide series, only one of which is listed under "Special Temperance Subjects".[961] While Sims's ballad was certainly a popular piece for public recitation, it might not have propagated temperance and piousness in strong enough language.

Adaptations by Bamforth: Poor Children between the Picturesque and the Authentic

Lucerna – The Magic Lantern Web Resource lists three adaptations of *The Road to Heaven* by two different producers, York & Son of London and Bamforth of Holmfirth. All three series were made in the life model genre. The production dates, number of slides and slide titles for the series were reconstructed using copyright entries from Stationers' Hall and slide catalogues from producers and distributors. The amount of information about a given slide set in catalogues of producers and retailers or in lists of slides distributed by organizations with lending departments varies greatly between sources. While the name and number of slides are the minimal information required for purchase or hire, the producer of a slide set is seldom specified but can often be inferred. Titles for the individual slides in a set aren't included in lists but usually in catalogues although sometimes they are replaced by a short summary of the plot as in the case of the Riley Bros. 1908 catalogue.

A slide set called THE ROAD TO HEAVEN made up of six slides (the first one repeated during projection) with slide titles taken from Sims's poem was advertised in the Riley Bros. Catalogue of 1891 for the coming lantern season.[962] The same set of six life model slides with Sims's reading was still advertised in their 1908 catalogue as "the touching story of two miserable Slum Children".[963] Two versions of THE ROAD TO HEAVEN were offered for hire by the Church of England Temperance Society for the 1890–1891 season, one version with six slides listed under "Special Temperance Subjects" and one version with eight slides.[964] The 1912 catalogue of Scottish lantern and slide dealer J. Lizars also lists a version of THE ROAD TO HEAVEN composed of six slides with slide titles taken from the Sims ballad.[965] Robert Craven's reading for THE ROAD TO HEAVEN as published by Bamforth in 1887 specifically lists seven slides, two of them repeated during projection. Such a version with seven

---

961   See Stead, "A Magic Lantern Mission", 565.

962   *Catalogue of Photographic Lantern Transparencies and Apparatus* (Bradford: Riley Brothers, 1891), 33.

963   *Catalogue of Optical Lantern Slides* (Bradford: Riley Brothers Ltd, [1908]), 15.

964   Quoted in Stead, "A Magic Lantern Mission", 565.

965   See Lucerna record for THE ROAD TO HEAVEN (Bamforth, in or before 1887, 6 slides), (http://lucerna.exeter.ac.uk/set/index.php?id=3005584).

slides (one repeated) with a "Reading in Verse, by Robert Craven, C. M." was offered for hire or purchase in the catalogue of lantern and slide wholesaler J. Theobald & Co issued around 1893 and in the Band of Hope Catalogue of 1891.[966] Finally, copyright records show that another set with up to nine slides and slide titles from Sims's poem was produced by Bamforth in 1891 and advertised in their own catalogue published in 1908.[967]

Catalogues and other written sources thus indicate that there were likely three distinct versions of THE ROAD TO HEAVEN produced by Bamforth. Two as recitation pieces for Sims's poem: one slide set with six slides (Bamforth A) produced before 1890 and a newer version with up to nine slides produced in 1891 (Bamforth B). It was not uncommon for Bamforth to produce several versions of a slide set with a larger number of slides or different illustrations. In addition, a version of the slide set with Robert Craven's alternative reading and comprising seven slides was produced by Bamforth in or after 1887 (Bamforth C). These three slide sets reconstructed from contemporaneous sources will thus be referred to as nominal versions of THE ROAD TO HEAVEN. It is necessary to distinguish between the different adaptations of a source text in various slide sets and the different iterations of a slide set produced from the same negatives over time. I propose that *versions* refer to slide sets made by one producer that consist of distinct slides (as far as the number of slides in a set or their sequence is concerned), and that *variants* refer to different iterations of a slide or set produced from the same negatives. Most versions will thus have multiple variants but not each variant constitutes a different version of a slide or slide set. The difficulty of studying a performance-based medium is that this does not account for the agency of operators and showpeople, who might have combined slides according to their own preference. Version thus refers to idealized (nominal) versions of slide series as they were produced and advertised in catalogues. In comparison with surviving versions of the slide set found in museums, collections or archives today, these nominal versions refer to an idealized and complete version of a slide set as it was presumably produced and advertised in the past.

From the slide titles found in catalogues, some conclusions with regards to the content of the images can be drawn. All three Bamforth versions show at least one image of the two boys "cuddling close together" (slide 2) and all three feature the climactic moment of the boy mistaking his doctor for God (slides 6 and 7). A variation of Jack's advice to Mike regarding the path to heaven is also included in all three: "'That there's *one* road to 'eaven,' he said" (version A, slide 4), "'That there's one road to 'eaven,' he said, as he pointed down" (version B, slide 4) and "'There, look,' said he, 'look at them waters below'"

---

966   *J. Theobald and Company's Extra Special Illustrated Catalogue of Magic Lanterns*, 138, and *Complete Catalogue of Lantern Slides*, UK Band of Hope Union, Section C, 16.

967   See Crangle, *Hybrid Texts*, 246–248. Two slides are listed as numbers 5a and 5b – lower case letters usually marked effect slides – and were apparently optional, which explains why the set is also listed in catalogues as having seven slides.

Fig. 36: Detail of collation matrix for Bamforth versions of THE ROAD TO HEAVEN, John Finney Collection, Cinémathèque française Collection, illuminago Collection / Karin Bienek and Ludwig Vogl-Bienek, Frankfurt am Main.

(version C, slide 4). After that, however, only versions B and C explicitly picture the boy falling into the water with "When he seemed to lose his balance, gave a short, shrill cry and fell" (version B, slide 5) and "His balance he lost and down, down he fell" (version C, slide 5). Version A on the other hand appears to cut directly to the hospital with a slide titled "His forehead was cut and bleeding but a vestige of life we found" (slide 5). Most of the surviving artefacts cannot be neatly divided and attributed to three distinct versions. James Bamforth registered three photographs for copyright in 1888 and another five in 1891, the latter thus clearly belonged to the Bamforth B version. But since most surviving slide sets are either fragmented and / or hybrid versions assembled by collectors and heritage institutions, they cannot easily be matched to the catalogues of the Victorian period.

The following observations are based on a collation matrix of eight surviving slide series (most of them hybrid) spread over four private and two public collections.[968] I am assuming that those slide numbers written in typescript on round slips of paper and affixed to the dark paper masks of the slides correspond

968 Three series are in the illuminago Collection (3, 7 and 7 slides). One is in the John Finney Collection (9 slides), digital images are available via the Lucerna database (http://lucerna.exeter.ac.uk/set/index.php?id=3002625). One is held at the Cinémathèque française (8 slides), digital reproductions are available at Laterna Magica (http://www.laternamagica.fr/resultat.plaques.php?id_serie=37). In addition, there is one set in the Bamforth Collection of the Kirklees Museums and Galleries (6 slides), the Willem Wagenaar Collection (7 slides) and the Mervyn Heard Collection (8 slides), all of which were digitized by Ludwig Vogl-Bienek, senior researcher at the *Screen1900* research focus at the University of Trier for a DFG-funded research project.

to the 'official' slide numbers as they are listed in Bamforth's own catalogue and in other catalogues.[969]

A complete set of slides from the second Bamforth version (Bamforth B, 1891, 7–9 slides) is presented in the Lucerna database from the John Finney Collection (see first line of matrix, Fig. 36).[970] The printed slide numbers and copyright notices as well as the consistent colouring and the rounded edges of the paper masks appear to confirm that the surviving slide set is both complete and matches the historical records. A different surviving slide set from the collection of the Cinémathèque française (see second line of matrix, Fig. 36) is made up of eight slides, the associated reading is Robert Craven's rewriting of *The Road to Heaven*. Five out of the eight slide numbers are handwritten on paper slips and the shape of the paper masks on two of the slides differ from the other six.[971] It appears to be a hybrid but complete version of one of the earlier slide sets produced by Bamforth before 1888. It is not clear from the copyright records which slides apart from the three registered in 1888 formed part of the earlier versions of THE ROAD TO HEAVEN. The photographs in four of the slides (numbers 1, 3, 6 and 7) are identical in both the Cinémathèque (c. 1887) and the Finney version (1891) so it seems likely that Bamforth replaced three slides from the older slide sets with newer photographs and added an additional two slides (5a and 5b) showing the boy in the water.

There are four variants of the first slide found in as many archival versions (Wagenaar, Finney, Heard and Cinémathèque), three in colour and one in black-and-white.[972] In the other four surviving slide sets the first slide is missing. The image shows a boy lying in a hospital bed, his whole body except for his head covered by a white blanket, his eyes closed. A nurse is holding a cloth over his head seemingly about to cover his face. Two men are standing on the other side of the bed, leaning slightly down towards the boy with their backs turned to the viewer. The background wall is decorated with Christmas mottoes adorned with holly to mark the festive season. The image matches the description of a photograph registered for copyright by James Bamforth on 16 August 1888: "Photograph illustrating a scene from a set of lantern slides entitled 'The Road to Heaven', interior of hospital ward, with boy in bed, nurse

---

969   In several cases slide numbers were entirely missing or not visible in the digital reproduction, in others handwritten numbers were affixed to the slides to replace a printed one. In almost all cases these slides could be matched with other variants of the same slide (meaning differently coloured but with the same motif) carrying a printed number.

970   THE ROAD TO HEAVEN (Bamforth, 1891, 7–9 slides), (http://lucerna.exeter.ac. uk/set/index.php?id=3002625).

971   The final slide has a handwritten number "8" affixed to it and is a variant of slide number 1 from the same set. In place of an additional eighth slide, historical catalogues call for a repetition of the first slide (the image of a boy lying in a hospital bed) during projection.

972   Surviving slide sets found in collections are frequently either fragmented or hybrids of multiple versions of a series or variants of a slide. Such surviving slide sets will be referred to as distinct versions within a collection (e.g., the Cinémathèque française version, the illuminago version).

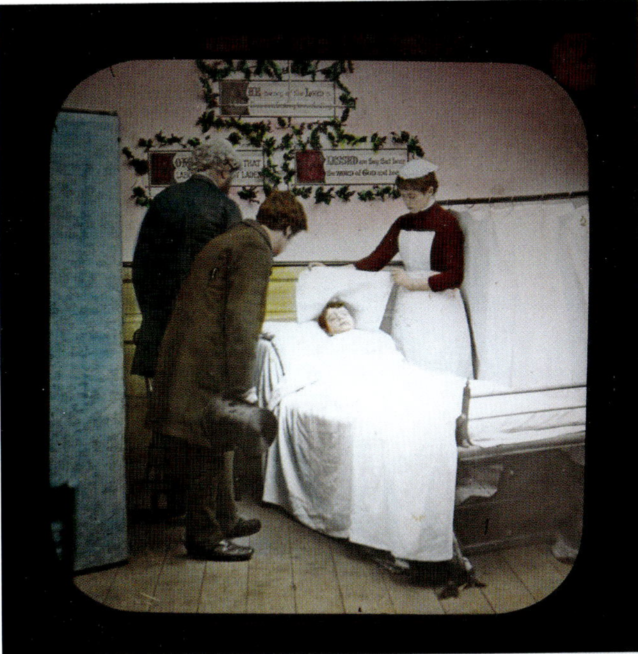

Fig. 37: Slide 1 of THE ROAD TO HEAVEN (Bamforth B, 1891, 7-9 slides),
John Finney Collection, reproduced with permission.

standing on one side and two gentlemen on the other."[973] Bamforth used the
same setting and props – even the same Christmas mottoes – and some of the
same actors to photograph a slide for another adaptation called THE NEWSBOY'S
DEBT. The two life model slide series were thus photographed in the same
year, probably in 1887 or earlier.[974] The associated verses in the Sims reading
"So poor little Mike is sleeping the last long sleep of all" / "Let me look at him,
doctor – poor little London waif" and the Craven reading "Let me look at him,
doctor, at least once more" thrust viewers into the narrative without pream-
ble.[975] Three of the four persons depicted in the image are identified with these
words as the narrator, doctor and child protagonist, respectively. The two men

973   The National Archives: "Record COPY 1/393/266", *Records of the Copyright Office, Stationers' Company*
      (http://discovery.nationalarchives.gov.uk/details/record?catid=-4344088&catln=7). The paper copies of
      the copyright entries at Stationers' Hall held at the National Archive in Kew have a copy of the original
      photo pinned to them. These records and photographs have not been digitized yet but it can be inferred
      from the descriptions which slides they are referring to.

974   Slide number 6 from THE NEWSBOY'S DEBT (Bamforth, 1880s) was registered for copyright in July of
      1888. The National Archives: "Record COPY 1/393/155" (http://discovery.nationalarchives.gov.uk/de-
      tails/r/C9083829) and an associated reading by a Hannah R. Hudson appeared in the first series of the
      Short Lantern Readings published by Bamforth in 1887.

975   The slide titles (i.e. the verses associated with the respective slide) are taken from Lucerna for Sims's
      ballad and differ slightly between the two Bamforth versions. The verses from Robert Craven's reading
      are taken from the Band of Hope Catalogue for 1891–1892 and confirmed by the J. Theobald & Co
      catalogue dated around 1893.

Fig. 38: Slide 6 of THE NEWSBOY'S DEBT (Bamforth, c. 1887, 6 slides),
Nicholas Hiley Collection, reproduced with permission.

are notably turning their faces away from the camera and are angling towards the boy, their faces hidden. However, the top hat that one of them is holding denotes status and respectability, while at the same time any signs of poverty in the dead boy are covered by the large white blanket.

Dead and dying children were a popular motif both in Sims's ballads and in Victorian popular culture. In his study *The Image of Childhood: Representations of the Child in Painting and Literature, 1700–1900*, art historian Michael Benton describes dying and orphaned children as "ubiquitous images of Victorian art and literature".[976] Prolonged and sentimental death scenes in particular were a staple of both Dickens and Sims's writing:

> Dickens's description of the death of Little Nell is merely his most affecting and memorable one; in his novels, the child mortality rate is high. So it is in the popular poetry of the time, with George Sims's *Billy's Rose* perhaps narrowly edging out Edward Farmer's *Little Jim* as the most mawkish.[977]

Luke Fildes's painting *The Doctor* (1891), first exhibited in the same year that Bamforth produced their adaptation of *The Road to Heaven*, and Henry Peach

---

976 Michael Benton, "The Image of Childhood: Representations of the Child in Painting and Literature, 1700–1900", *Children's Literature in Education*, vol. 27, no. 1 (January 1996): 35–60, here 55.

977 Ibid. On *Billy's Rose* in lantern slide series and cinematic adaptations, see Ine van Dooren and Amy Sargeant, "Dead Babies: Representations of Infant Mortality Before the First World War", in Toulmin and Popple (ed.), *Visual Delights – Two*, 73–86, here 73–75.

Fig. 39: Henry Peach Robinson - *Fading Away* (1858), Albumen silver print,
Public domain, Courtesy of the George Eastman Museum.

Robinson's composite photograph *Fading Away* (1858) presented idealized representations of Victorian physicians and the coming of death.[978] Unlike the boy in the Bamforth slide, the dying girl and woman are depicted in their homes and with family members. Mike on the other hand is bodily removed from his parents while in the accompanying recitation he is referred to as "Poor little baby outcast, poor little waif of sin!" (Sims) and "the poor waif" (Craven). This follows a common pattern in reform literature and writings about child poverty of the time, according to historian Lydia Murdoch:

> The common phrases used to describe poor children accented their alleged separation from parents and lack of connection to established, stable communities. They were 'waifs and strays,' or 'nobody's children,' or 'street arabs' who wandered nomadically through the urban landscape, sleeping under archways and on rooftops.[979]

Mike and Jack's situation is revealed in the second slide of the Bamforth series. Here, two distinct versions in multiple variants survive in the six collections. One image, shot frontally, depicts two boys seated on a bench next to a lamppost. They are "Cuddling close together, crouched on a big stone seat", like the corresponding verse in Sims's poem suggest. The image of the two

---

978   Fildes attempted to faithfully reproduce the setting of a rural cottage and even built a replica of an actual fisherman's home in Devon that he had sketched before. See Heather Birchall, "Sir Luke Fildes. *The Doctor*" (September 2003), (accessed on 14 December 2020, http://www.tate.org.uk/art/artworks/fildes-the-doctor-n01522).

979   Lydia Murdoch, *Imagined Orphans: Poor Families, Child Welfare, and Contested Citizenship in London* (New Brunswick, New Jersey, London: Rutgers University Press, 2006), 1.

Fig. 40: Slide 2 of THE ROAD TO HEAVEN (Bamforth, before 1888), Cinémathèque française Collection, reproduced with permission.

boys was supposed to be projected onto the screen for about eighteen verses of Sims's poem and, since the slide was to be repeated once, a combined 40 verses of Craven's reading.[980] This gave audiences ample time to study the pair, who are positioned in the centre of the image and depicted frontally. The smaller one is holding a broomstick, his feet are bare and one foot is wrapped in white bandages. The taller boy's face is turned down and hidden under a wide-brimmed cap.[981] This serves to direct the viewer's attention towards the smaller boy. His bare feet, ragged clothes and crutch reveal the boy as very poor but also signal to viewers that he is worthy of their empathy – or even charity.

As literary historian Deborah Wynne points out, many Victorians were afraid of being deceived by imposters undeserving of their benevolence: "Fears of wasting one's emotions on the 'undeserving' poor ran through many Victorian narratives of poverty, but these were allayed when the sufferer was a child."[982]

---

980 Assuming that operators followed the suggestions for staging the series found on the artefacts (slide numbers and titles glued to the slides), in readings and in catalogues – which sometimes differed from one another. Individual performers might have altered the succession of images or changed the reading according to their own preferences, however, since Sims's poem was a well-known recitation piece specifically composed for public performances, his text would most probably have been recited in full.

981 Variants of this slide exist in the Cinémathèque française, the Mervyn Heard and the Kirklees Museums and Galleries versions of the series.

982 Deborah Wynne, "Reading Victorian Rags: Recycling, Redemption, and Dickens's Ragged Children", *Journal of Victorian Culture*, vol. 20, no. 1 (2015): 34–49, here 40.

Thus, similar images of poor children were used for raising money directly. Collection boxes for the Church of England Waifs and Strays Society, funded in the early 1880s to provide homes for street children, featured an image of a boy and girl, their clothes ragged and their feet bare, crouched together on a doorstep.[983] Their clean, almost rosy faces and naked limbs appear innocent and non-threatening to support the appeal to Christian benevolence. The East End Juvenile Mission founded by Dr Thomas Barnardo in 1867 famously raised funds for their homes for destitute boys (and later girls) with carefully arranged photographs of homeless children. Depicting the children before and after they had entered the Barnardo Homes, these images were sold as postcards, placed on collection boxes and projected as lantern slides.[984] The visual clues to suggest authentic poverty were centred around the children's ragged clothes and their bare feet:

> Barnardo's photographs intentionally underscored the raggedness of the children's clothing. Raggedness – ripped and torn clothing that exposed the bodies and extremities of children – was not only an effective visual marker of poverty, but could also be a disturbingly erotic sign.[985]

Some of the photographs taken for the Barnardo Homes became the subject of an arbitration case brought against Thomas Barnardo in 1877. While the more serious charges like misappropriation of funds or abuse of children were dismissed, Barnardo was reprimanded for "producing 'fictitious representations of destitution' for 'the purposes of obtaining money'".[986] "Fictitious representations of destitution" weren't frowned upon of per se, in fact, even philanthropic writers and social investigators regularly blurred the lines between factual accuracy and narrative invention, as historian Seth Koven notes:

> If the experience of finding the same story in a novel and a philanthropic report made each narrative seem more authentic and true, it must also have confused readers' expectations about the relationship between facts and fictions. This confusion was part of a much broader problem confronting readers in an age when many novelists, not just writers of evangelical tracts, drew on reports produced by social investigators whose authors, for their part, often deployed novelistic conventions in presenting their own 'facts.'[987]

983   The Waifs and Strays Society also appealed directly to children in better-off households who kept "Penny a Week" boxes for one year and were instructed on printed labels on the sides of the box to "give a thank-offering each week for your happy home" and place "a small additional offering on Christmas Day, Ash Wednesday, Easter Day, and your Birthday".

984   On the use of lantern slides by Barnardo, see Eifler, *The Great Gun of the Lantern*, 119–120. On the iconography of Barnardo's photographs, see Murdoch, *Imagined Orphans*, 12–42, and Lindsay Smith, "The Shoe-Black to the Crossing Sweeper: Victorian Street Arabs and Photography", *Textual Practice*, vol. 10, no. 1 (1996): 29–55.

985   Seth Koven, "Dr. Barnardo's 'Artistic Fictions': Photography, Sexuality, and the Ragged Child in Victorian London", *Radical History Review*, issue 69 (Fall 1997): 6–45, here 30. In *The Road to Heaven*, George Sims merely hints at the dangers of sexual abuse and exploitation, which threatened the innocence of street children in the verses: "It's better he died in the ward here, better a thousand times / Than have wandered back to the alley, with its squalor and nameless crimes / Too young for the slum to sully, he's gone to the wonderland." St. 2, v. 3–4, p. 59 and st. 3, v. 1, p. 60.

986   Koven, "Artistic Fictions", 25.

987   Ibid., 14.

Fig. 41: Slide 2 of THE NEW KINGDOM (Bamforth, 1897, 7–8 slides),
Philip and Rosemary Banham Collection, reproduced with permission.

Nor were photographs of poor children expected to only depict the factual
reality found in front of the camera. Indeed, a woodcut of Oscar Rejlander's
Poor Joe or *Night in Town*, "the most widely recognised image of the ragged
child" was used on publications by the Ragged School Union (later the
Shaftesbury Society) well into the 20th century.[988] The image, part of a series
of photographs of street urchins taken in Rejlander's studio in the early 1860s,
shows a young boy in torn clothes, sitting in a doorway, his bare feet and
exposed shoulder turned towards the viewer (see Fig. 2). His head lies on his
forearms which rest on his knees while his face remains hidden. While
Rejlander chose his models from a nearby Ragged School in Chalk Farm and
their bare feet suggested authentic poverty, the composition, lighting, poses
and arrangement of their ragged clothes emulated genre paintings like Bartolomé Esteban Murillo's *Two Peasant Boys and a Negro Boy*. The barefooted
boy later became a quintessential figure of Victorian poverty – especially in
picturesque poses. These picturesque elements were even more pronounced
in the well-lit studio photographs of life model slides series like the song set
THE NEW KINGDOM (Bamforth, 1897, 7–8 slides). The series was almost
entirely photographed on the same bench and with the same painted background as THE ROAD TO HEAVEN. Five slides show a barefooted but clean

---

988 Murdoch, *Imagined Orphans*, 21. See also Koven, "Artistic Fictions", 43, note 58.

crossing-sweep and a young flower girl with blonde curls who are cuddling close together and appear almost like dolls, striking examples of picturesque poverty.[989]

Homeless children were a conspicuous presence on London's streets throughout the Victorian period: "Such independent children, sometimes living rough but often in some sort of household, earned a precarious living through service, entertainment, trade, foraging, begging and theft."[990] Henry Mayhew devoted an entire chapter of *London Labour and the London Poor* to "The Children Street Sellers" and their particular "pursuits, morals, dwellings, diet, amusements, clothing and propensities; they demanded a full ethnographic study".[991] As historian Hugh Cunningham points out, these 'savage' children were sometimes considered a threat to the future of the country but "they came also to be pitied, to be seen as 'waifs and strays' or 'ragamuffins' in need of rescue for a proper childhood; and having at the same time a beauty and a fragility and a freedom from social conventions which made them a picturesque feature of the urban scene".[992] By the 1870s, they had even become a part of the picturesque appeal of London for travellers like Gustave Doré or Hippolyte Taine.[993] In *London. A Pilgrimage* (1872), Blanchard Jerrold described them with a characteristic mixture of sympathy and amusement:

> It is on the day of the boat-race that the boys of London are seen in all their glory, and in all their astonishing and picturesque varieties. To watch them on the parapets of the bridges, dangling from the arches, swinging from the frailest boughs of trees, wading amid the rushes, paddling in the mud; scrambling, racing, fighting, shouting along the roads and river paths, or through the furze of Putney Common, is a suggestive as well as an amusing sight. We studied them in all the rich picturesqueness of rags – poor, hungry, idle little fellows! – as they worked valiantly, trying to earn a few pence by disentangling the carriages and leading them to their owners, after the event of the day was over.[994]

An alternative version of slide number 2 of THE ROAD TO HEAVEN appears in several surviving versions of the series from three different collections.[995] The

---

989   The same backgrounds and similar poses were also used for several slides (nos. 20–27) from the service of song WON BY A CHILD (Bamforth, 1894, 41–46 slides) to illustrate the religious conversion of the protagonist, a homeless boy, by a poor old woman who dies after they have to spend the night huddled together on the stone seat of the bridge. See Vogl-Bienek, *Lichtspiele*, 217–221 for a longer discussion of the series.

990   Davin, "Waif Stories", 70.

991   Cunningham, *Representations of Childhood*, 122.

992   Ibid., 5. The term "street arabs", also frequently used to refer to these children highlighted their independence but also their "threatening outsider status" by naming them a literal 'race' apart. Davin, "Waif Stories", 70. It was coined by Thomas Guthrie in his *Plea for Ragged Schools*: "These Arabs of the city are wild as those of the desert, and must be broken into three habits, – those of discipline, learning, and industry, not to speak of cleanliness." Thomas Guthrie, *A Plea for Ragged Schools, or, Prevention Better Than Cure*, 3rd edition (Edinburgh: John Elder, 1847), 19.

993   See Cunningham, *Representations of Childhood*, 117.

994   Doré and Jerrold, *London*, 62.

995   Variants of the slide exist in the illuminago collection (version 1), the John Finney collection (here, the image is inverted) and the Willem Wagenaar collection (in black and white).

Fig. 42: Slide 2 of The Road to Heaven (Bamforth B, 1891, 7-9 slides), John Finney Collection, reproduced with permission.

image matches a copyright entry by James Bamforth dated 17 November 1891 with the following description: "Photograph to illustrate story 'Road to Heaven' two boys (one a cripple) seated in recess of bridge, man standing by."[996] Presumably, the slide formed part of Bamforth's newer version of The Road to Heaven (Bamforth B, 7–9 slides) released for the lantern season of 1891–1892. In comparison to the earlier version, the focus of the visual storytelling notably shifts. The image no longer shows the two boys as the narrator would perceive them, instead, both the hidden observer and his subjects are presented to the viewer as they would appear on a theatre stage. The well-lit studio setting of the photograph could not match Sims's description of the scene, "I stood where the shadows hid me, and peered about until / I could see two ragged urchins, blue with the icy chill."[997] The two boys are taller than their counterparts in the first version, both of their faces are visible, their heads slightly lowered. Mike's feet are still bare, one leg now bandaged up to the knee while his clothes appear in worse condition than those of his friend. A well-dressed man in a top hat is entering the scene from the right (left in the Finney version), leaning slightly towards the pair, one hand placed on the bridge's parapet and the other on the side of the wall. The same man,

996   The National Archives: "Record COPY 1/406/472", *Records of the Copyright Office, Stationers' Company* (http://discovery.nationalarchives.gov.uk/details/record?catid=-4532546&catln=7).

997   St. 9, v. 1–2, p. 62.

wearing a similar hat, appears in a Bamforth adaptation of another Sims ballad, IN THE HARBOUR (1890, 9 slides) where he plays a silent interlocutor who listens to the story of "Crazy Kate" as it is relayed by the boatman.

Such a character was a common narrative device in Sims's ballads, someone "who is not himself one of the down-home 'folks', through whom Sims would often manage the intrusiveness of his ballads' social investigation", as Joss Marsh and David Francis state.[998] In the ballad *The Road to Heaven* the narrator character can be read as ambiguous. His motivations for roaming London's bridges on a bitterly cold Christmas Eve seem dubious. While he claims to be "looking about for a collie – a favourite dog I'd lost", the precious animal isn't mentioned again after he stumbles upon the two homeless boys.[999] And while he claims to have "listened and heard / The talk of the little arabs – listened to every word" from his hiding place in the shadows, he conveniently misses the reason for Mike's fall into the Thames.[1000] Contemporaneous audiences might have been reminded of evangelical missionary Thomas Barnardo. Barnardo would search London's streets at night together with a policeman to look for homeless children who could then be brought to one of his homes. In reports he wrote for Christian publications, he described himself as a hunter looking for prey: "Squalid and overcrowded London streets and alleys, the haunts of the very poorest, have been for a long time our busiest hunting-grounds. In them have we many a time discovered and captured game which more than repaid all energy expended and inconvenience experienced in its pursuit."[1001] The narrator in Sims's *The Road to Heaven* relates how he came across the two boys on the dark bridge in similar terms: "Some ragged boys, so they told me, had been seen with one [dog] that night / In one of the bridge recesses, so I hunted left and right."[1002] And Mike's innocent misconceptions about heaven and Christianity in Sims's poem echo statements Barnardo attributed to his "first arab", a boy named Jim Jarvis: "'Have you ever thought that there is another world brighter than this, where there will be no more hunger, and little boys will never be beaten and ill-treated?' 'Ah, that's 'eaven, sir.' [...] 'But, sir, will I 'ave a father an' mother there to look arter me, as some boys has down here as I knows on?' [...] 'But, sir' – and there came a look of earnest inquiry into his face – 'will 'Swearing' Dick' be there? And will there be any bobbies?'"[1003] In the lantern slide adaptation by Bamforth, the narrator appears like a foreign body. He does not visibly interact (through touches, gestures or facial expression) with any of the other characters (doctor, nurse, boatman) or the

---

998 Marsh and Francis, "Poetry of Poverty", 69.

999 St. 5, v. 2, p. 60.

1000 St. 11, v. 3–4, p. 62.

1001 Thomas J. Barnardo, "A Midnight Ramble Near Drury-Lane", *The Christian* (14 March 1872): 9–10, here 9.

1002 St. 5, v. 3–4, p. 60.

1003 Thomas J. Barnardo, "How It All Happened", *The Christian* (22 August 1872): 6–7, here 7.

Fig. 43: Slide 3 of THE ROAD TO HEAVEN (Bamforth B, 1891,
7–9 slides), John Finney Collection, reproduced with permission.

poor boy, who is the subject of his dramatic tale. His face and body are notably angled away from the camera in all of the slides the character appears in.

There are seven surviving variants of the third slide from THE ROAD TO HEAVEN found in all six collections.[1004] The image shows two adults standing on either side of a young boy (it appears to be the same boy photographed for slide 1 and the earlier version of slide 2). The verses that correspond to the image provide a clear interpretation of the domestic scene: "How he was starved and beaten – 'twas a tale one's heart to rend / He'd a drunken father and mother, who sent him out to beg" (Sims) and "He'd a drunken father and mother to fight / Who sent him each morning into the street / To see with what sympathy he would meet" (Craven).[1005] The parents of street orphan Mike are easily recognisable as bad characters even without the accompanying verses. Their drunkenness and indifference towards their son are mirrored by their neglected clothing. The father's hat is askew and his jacket is torn while the

---

1004 Four surviving slides show the man standing on the left side while three show the image inverted with the man standing on the right. Judging from the copyright slips, printed slide numbers and paper bindings, it appears that the slides were produced and distributed in both variants, not accidentally inverted by collectors. Whether this indicates an error made during the reproduction process at Bamforth or an intentional variation is unclear. One might assume that experienced operators would have sought to avoid errors in continuity – for example Mike's bandage shifting from the left to the right foot in the course of the series.

1005 Sims, st. 13, v. 4 through st. 14, v. 1, p. 63; Craven, v. 52–54, p. 11.

mother's long hair is in a state of disarray, which marks their alcoholism, while Mike's ragged jacket, comically large pants and missing shoe emphasize their parental neglect.[1006] The effect is reinforced by their cold looks and the father's clenched fist, all of which communicate to the audience that the boy is being mistreated by his parents. As Ine van Dooren and Amy Sargeant remark: "Life model lantern slides depicting pathetic subjects employ a narrative structured by clear contrasts and absolute opposites: Good and Bad; Temperance and Intemperance; Sin and Redemption."[1007] The life model slide genre thus followed the logic of contemporaneous melodrama as described by literary historian Juliet John: "It depends on an externalised aesthetics which simplifies and externalises that which is normally invisible or hidden. Character, for example, is transparent and one-dimensional. Good people look good and bad people look bad (and often ugly)."[1008]

Like the barefooted boy, the drunkard was also a recurring character in depictions of poverty throughout the Victorian period. Usually an able-bodied, undeserving poor character, his alcoholism often served as an explanation for the descent into poverty, illness and, ultimately, death.[1009] Sir Luke Fildes's painting *Applicants for Admission to a Casual Ward* (1874) shows a queue of mostly poor women and children waiting for a night's shelter (see Fig. 12).[1010] In between these sympathetic poor characters a tall man stands with his legs spread wide, a large top hat sitting awkwardly on his bent head, his eyes closed and hands shoved deep into his pockets. His large belly, poking out from a worn-out jacket, and dishevelled shirt provide a stark contrast to the huddling figures and half-starved children next to him. In an attempt to recreate the scene faithfully, Fildes had asked actual applicants to the casual ward to pose for him in his studio. As his son later remembered, this posed some difficulty since many of the homeless people were suspicious of the painter and hesitant to enter his workshop:

> This difficulty, however, did not occur with the big old Boozer in the middle of the queue, for whom a pint mug of porter at his feet, replenished at intervals by the pot-boy from the nearest pub, was an ample inducement. The big old Boozer

---

1006 For other examples of depictions of alcoholism and drunkenness in lantern slides, see Vogl-Bienek, "From Life", 476 and G.A. Household (ed.), *To Catch a Sunbeam: Victorian Reality through the Magic Lantern. From the collection of L.M.H. Smith* (London: Joseph, 1979), 31–32.

1007 Van Dooren and Sargeant, "Dead Babies", 77.

1008 John, "Melodrama and its Criticism", 3.

1009 The most prominent example is probably George Cruikshank's series of prints titled *The Bottle* (1847) and the sequel *The Drunkard's Children* (1848), which show the descent of a family into poverty, murder and suicide caused by a father's alcoholism. Both series were transferred to lantern slides by at least four different slide producers. Joss Marsh thus fittingly calls Cruikshank's tale "the work that launched the Temperance movement into lantern propaganda". Marsh, "Dickensian Dissolving Views", 23. On THE BOTTLE and other examples of temperance slide sets, see Vogl-Bienek, *Lichtspiele*, 171–177. On the temperance movement and the magic lantern, see Richard Crangle and Mervyn Heard, "The Temperance Phantasmagoria", in Crangle, Heard and van Dooren (ed.), *Realms of Light*, 46–55.

1010 The painting is based on an engraving by Fildes titled *Houseless and Hungry* (1869) and published in the illustrated London newspaper *The Graphic*. See Rosen, "Posed as Rogues", 12.

had always to be put in quarantine by being made to stand on sheets of brown paper sprinkled with Keating's Powder.[1011]

James Bamforth similarly recruited regulars at the local pub to pose for his lantern slides: "A public-house interior is, perhaps, the easiest possible scene to fill with realistic sitters, for though Holmfirth is a busy little town there are always some idlers in the nearest 'pub,' and they know that whatever else in the studio may be a fraud the beer is real."[1012] A similar comment appears in another article on the production of lantern slides at Bamforth published in 1900: "Thus it has happened that some of his bold, bad villains have been really most respectable and law-abiding townsmen, while some of the awful drunkards have been in private life the most sober of men. At the same time it must be admitted that the taproom of the local public-house has afforded some excellent models."[1013] These anecdotes further highlight the moral decay of the drunkard and assure that the fictional character – however authentic he (or she) may be – is not met with empathy but rather disgust and outrage.

The fourth and fifth slide are the only two included in all eight surviving versions of THE ROAD TO HEAVEN.[1014] From the copyright entries at Stationers' Hall, two distinct versions of both slides can be dated and attributed to the respective slide series. On 16 August 1888 James Bamforth registered a "Photograph illustrating a scene from a set of lantern slides entitled 'The Road to Heaven' parapet of bridge with man leaning over and a boy with crutch sitting down".[1015] Slide variants found in the illuminago, Willem Wagenaar and Kirklees Museums and Galleries collection versions show a tall figure standing on the left, his back turned to the camera, his face hidden, wearing a wide-brimmed hat.[1016] The small boy sitting next to him, looking over the edge of the wall, is shown in profile with a makeshift crutch and bandaged left foot. He is wearing the same hat, shawl and torn jacket and appears to be the same actor as in the second (Bamforth A, C) and third slide (Bamforth A, B, C) of the set. A different version of the fourth slide was registered for copyright on 13 November 1891 with the following description: "Photograph 'Road to Heaven', two boys, one a cripple seated on bridge, man standing."[1017] Here, as

1011 Luke Val Fildes, *Luke Fildes, R.A.: A Victorian Painter* (London: Michael Joseph, 1968), 25.

1012 *The Photogram* (February 1899): 76. Curiously, the man posing as the drunken father for THE ROAD TO HEAVEN appears in an accompanying photograph and is cited as an example of one of the neighbors "harmless enough in real life, who make beautiful models as 'leading drunkards,' wife-beaters etc., and who are quite willing to oblige by doing so". Ibid., 78.

1013 Reynolds, "Sentiment to Order", 340.

1014 The third surviving version of THE ROAD TO HEAVEN in the illuminago collection consists only of slides 4 and 5 from one of the earlier Bamforth versions of the set.

1015 The National Archives: "Record COPY 1/393/267", *Records of the Copyright Office, Stationers' Company* (http://discovery.nationalarchives.gov.uk/details/record?catid=-4344089&catln=7).

1016 In the Cinémathèque française version of the slide the image is inverted, the taller boy standing on the right and Mike sitting on the left.

1017 The form was completed on 13 November with the registration stamp dating from the 17 November. See The National Archives: "Record COPY 1/406/473" (http://discovery.nationalarchives. gov.uk/details/r/C9252376).

Fig. 44: Slide 4 of THE ROAD TO HEAVEN (Bamforth B, 1891, 7–9 slides),
John Finney Collection, reproduced with permission.

in the later version of the second slide, the narrator is shown watching the two boys whose conversation he is eavesdropping on, unbeknownst to them.[1018]

The fifth slide marks the dramatic climax of the ballad as Mike is shown falling headfirst over the bridge's parapet, only his naked feet and legs still visible over the stonework. The camera's perspective and positioning of the actors mirror those of the fourth slide in both versions. One shows only the falling Mike and the taller boy, his hands raised in a dramatic gesture (Bamforth A and C).[1019] The second, later version (Bamforth B) leaves the taller boy's position unchanged only leaning further over the stonework, while the narrator has moved closer to the pair and is the one to raise his arms, stretching them out towards the falling Mike in vain.[1020]

1018 Variants of this slide are found in the Mervyn Heard, illuminago and John Finney collections.

1019 It was registered for copyright as "Photograph illustrating a scene from a set of lantern slides entitled 'The Road to Heaven', parapet of bridge boy falling over and man holding up his hands" on 16 August 1888. The National Archives: "Record COPY 1/393/265" (http://discovery.nationalarchives.gov.uk/details/record?catid=-4344087&catln=7). Variants of this slide are found in the illuminago, Cinémathèque française, Mervyn Heard and Kirklees Museums and Galleries collections.

1020 The slide was registered for copyright as "Photograph 'Road to Heaven', two boys, one a cripple, who has jumped over bridge, man looking after him" on 13 November 1891. The National Archives: "Record COPY 1/406/474" (http://discovery.nationalarchives.gov.uk/details/record?catid=-4532548&catln=7). Variants of this slide are found in the John Finney, illuminago (two variants) and Willem Wagenaar collections.

Fig. 45: Slide 5 of THE ROAD TO HEAVEN (Bamforth, before 1888),
Cinémathèque française Collection, reproduced with permission.

Any ambiguities regarding the exact circumstances of Mike's fall into the Thames present in George Sims's ballad ("He'd stood but a moment looking – how it happened I cannot tell") are absent from this depiction.[1021] The frantic hand gestures of the other characters and Mike's outstretched legs signal that his plunge is an unfortunate accident and not an unconscious or conscious suicide attempt. This becomes clear especially in comparison with a contemporaneous depiction of a woman jumping to her death from a London bridge. The final plate of George Cruikshank's temperance story *The Drunkard's Children* (1848) depicts her in mid-air in front of the bridge's arch, her hands flung desperately over her eyes, her clothes and hair flowing in the wind as she is plunging to her death. The image was also reproduced as a lantern slide in the 1880s by several producers who adapted Cruikshank's popular plates for the magic lantern.

While the buildup to the dramatic event of the ballad is fairly similar in all three reconstructed versions of THE ROAD TO HEAVEN by Bamforth, the narrative resolution is managed differently in each iteration of the series. In version A (before 1890, 6 slides) there is no slide depicting the boy's fall, judging from the slide titles. The fourth slide is titled "'That there's one road to 'eaven,' he said", referring to the two boys looking down at the water from the bridge's

---

1021 St. 18, v. 1, p. 65.

Fig. 46: Slide 5 of THE ROAD TO HEAVEN (Bamforth B, 1891, 7–9 slides), John Finney Collection, reproduced with permission.

Fig. 47: Slide 8 of THE DRUNKARD'S CHILDREN (York & Son, in or before 1888, 8 slides), Philip and Rosemary Banham Collection, reproduced with permission.

coping. The fifth slide, titled "His forehead was cut and bleeding but a vestige of life we found", jumps directly to the boy's rescue at the hospital. It seems likely that slide 5 in version A corresponds to slide 6 in versions B and C ("When they brought him here he was senseless, but slowly the child came round"). That slide shows the unconscious boy, his face bleeding from multiple wounds, as he is being carried to a hospital bed by a boatman; a nurse is opening her arms to welcome the patient while the narrator appears to be walking into the scene from the opposite direction.[1022] Notably, all three adults are either bowing their heads or turning them away from the camera. The arrangement appears to have followed established principles of life model slide composition as described by Richard Crangle: "Characters were often positioned with their backs to the camera, particularly in the case of extras, or were positioned relative to the background or other characters as though caught in mid-action, and sometimes caught in motion."[1023] All of this contributed to a realistic impression, as actors "were arranged to simulate instantaneously-arrested stages of everyday movement and situations into which the camera happened to have intruded, rather than situations created with only their framing and visual status in mind (although framing remained important)".[1024]

The sixth and final slide (although, notably, not the final screen image) of Bamforth version A is titled "Then to the kind old doctor, 'please are you God,' he said", according to the Riley catalogue. Slide number 7 from the Cinémathèque version of the set shows the boy in a hospital bed together with a sitting doctor and another man (the narrator) leaning over him.[1025] However, the handwritten number 7 attached to the slide appears to cover a typewritten number 6 on a round paper slip under the coverglass.[1026] The slide title for slide number 7 of version Bamforth C (in or before 1887, 7 slides) is given as "He ventured to ask him, 'Please sir, are you God'" in the Band of Hope Catalogue. Since both titles potentially match the image, it may have originally formed part of either version. This implicitly confirms the existence of Bamforth version A (before 1890, 6 slides) from the surviving artefacts although it remains unclear exactly which of the surviving slides formed part of the nominal set.

To conclude the narrative, Bamforth version A of THE ROAD TO HEAVEN called for a repetition of the first slide (showing the deceased boy in the hospital bed) during projection, accompanied by the verse "And now he is safe for ever,

---

1022 Variants of this slide are found in all six collections. The matching nurse's uniform, similar props and recurring Christmas mottoes on the background wall all indicate that the photograph was taken around the same time as the negatives for the first slide, which was registered for copyright in August of 1888. The image could thus easily have formed part of all three versions of the series.

1023 Crangle, *Hybrid Texts*, 146.

1024 Ibid.

1025 Variants of this slide are found in all six collections, four with a printed slide number 7 on them.

1026 A consultation of the physical artefact could bring clarity in this matter.

Fig. 48: Slide 6 of THE ROAD TO HEAVEN (Bamforth B, 1891, 7-9 slides), John Finney Collection, reproduced with permission.

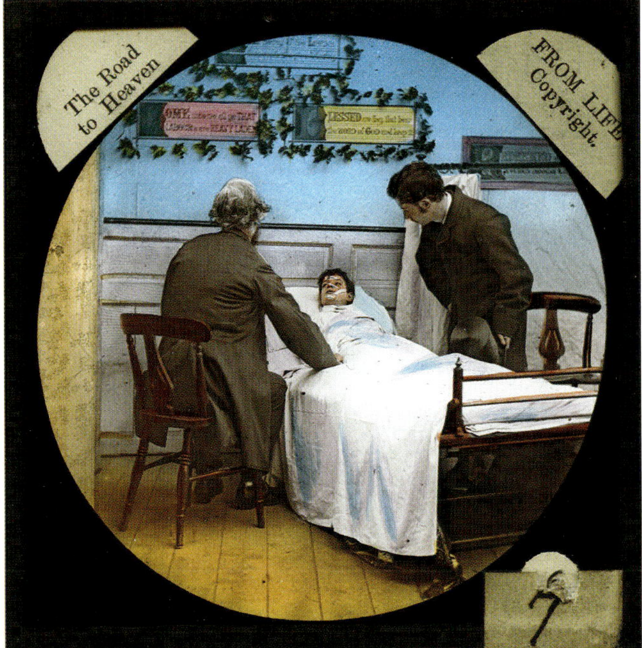

Fig. 49: Slide 7 of THE ROAD TO HEAVEN (Bamforth, before 1888), Cinémathèque française Collection, reproduced with permission.

where such as he are best [sic]".[1027] Over the course of the ballad Mike is thus transformed from the "poor little waif" of the first slide to one who is blessed in death. Ine van Dooren and Amy Sargeant describe the idea of a "good death" as expressed frequently in Victorian representations of dying children:

> The death of a child is often depicted as an exemplary, good death, relieved of the physical decay, moral dilemmas and emotional sorrow which is the burden of a full life's span. It may even be seen as a welcome respite, with Jesus and the angels (as in Sims's *Billy's Rose*) beckoning to a comfortably domestic heaven beyond the grave.[1028]

They note, however, that these deaths often serve "a narrative or moral purpose", like reuniting estranged lovers and families or reforming drunk parents.[1029] An aspect that is notably absent from Sims's version of *The Road to Heaven*. Mike's death is completely self-contained and serves only as a satisfying narrative resolution for his own tragic story. Robert Craven, in his rewriting of Sims's ballad for Bamforth (version C, in or before 1887, 7 slides) clearly attempts to establish a purpose for Mike's death. As the first stanza reveals, his story served as a catalyst for the narrator's temperance activism and could resonate even beyond the narrative:

> I don't know whether you'll care to know
> The poor lad's tale but it moved me so –
> I thought of the thousands in similar plight,
> And longed for the power their wrongs to right;
> I thought I might help in some humble way,
> The demon, that causes these horrors, to lay,
> And it may do the same to you very like,
> When you hear the story of poor crippled Mike.[1030]

Sargeant and van Dooren also note that a "good death" could be "a relief, a wish come true, a glorious reward, eternal happiness free from all care" for the dying children themselves.[1031] This idea is mirrored in the last verses of Craven's reading that accompanied a repetition of the first slide during projection. Mike's death, following his conversion, brings the boy happiness and relief from past abuses and Craven even places friends by his bedside (who are not depicted in the slide image): "And there in that hospital ward he lay / 'Til the cold earth should hide his body away / While his friends take a farewell look at the face / In which his past sufferings they can trace / But which are eclipsed by the smile of joy / That rests on the face of the now happy boy."[1032]

Version B (Bamforth, 1891, 9 slides) of THE ROAD TO HEAVEN does not call for a repetition of the first slide during projection and ends the visual narrative

---

1027 St. 23, v. 4, p. 66.

1028 Van Dooren and Sargeant, "Dead Babies", 78.

1029 Ibid., 80.

1030 Craven, v. 17–24, p. 10.

1031 Van Dooren and Sargeant, "Dead Babies", 78.

1032 Craven, v. 143–148, p. 13.

with slide number 7, the image of the boy, still alive, looking up at his doctor in confusion: "Then to the kind old doctor, 'Please are you God?' he said." This was preceded by slide number 6, which shows the boy being carried to the hospital, with the associated verses "When they brought him here he was senseless, but slowly the child came round". In between Mike's fall from the bridge and his arrival at the hospital, two additional slides were added in version B. Registered for copyright in June and July of 1891 and marked 5a and 5b, they add a new dramatic element to the visual story-telling of the series.[1033] Slide 5a shows an impressive perspective view of the bridge's stonework, the boy in front of it almost submerged in the 'water' with his eyes closed, one arm stretched out above his head.[1034] His pose is almost identical to a slide from the York & Son adaptation of the ballad, which will be discussed in the following section. This confirms Richard Crangle's assertion that "manufacturers appear to have had few scruples about re-using or blatantly copying each other's images and conceptions of a scene".[1035] This was apparently also the case for slide 5b of Bamforth version B which was photographed in front of the same bridge background as slide 5a. It shows two men in a small boat, one of them lifting the boy from the water by the collar of his jacket, the other reaching for him with both arms.[1036] York & Son had registered a slide with a similar composition for copyright one year earlier: "Photograph of Buttress of Bridge with two men in boat rescuing boy in water, Illustrating the story 'The Road to Heaven' by G R Sims."[1037]

Adaptation by York & Son

The manufacturer of lantern slides York & Son produced and distributed their own version of THE ROAD TO HEAVEN in 1890.[1038] It was quickly listed in distribution catalogues of slide retailers in England, the Netherlands and the United States of America.[1039] A surviving version missing one slide (number

---

1033 The numbering is somewhat curious. Bamforth usually added lowercase letters to slide numbers to mark slides with **optional** projection effects like dream sequences or superimpositions. The slide titles indicate that during performance, the images would have appeared on the screen for a mere two lines each. This could mean that the ballad recital would have been interrupted after the fifth slide to heighten the dramatic effect of Mike's fall into the Thames – possibly by adding musical accompaniment. I am thankful to Ludwig Vogl-Bienek for pointing this out to me.

1034 The National Archives: "Record COPY 1/404/469", *Records of the Copyright Office, Stationers' Company* (http://discovery.national archives.gov.uk/details/record?catid=-4406931& catln=7). Variants of this slide are found in the illuminago and the John Finney collections.

1035 Crangle, *Hybrid Texts*, 139.

1036 Variants of this slide survive in the illuminago (two variants), the John Finney and Mervyn Heard collections.

1037 Registered on 14 August 1890. The National Archives: "Record COPY 1/401/242" (http://discovery.na-tionalarchives.gov.uk/details/r/C9144168).

1038 All eight slides of the set were registered for copyright in the right order on 14 August 1890. The National Archives: "Record COPY 1/401/236–243" (http://discovery.nationalarchives.gov.uk/browse/r/h/ C9144162).

1039 UK Band of Hope Union, 1891, Section B, 142; Church of England Temperance Society quoted in Stead, "Magic Lantern Mission", 565; *Catalogue and Price List of Stereopticons, Dissolving-View Apparatus, Magic Lanterns, and Artistically-Colored Photographic Views on Glass* (New York: T.H. McAllister, 1891), 186.

Fig. 50: Slide 5a of THE ROAD TO HEAVEN (Bamforth B, 1891, 7–9 slides), John Finney Collection, reproduced with permission.

Fig. 51: Slide 6 of THE ROAD TO HEAVEN (York & Son, 1890, 8 slides), Nicholas Hiley Collection, reproduced with permission.

Fig. 52: Slide 5b of THE ROAD TO HEAVEN (Bamforth B, 1891, 7–9 slides), John Finney Collection, reproduced with permission.

Fig. 53: Slide 7 of THE ROAD TO HEAVEN (York & Son, 1890, 8 slides), Nicholas Hiley Collection, reproduced with permission.

7, titled "They dragged his body out") is found in the Gwen Sebus collection, while a complete version of eight slides survives in the Nicholas Hiley Collection. The incidents from the ballad selected for illustration are almost identical to the Bamforth versions and the pictorial composition of most slides is similar as well. The series differ mostly in details, the use of different perspectives and the quality of the painted backgrounds. In general, York's painted backdrops were more detailed and realistic, as Richard Crangle notes: "Life Model slides by York, in particular, are instantly recognisable by their highly-detailed background scenes, especially in interior views, their conspicuous use of interior perspective effects, and the inclusion of ceiling detail in room interiors."[1040] Such perspective effects are used to represent the hospital ward in the first slide of the ROAD TO HEAVEN series. While the Bamforth slide is centred on the dead boy in his bed with the other characters grouped around him, the York & Son slide presents the doctor and narrator in conversation in the foreground, with a nurse walking away from the scene with a tray in her hands in the middle plane.[1041] The painted background uses a combination of details (chairs, paintings, curtains, a small sculpture) on the left side and a vanishing point on the right side of the image to create the illusion of depth. The dead Mike is notably hidden from view behind a folding screen in a literal adaptation of the opening verses of the Sims ballad: "How is the boy this morning? Why do you shake your head? / Ah! I can see what's happened – there's a screen drawn round the bed."[1042] Slides 2 through 5 of York and Son's THE ROAD TO HEAVEN all follow the same compositional principle. The images are split into a bottom and a top half by the bridge's balustrade which appears to be a skilful combination of the painted backdrop and furniture placed in the studio. The background itself is much less detailed than in the first and last slide, the buildings and chimneys of nightly London appearing dimly lit and out of focus. The characters are all completely visible in the frame, posed in the middle plane. The changing scenes are presented in wide shots, almost as they would appear on a theatre stage. In that they resemble the later Bamforth version B produced in 1891 while in the earlier Bamforth versions A and C, the boys are shown in a sort of close-up that almost fills the entire picture. This gave viewers a chance to study their run-down appearance and ragged clothes more closely while the wide perspective highlights the characters' actions and their relationships instead.

Unlike the Bamforth versions, the York & Son set foregoes any depiction of Mike's living situation or his parents in favour of a literal adaptation of various scenes described in the ballad. The second slide of the York & Son version thus

---

1040 Crangle, *Hybrid Texts*, 141.

1041 The bearded man holding a walking stick, who acts as the narrator in this slide set, also appeared in at least two other adaptations of Sims's ballads by York & Son. As the (almost) silent interlocutor in THE LIFEBOAT (1886, 7 slides) and again as the narrator (a School Board officer) in THE MAGIC WAND (1889, 9 slides).

1042 St. 1, v. 1–2, p. 59.

shows two boys, both of them barefoot, sitting with a dog at the foot of a stone bench accompanied by the verses "I was looking about for a collie – a favourite dog I'd lost / Some ragged boys, so they told me, had been seen with one that night / In one of the bridge recesses, so I hunted left and right."[1043] The fourth slide pictures Mike leaning on his crutch begging from an older gentleman as the verses "He'd a drunken father and mother, who sent him out to beg / Though he'd just got over a fever, and was lame with a withered leg" are recited.[1044] This combination of images and spoken words establishes Mike as a helpless and deserving poor character worthy of charity and empathy.[1045] Interestingly, it is the only slide of the set that shows the boy actually using his crutch to support himself, thus putting his illness on display for the viewer. The boy also looks very small in comparison with the portly gentleman standing next to him.

In the third slide of the series the two boys appear to be almost the same height with their clothes and hats much tidier than in the Bamforth versions. Their pose is not without a picturesque quality: One is reclining against the stone-work, his legs crossed, and the other is lying on the bench, his legs stretched out, holding a long crutch in one hand while he leans into the sitting boy's chest as the narrator observes the scene from the right. The careful arrange-ment of their poses is contrasted with their more natural positions in the fifth slide, which shows both of them seated atop the bridge's parapet, Mike leaning halfway over the edge as Jack points down with one arm. The narrator on the right is now bending towards the pair but makes no effort to intervene. The boys' physical closeness in the third slide matches the descriptive verses ("One was singing the carol, when the other, with big round eyes – It was Mike – looked up in wonder") and suggests their loving connection.[1046] Their respec-tive positions mark Jack as the stronger of the two, caring for his weaker, handicapped friend.[1047] Such "loving relationships" between waif children were frequently depicted in popular waif stories of the time, according to literary historian Anna Davin:

> The waifs huddle against each other for warmth and comfort, sleep in each other's arms, kiss and soothe each other, fear for and make sacrifices for each other. The older ones take economic responsibility, struggling to earn enough for rent and their daily food, however meagre; and at the same time, girl or boy, they mother the younger ones. […] Similar loving relationships in some cases develop between

---

1043 St. 5, v. 2–4, p. 60.

1044 St. 14, v. 1–2, p. 63.

1045 That street children and their various efforts to make money were also seen as a nuisance is evident in *Punch* cartoons of the time that depict crossing-sweepers and cart-wheelers in particular as obstacles in London's traffic. See Cunningham, *Representations of Childhood*, 116–119.

1046 St. 10, v. 1–2, p. 62.

1047 Homeless and orphaned children were also typical characters of melodrama, the physically stronger protecting the smaller and weaker one. George Sims reused this trope for his play *Two Little Vagabonds* in 1896, which also featured a prolonged death scene for one of them. See Crozier, *Notions of Childhood*, 91 and 114–124.

Fig. 54: Slide 1 of THE ROAD TO HEAVEN (York & Son, 1890, 8 slides), Nicholas Hiley Collection, reproduced with permission.

Fig. 55: Slide 3 of THE ROAD TO HEAVEN (York & Son, 1890, 8 slides), Nicholas Hiley Collection, reproduced with permission.

children who are not siblings; they are not the less intense, but for reasons of propriety, no doubt, they are then usually between children of the same sex.[1048]

In the context of the Christmas setting evoked by the ballad, the image of the two boys moves towards a sentimentalizing depiction of street children popularized from the 1870s in paintings by Augustus Edwin Mulready.[1049] His *A London Crossing Sweeper and Flower Girl* (1884) presents a picturesque pair of street children in a bridge recess, their faces white as marble while the lights of London provide a romantic backdrop. Similarly, *A Recess on a London Bridge* (1879) shows a rosy-cheeked homeless boy, reclining in a bridge recess under a starry sky, his eyes closed peacefully, his ripped trousers and oversized shirt draped decoratively around his light, clean skin.

Unlike in Bamforth versions B and C the dramatic event of the ballad, Mike's fall into the Thames, is not depicted in the York & Son version. The same stone bench was used for the depiction of a female suicide in an another slide set, THE GIN FIEND (York & Son, in or before 1888, 4 slides).[1050] The second slide of the set shows a woman standing on the bench with her back to the viewer, her long hair loose, one arm raised dramatically to her forehead to signal her despair and impending jump. And York & Son's adaptation of Thomas Hood's *The Bridge of Sighs* used the same backgrounds and almost identical positioning of characters as slides 5 and 6 of THE ROAD TO HEAVEN to depict the protagonist's suicide.[1051] After leaning over the coping in slide 5, the boy is shown adrift next to the bridge's pillar and arch in the following image, his body already half submerged in the water (see Fig. 50).

The eighth and final slide of the set uses the same painted background and almost identical point of view as the first one but reveals a hospital bed in the middle plane and shows other young patients in their beds in the background (not visible in the first slide through careful placement of the actors). The ward is now decorated with "mistletoe green and holly, in honour of Christmas Day".[1052] The boy's body remains almost completely hidden under the large blankets, one arm flung across his forehead ("And, as he looked about him, came the kind old surgeon through / Mike gazed at his face a moment, put his hand to his fevered head") as the doctor slightly lifts his right hand, appearing to check for a pulse while the nurse and narrator look on.[1053] As in the other slides (and in contrast to the Bamforth versions), the entire scene is depicted

---

1048 Davin, "Waif Stories", 86.

1049 See Cunningham, *Representations of Childhood,* 159. "[Mulready] painted many small pictures of starving waifs, street beggars and flower girls. He idealised his subjects, giving them stage rags and winsome expressions without a hint of malnutrition." Ibid., 159–160.

1050 For digital reproductions, see the Lucerna record for the slide set (http://lucerna.exeter.ac.uk/set/index.php? id=3004474).

1051 See reproductions of the four slides from the series included in Peter Delpeut et al., *Laterna Magica* (Amsterdam: Nederlands Filmmuseum & Skrien, 1989), 28–29.

1052 St. 20, v. 1–2, p. 65.

1053 St. 22, v. 2–3, p. 66.

Fig. 56: Slide 5 of THE ROAD TO HEAVEN (York & Son, 1890, 8 slides), Nicholas Hiley Collection, reproduced with permission.

Fig. 57: Slide 8 of THE ROAD TO HEAVEN (York & Son, 1890, 8 slides), Nicholas Hiley Collection, reproduced with permission.

in a wide shot, the persons presented from head to toe in the middle distance with the studio floor visible in the foreground.

In conclusion, the York & Son adaptation of *The Road to Heaven* depicts the events described in Sims's ballad more faithfully than the Bamforth versions, in particular through the use of detail (the dog, the hospital screen). All four series were clearly influenced by contemporaneous depictions of poor children, whether in paintings or popular literature, and show elements of a picturesque poverty in the costumes and poses selected for the two homeless boys.

Reception Contexts and Other Adaptations

Public recitations and readings of poems, ballads and excerpts of famous plays were popularized throughout the 19th century. This included a wide range of practices like elocutionary competitions, mixed concerts and educational exercises in diverse venues like schoolrooms, public halls or the variety entertainment of the music halls.[1054] Frequently but not always, recitations were accompanied by visual illustrations in the form of magic lantern slides. As film projectors slowly entered lantern culture, professional reciters increasingly worked cinematographic images into their elocutionary practices. They formed part of what Stephen Bottomore has called an "'experimental' era for live audio" in early British cinema and "a time of quite significant experimentation in the relationship between the human voice and the new moving pictures" that lasted well into the 1910s.[1055] Performers like Eric Williams or Mr and Mrs Dove Paterson and companies like the Clarendon Film Co. and the American Poem-o-Graph Company experimented with various combinations of spoken words and films. The Clarendon Film Co. introduced their "speaking pictures" in December of 1913. Hailed as the "latest thing in cinematography" by *The Cinema*, these films illustrated famous monologues and poems which were simultaneously recited during film exhibition by speakers hidden from view.[1056] The American Novelty Poem-o-Graph Company of Cleveland, Ohio, purchased the rights to produce a "human-voice talking picture" of George Sims's ballad *In the Workhouse. Christmas Day* in 1913 that was "met with great success wherever it has been shown".[1057] Eric Williams was a professional elocutionist who appeared in specially produced film adaptations of selected poems which he would recite synchronously during projection. His repertoire also included a version of George Sims's *The Lifeboat* produced in 1914.[1058]

1054 See Kirkpatrick, "Wild Reciter", 59–71. On recitation as part of the Victorian school curriculum, see Robson, "Burning Deck", 148–162.

1055 Stephen Bottomore, "Eric Williams: Speaking to Pictures", in Julie Brown and Annette Davison (ed.), *The Sounds of the Silents in Britain* (New York: Oxford University Press, 2013), 55–71, here 55 and 57.

1056 "Clarendon Speaking Pictures", *The Cinema*, vol. 5, no. 61 (11 December 1913): 32.

1057 *The Billboard* (23 August 1913): 15, and *Motion Picture News*, vol. 9, no. 5 (7 February 1914): 28.

1058 On Dove Paterson, see Trevor Griffiths, "Sounding Scottish: Sound Practices and Silent Cinema in Scotland", in Brown and Davison (ed.), *The Sounds of the Silents*, 76–81.

An analysis of newspaper reports and advertisements for magic lantern shows featuring recitations or readings of *The Road to Heaven* between 1888 and 1914 reveals both a continuity of elocutionary practices and a rapidly changing media landscape around the turn of the century and in the 1910s.[1059] The varying performance contexts give an indication of how the lantern slide series and the ballad were presented to contemporary audiences over time. The number of reports found over this 26-year period is too small to allow for a quantitative interpretation but with more than 110 individual performances it reveals general tendencies and offers material for qualitative analysis of shows given by individual performers over time.[1060] The reports also reveal a broad range of terms used to describe the projection apparatus. It was usually referred to as "lantern" or "magic lantern" but also as "oxy-hydrogen light", "oxy hydrogen limelight lantern" or in one case "powerful oxy-hydrogen bi-unial lantern".[1061] Similarly, the glass images were often simply called "slides" or "lantern slides" but also frequently referred to as "views", "pictures", "transparencies", "illustrations" or "dissolving views". The projection surface, if it was mentioned at all, was only called either "screen" or "sheet". As far as the geographical distribution is concerned, reports mentioned performances both in larger cities and smaller towns (e.g., Sunderland, Northampton, Aberdeen, Dundee, Belfast) as well as small villages (e.g., Innerleithen, Richhill, Kincardine O'Neil, East Pennard) across England, Scotland and Northern Ireland.[1062] And while recitations were given all year round, lantern events with projected images tended to take place during the autumn and winter months (roughly between September and March).[1063]

Reports about public recitations of *The Road to Heaven* in various performance contexts indicate that it entered the repertoire of professional and amateur reciters shortly after its first publication in December of 1882. From January 1883 recitations of *The Road to Heaven* were included in varied entertainments together with songs and musical performances or in religious contexts and by

---

1059 By contrast, only a single report explicitly mentioned THE ROAD TO HEAVEN in *The Sunday School Chronicle* between the years of 1883 and 1900. See event entry in Lucerna – The Magic Lantern Web Resource (http://lucerna.exeter.ac.uk/event/index.php?language=EN&id=7004198).

1060 Found with the search phrase "road to heaven" and the starting date 24 December 1882 (first publication of ballad) and ending date 31 December 1914 in the British Newspaper Archive in January and February of 2017. That same search yielded more than 2,900 individual hits in August of 2017. The number of performances (111) refers only to those that explicitly mentioned illustrated recitations either with lantern slides or film images – the number of 'plain' recitations was much higher.

1061 The term "magic lantern" had established itself in England by the 1890s at the latest. See Crangle, *Hybrid Texts*, 118. For a list of more than 25 names used for the apparatus by different English instrument makers in the late 1880s, see *The Optical Magic Lantern Journal and Photographic Enlarger*, vol. 1, no. 1 (15 June 1889): 2–3.

1062 As noted in chapter four, this might have less to do with a prevalence of lantern shows in these areas and more with the types of newspapers and reporting found there and the quality of the material selected for digitization. The only report about an illustrated performance of *The Road to Heaven* given in London came from a local paper for the district of Shoreditch and the borough of Hackney. For newspaper reports on performances in New Zealand, see Lydia Jakobs, *George R. Sims' viktorianische Armutsballaden im Medium der Projektionskunst*, MA diss. (Trier: University of Trier, 2011), 54–56.

1063 This roughly matches the dates of the so-called lantern season. See Crangle, *Hybrid Texts*, 123.

temperance organizations like the I.O.G.T. (International Order of Good Templars) and the Band of Hope. Recitations of the ballad during concerts, elocutionary competitions and performances or varied entertainments continued throughout the 1880s and 1890s. The first report of a recitation accompanied by magic lantern slides appeared on 17 November 1888 in the *Cheshire Observer*, the same year that Bamforth registered photographs from their earlier version of THE ROAD TO HEAVEN for copyright.[1064] At the "annual tea meeting" of the Presbyterian Church in Chester attended by more than 300 people, a Mr Llew Wynne recited a number of pieces (including two Sims ballads) and managed the lantern during a "musical and elocutionary entertainment, illustrated by oxy-hydrogen transparencies".[1065] After that date, illustrated recitals and traditional ones ran in parallel with the bulk of reports on illustrated performances dating from the 1890s.[1066] Between 1900 and 1909, a significantly larger number of 'plain' recitations were given at religious events or concerts as well as elocutionary competitions and by professional reciters. Even throughout the 1910s recitations were still given as part of musical and temperance evenings or sacred concerts.

Most reports on recitations of the ballad foregrounded the abilities of the respective reciters, performers and elocutionists while the content of the mostly familiar pieces was of secondary importance. A report from the *Derry Journal* gives an idea of the required talents and the effect on the audience attributed to a good reciter. A Mr Warden, lessee of the Derry Opera House, performed *The Road to Heaven* following a "farcical eccentricity" and "burlesque extravaganza" presented by a touring acting company:

> We have never heard Mr. Warden to better effect. There was all the grace of movement, the charm of voice and presence, and singular impressiveness in the rendering that have long marked Mr. Warden distinguished as an actor and elocutionist. Mr. Warden seemed rapt in the feeling of the touching recital, and he carried the audience with him to the very realism of the scene depicted.[1067]

That same Mr J.F. Warden was also praised in the *Belfast News-Letter* for his restrained delivery of the ballad, which still allowed for the required pathos, one week earlier at the New Theatre Royal in Belfast:

> The unaffected style of Mr. Warden is particularly well suited to such a poem, for, if recited in the florid manner which some elocutionists consider essential to good effect, the ballad would only become ludicrous. Last evening, the deepest tenderness and the most genuine pathos were imparted to every stanza.[1068]

1064 Apart from events predating York's version of THE ROAD TO HEAVEN (1890, 8 slides) it is usually not possible to deduce which version of the slide series was shown at a specific event or – unless George Sims is explicitly mentioned – which reading accompanied the images.

1065 *Cheshire Observer* (17 November 1888): 5.

1066 A total of 74 reports between 1890 and 1899.

1067 *Derry Journal* (18 February 1884): 8. See also *Derry Journal* (15 February 1884): 5 for announcement.

1068 *Belfast News-Letter* (9 February 1884): 5.

Apart from such theatrical entertainments, the ballad was also frequently recited in temperance contexts. It was presented both alongside religious songs and other recitations during entertaining soirées and paired with personal stories and lectures for instructive events that stressed the dangers of alcohol and benefits of teetotalism. Organizations like the Band of Hope and the Church of England Temperance Society obviously recognized the tragic story as a valuable piece of propaganda.[1069] They also recognized the potential of projected images and made extensive use of lantern and cinematographic projections and had their own lantern departments and stocks of slides that were hired out to local branches.

The organizers and performers mentioned in reports about lantern events featuring the various versions of THE ROAD TO HEAVEN fall into four categories: National and regional temperance organizations like the Church of England Temperance Society and the Band of Hope or the Gibraltar Gospel Total Abstinence Society and the Independent Order of Rechabites included recitations in their magic lantern entertainments or regular meetings (usually held on weeknights), sometimes combined with medical or instructional slides (e.g. on the production of tea and sugar). Religious organizations and church missionary societies like the Sunday School Union, the Church Army Mission, the Wesleyan Lay Mission and the Sandy Baptist Christian Endeavour Society combined the illustrated ballad with longer services of song.[1070] Local chapels or churches also included it in concerts given in aid of church renovations or other funds connected to various missionary and social activities. THE ROAD TO HEAVEN was also performed in various institutions connected with poor relief during magic lantern entertainments that combined illustrated recitals, live music, travelogues and projection effects like chromatropes with comic and topical slides.[1071] Reports mention a diverse range of public and private institutions and initiatives from workhouses and hospital wards to convalescent homes and private homes for the insane; from Sailor's Rest and Working Men's Missions to Tea to Old People and Old Couples' Treats. At these events, attendees were often given free food (buns, apples, oranges, sandwiches, Christmas pudding) and drink (tea) or sometimes gifts and money around Christmastime. Lastly, individual performers, elocutionists and lecturers (e.g.,

---

1069 This might explain why it was chosen for adaptation to the magic lantern and why Bamforth supplied an alternative reading more suited to the message of abstinence and religious devotion. As Richard Crangle and Mervyn Heard have pointed out, Bamforth specifically targeted religious organizations: "The slide producer Bamforth and the slide hirer Riley Brothers, both run by Methodists, are good examples of businesses which did well, directly or indirectly, from the temperance movement." Crangle and Heard, "Temperance Phantasmagoria", 53.

1070 Services of song were illustrated church services composed of biblical and religious narratives – depicted in life model slides – interspersed with songs and hymns to be sung by the congregation. See also David Robinson, "Services of Song", in David Robinson, Stephen Herbert and Richard Crangle (ed.), *Encyclopaedia of the Magic Lantern* (Ripon, North Yorkshire: The Magic Lantern Society, 2001), 276.

1071 The other items included in lantern shows with THE ROAD TO HEAVEN were quite varied. Many included other adaptations of Sims's ballads, the most popular of which were IN THE SIGNAL BOX and THE LIFEBOAT with BILLY'S ROSE also mentioned multiple times.

a professor of phrenology) – sometimes connected with temperance or religious organizations or with special lantern initiatives like the Leicester Lantern Mission and the National Society of Lanternists – included the ballad in their lantern programmes.

Admission appears to have been either free or relatively cheap (one penny) for most events, announcements rarely mention ticket prices but do sometimes call for collections at the door for expenses incurred.[1072] A surprising number of events took place on Sundays either as religious lantern services, illustrated "sacred recitals" and lectures, or concerts of elocutionists (both male and female) and musical performers. Audience numbers were rarely mentioned, but in those cases they ranged between 80 and 300 people. From 1898, lantern events occasionally included "cinematograph exhibitions", with "animated pictures" gaining popularity in the late 1900s and 1910s as elocutionists in particular experimented with various combinations of spoken words and moving images.[1073]

One of them was Dove Paterson a popular elocutionist and cinematographer from Aberdeen. Born in Newburgh, Aberdeenshire, Paterson was a former salesman who started his career in popular entertainments with readings and recitals of Scottish and English poems in the 1880s. He was probably the first to publicly recite Sims's *The Road to Heaven* in Scotland shortly after it was first published in *The Referee*.[1074] The *Aberdeen Evening Express* reported on an evening of dramatic recitals interspersed with songs and piano music given "under the auspices of the Aberdeen Drapers' Assistants' Literary and Musical Association" on 16 January 1883.[1075] Paterson's selection also included another Sims ballad, *In the Signal-box*, and classics like *The Charge of the Light Brigade* and Thomas Hood's *The Bridge of Sighs*. The latter was perhaps the most famous description of a suicide by drowning of the Victorian period. In reception contexts like these, the dramatic stories and tragic deaths of desperate poor characters became exercises for the reciter's "dramatic ability" and presented an "excellent entertainment" for the audience.[1076] Similarly, a report on an evening event by the Nelson Street Church Literary Association in March of 1886 praised Paterson for his "well-known ability and feeling" in reciting *The Road to Heaven* among other recitation pieces by Tennyson and Scott.[1077] Throughout the 1880s and 1890s Paterson performed regularly in Scotland at

1072 For an example, see a report on a "Happy Evening for the People" concert in the *Lisburn Herald, and Antrim and Down Advertiser* (5 January 1895): 4. Here, regular ticket prices were threepence and sixpence with special reserved shilling seats.

1073 See *Aberdeen Press and Journal* (29 March 1898): 7 for an early example of a "cinematograph exhibition" combined with "limelight views" at a temperance meeting.

1074 The ballad was reprinted in two regional newspapers, the *Aberdeen Evening Express* (27 December 1882): 4, and the *Aberdeen Press and Journal* (30 December 1882): 6.

1075 *Aberdeen Evening Express* (17 January 1883): 4.

1076 Ibid.

1077 "Aberdeen. Dramatic and Organ Recitals", *Aberdeen Free Press* (3 March 1886): 4.

concerts and entertainment evenings, sometimes illustrated with magic lantern slides. Newspaper announcements point to different audiences (younger and poorer) and reception contexts if projected images were a prominent aspect or even the main attraction of an event. In April of 1888 Paterson (supposedly) read selected pieces followed by a "magic-lantern exhibition of 'John Ploughman's Pictures'" during a "social meeting for farm servants" held in Foveran, a small town north of Aberdeen.[1078] Paterson was also actively involved in the efforts of the Aberdeen Temperance Society and participated in their efforts of "providing a healthy entertainment of an interesting character for young people" on New Year's Day in 1889.[1079] He was to give the connective readings during a "lime light exhibition" in Aberdeen's Music Hall with multiple lanterns and lantern slides "procured from London" projected onto "a large sheet specially made for the Society".[1080] And in April of 1905 Dove Paterson and his son Leo, who operated the lantern, presented a "pictorial recital" and a selection of his photographs to patients at the Royal Infirmary, Aberdeen.[1081] For this event, two humorous films (called "series of pictures") entitled THE BUSY BOYS OF BON-ACCORD and TURNIP FREAKS were provided by a local lantern and slide dealer, Walker and Co. of Bridge Street, Aberdeen.[1082]

Dove Paterson soon owned his own cinematograph, sometimes operated by his son Leo while he acted as lecturer or described the images, and from October of 1907 Paterson regularly showcased the "electro-cinematograph machine" at the old Alhambra Musical Hall in Aberdeen.[1083] Paterson continued to perform as an elocutionist and cinematograph operator even after he became one of Aberdeen's first cinema proprietors in 1908. At the Gaiety Theatre, Shiprow, Paterson also developed a practice of "speaking to pictures" together with a female elocutionist with both of them positioned behind the screen.[1084] Dramatic recitations of *The Road to Heaven*, often illustrated with slides, formed part of their repertoire for concerts or interludes at film programmes or "picture services", although the reciting now fell to Marie Pascoe

---

1078 *Aberdeen People's Journal* (31 March 1888): 5.

1079 Announcement for "New Year's Entertainment for Children", *Aberdeen Free Press* (27 December 1889): 6. By New Year's Day of 1901, the Aberdeen Temperance Society's festival for children, programmed by Dove Paterson also included "a cinematograph exhibition". "The Temperance Festival", *Aberdeen People's Journal* (21 December 1901): 7.

1080 Ibid.

1081 "Pictorial Recital at Royal Infirmary", *Aberdeen Press and Journal* (10 April 1905): 7. The images were accompanied by piano music from one of the infirmary's nurses.

1082 Walker frequently collaborated with Paterson and might have introduced him to the moving images of the cinematograph. In October 1897, William Walker presented a combined "cinematograph and optical lantern exhibition" to the royal family and Court at Balmoral. "Cinematograph Exhibition at Balmoral", *Aberdeen Press and Journal* (27 October 1897): 8. One year later, an announcement for a benefit concert where Dove Paterson was listed among the performers touted Walker & Co.'s "famous cinematograph" with "new local and other pictures", which were to be presented during "the largest exhibition ever given in the city". *Aberdeen Press and Journal* (13 October 1898): 1.

1083 See "The Alhambra Hall Decorations", *Aberdeen Press and Journal* (10 October 1907): 4, and "The Alhambra", *Aberdeen Press and Journal* (19 May 1908): 4.

1084 Griffiths, "Sounding Scottish", 79–80.

(the future Mrs Dove Paterson).[1085] Press reports about these events from the 1910s show that the cinema benefits and benefit concerts were aimed at quite different audiences. At the Gaiety picture theatre those who donated to the Gale Relief Fund for victims of a shipwreck in January of 1912 were described as "the large-hearted patrons of Mr Dove Paterson's place of entertainment – all-working class people".[1086] In contrast, a sacred concert at the Music Hall for the same fund held the same week called for silver collections at the door and offered a "Golden Square door" for contributors willing and able to give one shilling.[1087] The programme included an illustrated recital of *The Road to Heaven* by Mrs Dove Paterson, who was praised for her "splendid elocutionary gift".[1088] The concert followed an interesting controversy centred around the refusal of the Aberdeen magistrates to allow the exhibition of cinematograph pictures on Sundays – even alongside the sacred songs and recitals and even if it was for charitable purposes.[1089] Paterson, who had told the *Aberdeen Journal* about his plans to show four cinematograph films at the sacred concert (sacred being the operative word), was thus only "permitted to put on lantern slides".[1090] A recitation of *The Road to Heaven* illustrated with moving images was finally given by Mrs Paterson as part of a Christmas entertainment and dinner for poor school children in 1913. The ballad was now described as "Dagonet's well-known Christmas story" and considered suitable for entertaining children.[1091]

Like *In the Workhouse*, George Sims's ballad *The Road to Heaven* presents the tragic fate of an individual deserving poor character. In contrast to the former, however, Mike's misery is not the result of a failed poor law (public) but rather explicitly blamed on the behaviour of other poor characters (personal). Both George Sims and Robert Craven highlight the moral corruption and alcoholism of the boys' parents, a common trope in philanthropic literature of the time. As historian Lydia Murdoch argues, missionaries like Dr Barnardo attempted to justify the separation of poor parents from their children by

---

1085 See reports on two picture services at the Gaiety in aid of the Aberdeen Lifeboat Fund in October 1910 in the *Aberdeen Press and Journal* (30 September 1910): 4, and *Aberdeen Press and Journal* (3 October 1910): 6. And on a concert and "cinematograph display" at the Corporation Lodging-House in the *Aberdeen Press and Journal* (20 March 1911): 8.

1086 "The Gaiety Fund", *Aberdeen Press and Journal* (24 January 1912): 7.

1087 A report in the *Aberdeen Press and Journal* described the audience as follows: "Many prominent citizens were present, and the whole tone of the concert was deeply touching and appropriate to the occasion, the affecting songs and beautiful coloured pictures appealing to all hearts." "Sacred Concert in Music Hall", *Aberdeen Press and Journal* (29 January 1912): 4.

1088 See "The Music Hall Concert", *Aberdeen Press and Journal* (27 January 1912): 6, and "Sacred Concert in Music Hall", *Aberdeen Press and Journal* (29 January 1912): 4.

1089 See "Sunday Cinematograph Entertainments", *Aberdeen Press and Journal* (27 January 1912): 8. The Cinematograph Act of 1909 expressly allowed cinemas to open for charity performances and sub-let their venue to charitable organizations on Sundays. See Burrows, *The British Cinema Boom*, 87–88.

1090 "Sacred Concert in Music Hall", *Aberdeen Press and Journal* (29 January 1912): 4.

1091 "Entertainments to City Children", *Aberdeen Press and Journal* (26 December 1913): 6.

presenting the children in their care either as "imagined orphans" or victims of domestic abuse:

> By scripting the evolution of poor children in melodramatic terms of rescue and reformation, philanthropists produced narratives that focused on individual and family pathologies rather than on the broader structural causes of poverty. For Barnardo and other innovative philanthropic reformers who were willing to extend child welfare beyond the services available under the poor law, saving poor children depended on the supposed absence or removal of their parents.[1092]

The solution to the 'problem' of poor children in London's streets was thus not political change but rather personal charity and the promotion of temperance. Accordingly, recitations and illustrated recitals of *The Road to Heaven* in temperance and charitable contexts appear to have remained constant over time – unlike the changing political implications of *In the Workhouse* outlined in the previous chapter.

This chapter has shown how popular images of poor children often combined visual clues of authentic poverty with compositional principles drawn from existing pictorial conventions. Poor children were mostly considered innocent and non-threatening deserving poor characters and thus uniquely suited to make audiences sympathetic to the plight of the poor. At the same time, they were sentimentalized with images of red-faced, bare-footed children in dramatic poses or huddled close together that presented their poverty as picturesque. Poor children made for pretty pictures and suffering poor children reached the hearts (and purses) of viewers.

1092 Murdoch, *Imagined Orphans*, 14.

Perspectives

Representations of poverty enjoyed a remarkable mobility across media and a wide popularity across British society in the Victorian period and beyond. Whether in novels or newspapers, illustrated magazines or paintings, sociological surveys or medical enquiries, lantern slides or films, "the poor" were objects of social concerns and Christian charity but also of entertainment. The poor and the working class were by no means a homogenous group and in London's densely populated centre were often forced to compete for the same living spaces. George Sims described the considerable hardships this caused for those displaced by slum clearances in *Three Brass Balls*:

> Sorrowfully the outcasts come from the rookery that has been their home for years. Vile and awful as the dens were, they have become attached to them; they have grown used to the foul air, the reeking walls, and the crumbling staircases. […] The bulk of the last lingerers have passed away, some to other rookeries, some to the workhouse, some to shelter which they have procured at the cost of half their poor earnings. Day by day, as the old haunts of the poor are destroyed to make room for palatial 'model lodgings' and 'artisans' dwellings,' it has become a harder task for them to find shelter. The gorgeous buildings reared on the site of their vaunted homes are far beyond their humble means, and the few existing places of the old-fashioned sort are crammed to suffocation.[1093]

The entire collection of short stories centred around pawned objects and the lives of those who need to monetize them. Sims's description of this economy of poverty represents the daily and often mundane struggles of living while poor:

> To the reckless and the unthrifty this is but a depot – a place to be visited from time to time with a light heart when the week's money has gone in drink, or a day's outing calls for more cash in hand. The regular customers crowd at certain periods and sacrifice their household gods with no thought of sacrilege, intending to redeem them and sacrifice them again, and looking upon the proceeding as an ordinary transaction of everyday life.[1094]

The "reckless and unthrifty" also mark the other end of the spectrum of poverty, the so-called "residuum" that threatened to contaminate and corrupt the working poor and their children. Such fears were repeatedly evoked in the 1880s, as Gareth Stedman Jones has shown:

1093 Sims, *Three Brass Balls*, 145–146.

1094 Ibid., 3. The titular three brass balls refer to the sign sometimes put up beside the doors of pawnshops like the one that Sims observed from his work at his father's office. See Sims, *My Life*, 36.

> The evidence of Sims, Mearns, and the Royal Commission on Housing revealed that the chronically poor 'residuum', far from being a dwindling enclave, in fact composed a substantial proportion of working-class London. [...] Herded into slums where religion, propriety, and civilization were impossible, interspersed with criminals and prostitutes, deprived of light and air, craving for drink and 'cheap excitement', the 'residuum' was large enough to engulf civilized London.[1095]

This book has identified in George R. Sims's works two modes of representing poverty – likewise located on a spectrum. Picturesque poverty, often associated with innocence and childhood in depictions that could be appreciated for their artistic merit but could also arouse sentiments such as pity and Christian charity. And authentic poverty, frequently associated with dirt, sickness and sexual depravity that shocked readers or viewers and served as a call to action.[1096] I have argued that both are the result of artistic strategies activated (or nullified) at the moment of reception. They are thus both historically contingent and subject to changing interpretations, depending both on the wider social and cultural context and more narrowly on the media conventions and specific exhibition practices. George Sims's ballad *In the Workhouse. Christmas Day,* first published in 1877 and frequently recited in contexts of religious and political agitation, lost much of its political radicalism after the welfare reforms of the 1910s. Reviews of the 1914 film adaptation instead stressed its potential to elicit an emotional, even cathartic response to the depiction of "the harshness of workhouse 'relief,' now largely mitigated".[1097] In contrast, recitations of the ballad given in the context of elocution and spoken performance over the same time period were usually judged by their style, textual accuracy and (suitably contained) emotional delivery rather than the political implications of the text.

For the purposes of this study, the picturesque was defined as an aesthetic operation that transforms a perceived social reality (whether a landscape, a cityscape, or a group of people) into an image that evokes pleasure – even if the subject itself is not pleasurable.[1098] The adjective picturesque was originally applied to travel destinations and landscapes that either conformed to or were modelled according to picturesque principles that valued "variety and contrast, light and shade, fragmentation, intricacy".[1099] Picturesque travel was popular-

---

1095 Stedman Jones, *Outcast London*, 283.

1096 There are also examples of the opposite. Italian *banditti* were sometimes considered a picturesque element of the Italian countryside and viewed as romantic outlaws – despite the very real danger they posed. Magic lantern slides with their often highly pictorial composition and artificial poses could still strive for realistic representations of the homes of the honest poor and of innocent children.

1097 "A Mixed Program. At A Composite Trade Show", *Kinematograph and Lantern Weekly*, vol. 16, no. 393 (5 November 1914): 55.

1098 Sometimes that transformation is meant literally. As literary historian Nancy Hill points out, the desire for a picturesque aesthetic significantly reshaped English landscapes in the 18th and influenced town planning in the 19th century. See Hill, *Dickens' Picturesque*, 9.

1099 Francesca Orestano, "Charles Dickens and Italy: The 'New Picturesque'", in Michael Hollington and Francesca Orestano (ed.), *Dickens and Italy: Little Dorrit and Pictures from Italy* (Newcastle-upon-Tyne: Cambridge Scholars Publishing, 2020), 49–67, here 53.

ized throughout the 18th century and from its inception included scenes of rural dilapidation and human misery like the slums of Naples or "gypsy encampments" in the English countryside. The authentic was defined as the result of authenticating strategies activated at the moment of reception. Some of these strategies were identified in analyses of Henry Mayhew's *London Labour and the London Poor* and George Sims's *How the Poor Live* (1883). They include the use of direct quotes and colloquial language (which could, however, also be picturesque), references to a personal familiarity of the authors with their subject and an abundance of detail in descriptions of poor homes. The authentic mode tended to present poverty as a social problem that threatened the stability of the "English race" and nation, while the picturesque often represented poverty as an expected part of everyday life in the city. The latter tended to value the formal, carefully constructed and composed image, while the former often attempted an immediate and direct representation and a confrontation with reality. Contrary to intuition, the photographically illustrated representations of poverty discussed in this book were not necessarily considered more authentic by contemporary reviewers and commentators than written accounts that relied on first-hand observations, direct quotes and detailed visual descriptions.

The status of being poor – through no fault of one's own – while pitiable also rendered one deserving of Christian charity in the form of almsgiving and parish assistance in the form of money or goods. But that was only true if a poor person was what they claimed to be – sick, old, unable to work – and not idle, lazy or unwilling to work; or, in other words, if their poverty was authentic. Otherwise, Christian charity and parish money would be misplaced and fraud would be encouraged. If they were to be perceived as authentic and arouse sympathy or affect political change, representations of poverty thus needed to affirm both the authenticity of the depiction (that they were showing what they claimed to be showing) and the authenticity of those depicted (that they were what they claimed to be). Similar to travel accounts, descriptions of 'hidden' poverty (in workhouses, slum buildings and common lodging-houses) presented a strange and foreign environment to audiences unable or unwilling to gain first-hand knowledge. Authenticating strategies combined with appropriate reception contexts suggested that such knowledge could be gained without the dangers – and possibilities of fraud – generally associated with poor neighbourhoods. The proliferation of illustrated newspapers and magazines and of photographic lantern slides increasingly offered readers and viewers experiences of armchair travel and virtual slumming.[1100]

This study also touches on ongoing discussions within the field of adaptation studies. George Sims's ballads were selected for adaptation by slide producers like Bamforth and York & Son for their popularity and in response to the widespread practices of public recitation and elocution. The preferred genre

1100 On virtual slumming, see Vogl-Bienek, *Lichtspiele*, 222–239.

were the photographic life model slides, which showed people in decorated sets posed in carefully composed groups to illustrate the pivotal events of a narrative. As series of illustrative images that depended on an accompanying recitation (or song) to produce a continuous narration, life model slides represent a special type of adaptation. Adaptation scholar Brian McFarlane has stressed the "central importance" of narrative for both novels and films and identified it as "the chief transferable element" in adaptations from one to the other. McFarlane's definition of narrative as "a series of events, causally linked, involving a continuing set of characters which influence and are influenced by the course of events" could easily include the visual narration of life model slide sets.[1101] They establish protagonists as characters that appear in all (or most) slides of a set, who are usually posed in interaction with other characters and props to signal actions, reactions and relations – even without the accompanying oral narration. George Sims's popular ballads with their stress on plot over characterization were thus well suited for adaptation in a lantern genre that favoured simple visual storytelling reminiscent of popular melodrama. They usually centred around a dramatic situation or past event in the life of the protagonist, which, following McFarlane's distinction between "transfer" and "adaptation proper", could be transferred directly to the projection screen:

> Broadly, a distinction has been made between those novelistic elements which can be *transferred* and those which require *adaptation proper*, the former essentially concerned with *narrative*, which functions irrespective of medium, and the latter with *enunciation*, which calls for consideration of two different signifying systems. By narrative is meant a series of (more or less) causally connected events working towards the illumination of a larger, underlying pattern which shapes the whole work, while enunciation comprehends all those elements of the work responsible for the display of this narrative.[1102]

George Sims's ballad formula relied heavily on characterization and authentification of characters through speech and dialect, which (depending on the abilities of the reciter) augmented the visualizations of the slides. The medium specificity of early cinema meant that adaptations of Sims's ballads for the movie screen required "adaptation proper", to replace the missing text and sound in the form of scenarios or film scripts (THE MAGIC WAND, OSTLER JOE) and intertitles (CHRISTMAS DAY IN THE WORKHOUSE, SIR RUPERT'S WIFE). Or a straightforward transfer of the practices of recitation to the theatre as efforts at synchronized elocution by Eric Williams (THE LIFEBOAT) and Dove Paterson (THE ROAD TO HEAVEN) indicate.

The adaptations of two ballads discussed in detail in this study show that the transfer or adaptation of a written (or spoken) text to a visual medium inevitably amounted to a reduction of ambiguities. The protagonist of *In the Workhouse. Christmas Day* is established unequivocally as a reliable narrator both in the lantern and film adaptation of the ballad. Scenes depict and thus confirm

1101 McFarlane, *Novel to Film*, 12.

1102 Ibid., 195.

his perspective on pivotal aspects of the narrative (e.g., that he did not steal from a baker's shop and was forcibly driven away from the workhouse gate), where lines like "'He's drunk!' said the workhouse master / 'Or else he's mad and raves'." or "Just let me have the fit out / It's only on Christmas Day / That the black past comes to goad me / And prey on my burning brain" in the ballad leave the possibility (however slim) of an unreliability.[1103] In the case of *The Road to Heaven*, possible ambiguities of the source text – like the dubious role of the narrator – necessarily disappeared in the studio photographs for the lantern adaptation, which show the narrator actively trying to save the unfortunate Mike. Adaptations of written texts in visual media usually open the subject to a wider circle of recipients (in case of the art of projection and early cinema, this meant working-class audiences in particular). The life model slide adaptations of Sims's ballads were often used by Christian and temperance organizations in their missionary work. Their causes left little room for ambiguities, thus an alternative reading for THE ROAD TO HEAVEN distributed by Bamforth formulated its evangelical message much more directly and aggressively than Sims's original.

The adaptations made of George Sims's ballad *The Road to Heaven* for the magic lantern also make an excellent case for the study of the historical art of projection in the Victorian and Edwardian period. An ever-growing number of contemporaneous sources from the British Isles is becoming accessible online. Personal data (addresses, birth dates, occupations, number of dependents) for many citizens is available from various censuses, through which researchers can identify and track individual performers, lecturers or others persons connected to the historical art of projection.[1104] Catalogues of magic lantern makers and slide manufacturers, distributors and organizations that used the art of projection for their own means are available as digital reproductions, allowing researchers to reconstruct the production, distribution and exhibition of lantern slides sets. And lastly, reports about lantern performances, religious and temperance events or other types of entertainments using the art of projection appeared in local and regional newspapers, the trade press and periodicals of charitable organizations all of which are continuously being digitized.[1105] The surviving artefacts (lantern slide series, slide readings, apparatuses) on the other hand are often scattered across museum collections, film and photographic archives and private collections.[1106] The field also yet lacks universal photographic and metadata standards for the digitization of lantern

---

1103 St. 6, v. 3–4 and st. 7, v. 3–6, respectively.

1104 Basic search functions are available free of charge for the English censuses between 1841 and 1911 (https://www.ukcensusonline.com). The National Archives of Ireland provide a similar search function for the 1901 and 1911 censuses (http://www.census.nationalarchives.ie/).

1105 It should be noted that women are often harder to find and track in newspaper and magazine databases as they were seldom referred to by their proper names but rather as, e.g., Mrs George Sims.

1106 For a list of the types of heritage institutions that hold magic lantern slides, see Francisco Javier Frutos Esteban, *Los ecos de una lámpara maravillosa. La linterna mágica en su contexto mediático* (Salamanca: Ediciones Universidad de Salamanca, 2010), 158–160.

slides, which can be attributed to the wide range of institutions from regional museums to national libraries that hold lantern slides as part of their collections.[1107] Individual and institutional collections are being digitized and made accessible online at a growing rate but critical or study editions of slide sets that collate and compare multiple versions of a series are still a rarity.[1108]

In her essay *The Comparative Method and Images*, Kari Kraus argues that methods developed in textual scholarship "for comparing variants between two or more related texts with the purpose of reconstructing their genealogy and archetype" can be made fruitful for the study of images.[1109] Kraus defines the objects and objectives of this "picture criticism" as follows:

> The types of images that are relevant to picture criticism are those for which multiple representations exist. Our concern is less with original paintings and drawings than with manual or mechanical reproductions of them, including engravings, slides, photographs, digital copies, or hand-drawn illustrations: pictorial artifacts that persist in time and space by virtue of being iterable rather than durable. It is not the reproductions per se that are of interest so much as the relationships among them; their points of agreement and disagreement; their manner of production, mode of dissemination, and connection to the original.[1110]

The study of surviving artefacts of the historical art of projection has much to gain from the comparative method. Where even the most basic information (manufacturer, date of manufacture, series a slide forms part of) is often unknown, the possibilities offered by the collation (systematically comparing two or more objects) and collocation (placing objects side by side for direct comparison) of digital surrogates are remarkable.[1111] Tentative dating is sometimes possible by comparing the colouring, binding, copyright slips and even the print of the slide numbers (serifs or no serifs) in multiple variants of a slide. Thus, ideally, digital surrogates of lantern slides should provide a facsimile of the entire artefact, not only the picture surface. While a digital copy of a lantern slide cannot replace the physical artefact, it can be more useful for answering certain research questions. High-resolution digital images of glass lantern slides allow users to examine details not visible when looking at the glass slides themselves with the naked eye.

1107 Javier Frutos Esteban and Carmen López San Segundo give a good overview and classify the different types of institutions and private collections that retain lantern slides in "Un fondo patrimonial en la sombra: la Linterna Mágica", *E-rph: Revista electrónica de Patrimonio Histórico*, no. 2 (2008): 9–15. For a provisional overview of digital collections of lantern slides, see Wikipedia: "List of Lantern Slide Collections" (https://en.wikipedia.org/ wiki/List_of_lantern_slide_collections).

1108 See the model critical edition of ORA PRO NOBIS (Bamforth, multiple versions) edited by Ludwig Vogl-Bienek for eLaterna: Historical Art of Projection (https://elaterna.uni-trier.de/#/ce/130169).

1109 Kari Kraus, "Picture Criticism: Textual Studies and the Image", in Neil Freistat and Julia Flanders (ed.), *The Cambridge Companion to Textual Scholarship* (Cambridge, New York: Cambridge University Press, 2013), 236–256, here 237.

1110 Ibid., 239.

1111 On collation and collocation, see ibid., 240.

Digital copies are increasingly replacing direct access to manuscripts or newspapers. Potentially, digital files can be copied indefinitely without any loss of picture quality. This allows for a wider dissemination of and better access to archival sources than ever before without risking deterioration of the fragile source material. As Vanessa Toulmin, founder of the National Fairground and Circus Archive notes, "regardless of the issues involving resolution, formats and means of creating back up copies, ultimately digitization of the collections improves both preservation and access".[1112] What will become of digital files in the long run as file formats change and server space potentially becomes scarce remains to be seen. Providing long-term sustainable (and ideally open) access will prove one of the biggest challenges for digitization efforts in the coming decades. Producing and distributing digital copies of artefacts (whether texts or images) is ultimately a means of enabling private digital collections of material to survive alongside institutional archives. If digital data is distributed freely and independent of the resource it is hosted in, that is bound to create multiple copies by virtue of images and texts being downloaded. Users will – intentionally or unintentionally – create their own digital archives. Even if the files will end up forgotten in unlabelled 'boxes' in their digital attic, they have the potential to be rediscovered and brought to light again – just like their analogue predecessors were decades ago.

Finally, this study has demonstrated that digital resources produce the best research results when used alongside more traditional archival resources. As digitization engulfs ever wider areas of historical material, the function of the researcher as the one to "fill in the gaps" becomes more pronounced. Locating the correspondence printed in response to Sims's *How the Poor Live* (1883) and reestablishing the original publication context of his ballads required access to physical copies of the *Pictorial World* and microfilms of *The Referee* held at the British Library, since neither newspaper has been digitized so far.[1113] It will be the function of the critical researcher to extract the most relevant results from digital resources but also to locate alternative discourses outside the digital canon.

1112 Vanessa Toulmin, "Digitization and Access", in Martin Loiperdinger (ed.), *Celluloid Goes Digital: Historical-Critical Editions of Films on DVD and the Internet* (Trier: Wissenschaftlicher Verlag Trier, 2003), 29–34, here 30.

1113 Selected volumes of *The Referee* have since been made digitally available in the British Newspaper Archive, although the years 1913 through 1928 from the British Library's holdings are still missing.

Appendices

Appendix A: Dates of First Publication for Selected Works by George R. Sims

Date	Title	*Periodical / Newspaper*	Volume / Issue	Page no.
9 December 1877	Told to the Missionary	*The Referee*		5
23 December 1877	In the Workhouse. Christmas Day	*The Referee*		5
30 December 1877	Jack's Story[1114]	*The Referee*		5
6 January 1878	Sal Grogan's Face	*The Referee*		5
20 January 1878	In the Shipka Pass	*The Referee*		5
3 February 1878	The Level Crossing	*The Referee*		7
10 March 1878	During Her Majesty's Pleasure	*The Referee*		7
21 April 1878	In A Cellar in Soho	*The Referee*		3
2 June 1878	Orinska	*The Referee*		7
30 June 1878	Two Women	*The Referee*		3
21 July 1878	The Last Letter	*The Referee*		3
11 August 1878	Billy's Rose	*The Referee*		7
15 September 1878	Moll Jarvis O'Morley: A Constable's Tale	*The Referee*		3
20 October 1878	Polly	*The Referee*		2–3
8 December 1878	An Old Fool: A Fashionable Conversation	*The Referee*		4
15 December 1878	Grundy's Grumble	*The Referee*		4
12 January 1879	Kate Maloney	*The Referee*		5
26 January 1879	A Fellow-Feeling	*The Referee*		5
3 November 1879	Fallen by the Way	*The Referee*		3
16 November 1879	The Matron's Story	*The Referee*		3
7 December 1879	Sir Rupert's Wife	*The Referee*		8
29 December 1879	A Christmas Story	*The Referee*		8
18 January 1880	One Winter Night	*The Referee*		8
February 1880	Sensational Science	*Time: A Monthly Miscellany of Interesting & Amusing Literature*	vol. II	608–611
1 March 1880	Forgotten – A Last Interview	*The Theatre: A Monthly Review of the Drama, Music, and the Fine Arts*		164–166

28 March 1880	A Silver Wedding	*The Referee*		6–7
16 May 1880	A Last Look	*The Referee*		7
26 December 1880	In the Signal Box	*The Referee*		n. pag.
5 June 1881	The Lifeboat	*The Referee*		7–8
January 1882	The Street Tumblers	*The Theatre*		36–38
9 April 1882	A Bunch of Primroses	*The Referee*		7
28 May 1882	In the Harbour	*The Referee*		7
6 August 1882	Nellie's Prayer	*The Referee*		7
24 December 1882	The Road to Heaven	*The Referee*		7
1 January 1883	Ticket o' Leave	*The Theatre*		10–12
14 January 1883	The Old Actor's Story	*The Referee*		7
28 January 1883	A Man Hunt[1115]	*The Referee*		7
5 March 1883	The Workhouse Test	*The Referee*		7
2 June 1883	How the Poor Live Chapter I	*The Pictorial World. An Illustrated Weekly Newspaper*	vol. 2, no. 40	609–610
9 June 1883	How the Poor Live Chapter II	*The Pictorial World*	vol. 2, no. 41	637–638
16 June 1883	How the Poor Live Chapter III	*The Pictorial World*	vol. 2, no. 42	669–670
23 June 1883	How the Poor Live Chapter IV	*The Pictorial World*	vol. 2, no. 43	725–726
30 June 1883	How the Poor Live Chapter V	*The Pictorial World*	vol. 2, no. 44	725–726
7 July 1883	How the Poor Live Chapter VI	*The Pictorial World*	vol. 3, no. 45	21–22
14 July 1883	How the Poor Live Chapter VII	*The Pictorial World*	vol. 3, no. 46	41–42
21 July 1883	How the Poor Live Chapter VIII	*The Pictorial World*	vol. 3, no. 47	73–74
28 July 1883	How the Poor Live Chapter IX	*The Pictorial World*	vol. 3, no. 48	97–98
4 August 1883	How the Poor Live Chapter X	*The Pictorial World*	vol. 3, no. 49	121–122
11 August 1883	How the Poor Live Chapter XI	*The Pictorial World*	vol. 3, no. 50	145–146
18 August 1883	How the Poor Live Chapter XII	*The Pictorial World*	vol. 3, no. 51	173–174
25 August 1883	How the Poor Live Chapter XIII	*The Pictorial World*	vol. 3, no. 52	201–202
8 November 1883	Horrible London Letter I	*London Daily News*		5
14 November 1883	Horrible London Letter II	*London Daily News*		5
19 November 1883	Horrible London Letter III	*London Daily News*		5
23 November 1883	Horrible London Letter IV	*London Daily News*		5
7 December 1883	Horrible London Letter V	*London Daily News*		5
23 December 1883	Charity: A Problem	*The Referee*		7

Date	Title	Publication	Volume	Pages
28 December 1884	A Sister's Story	*The Referee*	1	
27 December 1885	A Lancashire Lad	*The Referee*	1	
26 December 1886	The Land of Gold	*The Referee*	5	
25 December 1887	The Parson's Fight	*The Referee*	5	
23 December 1888	Seth the Ganger	*The Referee*	7	
22 December 1889	Mabel May	*The Referee*	7	
23 October 1901 – 4 March 1903	Living London: Its Work and Its Play, Its Humour and Its Pathos, Its Sights and Its Scenes	36 fortnightly instalments	vols 1–36	
April 1904	Off the Track in London Chapter I. In Alien-Land	*The Strand Magazine*	vol. 27, no. 160	416–423
May 1904	Off the Track in London Chapter II. In the Royal Borough of Kensington	*The Strand Magazine*	vol. 27, no. 161	545–551
June 1904	Off the Track in London Chapter III. In Hidden Camberwell	*The Strand Magazine*	vol. 27, no. 162	666–672
July 1904	Off the Track in London Chapter IV. "Down Town" in Rotherhithe	*The Strand Magazine*	vol. 28, no. 163	34–40
August 1904	Off the Track in London Chapter V. The Shadow of St. Stephen's	*The Strand Magazine*	vol. 28, no. 164	152–158
September 1904	Off the Track in London Chapter V. [sic] Round Hackney Wick	*The Strand Magazine*	vol. 28, no. 165	323–329
12 October 1904 – 28 February 1906	Living London: Its Work and Its Play, Its Humour and Its Pathos, Its Sights and Its Scenes	New, updated edition in 37 fortnightly instalments	vols 1–37	
March 1905	Trips About Town Chapter I. A Saunter in Soho	*The Strand Magazine*	vol. 29, no. 171	273–280
April 1905	Trips About Town Chapter II. In Bethnal Green	*The Strand Magazine*	vol. 29, no. 172	462–468
May 1905	Trips About Town Chapter III. Round Little Italy	*The Strand Magazine*	vol. 29, no. 173	510–516
June 1905	Trips About Town Chapter IV. Round St. George in the East	*The Strand Magazine*	vol. 29, no. 174	685–691
July 1905	Trips About Town Chapter V. In Limehouse and the Isle of Dogs	*The Strand Magazine*	vol. 30, no. 175	35–42
September 1905	Trips About Town Chapter VI. In the Heart of Hoxton	*The Strand Magazine*	vol. 30, no. 177	325–331
19 October 1913	The Picture Show	*The Referee*	13	

Appendix B: Magic Lantern Adaptations of Works by George R. Sims

Date of first production	TITLE *original title*	Producer	No. of Slides	Image Type
in/before 1884	OUTCAST LONDON: OR, HOW THE POOR LIVE	York & Son	40	Photograph
1886	IN THE SIGNAL BOX	York & Son	6	Life Model
in/before 1887	THE ROAD TO HEAVEN	Bamforth	8	Life Model
1887–1888	BILLY'S ROSE	York & Son	10	Life Model
in/before 1888	THE FAIRY WAND *The Magic Wand*	J.H. Steward	24	Photograph
in/before 1888	THE LIFEBOAT	Newton & Co	9	Unknown
1888	KATE MALONEY	York & Son	6	Life Model
1888	THE LEVEL CROSSING	York & Son	9	Life Model
in/before 1889	THE LIFEBOAT	York & Son	7	Life Model
1889	A BUNCH OF PRIMROSES	Bamforth	7	Life Model
1889	A BUNCH OF PRIMROSES	York & Son	9	Life Model
1889	IN THE SIGNAL BOX	Bamforth	9	Life Model
1889	THE MAGIC WAND	Bamforth	6	Life Model
1889	THE MAGIC WAND	York & Son	9	Life Model
1889	TICKET OF LEAVE	York & Son	11	Life Model
1889	TOLD TO THE MISSIONARY	Bamforth	4	Life Model
before 1890	THE ROAD TO HEAVEN	Bamforth	6	Life Model
1890	IN THE HARBOUR	Bamforth	9	Life Model
1890	IN THE WORKHOUSE *In the Workhouse. Christmas Day*	Bamforth	9	Life Model
1890	NELLIE'S PRAYER	Bamforth	13	Life Model
1890	THE LAND OF GOLD	Bamforth	16	Life Model
1890	THE MATRON'S STORY	Bamforth	12	Life Model
1890	THE ROAD TO HEAVEN	York & Son	8	Life Model
1890	THE STREET TUMBLERS	Bamforth	10	Life Model
1891	ONE WINTER NIGHT	Bamforth	9	Life Model
1891	THE ROAD TO HEAVEN	Bamforth	7–9	Life Model
in/before 1892	OSTLER JOE	Green	10	Life Model
1892	OLD PARSON RAYNE	York & Son	12	Life Model
1892	THE LIGHTS OF LONDON	York & Son	4	Life Model
in/before 1893	MRS THREE-DOORS-UP	York & Son	12	Drawing/Painting
1893	A MAN HUNT	Bamforth	8	Life Model
1893	A MUSICAL BOX	York & Son	12	Life Model
1893	A SUIT OF BLACK	York & Son	12	Life Model
1893	THE FATAL SNEEZE	Bamforth	14	Drawing/Painting
1894	A DRESS SUIT	York & Son	12	Life Model
1898	BILLY'S ROSE	Bamforth	17	Life Model
1899	A CHRISTMAS STORY	Bamforth	17	Life Model
1899	A MUSLIN FROCK	Bamforth	25	Life Model
1899	IN THE SIGNAL BOX	Bamforth	27	Life Model
1899	OSTLER JOE	Bamforth	14	Life Model

1899	THE LIFEBOAT	Bamforth	20	Life Model
1899	THE OLD ACTOR'S STORY	Bamforth	26	Life Model
1903	NELLIE'S PRAYER	Bamforth	25	Life Model
1909	FALLEN BY THE WAY	Bamforth	22	Life Model
in/before 1912	THE LIFEBOAT	Newton & Co.	20	Unknown
n.d.	NELLIE'S PRAYER	J. Theobald & Co.	12	Drawing/Painting
n.d.	THE PARSON'S FIGHT	York & Son	12	Life Model

See Lucerna – The Magic Lantern Web Resource: "Sims, George R. (1847–1922)" (http://lucerna.exeter.ac.uk/person/index.php?id=6001550)

Appendix C: Film Adaptations of Works by George R. Sims

Date	TITLE *original title (if different)*	Producer	Director
1904	LIVING LONDON	Charles Urban Trading Company	
1908	OSTLER JOE	American Mutoscope and Biograph	
1908	LADY LETMERE'S JEWELLERY	Gaumont	
1909	THE MARTYRDOM OF ADOLF BECK	Gaumont	
1911	THE PRICE *Ostler Joe*	Rex Motion Picture	Edwin S. Porter
1912	THE MAGIC WAND	Essanay	
1912	OSTLER JOE	Edison	J. Searle Dawley
1912	OSTLER JOE	Comet	
1913	CHRISTMAS DAY IN THE WORKHOUSE	American Novelty Poem-o-graph	
1914	THE LIFEBOAT	Eric Williams Speaking Pictures	
1914	THE LIGHTS O' LONDON	Magnet (Barker Motion Photography)	Bert Haldane
1914	THE LIGHTS O' LONDON	World	
1914	THE ROMANY RYE	Leonard	
1914	HARBOUR LIGHTS	Neptune	Percy Nash
1914	CHRISTMAS DAY IN THE WORKHOUSE	G.B. Samuelson	George Pearson
1914	IN THE RANKS	Neptune	Percy Nash
1915	THE ROMANY RYE	Neptune	Percy Nash
1915	THE TRUMPET CALL	Neptune	Percy Nash
1915	MASTER AND MAN	Neptune	Percy Nash
1915	THE NIGHTBIRDS OF LONDON	Hepworth Manufacturing Company	Frank Wilson
1920	THE LIGHTS OF HOME	Screen Plays	Fred Paul
1920	THE ENGLISH ROSE	British Standard (Whincup)	Fred Paul
1920	THE EVER-OPEN DOOR	Ideal Film Company	Fred Goodwins
1921	THE GREAT DAY	Famous Players-Lasky British	Hugh Ford

1922	HIS OTHER WIFE	British Exhibitors Films	
1922	IN THE SIGNAL BOX	Master Film Company	Harry Parkinson
1922	THE STREET TUMBLERS	Master Film Company	George Wynn
1922	THE OLD ACTOR'S STORY	Master Film Company	Harry Parkinson
1922	THE ROAD TO HEAVEN	Master Film Company	Challis Sanderson
1922	THE PARSON'S FIGHT	Master Film Company	Edwin J. Collins
1922	THE MAGIC WAND	Master Film Company	George Wynn
1922	SIR RUPERT'S WIFE	Master Film Company	Challis Sanderson
1922	A TICKET O' LEAVE	Master Film Company	Edwin J. Collins
1922	BILLIE'S ROSE	Master Film Company	Challis Sanderson
1922	SAL GROGAN'S FACE	Master Film Company	Edwin J. Collins
1922	FALLEN BY THE WAY	Master Film Company	Challis Sanderson
1922	THE LIGHTS O' LONDON	Master Film Company	Edwin J. Collins
1923	THE HARBOUR LIGHTS	Ideal Films	Tom Terriss
1923	THE LIGHTS OF LONDON	Gaumont	Charles Calvert

1114 The ballad was published with the following note: "This is the only correct and properly authorised version of *Jack's Story*. In a more or less garbled and mutilated form, this poem has been privately circulated for some time, and for every fresh version there has been forthcoming a fresh author. For the purpose of setting these disputes at rest, we publish, for the first time, the story as properly told, and append the author's pseudonym." According to Sims's autobiography, the ballad was first published in an American newspaper and was the first of the Dagonet ballads. See Sims, *My Life*, 43–44.

1115 The ballad *A Man Hunt* appeared within Sims's "Mustard and Cress" column (instead of next to it) and the previous paragraph read: "That was a terrible case the other day of the poor old woman who stole a piece of beef, repented, took it back, and was given into custody and sent to prison. In this instance an investigation showed how sorely the poor starving creature had been tempted – how her mind had been unhinged by sorrow and starvation; and she was released. But in how many cases does the poor devil who yields to the sudden temptation get his or her story sifted? I saw an emaciated wretch seize a loaf the other day and rush away with it. He was pursued by a howling crowd, knocked down, kicked, and almost torn to pieces before the police secured him. A Man Hunt seems to call all the latent savagery of the rougher population into play."

Reference Works

Blum, Daniel, *A Pictorial History of the Silent Screen* (New York: G.P. Putnam, 1953)

Gifford, Denis, *Books and Plays in Films, 1896–1915: Literary, Theatrical and Artistic Sources of the First Twenty Years of Motion Pictures* (London: Mansell, 1991)

Low, Rachael, *The History of British Film*, vol. 2, *The History of the British Film 1906–1914* (London: George Allen & Unwin, 1949)

Low, Rachael, *The History of British Film*, vol. 3, *The History of the British Film 1914–1918* (London: George Allen & Unwin, 1950)

Low, Rachael, *The History of British Film*, vol. 4, *The History of the British Film 1918–1929* (London: George Allen & Unwin, 1971)

Mayer, David, "The Victorian Stage on Film", *Nineteenth Century Theatre*, vol. 16, no. 2 (1988): 111–122

Newspaper and Magazine Articles, Advertisements, Lists

The Era (8 October 1904): 35

Moving Pictures News, vol. 6, no. 14 (5 October 1912): 27

The Moving Picture World, vol. 14, no. 3 (19 October 1912): 244

The Billboard (23 August 1913): 15

The Bioscope (12 March 1914): 1145

The Bioscope (9 April 1914): 217

The Bioscope (10 September 1914): 937

The Bioscope (8 October 1914): 150–151

Motion Picture News, vol. IX, no. 5 (7 February 1914): 28

Pictures and the Picturegoer (21 August 1915): 394

Kinematograph Weekly (30 March 1922): 60

Variety (27 October 1922): 42

Appendix D: Transcript of Letter Sent to George R. Sims by Frederick Barnard
(Rylands Library, Manchester, Archive reference GB 133 GRS/10/3/4)

——

For I am such an art-less Thing!

~~WARRINGTON HOUSE~~ out
~~STEELE'S ROAD~~
~~HAVERSTOCK HILL~~[1116]

Dear G.R.S.

Who are the proprietors of the "Pictorial World" our magic lantern friend speaks of?

Whoever or whichever they are or may be they have "doubled" in a way highly creditable to them as business men.

Had he or they been the simple hustling artists I should have dubbed him or them as b——y [bloody] thieves, but not being so – it's superfluous –

The ways of the business bloke to me are a simple marvel. How we should "lose £100 & a splendid advt. for the book" on the chance of a run on a magic lantern show when I am offered £50 for my share in the thing is to me in my present state of ignorance an utter staggerer.

Blow business & long live art.

Yours always

FBarnard

G.R. Sims Esq.

——

I want to thank Richard Crangle, who was able to decipher the terrible handwriting.

1116 According to Richard Crangle this was Frederick Barnard's address between 1875 and 1888, after which date he was not listed there in the London electoral roll. He notes that the crossing out of the address and handwritten "out" might suggest the letter was written soon after Barnard moved – sometime in or before 1888. (Private e-mail correspondence on 3 July 2014).

Bibliography

Note: Unless they are referenced in the main text or in multiple footnotes, individual works are not repeated here. Individual articles from historical newspapers and magazines (except for portraits of Sims and Bamforth) are not included in this list but rather cited in full whenever they are referenced in the text. Unless otherwise specified, all online resources were last accessed on 29 May 2021.

Primary Sources

Andrews, Malcolm (ed.), *The Picturesque: Literary Sources & Documents*, 3 volumes (Mountfield: Helm Information, 1994)

Booth, Michael (ed.), *The Lights o' London and Other Victorian Plays* (Oxford, New York: Oxford University Press, 1995)

Calder-Marshall, Arthur (ed.), *Prepare to Shed Them Now: The Ballads of George R. Sims* (London: Hutchinson, 1968)

Craven, Robert, "The Road to Heaven", *Short Lantern Readings*, series no. 4 (Holmfirth: Bamforth, 1887): 10–13

Dickens, Charles, "A Walk in a Workhouse", *Household Words*, vol. 1, no. 9 (25 May 1850): 204–207

Dickens, Charles, *The Adventures of Oliver Twist* (London: Chapman and Hall, 1866)

Doré, Gustave, and Blanchard Jerrold, *London. A Pilgrimage* (London: Grant & Co, 1872) Digital edition http://gallica.bnf.fr/ark:/12148/bpt6k10470488.r=london%20a%20 pilgrimage

Gilpin, William, *A Dialogue upon the Gardens of the Right Honourable the Lord Viscount Cobham at Stow in Buckinghamshire* (London: Printed for B. Seeley, Sold by J. and J. Rivington, 1748) Digital edition
https://www.gale.com/primary-sources/eighteenth-century-collections-online

Gilpin, William, "Observations on the River Wye in the Summer of 1770", reprinted in Malcolm Andrews (ed.), *The Picturesque: Literary Sources & Documents*, vol. 1: *The Idea of the Picturesque and the Vogue for Scenic Tourism* (Mountfield: Helm Information, 1994), 241–278

Gray, Thomas, "Journal in the Lakes", in Edmund Gosse (ed.), *The Works of Thomas Gray in Prose and Verse*, vol. 1, reprint of 1884 edition (New York: AMS Press, 1986), 249–281

Keating, Peter (ed.), *The Working Classes in Victorian Fiction* (London: Routledge, 1971)

Keating, Peter (ed.), *Into Unknown England, 1866–1913: Selections from the Social Explorers* (Manchester: Manchester University Press, 1976)

Mayhew, Henry, *London Labour and the London Poor*, vol. 1: *The London Street-Folk* (London: George Woodfall and Son, 1851)
Digital edition https://archive.org/details/cu31924092592751

Mursell, Arthur, *Hard Lines. An Address Delivered in the Birmingham Music Hall, on Sunday, February 8th 1880* (Manchester and London: John Heywood, 1880)

Pearson, George, *Flashback: The Autobiography of a British Filmmaker* (London: George Allen & Unwin, 1957)

Price, Uvedale, *Essays on the Picturesque, As Compared with the Sublime and the Beautiful; And, on the Use of Studying Pictures, For the Purpose of Improving Real Landscape*, vol. 1 (London: J. Mawman, 1810)
Digital edition https://archive.org/stream/essaysonpictures01priciala

Price, Uvedale, *Essays on the Picturesque, As Compared with the Sublime and the Beautiful; And, on the Use of Studying Pictures, For the Purpose of Improving Real Landscape*, vol. 3 (London: J. Mawman, 1810)
Digital edition https://archive.org/details/essaysonpictures03pric_0

Robinson, Henry Peach, *The Elements of a Pictorial Photograph* (Bradford: Percy Lund, 1896)
Digital edition https://archive.org/stream/elementsapictor00robigoog

Rogers, Frederick, *Labour, Life and Literature. Some Memories of Sixty Years* (London: Smith, Elder & Co, 1913)

Ruskin, John, *The Seven Lamps of Architecture*, 6th edition (Orpington, Kent: George Allen, 1889)

Ruskin, John, *Modern Painters*, vol. 5: *Of Mountain Beauty* (London: George Allen, 1906)
Digital edition https://archive.org/details/modernpainters01ruskgoog

Sims, George Robert, *Ballads of Babylon* (London: J.P. Fuller, 1880)
Digital edition https://archive.org/details/balladsbabylon00simsgoog

Sims, George Robert, *Three Brass Balls* (London: J.P. Fuller, 1880)
Digital edition https://archive.org/details/ 22176718.3066.emory.edu

Sims, George Robert, *The Social Kaleidoscope*, First and second series (London: J.P. Fuller, 1881)

Sims, George Robert, *How the Poor Live* (London: Chatto & Windus, 1883)

Sims, George Robert, *The Lifeboat and Other Poems* (London: J.P. Fuller, 1883)

Sims, George Robert, "An Autobiography", *The Theatre* (July 1884): 14–17

Sims, George Robert, *The Dagonet Reciter and Reader; Being Readings and Recitations in Prose and Verse, Selected from His Own Works by G.R. Sims* (London: Chatto & Windus, 1888)

Sims, George Robert, *The Land of Gold and Other Poems* (London: J.P. Fuller, 1888)

Sims, George Robert, *How the Poor Live and Horrible London* (London: Chatto & Windus, 1889) Digital edition https://archive.org/details/howpoorliveandho00sims

Sims, George Robert (ed.), *Living London: Its Work and Its Play, Its Humour and Its Pathos, Its Sights and Its Scenes*, 3 volumes (London etc.: Cassell & Co., 1902–1903)

Sims, George Robert, "Off the Track in London. I. In Alien Land", *Strand Magazine*, vol. 27, no. 160 (1904): 416–423

Sims, George Robert, "Trips About Town. III. Round Little Italy", *Strand Magazine*, vol. 29, no. 173 (May 1905): 510–516

Sims, George Robert, *Socialism and Human Nature*, Anti-Socialist Tracts, no. 3 (London: Anti-Socialist Union Publication Department, 1909)

Sims, George Robert, *Off the Track in London* (London: Jarrold & Sons, 1911)

Sims, George Robert, *My Life: Sixty Years' Recollections of Bohemian London* (London: Eveleigh Nash, 1917)
Digital edition https://archive.org/details/mylifesixtyyears00simsuoft

Thomson, John, and Adolphe Smith, *Street Life in London* (London: Sampson Low, Marston, Searle & Rivington, 1877, Reprint New York, London: Benjamin Blom, 1969)
Digital edition http://www.archive.org/details/streetlifeinlond00thom

Woolmer, D. L., "Scenes from London Slum-Land", in George R. Sims (ed.), *Living London: Its Work and Its Play, Its Humour and Its Pathos, Its Sights and Its Scenes*, vol. 3 (London etc.: Cassell & Co., 1903), 109–114

Government Publications

An Act for the Amendment and Better Administration of the Laws Relating to the Poor of England and Wales: With Explanatory Notes and a Copious Index, 2nd edition (London: B. Fellowes, 1834)

Copyright Act, 1911, Part I, Section 1.2 (d), (https://www.legislation.gov.uk/ukpga/1911/46/pdfs/ukpga_19110046_en.pdf)

First Report of Her Majesty's Commissioners for Inquiring into the Housing of the Working Classes (London: Eyre and Spottiswoode, 1885)

Contemporaneous Articles on Sims

"About Well-Known People, Mr. George R. Sims", *Unknown Magazine*, vol. 7, no. 161 (16 January 1892) (George R. Sims Collection, Rylands Library, Manchester, GB 133 GRS/10/3: 123)

Archer, William, *English Dramatists of To-day* (London: Sampson Low, Marston, Searle, & Rivington, 1882)

Black, Helen C., "Half-Hours with Celebrities. Mr. George R. Sims", *Lloyd's Weekly* (30 June 1885): 8

"G.R. Sims. Journalist, Dramatist and Bohemian", *The Times* (6 September 1922): 12

J.L.O., "Mr. G.R. Sims at Home", *Booksellers' Supplement to the Newsagent & Booksellers' Review* (7 September 1895): 38–40

Keating, Joseph, "George R. Sims", *The Idler* (September 1904): 284–288

Latey, John, "G.R. Sims at Home to *The Sketch*", *The Sketch* (12 February 1902): 140–141

Morton Lane, Anne, "'Dagonet' at Home", *The Princess* (9 November 1895): 2–5

"Mr. George Robert Sims", *The Search Light* (1892): 74 (George R. Sims Collection, Rylands Library, Manchester, GB 133 GRS/10/3: 117)

"Mr. G.R. Sims Interviewed by G.S. Edwards", *Illustrated Sporting and Dramatic News*, vol. 46, no. 1221 (6 February 1897): 896–898

"Mr. George R. Sims's New Melodrama, 'The Last Chance'", *Pall Mall Gazette*, vol. 41, no. 6260, supplement no. 41 (7 April 1885): 19

Pearce, John, "Mr. George R. Sims", *'House and Home' Popular Biographies*, no. 1 (1882): 3–12

Pry, Paul, "Lions of the Day in Their Dens. No. 14 – Mr. Geo. R. Sims in Regent's Park", *Judy, or the London Serio-Comic Journal* (17 September 1890): 137

Sala, Mrs. George Augustus, "Famous People I Have Met", *The Gentlewoman* (11 July 1891): 42

Whibley, Charles, "Modern Men. George R. Sims", *The Scots Observer* (23 November 1889): 11–12

"Workers and Their Work – No. III. Mr. George R. Sims, Journalist and Playwright", *Pearson's Weekly* (19 September 1891): 135

Reports on Bamforth

Brierly, Harwood, "Among Life-Models", *Newcastle Courant* (18 November 1899): 2

"Life Model Studies. No. I – A Peep Behind Some Scenes", *The Photogram* (February 1899): 46–48

"Life Model Studies. No. II – The Models Themselves", *The Photogram* (February 1899): 76–78

Reynolds, Philip, "Sentiment to Order", *Harmsworth Magazine*, vol. 5, no. 28 (October 1900): 337–343

Saunders, Alfred, "Prominent Men in the Lantern World: New Series, No. 1. Mr James Bamforth, of Holmfirth, Yorkshire", *The Optical Magic Lantern Journal*, vol. 13, no. 151 (October 1902): 7–9

Catalogues

Catalogue and Price List of Stereopticons, Dissolving-View Apparatus, Magic Lanterns, and Artistically-Colored Photographic Views on Glass (New York: T.H. McAllister, 1891)

Catalogue of Lantern Slides (London: York & Son, after 1901)

Catalogue of Optical Lantern Slides (Bradford: Riley Brothers Ltd, [1908])

Catalogue of Photographic Lantern Transparencies and Apparatus (Bradford: Riley Brothers, 1891)

Complete Catalogue of Lantern Slides, Dissolving Views, Magic Lanterns etc. (London: UK Band of Hope Union, 1891)

J. Theobald and Company's Extra Special Illustrated Catalogue of Magic Lanterns, Slides and Apparatus (London: Theobald & Co., c. 1893)

Secondary Sources

Abel, Richard, *Menus for Movieland: Newspapers and the Emergence of American Film Culture, 1913–1916* (Oakland: University of California Press, 2015)

Andrews, Malcolm, "Introduction", in Malcolm Andrews (ed.), *The Picturesque: Literary Sources & Documents*, vol. 1: *The Idea of the Picturesque and the Vogue for Scenic Tourism* (Mountfield: Helm Information, 1994), 3–37

Andrews, Malcolm, "The Metropolitan Picturesque", in Stephen Copley and Peter Garside (ed.), *The Politics of the Picturesque: Literature, Landscape and Aesthetics since 1770* (Cambridge: Cambridge University Press, 1994), 282–298

Anstruther, Ian, *The Scandal of the Andover Workhouse* (London: Bles, 1973)

Arlitsch, Kenning, and John Herbert, "Microfilm, Paper, and OCR: Issues in Newspaper Digitization: The Utah Digital Newspapers Program", *Microform & Imaging Review*, vol. 33, no. 2 (2004): 59–67

Armstrong, Nancy, *Fiction in the Age of Photography: The Legacy of British Realism* (Cambridge, Mass.: Harvard University Press, 1999)

Ashforth, David, "The Urban Poor Law", in Derek Fraser (ed.), *The New Poor Law in the Nineteenth Century* (London, Basingstoke: Macmillan, 1976), 128–148

Bailey, Peter, "Ally Sloper's Half-Holiday: Comic Art in the 1880s", *History Workshop Journal*, vol. 16, no. 1 (October 1983): 4–32

Bakker, Gerben, *Entertainment Industrialised: The Emergence of the International Film Industry, 1890–1940* (Cambridge etc.: Cambridge University Press, 2008)

Barnes, John, "The History of the Magic Lantern", in Dennis Crompton, Richard Franklin and Stephen Herbert (ed.), *Servants of Light: The Book of the Lantern* (Ripon, North Yorkshire: The Magic Lantern Society, 1997), 8–33

Benton, Michael, "The Image of Childhood: Representations of the Child in Painting and Literature, 1700–1900", *Children's Literature in Education*, vol. 27, no. 1 (January 1996): 35–60

Berg, Jan, "Techniken der medialen Authentifizierung Jahrhunderte vor Erfindung des 'Dokumentarischen'", in Ursula von Keitz and Kay Hoffmann (ed.), *Die Einübung des dokumentarischen Blicks. 'Fiction Film' und 'Non Fiction Film' zwischen Wahrheitsanspruch und expressiver Sachlichkeit 1895–1945* (Marburg: Schüren, 2001), 51–70

Bernstein, Carol, *The Celebration of Scandal: Toward the Sublime in Victorian Urban Fiction* (University Park, Pa.: The Pennsylvania State University Press, 1991)

Bertellini, Giorgio, *Italy in Early American Cinema: Race, Landscape, and the Picturesque* (Bloomington: Indiana University Press, 2010)

Bingham, Adrian, "The Digitization of Newspaper Archives: Opportunities and Challenges for Historians", *Twentieth Century British History*, vol. 21, no. 2 (2010): 225–231

Booth, Michael, "Introduction", in Michael Booth (ed.), *The Lights o' London and Other Victorian Plays* (Oxford, New York: Oxford University Press, 1995), ix–xxvi

Bibliography

Borgo Ton, Mary, "Magic Lantern Shows through a Macroscopic Lens: Topic Modelling and Mapping as Methods for Media Archaeology", *Early Popular Visual Culture*, vol. 17, nos. 3–4 (2019): 341–360

Bottomore, Stephen, "George R. Sims and the Film as Evidence", in Andrew Shail (ed.), *Reading the Cinematograph: The Cinema in British Short Fiction 1896–1912* (Exeter: University of Exeter Press, 2010), 19–36

Bottomore, Stephen, "Eric Williams: Speaking to Pictures", in Julie Brown and Annette Davison (ed.), *The Sounds of the Silents in Britain* (New York: Oxford University Press, 2013), 55–71

Bottomore, Stephen, "The Lantern and Cinematograph for Political Persuasion before WWI: Towards an Introduction and Typology", in Richard Crangle and Ludwig Vogl-Bienek (ed.), *Screen Culture and the Social Question 1880–1914* (New Barnet: John Libbey Publishing, 2014), 20–33

Boyd, Kelly, and Rohan McWilliam (ed.), *The Victorian Studies Reader* (London, New York: Routledge, 2007)

Boyd, Kelly, and Rohan McWilliam, "Introduction. Rethinking the Victorians", in Kelly Boyd and Rohan McWilliam (ed.), *The Victorian Studies Reader* (London, New York: Routledge, 2007), 1–47

Brake, Laurel, "Half Full and Half Empty", Digital Forum, *Journal of Victorian Culture*, vol. 17, no. 2 (2012): 222–229

Bramen, Carrie Tirado, "The Urban Picturesque and the Spectacle of Americanization", *American Quarterly*, vol. 52, no. 3 (2000): 444–477

Bratton, Jacqueline Susan, *The Victorian Popular Ballad* (Totowa, New Jersey: Rowman and Littlefield, 1975)

Braun, Caroline (née Henkes), "Early Christmas Films in the Tradition of the Magic Lantern", in Richard Crangle and Ludwig Vogl-Bienek (ed.), *Screen Culture and the Social Question 1880–1914* (New Barnet: John Libbey Publishing, 2014), 96–110

Brewster, Ben, and Lea Jacobs, *Theatre to Cinema: Stage Pictorialism and the Early Feature Film* (Oxford: Oxford University Press, 1997)

Brosch, Renate, "Introduction. Victorian Visual Culture", in Renate Brosch (ed.), *Victorian Visual Culture* (Heidelberg: Universitätsverlag Winter, 2008), 7–20

Brown, Julie, and Annette Davison (ed.), *The Sounds of the Silents in Britain* (New York: Oxford University Press, 2013)

Brundage, Anthony, *The English Poor Laws, 1700–1930* (Basingstoke, New York: Palgrave, 2002)

Burrows, Jon, *Legitimate Cinema: Theatre Stars in Silent British Films 1908–1918* (Exeter: University of Exeter Press, 2003)

Burrows, Jon, *The British Cinema Boom, 1909–1914: A Commercial History* (London: Palgrave Macmillan, 2017)

Calder-Marshall, Arthur, "Introduction. George R. Sims", in Arthur Calder-Marshall (ed.), *Prepare to Shed Them Now: The Ballads of George R. Sims* (London: Hutchinson, 1968), 1–48

Christ, Carol, and John Jordan (ed.), *Victorian Literature and the Victorian Visual Imagination* (Berkeley, Los Angeles, London: University of California Press, 1995)

Christie, Ian (ed.), *Audiences: Defining and Researching Screen Entertainment Reception* (Amsterdam: Amsterdam University Press, 2012)

Connelly, Mark, *Christmas: A Social History* (London and New York: I.B. Tauris, 1999)

Cook, Olive, *Movement in Two Dimensions* (London, 1963), reprinted in Stephen Herbert (ed.), *A History of Pre-Cinema*, vol. 3 (London and New York: Routledge, 2000)

Copinger, Walter Arthur, *The Law of Copyright, in Works of Literature and Art: Including that of the Drama, Music, Engraving, Sculpture, Painting, Photography, and Ornamental and Useful Designs*, 2nd edition (London: Stevens and Haynes, 1881)
Digital edition https://archive.org/details/cu31924022164341

Copinger, Walter Arthur, *The Law of Copyright, in Works of Literature, Art, Architecture, Photography, Music and the Drama: Including Chapters on Mechanical Contrivances and Cinematographs*, 5th edition (London: Stevens and Haynes, 1915) Digital edition https://archive.org/details/cu31924022164341

Crangle, Richard, *Hybrid Texts: Modes of Representation in the Early Moving Picture and Some Related Media in Britain*, PhD diss. (University of Exeter, 1996)

Crangle, Richard, "Zweidimensionales Leben. Die britischen Life model-Dias", translated by Jens Ruchatz, *Fotogeschichte*, vol. 19, no. 74 (1999): 25–34

Crangle, Richard, "What Do Those Old Slides Mean? or Why the Magic Lantern is Not an Important Part of Cinema History", in Simon Popple and Vanessa Toulmin (ed.), *Visual Delights: Essays on the Popular and Projected Image in the 19th Century* (Trowbridge: Flicks Books, 2000), 16–24

Crangle, Richard, "'Next Slide Please': The Lantern Lecture in Britain, 1890–1910", in Richard Abel and Rick Altman (ed.), *The Sounds of Early Cinema* (Bloomington: Indiana University Press, 2001), 39–47

Crangle, Richard, "The Lucerna Magic Lantern Web Resource", in Richard Crangle and Ludwig Vogl-Bienek (ed.), *Screen Culture and the Social Question 1880–1914* (New Barnet: John Libbey Publishing, 2014), 190–202

Crangle, Richard, and Mervyn Heard, "The Temperance Phantasmagoria", in Richard Crangle, Mervyn Heard and Ine van Dooren (ed.), *Realms of Light: Uses and Perceptions of the Magic Lantern from the 17th to the 21st Century* (London: The Magic Lantern Society, 2005), 46–55

Crangle, Richard, Mervyn Heard and Ine van Dooren (ed.), *Realms of Light: Uses and Perceptions of the Magic Lantern from the 17th to the 21st Century* (London: The Magic Lantern Society, 2005)

Crangle, Richard, and Ludwig Vogl-Bienek (ed.), *Screen Culture and the Social Question 1880–1914* (New Barnet: John Libbey Publishing, 2014)

Crozier, Brian, *Notions of Childhood in London Theatre, 1880–1905*, PhD diss. (University of Cambridge, 1981)

Cunningham, Hugh, *The Children of the Poor: Representations of Childhood since the Seventeenth Century* (Cambridge: Blackwell, 1991)

Daunton, Martin, "Society and Economic Life", in Colin Matthew (ed.), *The Nineteenth Century: The British Isles, 1815–1901* (Oxford: Oxford University Press, 2005), 41–82

Davin, Anna, "Waif Stories in Late Nineteenth-Century England", *History Workshop Journal*, no. 52 (Autumn 2001): 67–98

De Maré, Eric, *The London Doré Saw: A Victorian Evocation* (London: Allen Lane, 1973)

Deegan, Marilyn, and Kathryn Sutherland, *Transferred Illusions: Digital Technology and the Forms of Print* (Farnham/Burlington: Ashgate, 2009).

Dellmann, Sarah, *Images of Dutchness: Popular Visual Culture, Early Cinema and the Emergence of a National Cliché* (Amsterdam: Amsterdam University Press, 2018)

Dellmann, Sarah, "Analogue Objects Online. Epistemological Reflections on Digital Reproductions of Lantern Slides", *Early Popular Visual Culture*, vol. 17, nos. 3–4 (2019): 322–340

Denisoff, Dennis, "Popular Culture", in Francis O'Gorman (ed.), *The Cambridge Companion to Victorian Culture* (Cambridge: Cambridge University Press, 2010), 135–155

Donovan, Stephen, and Matthew Rubery (ed.), *Secret Commissions: An Anthology of Victorian Investigative Journalism* (Peterborough, Ontario etc.: Broadview Press, 2012)

Dooren, Ine van, *Devices and Desires: The Magic Lantern and the Life Model Drama Presentations in a History of Screen Practices*, MA diss. (University of East Anglia, 1989/1990)

Dooren, Ine van, and Amy Sargeant, "Dead Babies: Representations of Infant Mortality Before the First World War", in Vanessa Toulmin and Simon Popple (ed.), *Visual Delights – Two: Exhibition and Reception* (Eastleigh: John Libbey, 2005), 73–86

Dyos, Harold James, "The Slums of Victorian London", *Victorian Studies*, vol. 11, no. 1 (1967): 5–40

Dyos, Harold James, and David Alec Reeder, "Slums and Suburbs", in Harold James Dyos and Michael Wolff (ed.), *The Victorian City: Images and Realities*, vol. 1 (London and Boston: Routledge and Kegan Paul, 1973), 359–386

Dyos, Harold James, and Michael Wolff (ed.), *The Victorian City: Images and Realities*, 2 volumes (London and Boston: Routledge and Kegan Paul, 1973)

Edsall, Nicholas, *The Anti-Poor Law Movement* (Manchester: Manchester University Press, 1971)

Eifler, Karen, "Between Attraction and Instruction: Lantern Shows in British Poor Relief", *Early Popular Visual Culture*, vol. 8, no. 4 (2010): 363–384

Eifler, Karen, *The Great Gun of the Lantern. Lichtbildereinsatz sozialer Organisationen in Großbritannien, 1875–1914* (Marburg: Schüren, 2017)

Elsaesser, Thomas, and Adam Barker (ed.), *Early Cinema: Space, Frame, Narrative* (London: British Film Institute, 1990)

Fildes, Luke Val, *Luke Fildes, R.A.: A Victorian Painter* (London: Michael Joseph, 1968)

Fox, Celina, "The Development of Social Reportage in English Periodical Illustration during the 1840s and Early 1850s", *Past and Present*, vol. 74, no. 1 (1977): 90–111

Fraser, Derek (ed.), *The New Poor Law in the Nineteenth Century* (London, Basingstoke: Macmillan, 1976)

Fraser, Derek, "Introduction", in Derek Fraser (ed.), *The New Poor Law in the Nineteenth Century* (London, Basingstoke: Macmillan, 1976), 1–24

Freeman, Nicholas, *Conceiving the City: London, Literature, and Art 1870–1914* (Oxford: Oxford University Press, 2007)

Frenk, Joachim, "'We have learned the value of poverty': (Re-)Presentations of the Poor in Nineteenth-Century Melodramas", in Barbara Korte and Frédéric Regard (ed.), *Narrating Poverty and Precarity in Britain* (Berlin, Boston: Walter de Gruyter, 2014), 57–74

Fuchs, Rachel, *Gender and Poverty in Nineteenth Century Europe* (Cambridge: Cambridge University Press, 2005)

Funk, Wolfgang, Florian Groß and Irmtraud Huber, "Exploring the Empty Plinth", in Wolfgang Funk, Florian Groß and Irmtraud Huber (ed.), *The Aesthetics of Authenticity: Medial Constructions of the Real* (Bielefeld: transcript Verlag, 2012), 9–21

Gärtner, Torsten, "The Sunday School Chronicle – eine Quelle zur Nutzung der Laterna Magica in englischen Sonntagsschulen", in Frank Kessler, Sabine Lenk and Martin Loiperdinger (ed.), *KINtop. Jahrbuch zur Erforschung des frühen Films* 14 / 15: *Quellen und Perspektiven / Sources and Perspectives* (Frankfurt am Main, Basel: Stroemfeld, 2006), 25–35

Gärtner, Torsten, "The Church on Wheels. Travelling Magic Lantern Mission in Late Victorian England", in Martin Loiperdinger (ed.), *Travelling Cinema in Europe: Sources and Perspectives* (Frankfurt am Main: Stroemfeld, 2008), 128–142

Gaudreault, André, "Showing and Telling: Image and Word in Early Cinema", in Thomas Elsaesser and Adam Barker (ed.), *Early Cinema: Space, Frame, Narrative* (London: British Film Institute, 1990), 274–281

Gestrich, Andreas, Steven King and Lutz Raphael (ed.), *Being Poor in Modern Europe: Historical Perspectives 1800–1940* (Oxford etc.: Lang, 2006)

Gestrich, Andreas, Steven King and Lutz Raphael, "The Experience of Being Poor in Nineteenth- and Early-Twentieth-Century Europe", in Andreas Gestrich, Steven King and Lutz Raphael (ed.), *Being Poor in Modern Europe: Historical Perspectives 1800–1940* (Oxford etc.: Lang, 2006), 17–40

Ghosh, Tanushree, "Gifting Pain: The Pleasures of Liberal Guilt in *London. A Pilgrimage* and *Street Life in London*", *Victorian Literature and Culture*, vol. 41, no. 1 (2013): 91–123

Ginn, Geoff, "Answering the 'Bitter Cry': Urban Description and Social Reform", *The London Journal*, vol. 31, no. 2 (2006): 179–200

Gray, Frank, "Engaging with the Magic Lantern's History", in Richard Crangle and Ludwig Vogl-Bienek (ed.), *Screen Culture and the Social Question, 1880–1914* (New Barnet: John Libbey Publishing, 2014), 172–180

Green, David, "Pauper Protests: Power and Resistance in Early Nineteenth-Century London Workhouses", *Social History*, vol. 31, no. 2 (May 2006): 137–159

Green, Jennifer Marion, "The Right Thing in the Right Place: P.H. Emerson and the Picturesque Photograph", in Carol Christ and John Jordan (ed.), *Victorian Literature and the Victorian Visual Imagination* (Berkeley, Los Angeles, London: University of California Press, 1995), 88–110

Green-Lewis, Jennifer, *Framing the Victorians: Photography and the Culture of Realism* (Ithaca, London: Cornell University Press, 1996)

Griffiths, Trevor, "Sounding Scottish: Sound Practices and Silent Cinema in Scotland", in Julie Brown and Annette Davison (ed.), *The Sounds of the Silents in Britain* (New York: Oxford University Press, 2013), 76–81

Groth, Helen, "Kaleidoscopic Vision in Late Victorian Bohemia: George Sims's *Social Kaleidoscope*", in Colette Colligan and Margaret Linley (ed.), *Media, Technology, and Literature in the Nineteenth Century: Image, Sound, Touch* (Farnham, Surrey, Burlington, Vermont: Ashgate, 2011), 91–104

Groth, Helen, *Moving Images: Nineteenth-Century Reading and Screen Practices* (Edinburgh: Edinburgh University Press, 2013)

Gunning, Tom, "The Cinema of Attractions: Early Film, Its Spectator and the Avant-Garde", in Thomas Elsaesser and Adam Barker (ed.), *Early Cinema: Space, Frame, Narrative* (London: British Film Institute, 1990), 56–62

Gunning, Tom, "Before Documentary: Early Nonfiction Films and the 'View' Aesthetic", in Daan Hertogs and Nico de Klerk (ed.), *Uncharted Territory: Essays on Early Nonfiction Film* (Amsterdam: Stichting Nederlands Filmmuseum, 1997), 9–24

Hattendorf, Manfred, *Dokumentarfilm und Authentizität. Ästhetik und Pragmatik einer Gattung* (Konstanz: Ölschläger, 1994)

Hewitt, Martin, "Why the Notion of Victorian Britain Does Make Sense", *Victorian Studies*, vol. 48, no. 3 (Spring 2006): 395–438

Higginbotham, Peter, *The Workhouse Cookbook* (Stroud: The History Press, 2008)

Higgins, Richard, "London on Stage: The Urban Melodrama of George Sims", *Literary London: Interdisciplinary Studies in the Representation of London*, vol. 4, no. 1 (March 2006) (http://literarylondon.org/the-literary-london-journal/archive-of-the-literary-londo n-journal/issue-4-1/london-on-stage-the-urban-melodrama-of-george-sims/)

Hiley, Nicholas, "'At the Picture Palace': The British Cinema Audience, 1895–1920", in Ian Christie (ed.), *Audiences: Defining and Researching Screen Entertainment Reception* (Amsterdam: Amsterdam University Press, 2012), 25–34

Hill, Nancy Klenk, *A Reformer's Art. Dickens' Picturesque and Grotesque Imagery* (London, Athens: Ohio University Press, 1981)

Himmelfarb, Gertrude, "Mayhew's Poor: A Problem of Identity", *Victorian Studies*, vol. 14, no. 3 (March 1971): 307–320

Himmelfarb, Gertrude, *Poverty and Compassion: The Moral Imagination of the Late Victorians* (New York: Alfred A. Knopf, 1991)

Himmelfarb, Gertrude, "In Defence of the Victorians", in Kelly Boyd and Rohan McWilliam (ed.), *The Victorian Studies Reader* (London, New York: Routledge, 2007), 209–219

Hobbs, Andrew, "When the Provincial Press Was the National Press (c.1836–1900)", *The International Journal of Regional and Local Studies*, vol. 5, no. 1 (Spring 2009): 16–43

Howarth, Janet, "Gender, Domesticity, and Sexual Politics", in Colin Matthew (ed.), *The Nineteenth Century: The British Isles, 1815–1901* (Oxford: Oxford University Press, 2005), 63–193

Hoy, Anne, and Katharina Harde-Tinnefeld, *Enzyklopädie der Fotografie* (Hamburg: National Geographic Deutschland, 2006)

Hughes, Lorna, *Digitizing Collections: Strategic Issues for the Information Manager* (London: Facet Publishing, 2004)

Humpherys, Anne, *Travels into Poor Man's Country: The Work of Henry Mayhew* (Athens, Georgia: University of Georgia Press, 1977)

Jackson, Sally, "The *Living London* Boom", *Senses of Cinema*, issue 49 (March 2009), (http://sensesofcinema.com/issues/issue-49/)

Jakobs, Lydia, *George R. Sims' viktorianische Armutsballaden im Medium der Projektionskunst*, MA diss. (Trier: Universität Trier, 2011)

Jakobson, Roman, *Language in Literature* (Cambridge, Mass., London: The Belknap Press of Harvard University Press, 1987)

John, Juliet, "Melodrama and its Criticism: An Essay in Memory of Sally Ledger", *19: Interdisciplinary Studies in the Long Nineteenth Century*, no. 8 (2009): 1–20

Jones, Aled, *Powers of the Press: Newspapers, Power and the Public in Nineteenth-Century England* (Aldershot, Hants: Scolar Press, 1996)

Kember, Joe, *Marketing Modernity* (Exeter: University of Exeter Press, 2009)

Kirkpatrick, Peter, "Hunting the Wild Reciter: Elocution and the Art of Recitation", in Joy Damousi and Desley Deacon (ed.), *Talking and Listening in the Age of Modernity: Essays on the History of Sound* (Canberra: The Australian National University Press, 2007), 59–71

Kirsten, Guido, *Filmischer Realismus* (Marburg: Schüren, 2013)

Koven, Seth, "Dr. Barnardo's 'Artistic Fictions': Photography, Sexuality, and the Ragged Child in Victorian London", *Radical History Review*, issue 69 (Fall 1997): 6–45

Koven, Seth, *Slumming: Sexual and Social Politics in Victorian London* (Princeton: Princeton University Press, 2004)

Kraus, Kari, "Picture Criticism: Textual Studies and the Image", in Neil Freistat and Julia Flanders (ed.), *The Cambridge Companion to Textual Scholarship* (Cambridge, New York: Cambridge University Press, 2013), 236–256

Lindner, Rolf, *Walks on the Wild Side. Eine Geschichte der Stadtforschung* (Frankfurt, New York: Campus Verlag, 2004)

Loiperdinger, Martin, "The Social Impact of Screen Culture 1880–1914", in Richard Crangle and Ludwig Vogl-Bienek (ed.), *Screen Culture and the Social Question, 1880–1914* (New Barnet: John Libbey Publishing, 2014), 8–19

Longmate, Norman, *The Workhouse* (London: Temple Smith, 1974)

Low, Rachael, *The History of British Film 1906–1914* (London: George Allen & Unwin, 1949)

Maltby, Richard, Daniel Bilereyst and Philippe Meers (ed.), *Explorations in New Cinema History: Approaches and Case Studies* (Malden, Mass., Oxford, Chichester, West Sussex: Wiley-Blackwell, 2011)

Marriott, John, *The Other Empire: Metropolis, India and Progress in the Colonial Imagination* (Manchester: Manchester University Press, 2003)

Marriott, John, and Masaie Matsumura (ed.), *The Metropolitan Poor. Semifactual Accounts, 1795–1910*, vol. 3: *People of the Abyss, 1885–1910* (London: Pickering & Chatto, 1999)

Marsh, Joss, "Dickensian 'Dissolving Views': The Magic Lantern, Visual Story-Telling and the Victorian Technological Imagination", in Jeffrey Geiger and Karin Littau (ed.), *Cinematicity in Media History* (Edinburgh: Edinburgh University Press, 2013), 21–34

Marsh, Joss, and David Francis, "'The Poetry of Poverty': The Magic Lantern and the Ballads of George R. Sims", in Richard Crangle and Ludwig Vogl-Bienek (ed.), *Screen Culture and the Social Question 1880–1914* (New Barnet: John Libbey Publishing, 2014), 64–81

Matthew, Colin (ed.), *The Nineteenth Century: The British Isles, 1815–1901* (Oxford: Oxford University Press, 2005)

Matthew, Colin, "Introduction: The United Kingdom and the Victorian Century, 1815–1901", in Colin Matthew (ed.), *The Nineteenth Century: The British Isles, 1815–1901* (Oxford: Oxford University Press, 2005), 1–38

Matthew, Colin, "Public Life and Politics", in Colin Matthew (ed.), *The Nineteenth Century: The British Isles, 1815–1901* (Oxford: Oxford University Press, 2005), 84–133

Mayer, David, "The Victorian Stage on Film", *Nineteenth Century Theatre*, vol. 16, no. 2 (Winter 1988): 111–122

McCord, Norman, "The Poor Law and Philanthropy", in Derek Fraser (ed.), *The New Poor Law in the Nineteenth Century* (London, Basingstoke: Macmillan, 1976), 87–110

McFarlane, Brian, *Novel to Film: An Introduction to the Theory of Adaptation* (Oxford: Clarendon Press, 1996)

McKernan, Luke, *Charles Urban: Pioneering the Non-Fiction Film in Britain and America, 1897–1925* (Exeter: University of Exeter Press, 2013)

McMillan, Robert, "James Bamforth. A Talk Given by Robert McMillan to the Magic Lantern Society of Great Britain on 29th April, 1978", *The New Magic Lantern Journal*, vol. 1, no. 2 (February 1979): 12–15

Meisel, Martin, *Realizations: Narrative, Pictorial, and Theatrical Arts in Nineteenth-Century England* (Princeton: Princeton University Press, 1983)

Moore, Paul S., "The Social Biograph: Newspapers as Archives of the Regional Mass Market for Movies", in Richard Maltby, Daniel Biltereyst and Philippe Meers (ed.), *Explorations in New Cinema History: Approaches and Case Studies* (Malden, Mass., Oxford, Chichester, West Sussex: Wiley-Blackwell, 2011), 263–279

Moore, Tara, "Starvation in Victorian Christmas Fiction", *Victorian Literature and Culture*, vol. 36, no. 2 (2008): 489–505

Morgan, Emily Kathryn, *'True Types of the London Poor': Adolphe Smith and John Thomson's 'Street Life in London'*, PhD diss. (University of Arizona, 2012)

Murdoch, Lydia, *Imagined Orphans: Poor Families, Child Welfare, and Contested Citizenship in London* (New Brunswick, New Jersey, London: Rutgers University Press, 2006)

Mussell, James, "Ownership, Institutions, and Methodology", *Journal of Victorian Culture*, vol. 13, no. 1 (2008): 94–100

Nadeau, Luis, *Encyclopedia of Printing, Photographic, and Photomechanical Processes*, 2 volumes (Fredericton, New Brunswick: Atelier Luis Nadeau, 1990)

Nicholson, Bob, "The Digital Turn: Exploring the Methodological Possibilities of Digital Newspaper Archives", *Media History*, vol. 19, no. 1 (2013): 59–73

O'Gorman, Francis (ed.), *The Cambridge Companion to Victorian Culture* (Cambridge: Cambridge University Press, 2010)

Orestano, Francesca, "Charles Dickens and Italy: The 'New Picturesque'", in Michael Hollington and Francesca Orestano (ed.), *Dickens and Italy: Little Dorrit and Pictures from Italy* (Newcastle-upon-Tyne: Cambridge Scholars Publishing, 2020), 49–67

Pellerin, Denis, and Brian May, *The Poor Man's Picture Gallery: Stereoscopy versus Paintings in the Victorian Era* (London: The London Stereoscopic Company, 2014)

Plunkett, John, "Moving Books / Moving Images: Optical Recreations and Children's Publishing 1800–1900", *19: Interdisciplinary Studies in the Long Nineteenth Century*, issue 5 (2007): 1–27
DOI: http://doi.org/10.16995/ntn.463

Pollock, Griselda, "Vicarious Excitements: *London. A Pilgrimage* by Gustave Doré and Blanchard Jerrold, 1872", *New Formations*, no. 4 (Spring 1988): 25–50

Popple, Simon, and Vanessa Toulmin (ed.), *Visual Delights: Essays on the Popular and Projected Image in the 19th Century* (Trowbridge: Flicks Books, 2000)

Prasch, Thomas, *Fixed Positions: Working-Class Subjects and Photographic Hegemony in Victorian Britain*, PhD diss. (Indiana University, 1994)

Price, Richard, "Does the Notion of Victorian England Make Sense?", in Derek Fraser (ed.), *Cities, Class and Communication: Essays in Honour of Asa Briggs* (Abingdon, Oxon, New York: Harvester Wheatsheaf, 1990), 152–171

Price, Richard, "Should We Abandon the Idea of the Victorian Period?", in Kelly Boyd and Rohan McWilliam (ed.), *The Victorian Studies Reader* (London, New York: Routledge, 2007), 51–65

Purchase, Sean, *Key Concepts in Victorian Literature* (Basingstoke, New York: Palgrave Macmillan, 2006)

Quennell, Peter, "Introduction", in Peter Quennell (ed.), *Mayhew's London* (London: Bracken Books, 1984, Reprint 1987), 17–28

Richardson, Ruth, *Dickens and the Workhouse: Oliver Twist and the London Poor* (Oxford: Oxford University Press, 2012)

Roberts, Phillip, "Building Media History from Fragments: A Material History of Philip Carpenter's Manufacturing Practice", *Early Popular Visual Culture*, vol. 14, no. 4 (2016): 319–339

Robson, Catherine, "Standing on the Burning Deck: Poetry, Performance, History", *PMLA / Publications of the Modern Language Association of America*, vol. 120, no. 1 (January 2005): 148–162

Roosevelt, Blanche, *Life and Reminiscences of Gustave Doré* (London: Cassell, 1885) Digital edition https://archive.org/details/lifeandreminisc00roosgoog

Rose, Michael, "The Disappearing Pauper: Victorian Attitudes to the Relief of the Poor", in Eric Sigworth (ed.), *In Search of Victorian Values: Aspects of Nineteenth-Century Thought and Society* (Manchester: Manchester University Press, 1988), 56–72

Rosen, George, "Disease, Debility, and Death", in Harold James Dyos and Michael Wolff (ed.), *The Victorian City: Images and Realities*, vol. 2 (London and Boston: Routledge and Kegan Paul, 1973), 625–667

Rosen, Jeff, "Posed as Rogues: The Crisis of Photographic Realism in John Thomson's *Street Life in London*", *Image*, vol. 36, nos. 3–4 (Fall / Winter 1993): 8–39

Rubery, Matthew, "Journalism", in Francis O'Gorman (ed.), *The Cambridge Companion to Victorian Culture* (Cambridge: Cambridge University Press, 2010), 177–194

Rubinstein, David, "Rogers, Frederick (1846–1915)", *Oxford Dictionary of National Biography* (Oxford: Oxford University Press, 2004), (accessed on 6 August 2014, http://www.oxforddnb.com/view/article/37909)

Sabatos, Terri, *Images of Death and Domesticity in Victorian Britain*, PhD diss. (Indiana University, 2001)

Saint, Andrew, "Cities, Architecture, and Art", in Colin Matthew (ed.), *The Nineteenth Century: The British Isles, 1815–1901* (Oxford: Oxford University Press, 2005), 255–291

Schierl, Thomas, "Der Schein der Authentizität: Journalistische Bildproduktion als nachfrageorientierte Produktion scheinbarer Authentizität", in Thomas Knieper and Marion Müller (ed.), *Authentizität und Inszenierung von Bilderwelten* (Köln: Herbert von Halem Verlag, 2003), 150–167

Schmandt, Peter, *Armenhaus und Obdachlosenasyl in der englischen Graphik und Malerei 1830–1880* (Marburg: Jonas Verlag, 1991)

Schmidt, Johann, *Ästhetik des Melodramas. Studien zu einem Genre des populären Theaters im England des 19. Jahrhunderts* (Heidelberg: Universitätsverlag Winter, 1986)

Schwarz, Werner Michael, Margarethe Szeless and Lisa Wögenstein, "Bilder des Elends in der Großstadt (1830–1930)", in Werner Schwarz, Margarethe Szeless and Lisa Wögenstein (ed.), *Ganz unten. Die Entdeckung des Elends: Wien, Berlin, London, Paris, New York* (Wien: Brandstätter, 2007), 9–17

Seltzer, Mark, "The Princess Casamassima: Realism and the Fantasy of Surveillance", *Nineteenth-Century Fiction*, vol. 35, no. 4 (March 1981): 506–534

Shail, Andrew, "Reading the Cinematograph: Short fiction and the Intermedial Spheres of Early Cinema", *Early Popular Visual Culture*, vol. 8, no. 1 (2010): 47–62

Shail, Andrew, "The Invention of Cinematic Celebrity in the United Kingdom", in André Gaudreault, Nicolas Dulac and Santiago Hidalgo (ed.), *A Companion to Early Cinema* (Chichester: Wiley-Blackwell, 2012), 460–486

Shesgreen, Sean, *Images of the Outcast* (Manchester: Manchester University Press, 2002)

Sivan, Gabriel, "George Berthold Samuelson (1889–1947): Britain's Jewish Film Pioneer", *Jewish Historical Studies*, vol. 44 (2012): 201–229

Stead, William Thomas, "A Magic Lantern Mission", *Review of Reviews*, vol. 2, no. 12 (December 1890): 561–567

Stedman Jones, Gareth, *Outcast London. A Study in the Relationship between Classes in Victorian Society* (Oxford: Clarendon Press, 1971)

Stein, Richard, "Street Figures: Victorian Urban Iconography", in Carol Christ and John Jordan (ed.), *Victorian Literature and the Victorian Visual Imagination* (Berkeley, Los Angeles, London: University of California Press, 1995), 233–263

Sukop, Sylvia, "Die soziale Wirklichkeit als Bild. John Thomsons *Street Life in London*", in Bodo von Dewitz and Roland Scotti (ed.), *Alles Wahrheit! Alles Lüge! Photographie und Wirklichkeit im 19. Jahrhundert. Die Sammlung Robert Lebeck* (Dresden: Verlag der Kunst, 1996), 201–209

Sutherland, Allan T., "The Yorkshire Pioneers", *Sight and Sound*, vol. 46, no. 1 (1977): 48–51

Sztaba, Wojciech, "Die Welt im Guckkasten. Fernsehen im achtzehnten Jahrhundert", in Harro Segeberg (ed.), *Die Mobilisierung des Sehens. Zur Vor- und Frühgeschichte des Films in Literatur und Kunst* (Munich: Fink, 1996), 97–112

Tanner, Simon, Trevor Muñoz and Pich Hemy Ros, "Measuring Mass Text Digitization Quality and Usefulness: Lessons Learned from Assessing the OCR Accuracy of the British Library's 19th Century Online Newspaper Archive", *D-Lib Magazine*, vol. 15, no. 7/8 (2009), (http://www.dlib.org/dlib/july09/munoz/07munoz.html)

Terras, Melissa, "Digitization and Digital Resources in the Humanities", in Claire Warwick, Melissa Terras and Julianne Nyhan (ed.), *Digital Humanities in Practice* (London: Facet Publishing, 2012), 47–70

Thissen, Judith, "Jewish Immigrant Audiences in New York City, 1905–14", in Melvyn Stokes and Richard Maltby (ed.), *American Movie Audiences: From the Turn of the Century to the Early Sound Era* (London: BFI Publishing, 1999), 15–28

Thissen, Judith, "Beyond the Nickelodeon: Cinemagoing, Everyday Life and Identity Politics", in Ian Christie (ed.), *Audiences: Defining and Researching Screen Entertainment Reception* (Amsterdam: Amsterdam University Press, 2012), 45–65

Thompson, Edward Palmer, and Eileen Yeo (ed.), *The Unknown Mayhew: Selections from the Morning Chronicle 1849–1850* (London: Merlin Press, 1971)

Thompson, Edward Palmer, "Mayhew and the *Morning Chronicle*", in Edward Palmer Thompson and Eileen Yeo (ed.), *The Unknown Mayhew: Selections from the Morning Chronicle 1849–1850* (London: Merlin Press, 1971), 11–50

Thompson, Kristin, *Exporting Entertainment: America in the World Film Market, 1907–1934* (London: British Film Institute, 1985)

Toulmin, Vanessa, "Digitization and Access", in Martin Loiperdinger (ed.), *Celluloid Goes Digital: Historical-Critical Editions of Films on DVD and the Internet* (Trier: Wissenschaftlicher Verlag Trier, 2003), 29–34

Toulmin, Vanessa, and Simon Popple (ed.), *Visual Delights – Two: Exhibition and Reception* (Eastleigh: John Libbey, 2005)

Vanhaelen, Angela, "Street Life in London and the Organization of Labour", *History of Photography*, vol. 26, no. 3 (Autumn 2002): 191–204

Vella, Stephen, "Newspapers", in Miriam Dobson and Benjamin Ziemann (ed.), *Reading Primary Sources: The Interpretation of Texts from Nineteenth- and Twentieth-Century History* (London, New York: Routledge, 2009), 192–208

Vogl-Bienek, Ludwig, "Die historische Projektionskunst: Eine offene geschichtliche Perspektive auf den Film als Aufführungsereignis", *KINtop – Jahrbuch zur Erforschung des frühen Films*, no. 3 (1994): 11–32

Vogl-Bienek, Ludwig, "'From Life': The Use of the Magic Lantern in Nineteenth-Century Social Work", in Andreas Gestrich, Steven King and Lutz Raphael (ed.), *Being Poor in Modern Europe: Historical Perspectives 1800–1940* (Oxford: Lang, 2006), 467–484

Vogl-Bienek, Ludwig, "Turning the Social Problem into Performance: Slumming and Screen Culture in Victorian Lantern Shows", in Marta Braun et al. (ed.), *Beyond the Screen: Institutions, Networks and Publics of Early Cinema* (New Barnet: John Libbey Publishing, 2012), 315–324

Vogl-Bienek, Ludwig, "A Lantern Lecture: Slum Life and Living Conditions of the Poor in Fictional and Documentary Lantern Slide Sets", in Richard Crangle and Ludwig Vogl-Bienek (ed.), *Screen Culture and the Social Question 1880–1914* (New Barnet: John Libbey Publishing, 2014), 34–63

Vogl-Bienek, Ludwig, *Lichtspiele im Schatten der Armut. Historische Projektionskunst und Soziale Frage* (Frankfurt am Main, Basel: Stroemfeld, 2016)

Waller, Philip, "Altercation Over Civil Society: The Bitter Cry of the Edwardian Middle Classes", in Jose Harris (ed.), *Civil Society in British History: Ideas, Identities, Institutions* (Oxford, New York: Oxford University Press, 2003), 115–134

Waller, Philip, "Sims, George Robert", in Henry Colin Gray Matthew and Brian Howard Harrison (ed.), *Oxford Dictionary of National Biography* (Oxford: Oxford University Press, 2004), 721–724

Warwick, Claire, Melissa Terras and Julianne Nyhan (ed.), *Digital Humanities in Practice* (London: Facet Publishing, 2012)

Wilson, Keith, "Surveying Victorian and Edwardian Londoners: George R. Sims' *Living London*", in Lawrence Phillips (ed.), *A Mighty Mass of Brick and Smoke: Victorian and Edwardian Representations of London* (Amsterdam: Rodopi, 2007), 131–149

Wohl, Anthony Stephen, "The Bitter Cry of Outcast London", *International Review of Social History*, vol. 13, no. 2 (1968): 189–245

Wohl, Anthony Stephen, "Unfit for Human Habitation", in Harold James Dyos and Michael Wolff (ed.), *The Victorian City: Images and Realities*, vol. 2 (London and Boston: Routledge and Kegan Paul, 1973), 603–624

Wohl, Anthony Stephen, *The Eternal Slum: Housing and Social Policy in Victorian London* (London: Edward Arnold, 1977)

Wood, Leslie, *The Miracle of the Movies* (London: Burke Publishing, 1947)

Woods, Alan, "Doré's London: Art and Evidence", *Art History*, vol. 1, no. 3 (1978): 341–359

Wright, David Graham, *Popular Radicalism: The Working Class Experience, 1780–1880* (London, New York: Longman, 1988)

Wynne, Deborah, "Reading Victorian Rags: Recycling, Redemption, and Dickens's Ragged Children", *Journal of Victorian Culture*, vol. 20, no. 1 (2015): 34–49

Yeo, Eileen, "Mayhew as a Social Investigator", in Edward Palmer Thompson and Eileen Yeo (ed.), *The Unknown Mayhew: Selections from the Morning Chronicle 1849–1850* (London: Merlin Press, 1971), 51–95

Zweig, Ronald, "Lessons from the Palestine Post Project", *Literary and Linguistic Computing*, vol. 13, no. 2 (June 1998): 89–95

Websites (unless otherwise specified, all websites were last accessed on 29 May 2021)

Archives Hub: "The George R. Sims Collection" (https://archiveshub.jisc.ac.uk/data/gb133-grs)

A Vision of Britain through Time: "Census Tables with Data for the Poor Law / Registration County" (http://www.visionofbritain.org.uk/unit/10097459).

Cinémathèque française: "Laterna Magica" (http://www.laternamagica.fr)

Cinema Treasures (www.cinematreasures.org)

eLaterna: Historical Art of Projection (https://elaterna.uni-trier.de)

Lucerna –The Magic Lantern Web Resource (http://lucerna.exeter.ac.uk)

Melton Prior Institute for reportage drawing & printing culture: Alexander Roob, "Gustave Doré in der Tradition der London – Reportage III: Dritte Männer", *Feature*, October 2016 (http://www.meltonpriorinstitut.org/pages/textarchive.php5?view=text&ID=122).

Media History Digital Library: "Magic Lantern and Lantern Slide Catalog Collection (1840s–1920s)" (http://mediahistoryproject.org/magiclantern)

Nineteenth Century UK Periodicals (https://www.gale.com/intl/primary-sources/19th-century-uk-periodicals)

Oxford English Dictionary Online (Oxford: Oxford University Press, January 2018), (http://www.oed.com)

Papers Past database, National Library of New Zealand (https://paperspast.natlib.govt.nz)

Periodicals Archive Online (https://www.proquest.com/pao)

The British Newspaper Archive (https://www.britishnewspaperarchive.co.uk)

The National Archives: *Records of the Copyright Office, Stationers' Company* (http://discovery.nationalarchives.gov.uk/browse/r/h/C59)

The National Archives of Ireland: "Census of Ireland 1901 / 1911 and Census Fragments and Substitutes, 1821–51" (http://www.census.nationalarchives.ie/)

The Waterloo Directory of English Newspapers & Periodicals: 1800–1900, third series (Waterloo, Ontario: North Waterloo Academic Press, 2009) (http://www.victorianperiodicals.com/series3/index.asp).

UK Census Online (https://www.ukcensusonline.com)

Wikipedia: "List of Lantern Slide Collections" (https://en.wikipedia. org/wiki/List_of_lantern_slide_collections)

Collections in Archives, Libraries

George R. Sims Collection, Rylands Library, Manchester

Lantern readings, Reuben Library, British Film Institute, London

Audio-Visual Material

DVD: *Screening the Poor 1888–1914* (Munich: Edition Filmmuseum, 2011)

DVD: *The Illustrated Bamforth Slide Catalogue*, compiled by Richard Crangle and Robert MacDonald (London: The Magic Lantern Society, 2009)

Newspapers

Church Army Gazette 1891–1895

The Referee 1877–1889; 1913–1914 (British Library, now available at British Newspaper Archive, https://www.britishnewspaperarchive.co.uk)

The Sunday School Chronicle 1883–1900

The Temperance Chronicle 1891–1900